SPARKNOTES™

SAT II U.S. History

2003–2004 Edition

Series Editor Ben Florman

Editor Margaret Welles

Contributor Matt Noble

Cover Design Dan O. Williams

Technology Tammy Hepps

This edition published by Spark Publishing

Spark Publishing
A Division of SparkNotes LLC
120 Fifth Avenue, 8th Floor
New York, NY 10011

02 03 04 05 SN 9 8 7 6 5 4 3 2 1

Please send all comments and questions or report errors to feedback@sparknotes.com.

Library of Congress information available upon request

Printed and bound in Canada

ISBN 1-58663-431-3

Welcome to SparkNotes Test Preparation™

SINCE YOU ARE LOOKING AT THIS BOOK, it seems safe to assume that you are thinking about taking the SAT II U.S. History test. It also seems likely that you want to earn as high a score as possible on the test. If these assumptions of ours are true, then you've picked up the right book.

In order to help you reach your goal of extreme success, the SparkNotes Guide to the SAT II U.S. History test includes:

The history you'll need to know for the test. This book is not designed to teach you all of American history; it's designed to teach you the history you need to know to do well on the SAT II U.S. History. We won't waste your study time by covering unnecessary topics. Yet while the history we teach is tailored to the test, we won't simply feed you facts and tell you to memorize them, as other books do. We'll teach you what you need to know so that you understand it: doing well on the SAT II U.S. History demands flexibility and understanding, not rigid memorization.

Critical-thinking skills and specific SAT II U.S. History test-taking strategies. An understanding of history is the most important ingredient for doing well on the SAT II U.S. History, but it also pays to know how to approach the test. We'll teach you critical-thinking skills and strategies that can help put your knowledge of history to the best use.

Five Full-Length Practice Tests (and a study method that will teach you how to transform practice tests into powerful study tools). Practice tests can and should be an extremely important part of your studying for any standardized test. Practice tests help you hone your test-taking skills; become comfortable with the format and time limits of the test; and track your progress. In addition, if you follow our methods for studying the practice tests you take, the tests can become an unparalleled study tool for helping you target and overcome your weaknesses.

General Information About SAT II Subject Tests. Beyond teaching you what you need to know to do well on a particular SAT II test, we think it's also important to discuss the SAT IIs in general. This first chapter of the book is dedicated to helping you figure out how the SAT II tests are used by colleges, which SAT II tests are right for you, when to take the tests, and how to register for them.

While other test prep companies actually write test preparation books as marketing tools to try to convince you to enroll in expensive courses, SparkNotes' goal is to teach you, so you don't need those courses. Our books are written with no hidden agenda, which frees us to help you get the best score you can.

Contents

SAT II U.S. HISTORY REVIEW

America Before the Europeans   35

The Colonial Period   39

Revolution and Constitution   59

A New Nation   75

The Age of Jackson   95

Cultural Trends: 1781–Mid-1800s   103

Westward Expansion and Sectional Strife   111

Civil War and Reconstruction   125

Industrial Revolution   139

The Age of Imperialism   151

The Progressive Era   157

World War I   167

The Roaring Twenties   175

The Great Depression and the New Deal   185

World War II   195

The 1950s:
Cold War, Civil Rights, and Social Trends   207

The 1960s   223

PRACTICE TESTS

Practice Tests Are Your Best Friends   319

ORIENTATION

Introduction to the SAT II

The SAT II Subject Tests are created and administered by the College Board and the Educational Testing Service (ETS), the two organizations responsible for producing the dreaded SAT I (which most people just call the SAT). The SAT II Subject Tests are meant to complement the SAT I. Whereas the three-hour-long SAT I tests your critical thinking skills by asking math and verbal questions, the one-hour-long SAT II Subject Tests examine your knowledge of a particular subject, such as U.S. History, Writing, Physics, or Biology.

In our opinion, the SAT II subject tests are "better" tests than the SAT I, since they cover a definitive topic rather than some ambiguous critical thinking skills that no one can define. You might wonder why we put "better" in quotes. (We're going to answer this question, whether you were wondering or not.) Well, just because the SAT II Subject tests do a better job of testing your knowledge of a useful subject, the tests aren't necessarily easier or demanding less study. A "better" test isn't guaranteed to be "better for you," in terms of how easy it will be.

In comparison to taking the SAT I, there are good things and bad things about taking an SAT II Subject test.

The Good

- Because SAT II Subject tests cover actual topics like U.S. History or Biology, you can study for them effectively. If you don't know a topic in U.S. history, such as the factors leading to the Louisiana Purchase, you can look it up and learn it. The SAT II tests are straightforward tests, which means that if you know your stuff, you will do well on them.

- Often, the classes you've taken in school have already prepared you well for the test. If you've taken a U.S. history course, then you've probably already covered most of the topics that are tested on the SAT II U.S. History test. All you need to do well on the test is to get some refreshing and refocusing, which this book provides.

- In studying for the History, Biology, or Chemistry SAT II tests, you really are learning History, Biology, and Chemistry. In other words, you are learning valuable, interesting knowledge. If learning is something you enjoy, you might actually find the process of studying for an SAT II test worthwhile and gratifying. It's hard to say the same about studying for the SAT I.

The Bad

- Because SAT II subject tests quiz you on specific knowledge, "beating" or "outsmarting" an SAT II test is much harder than outsmarting the SAT I. For the SAT I, you can use all sorts of tricks or strategies to figure out an answer. There are far fewer strategies to help you on the SAT II. Don't get us wrong: having test-taking skills *will* help you on an SAT II, but knowing the subject will help you much, much more. In other words, to do well on the SAT II, you can't just rely on your quick thinking and intelligence. You need to study!

Colleges and the SAT II Subject Tests

Stop for a second and think about why you would take an SAT II Subject test. Is it to prove to yourself how much you've learned in the year? That seems unlikely. Is it to prove to your teacher how much you've learned? No, you've got finals for that. Is it to win you a new car? You wish. No, there's only one reason to take an SAT II Subject Test: colleges want you to, and, sometimes, they require you to.

Colleges care about SAT II Subject tests for two related reasons. First, the tests demonstrate your interest, knowledge, and skill in specific topics. Second, because SAT II tests are standardized, they show how your knowledge of U.S. History (or Biology or Math) measures up to the knowledge of high school students nationwide. The grades you get in high school don't offer such a measurement to colleges: some high schools are more difficult than others, meaning that students of equal ability might receive different grades. Since SAT II tests are national tests, they provide colleges with a definite yardstick against which they can measure every applicant's knowledge and skills.

When it comes down to it, colleges like the SAT II tests because the tests make the colleges' job easier. The tests are the colleges' tool. But because you know how colleges use the SAT II, you can make the tests your tool as well. SAT II tests allow colleges to easily compare you to other applicants. This means that the SAT II tests provide you with an excellent chance to shine. If you got a 93 percent in U.S. History and some other kid in some high school across the country got a 91 percent, colleges won't know what to make of it. They won't know whose class was harder, whose teacher was a tough grader, or whose high school inflates grades. But if you get a 720 on the U.S. History SAT II, and that other kid gets a 650, colleges will recognize the difference in your scores.

The Importance of SAT II Tests in College Applications

Time for some perspective: SAT II tests are *not* the primary tools that colleges use to decide whether to admit an applicant. High school grades, extracurricular activities, and SAT or ACT scores are all more important to colleges than your scores on SAT II tests. If you take a lot of AP tests, it's likely that those will also be more important to colleges than SAT II tests. But because SAT II tests do provide colleges with such a nice and easy measurement tool, they are an important *part* of your application to college. Good SAT II scores can give your application the extra shove that pushes you from the maybe pile into the accepted pile.

College Placement

Occasionally, colleges use SAT II tests to determine placement. For example, if you do very well on the U.S. History SAT II, you might be exempted from a basic history class. Though colleges don't often use SAT II tests for placement purposes, it's worth it to find out whether the colleges to which you are applying do.

Scoring the SAT II Subject Tests

There are three different names for your U.S. History SAT II score. The "raw score" is a simple score of how you did on the test, like the grade you might receive on a normal test in school. The "percentile score" takes your raw score and compares it to the rest of the raw scores in the country for the same test. Percentile scores let you know how you did on the test in comparison to your peers. The "scaled score," which ranges from 200–800, compares your score to the scores received by all students who have ever taken that particular SAT II.

The Raw Score

You will never know your raw score on the SAT II that you take because the raw score is not included in the score report. But you should understand how the raw score is calculated, because this knowledge can affect your strategy for approaching the test.

A student's raw score is based solely on the number of questions that student got right, wrong, or left blank. A correct answer is worth 1 point; a question left blank yields 0 points; a wrong answer results in the loss of ¼ of a point.

Calculating the raw score is easy. Simply add up the number of questions you answered correctly and the number of questions answered incorrectly. Then multiply the number of wrong answers by ¼, and subtract this value from the number of right answers.

$$\text{raw score} = \text{\# of correct answers} - \frac{1}{4} \times \text{\# of wrong answers}$$

We'll explain how the way the raw score is calculated should affect your approach to the test in the chapter on strategy.

The Percentile Score

A student's percentile is based on the percentage of the total test-takers who received a lower raw score than he or she did. Let's say, for example, you had a friend named John Quincy Adams, and he received a score that placed him in the 37th percentile. This percentile score tells John that he scored better on the SAT II than 36 percent of the other students who took the same test; it also means that 63 percent of the students taking that test scored as well as or better than he did.

The Scaled Score

The scaled score takes the raw score and uses a formula to turn that raw score into the score from 200-800 that you've probably heard so much about. The curve to convert raw scores to scaled scores differs from SAT II test to SAT II test. For example, a raw score of 33 on the Math Ic will scale to about a 600, while the same raw score of 33 on the Math IIc will scale to about a 700. In fact, the scaled score can even vary between different editions of the *same* test. A raw score of 33 on the February 2002 Math IIc might scale to a 710, while a 33 in June 2002 might scale to a 690. These differences in scaled scores exist to accommodate for yearly differences in difficulty level of the test and student performance.

Which SAT II Subject Tests to Take

There are three types of SAT II tests: those you must take, those you should take, and those you shouldn't take.

- The SAT II tests you *must* take are those that are required by the colleges you are interested in.

- The SAT II tests you *should* take are tests that aren't required, but which you'll do well on, thereby impressing the colleges looking at your application.

- You *shouldn't* take the unrequired SAT II tests that cover a subject you don't feel confident about.

Determining Which SAT II Tests are Required

To find out if the colleges to which you are applying require that you take a particular SAT II test, you'll need to do a bit of research. Call the schools you are interested in, look at their web pages, or talk to your guidance counselor. Often, colleges request that you take the following SAT II tests:

- The Writing SAT II test

- One of the two Math SAT II tests (either Math Ic or Math IIc)

- Another SAT II in some other subject of your choice

Not all colleges follow these guidelines; you should take the time to research what tests you need to take in order to apply to the colleges that interest you.

Deciding if You Should Take an SAT II that isn't Required

To decide whether you should take a test that isn't required, know two things:

1. What a good score on that SAT II test is

2. Whether you can get that score or higher

Below, we have included a list of the most commonly taken SAT II tests and the average scaled score on each. If you feel confident that you can get a score that is significantly above the average (50 points is significant), taking the test will probably strengthen your college application. Please note that if you are hoping to attend an elite school, you might have to score significantly more than 50 points higher than the national average. The following list is just a general guideline. It's a good idea to call the schools that interest you; or talk to a guidance counselor to get a more precise idea of what score you should be shooting for.

TEST	AVERAGE SCORE
Writing	590-600
Literature	590-600
American History	580-590
World History	570-580
Math Ic	580-590
Math IIc	655-665
Biology E&M	590-600
Chemistry	605-615
Physics	635-645

As you decide which test to take, be realistic with yourself. Don't just assume you're going to do great without at least taking a practice test and seeing where you stand.

It's a good idea to take three SAT II tests that cover a range of subjects, such as one math, one humanities (history or writing), and one science. However, there's no real reason to take *more* than three SAT II tests. Once you've taken the SAT II tests you need to take, the best way to set yourself apart from other students is to take AP courses and tests. AP tests are harder than the SAT II tests, and as a result they carry quite a bit more distinction. AP tests show that you're excited and able to take on responsibility, and that you want to challenge yourself. SAT II tests give you the opportunity to show colleges that you can learn when you want to; AP tests give you the change to show colleges that you *want* to learn as much as you can.

When to Take an SAT II Subject Test

The best time to take an SAT II subject test is, naturally, right after you've finished a year-long course in that subject. If, for example, you take U.S. History in eleventh grade, then you should take the SAT II U.S. History near the end of that year, when the material is still fresh in your mind. (This rule does not apply for the Writing, Literature, and Foreign Language SAT II tests; it's best to take those after you've had as much study in the area as possible.)

Unless the colleges to which you are applying use the SAT II for placement purposes, there is no point in taking any SAT II tests after November of your senior year, since you won't get your scores back from ETS until after the college application deadline has passed.

ETS usually sets testing dates for SAT II subject tests in October, November, December, January, May, and June. However, not every subject test is administered in each of these months. To check when the test you want to take is being offered, visit the College Board website at www.collegeboard.com or do some research in your school's guidance office.

Registering for SAT II Tests

To register for the SAT II test(s) of your choice, you have to fill out some forms and pay a registration fee. We know, we know—it's ridiculous that *you* have to pay for a test that colleges require you to take in order to make *their* jobs easier. But, sadly, there isn't anything we, or you, can do about it. It is acceptable for you to grumble here about the unfairness of the world.

After grumbling, of course, you still have to register. There are two ways: online or by mail. To register online, go to www.collegeboard.com. To register by mail, fill out and send in the forms enclosed in the *Registration Bulletin*, which should be available in your high school's guidance office. You can also request a copy of the *Bulletin* by calling the College Board at (609) 771-7600, or writing to:

> College Board SAT Program
> P.O. Box 6200
> Princeton, NJ 08541-6200

You can register to take up to three SAT II tests for any given testing day. Unfortunately, even if you decide to take three tests in one day, you'll still have to pay a separate registration fee for each.

Introduction to the U.S. History SAT II

IMAGINE, FOR A MOMENT, two children playing tag in the forest. Who will win—the girl who never stumbles because she knows the placement of every tree and all the twists, turns, and hiding spots; or the kid who keeps falling down and tripping over roots because he doesn't pay any attention to the landscape? The answer is obvious. Even if the other kid is a little faster and more athletic, the girl will still win, because she knows how to navigate the landscape and use it to her advantage. This example of tag in the forest is extreme, but it illustrates the point: the structure of the SAT II is the forest; taking the test is the game of tag. And no one likes to lose at tag.

In this chapter we're going to describe the "landscape" of the U.S. History SAT II. In the next chapter, we will show you how to navigate and use the landscape to get the best score you can.

Content of the U.S. History SAT II

The U.S. History SAT II test covers 600 years of United States history, beginning with the period before Columbus' discovery of the New World and extending up to the present. There are two ways to organize and think about the 600 years of U.S. history covered on the test: by chronological eras, or by focusing on different aspects of history, such as political, social, or economic history.

11

Chronological Era

ETS breaks down the content of the test into three chronological eras, and tells how much of each the test covers:

Pre-Colombian to 1789	20%
1790–1898	40%
1899–present	40%

While these categories are helpful, they are overly broad. For example, the category Pre-Colombian to 1789 contains three distinct different time periods, each with its own characteristics: the Pre-Columbian period, the Colonial Period, and the American Revolution. The broad, chronological breakdowns provided by the ETS cover so much time that they aren't very sensible and won't be all that helpful in directing your study efforts.

We therefore created a test breakdown of our own in smaller, more cohesive chronological categories.

Pre-Columbian	1–3%
Colonial Period	10–14%
American Revolution and Constitution	8–12%
First Years of the New Nation	6–10%
Age of Jackson and Jacksonian Democracy	3–7%
Westward Expansion and Sectional Strife	6–10%
Civil War and Reconstruction	3–7%
Industrial Revolution	13–17%
American Imperialism	1–3%
Progressive Era	3–7%
Word War I	3–7%
The Roaring '20s	3–7%
The Great Depression and the New Deal	6–10%
World War II	5–9%
1950s: Cold War, Civil Rights	6–10%
1960s: Vietnam, Civil Rights, Social Movements	4–8%
1970s–Present	1–3%

This book is organized according to these seventeen categories, giving you the ability to focus on each time period to whatever degree you feel necessary. Also, each question in the practice tests at the back of this book has been categorized according to this breakdown, so that when you take practice tests, you can very precisely identify your weaknesses and then use this book to address them.

Aspects of History

The second way to think about the content covered by the test is in terms of thematic focus, regardless of time period. The test targets five types of historical knowledge:

Political history	32–36%
Economic history	18–20%
Social history	18–22%
Intellectual, cultural history	10–12%
Foreign policy	13–17%

In our opinion, this second way of categorizing the test is not as helpful as the breakdown by chronological era. For example, studying the economic history of the Industrial Revolution would be pointless without knowing any political history of the period. You can't really understand one without the other. Instead, you should use this breakdown to get a sense of where you should focus while studying a chronological era. In effect, this list tells you that when you are studying, you need to learn more than just the dates of major political events. You should also be familiar with social movements, cultural trends, and intellectual and artistic achievements.

Format of the U.S. History SAT II

The U.S. History SAT II test is a one-hour long test composed of 90–95 multiple-choice questions. The instructions for the test are very simple. You should memorize them so you don't waste time reading them on the day of the test.

> Directions: Each of the questions or incomplete statements below is followed by five suggested answers or completions. Select the one that is best in each case and then fill in the corresponding oval on the answer sheet.

Have you read the directions? Have you memorized them? (Don't lie to us). Have you memorized them? Good.

Basically, the instructions inform you of two simple things: all the questions on the test are five-choice multiple-choice questions, and you will have an answer sheet on which to mark down your answers.

Now for the shocker: the instructions don't cover many of the important aspects of the format and rules of the test. We're going to remedy that flaw that by providing you with a true understanding of the test's format.

- The questions on the test aren't organized by time period or difficulty. In other words, a difficult question about the Sherman Anti-Trust Act in the Industrial Revolution might be followed by an easy question about the causes of the War of 1812.

- You can skip around while taking the test. If, for example, you have a yearning to answer question 90 first, then question 1, then question 67, then 22… well, you could do that. But while it's silly to skip around for no reason, the ability to skip an occasional question can be very helpful.

- All questions are worth the same number of points, whether easy or difficult.

All of these facts can greatly affect your approach to taking the test, as we will explain in the next chapter on strategy.

The Four Types of Questions on the U.S. History SAT II

As the test directions imply, each question on the U.S. History SAT II follows the same basic format, involving a question and five possible answer choices. Within that basic format, though, there are four distinct types of questions:

1. Fact Questions

2. Trend Questions

3. EXCEPT Questions

4. Cartoons/Charts/Maps Questions

We provide answers and explanations to each of the sample questions we provide, but at this point, the answers themselves aren't essential. It's more important that you become familiar with each question type, so that you will be much less likely to be surprised by anything you encounter on the test. Prepare to get familiar.

Fact Questions

Fact questios test your knowledge of names and definitions, as well as your ability to recognize, describe, and explain specific acts or events and the people associated with them. In this type of question, you might be asked about the ramifications of one particular act, rather than the effects of a general legislative policy. The questions will cover all people from presidents to social revolutionaries to authors, and all time periods and themes, from the Great Awakening to Jimmy Carter's foreign policy to women's rights.

Example Fact Questions:

The Haymarket Riot of 1886:

(A) helped rouse public support and sympathy for unions

(B) contributed to the Knights of Labor's success in demanding higher wages and shorter work days

(C) effectively ruined the Knights of Labor, temporarily crippling the labor movement

(D) was violent but effective, as it forced the police to give strikers more liberty to express their grievances

(E) had little effect, since "scabs" went to work in place of those striking

Answer: (C) In the Haymarket Riot of 1886, laborers met in Chicago to protest police cruelty against strikers. The riot turned violent when one member of the Knights of Labor threw a bomb, killing a police officer. In all, nine people were killed and close to sixty injured. Many leaders of the Knights of Labor were convicted of inciting the riot, and public support plummeted, effectively destroying the union. In the aftermath, a general anti-union hysteria spread through the American public, portraying unions as violent and lawless.

The first immigrants to be blocked from entering the U.S. were:

(A) Polish

(B) Italians

(C) Irish

(D) Russians

(E) Chinese

Answer: (E) The Chinese Immigration Act was passed in 1882, preventing more Chinese from immigrating for the next six decades.

Trend Questions

Trend questions cover basic themes regarding groups, movements, and time periods. These questions test your abilities to draw connections between the facts that you know and to display a more nuanced and longer view of U.S. history. For example, you might be asked to spot connections between three listed acts, or to identify key issues during a listed span of years. Some Trend Questions will include quotations, asking you to identify a speaker's attitude and to fit that speaker into a larger historical context by associating him or her with a relevant political or social movement.

Example Regular Trend Question:

Which of the following best characterizes the Transcendentalists?

(A) they aimed to transcend nature and overcome man's inherent flaws

(B) they believed that, through the church, man could unite with God and achieve perfection

(C) they urged enlightenment through reason and the close study of scripture

(D) they believed that man could personally connect with God through oneness with nature

(E) they preached church reform and encouraged women to join the clergy

Answer: (B) Transcendentalists called for an individualistic approach to faith, shunning the institutional church and its restrictive disciplines. They urged instead that man commune with God through nature, through a personal and emotional response rather than an intellectualization of faith.

Example Quote Trend Question:

"With malice toward none; with charity for all; with firmness in the right, as God gives us to see the right, let us strive on to finish the work we are in; to bind up the nation's wounds; to care for him who shall have borne the battle, and for his widow and his orphan—to do all which may achieve and cherish a just and lasting peace among ourselves."

These words from 1864 best describe which of the following political agendas?

(A) a war relief program to help Civil War veterans and their loved ones

(B) a moderate Republican plan, known as the Ten Percent Plan, to ease Reconstruction and reunite the nation

(C) a religious plan to unite the nation through faith in God

(D) a Southern appeasement plan, drafted by Southern Congressmen, to help rehabilitate the South without military supervision or Northern intervention

(E) the aims of the Radical Republicans to reunite the nation through a long and punishing reform of the South

Answer: (B) Lincoln finished his second inaugural address with these words, expressing his desire to reunite the nation smoothly and quickly, without harsh punishment of the South. His plan for reconstruction of the South was moderate, known as the Ten Percent Plan, which allowed southern states to reenter the Union so long as ten percent of their voters pledged an oath of loyalty to the Union. Radical Republicans condemned this plan as too mild; they wanted to punish the South for seceding.

EXCEPT Questions

EXCEPT questions can be either fact- or trend-related, and are characterized by the use of the words EXCEPT, NOT, LEAST, INCORRECT, INCONSISTENT or something similar. These words will always appear in all caps.

EXCEPT questions can be tricky because the right answer is actually the *wrong* answer; it is the one answer among the five that doesn't fit. Though the idea is simple, as you're moving quickly through the test, it can be easy to get confused. If you are careful not to fall into a trap, though, the trickiness of the question actually makes it easier. On other questions, if you aren't sure of the answer, you have to eliminate four answer choices in order to get to the right one; on except questions, all you have to do is eliminate one—that one is the right answer.

Example EXCEPT questions:

The Populist Party supported all of the following EXCEPT:

(A)   graduated income tax
(B)   immigration restriction
(C)   public ownership of railroads, telephone, and telegraph systems
(D)   maintaining the gold standard, countering inflation
(E)   eight-hour work day

Answer: (D) The Populist Party vehemently opposed the gold standard, which served to limit the money in circulation and further aggravated farmers' debts and poverty. William Jennings Bryan, the Populist and Democratic candidate in the 1896 presidential election, condemned the gold standard as oppressive, declaring that the people, farmers and laborers in particular, should not be "crucified on this cross of gold." Bryan and the Populists pushed for a silver standard, which would create inflation and raise prices. They argued that increasing the money supply would help boost the struggling economy (and also make farmers' debts worth less).

Of the following, which was NOT a factor in the Panic of 1837?

(A)   overspeculation
(B)   inflation, followed by a tight contraction of credit
(C)   the successful recharter of the Second National Bank
(D)   recall of loans and Jackson's issuance of the Specie Circular
(E)   possible bank mismanagement

Answer: (C) Jackson vetoed the recharter of the Second National Bank, considering it corrupt and unconstitutional.

Cartoons / Charts / Maps Questions

This type of question presents you with an image—whether political cartoon, chart, or map—and asks you to interpret it in order to answer the question. Since the charts and maps tend to hold more information than a single question can test, read the question first so you know what to look for in the image. When you do look at the image, pay attention to all the information given. Look for a title or date attached to the image. Such things can help you place the image into a historical context, which will make deciphering the question easier. There are usually about 5–7 of this type of question on the test. Here's an example:

THE SPANISH BRUTE—ADDS MUTILATION TO MURDER.
By Hamilton in "Judge."

The above cartoon suggests that

(A)   the Spaniards used cruel guerilla tactics in the Spanish-American War
(B)   the Spanish tried to demoralize Americans by desecrating their grave sites
(C)   a disproportionate number of soldiers killed in the Spanish-American War were from Maine
(D)   Spain was a brutish colonial power that had to be punished for sinking the *Maine*
(E)   Americans attributed Spain's victory in the Spanish-American War to Spaniards' brutish, subhuman nature

Answer: (D) The cartoon shows Spain as a savage and brutal power hovering over a grave site for "Maine soldiers"—that is, for the 256 soldiers killed in the explosion of the U.S. naval ship, the *Maine*, off the coast of Havana in 1898. A 1976 investigation revealed that a fire onboard the ship had caused the blast, but in 1898 the U.S. government and general public were convinced that an underwater Spanish mine was to blame. Soon after the incident, the U.S. declared war on Spain to avenge both the loss of the *Maine* and Spain's well-publicized cruelty against Cuban nationalists, who had been fighting for independence from Spanish rule since 1895. The U.S. won the war within two months, securing Cuban independence.

Scoring and the U.S. History SAT II

Scoring on the U.S. History SAT II is the same as scoring for all other SAT II tests: for every right answer, you earn one point; for every wrong answer, you lose ¼ of a point; for every blank answer, you earn no points. Add all these points up, and you get your raw score. ETS then converts your raw score to a scaled score, according to a special curve tailored to the particular test that you take. We have included a generalized version of that table below. (Note that because ETS changes the curve slightly for each edition of the test, the table will be close to, but not exactly the same as, the table used by ETS.) You should use this chart to convert your raw scores on practice tests into a scaled score.

Raw Score	Scaled Score	Raw Score	Scaled Score	Raw Score	Scaled Score
90	800	55	650	21	450
89	800	54	640	20	440
88	800	53	640	19	440
87	800	52	630	18	430
86	800	51	630	17	430
85	800	50	620	16	420
84	800	49	610	15	420
83	800	48	600	14	410
82	800	47	600	13	410
81	790	46	590	12	400
80	790	45	590	11	400
79	790	44	580	10	390
78	780	43	570	9	390
77	780	42	570	8	380
76	770	41	560	7	380
75	770	40	560	6	370
74	760	39	550	5	370
73	760	38	540	4	360
72	750	37	540	3	360
71	740	36	530	2	350
70	740	35	530	1	340
69	730	34	520	0	340

68	720	33	520	−1	330
67	720	32	510	−2	320
66	710	31	510	−3	320
65	700	30	500	−4	310
64	700	29	490	−5	310
63	690	28	490	−6	300
62	690	27	480	−7	300
61	680	26	480	−8	290
59	670	25	470	−9	290
58	670	24	470	−10	280
57	660	23	460		
56	660	22	460		

In addition to its function as a conversion table, this chart contains crucial information: it tells you that you can do very well on the U.S. History SAT II without writing a perfect essay or answering every question correctly. In fact, you could skip some questions and get some other questions wrong and still earn a "perfect" score of 800.

For example, in a test of 95 questions, you could score:

- an 800 if you answered 87 right, 5 wrong, and left 3 blank

- a 750 if you answered 78 right, 10 wrong, and left 7 blank

- a 700 if you answered 72 right, 12 wrong, and left 11 blank

- a 650 if you answered 64 right, 20 wrong, and left 11 blank

- a 600 if you answered 56 right, 24 wrong, and left 15 blank

This chart should prove that when you're taking the test, you shouldn't imagine your score plummeting with every question you can't confidently answer. You can do very well on this test without knowing or answering everything. The key is to follow a strategy that ensures that you will get to see and answer all the questions you can answer correctly, and then intelligently guess on those questions about which you are a little unsure. We will discuss these strategies in the next chapter.

Strategies for Taking the U.S. History SAT II

A MACHINE, NOT A PERSON, WILL SCORE YOUR U.S. History SAT II test. The tabulating machine sees only the filled-in ovals on your answer sheet and does not care how you came to these answers; it just impassively notes whether your answers are correct. So whether you knew the correct answer right away or just took a lucky guess, the machine will award you one point. It doesn't award extra points if you've spent a really long time getting the right answer. It doesn't award points if you managed to get a tricky question right. Think of this scoring system as a message to you from the ETS: "We care only about your answers, and not any of the thought behind them."

So you should give ETS right answers, as many as possible, using whatever means possible. It's obvious that the U.S. History SAT II test allows you to show off your knowledge of U.S. history; but the test gives you the same opportunity to show off your fox-like cunning by figuring out what strategies will allow you to best display that knowledge. Remember, the SAT II test is your tool to get into college, so treat it as your tool. It wants right answers? Give it right answers by using whatever strategies you can.

Basic Rules of SAT II Test-Taking

There are some rules of strategy that apply to all SAT II tests. These rules are so obvious that we hesitate to even call them "strategies," but we're going to list them once, just to make sure that you've thought about them.

Avoid Carelessness

Avoiding carelessness probably sounds to you more like common sense than a sophisticated strategy. We don't disagree. But it is amazing how a timed test can warp and mangle common sense.

There are two types of carelessness, both of which will cost you points. The first type of carelessness results from moving too fast, whether that speed is caused by overconfidence or frantic fear. In speeding through the test, you make yourself vulnerable to misinterpreting the question, overlooking one of the answer choices, or simply making a logical mistake. As you take the test, make a conscious effort to approach it calmly, and not to move so quickly you become prone to making mistakes.

Whereas the first type of carelessness can be caused by overconfidence, the second results from frustration or lack of confidence. Some students take a defeatist attitude toward tests, assuming they won't be able to answer many of the questions. Such an attitude is a form of carelessness, because it causes the student to ignore reality. Just as the overconfident student assumes she can't be tricked and therefore gets tricked, the student without confidence assumes he can't answer questions and therefore at the first sign of difficulty gives up.

Both kinds of carelessness steal points from you. Avoid them.

Be Careful Gridding In Your Answers

The computer that scores SAT II tests is unmerciful. If you answered a question correctly, but somehow made a mistake in marking your answer grid, the computer will mark that question as wrong. If you skipped question 5, but put the answer to question 6 in row 5, and the answer to question 7 in row 6, etc., thereby throwing off your answers for an entire section . . . it gets ugly.

Some test prep books advise that you should fill in your answer sheet five questions at a time rather than one at a time. Some suggest that you do one question and then fill in the corresponding bubble. We think you should fill out the answer sheet whatever way feels most natural to you; just make sure you're careful while doing it. In our opinion, the best way to ensure that you're being careful is to talk silently to yourself. As you figure out an answer in the test booklet and transfer it over to the answer sheet, say to yourself: "Number 23, B. Number 24, E, Number 25, A."

How the U.S. History SAT II Tests History

Often, students think that studying history means memorizing lots of dates, names, and events. This sort of thinking will not serve you well on the U.S. History SAT II. Don't get us wrong: you do need to know facts, dates, and names for the U.S. History SAT II. But to do well on the test, you need to understand these facts, dates, and names within the contexts of larger historical eras, movements, or trends. That's why we broke our coverage of history into small historical eras, each of which contains coherent historical trends.

Thinking of history in terms of eras and movements within U.S. history will help you on the U.S. History SAT II by directing your study, making it more efficient, and organizing your knowledge in such a way that is perfectly suited to answering the types of questions that U.S. History SAT II asks.

Thinking in Eras Helps You Study

Thinking about history in terms of eras, movements, and trends provides organization for the information you learn. By thinking about history in terms of eras and trends, you create an outline in your mind. Then when you learn some new historical information, you can file it into that outline. Because this outline is structured, it will help you to remember and recall the things you learn, and to relate one era to another.

We'll make our point using an example. Imagine we had a box of 100 tacks, and we threw the tacks on the floor. Then we let you look at the tacks for 5 minutes. After that time, we ask you to go into another room and draw, on a piece of paper, where all of the tacks were. You probably wouldn't do a very good job of it, would you? But what if when you were looking at the tacks on the floor you noticed that they were organized into geometric shapes: 27 of the tacks were in a circle, 19 formed a triangle, another 28 formed a squiggly line, and 26 formed a hexagon. Then when you had to draw the tacks you'd do a pretty good job because though there are just as many tacks, now they're organized and easier to remember. All it would have taken was for you to notice the shapes in which the tacks were arranged. The same goes for history. All it takes is to always be aware of the trends the facts fit into.

Further, by always thinking of the facts you learn in terms of how they fit into an era or movement, you ensure that you remain engaged with the material you're studying. It's easy to read over a list of facts and think you've learned them, when really you've just looked at them and forgotten them. But if you are constantly trying to fit the facts you learn into an era or trend, you give yourself an active grip on those facts. You're not just reading them over; you're thinking about them. This engagement with the material will make your studying more efficient and fruitful.

Strategies

Thinking in Eras Helps You Answer U.S. History SAT II Questions

Many questions on the U.S. History SAT II will test broad thematic knowledge. These questions ask you about the "big picture" of history, and test your general knowledge of an era or movement. For these questions, just knowing particular facts isn't going to help you all that much. To answer these questions, you have to have studied the trends of history. For example, look at the question below:

> Which of the following best characterizes American foreign policy during the first half of Progressive Era, 1900 to 1910?
>
> (A)   aggressive intervention, through both military involvement and capitalist investment
> (B)   strict isolationism
> (C)   minimal diplomacy, as the U.S. focused almost exclusively on domestic reform
> (D)   primarily business-minded, aimed at expanding markets overseas
> (E)   alarmist and reactionary in nature, as the Red Scare swept the nation

This question doesn't care if you know a single fact or date. Instead, it tests to see if you understand the general situation of a particular era. Now, it is certainly true that in order to understand an era, you certainly have to know enough facts to understand the general trend, but you don't have to know *every* fact. There are a number of ways you could figure out the answer to this question. If you know that the U.S. won the Spanish-American War in 1898 and in the process arrived as a world power and took on an overseas empire, you would immediately know that the U.S. was heavily involved in foreign nations, sometimes through military means. Meaning the answer has to be (A). Alternately, you might have known that the president through many of those years was Teddy Roosevelt, who advocated "big stick" diplomacy. Again, that implies military intervention, giving you the answer (A). Note that you didn't have to know that one of the territories the U.S. gained in the Spanish American war was the Philippines, or that Roosevelt helped engineer a revolt in Panama.

Fact Questions Are Trend Questions in Disguise

But what about the more nitpicky questions that test you on precise facts and names? First, we've already discussed how thinking about history in terms of eras and trends will actually help you to remember individual facts. But knowing trends has an added importance: even if you aren't sure about a particular fact, understanding historical trends can still help you to answer a question that covers that fact. Let's say, for example, you are asked the following question, but don't remember the name John Calhoun:

John Calhoun most bitterly opposed Andrew Jackson's policies regarding

(A)   American involvement in Europe
(B)   slavery
(C)   income taxes
(D)   the nullification crisis
(E)   the Supreme Court

If you approach the test as if it's testing only a collection of facts, you might think that this question is testing something very specific: John Calhoun's political beliefs as opposed to Andrew Jackson's beliefs. If you don't even know who John Calhoun was, then how are you supposed to answer this question? You might very well just skip this question and move on, assuming you can't answer it.

But if you approach the test with the understanding that all facts fit into trends, then knowing who John Calhoun was becomes secondary to answering this question. You know that Calhoun opposed Andrew Jackson on this issue. You therefore know that this issue took place during Jackson's presidency, and you should know the general trends of Jackson's presidency: an emerging two-party system that vastly increased popular interest and participation in government; the development of a strong executive branch that included a spoils system in which a party rewarded its followers with political posts; sectional strife over tariffs that led to the nullification crisis; removal of the Cherokee Indians from Georgia. When you think of the Jacksonian Era, these few issues and trends should immediately leap to mind. With them, you can see that the answer to this question must be (D), the nullification crisis.

The SAT II will ask questions in ways you won't expect, forcing you to be flexible with your knowledge of history. Knowing facts alone does not make you flexible; knowing facts *and* themes does. So, while studying, always keep the larger picture in mind, and try to fit the facts you are learning into this larger picture. In some ways, studying for the SAT II U.S. History test should be like writing a story in your head, where you don't just come up with lists of facts, but rather connect them.

Strategy and Multiple Choice Questions

When you look at an SAT II U.S. History question, the answer is always right there in front of you. Of course, the test writers don't just *give* you the correct answer; they hide it among a bunch of incorrect answer choices. The important thing to realize is that there are two methods by which you can try to come to the correct answer:

1. Find the right answer.

2. Eliminate wrong answers until there's only one answer left.

In a perfect world, you would always see the right answer. And for many of the questions on the test, you probably will be able to pick out the right answer from among the five answer choices. But if you can't decide which question is the right answer, then you might want to work in the other direction and try to figure out which choices *can't* be the right answer.

Eliminating Wrong Answers: Thinking Contextually

We've already explained how thinking in terms of eras helps your studying, and will help you answer SAT questions. It can also help you eliminate wrong answers. Let's say you come across a question:

> Between the 1860s and 1890s, the United States changed in all of the following ways EXCEPT:
>
> (A) it became increasingly urban
> (B) labor unions became a powerful force in politics and in business, and gained widespread popular support
> (C) immigration significantly boosted the supply of workers
> (D) big corporations and monopolies thrived, often unchecked by the government
> (E) more women began to work outside of the home

What if you look at this question and just don't know the answer? Take a step back: identify the era the question covers to help you put the question into some historical context. In this case, knowing that "Between the 1860s and 1890s" roughly corresponds to the Industrial Revolution will help you remember the themes of that time period. What comes to mind when you ponder industrialization? Perhaps you think of big business and the rise in urbanization and immigration? If so, you can proceed to check off (A) and (C), since they're both clearly true. (Remember, for these EXCEPT questions, you are looking for the *wrong* answer, the answer that doesn't belong, so eliminate all the answers that are true.) The increased need for workers also likely had an effect on women, transforming some women from domestic to factory workers, allowing you to eliminate answer (E). Answer choice (D) might be a little trickier: yes, the first half of the answer is true because the Industrial Revolution spawned huge corporations like Carnegie's steel industry and Rockefeller's oil company, and the period is known as the "Era of Big Business"; but what about government regulation? Let's say you can't remember what government did with business during the Industrial Revolution, so you can't decide if (D) is true or false. As for (B), you may not know precisely what went on with unions during those years, so you can't say for sure whether that answer is right or wrong either.

So you are left with two possible answer choices: (B) and (D). You should be able to see that (B) and (D) are at odds with one another because if (B) were true, (D) would not be. If unions had been so politically powerful, they would have pushed for government to strictly regulate business and check the tyranny of monopolies (that is, the poor treatment of workers and the high prices of goods). In other words, if unions became so influential and popular during this period, then the Industrial Revolution would hardly be known as the "Era of Big Business," would it? Think again of what you remember about the trends of industrialization: big business was definitely a major one, whereas unions don't jar much in your memory. Armed with this knowledge of trends and eras, take a little leap of faith and guess that (B) is the right answer, the answer that doesn't fit with the other four.

Guess what? You guessed right!

Questions For Which You Can't Eliminate all Answers

Not all questions on the SAT II U.S. History test will work out quite as well as our last example. You might not always be able to use your knowledge of trends and eras to eliminate four answer choices, ensuring that you get the question right. But for almost every question you *will* likely be able to eliminate *at least one* answer. To see why this is important, move on to our discussion of guessing and the U.S. History SAT II.

Guessing and the U.S. History SAT II

Should you guess on the U.S. History SAT II? We'll begin to answer this question by posing a question of our own:

> Franklin Delano Roosevelt is holding five cards, numbered 1–5. Without telling you, he has selected one of the numbers as the "correct" card. If you pick a single card, what is the probability that you will choose the "correct" card?

The answer, of course, is one in five. But the answer is only important if you understand that the question precisely describes the situation you're in when you blindly guess the answer to any SAT II U.S. History question: you have a $\frac{1}{5}$ chance of getting the question right. If you were to guess on ten questions, according to probability you would get two questions right and eight questions wrong.

- 2 right answers gets you 2 raw points
- 8 wrong answers gets you $8 \times \frac{1}{4}$ points = –2 raw points

Those ten answers, therefore, net you a total of *0* points. This means that blind guessing is a complete waste of time, which is precisely what the ETS wants. They designed the scoring system so that blind guessing would be pointless.

Educated Guessing

But what if your guessing isn't blind? Here's a question about George Washington:

George Washington was born in the year

(A)   1730
(B)   1731
(C)   1732
(D)   1733
(E)   1977

You probably don't know what year George Washington was born (and you won't need to know such a minor fact for the SAT II test). But you probably do know that Washington was *not* born in 1977. Once you've eliminated "1977" as a possible answer, you have four choices from which to choose. Is it now worth it to guess? Probability states that if you are guessing between four choices you will correctly answer one question for every three you get wrong. For that one correct answer you'll get 1 point, and for the three incorrect answers you'll lose a total of ¾ of a point.

$$1 - \frac{3}{4} = \frac{1}{4}$$

This math indicates that if you can eliminate one answer, the odds of guessing turn in your favor: you become more likely to gain points than to lose points.

The rule for guessing on the U.S. History SAT II, therefore, is simple: *if you can eliminate even one answer-choice on a question, you should definitely guess.* And if you follow the above described contextual-thinking methods to eliminate answer choices, you should be able to eliminate at least one answer from almost every question.

Guessing as Partial Credit

Some students feel that guessing is similar to cheating, and that a correct guess is the same as getting credit where none is due. But instead of looking at guessing as an attempt to gain undeserved points, you should look at it as a form of partial credit. Take the example of the question about George Washington's birth. Most people taking the test will only know that Washington wasn't born in 1977, and will only be able to throw out that word as a possible answer, leaving them with a 1 in 4 chance of guessing correctly. But let's say that you also knew that Washington wasn't born in 1730. Don't you deserve something for that extra knowledge? Well, you do get something: you can throw out both "1977" and "1730" as answer choices, leaving you with a 1 in 3 chance of getting the question right if you guess. Your extra knowledge gives you better odds of getting this question right, exactly as extra knowledge should.

If You're Stumped

If you cannot eliminate even one answer choice and find yourself staring at a certain question with mounting panic, throw a circle around that nasty question and move on. If you have time, you can return to the question later. Remember, answering a hard question correctly doesn't earn you any more points than answering an easy question correctly. You want to be sure to see every question you can answer instead of running out of time by fixating on the really tough questions. While taking five minutes to solve a particularly difficult question might strike you as a moral victory when you're taking the test, you possibly could have used that same time to answer six other questions that would have vastly increased your score. Instead of getting bogged down on individual questions, you will do better if you learn to skip, and leave for later, the very difficult questions that you either can't answer or that will take an extremely long time to figure out.

Pacing: The Key to Scoring Well

Good pacing allows you to take the test, rather than letting the test take you. As we said earlier, the questions on the U.S. History SAT II test are not organized by difficulty or time period. You are as likely to come upon a question you can answer at the end of the test as you are at the beginning. Part of your job as you take the test is to make sure that you don't miss out on answering those questions near the end of the test that you could have answered if only you had more time.

By perfecting your pacing on practice tests, you can make sure that you will see every question on the test. And if you see every question on the test, then you can select which questions you will and won't answer, rather than running out of time before reaching the end of the test and letting the test decide, by default, which questions you won't answer.

In large part, pacing yourself entails putting into practice the strategies we've already discussed:

- Make sure not to get bogged down on one single question. If you find yourself wasting time on one question, circle it, move on, and come back to it later.

- Answer every question for which you know the answer, and make an educated guess for every question in which you can quickly eliminate at least two answer choices.

Learning to pace yourself is a crucial part of your preparation for the test. Students who know how to pace themselves take the test on their own terms. Students who don't know how to pace themselves enter the test already one step behind.

Setting a Target Score

You can make the job of pacing yourself much easier if you go into the test knowing how many questions you have to answer correctly in order to earn the score you want. So, what score do you want? Obviously, you should strive for the best score possible, but be realistic: consider how much you know about U.S. History and how well you do, generally, on SAT-type tests. You should also consider what exactly defines a good score at the colleges to which you're applying: is it a 620? a 680? Talk to the admissions offices of the colleges you might want to attend, do a little research in college guidebooks, or talk to your guidance counselor.

No matter how you do it, you should find out what the average score of a student going to the schools you want to attend is. Take that number and set your target score above it (you want to be above average, right?). Then take a look at this chart we showed you before.

You will get:

Score:	Right answers:	Wrong answers:	Blank answers:
800	83	5	2
750	74	8	8
700	66	12	15
650	59	16	15
600	52	20	18
550	44	24	22

So let's say the average score for the U.S. History SAT II, for the school you want to attend, is a 600. You should set your target at about 650. Looking at this chart, you can see that to get that score, you need to get 59 questions right, can absorb getting 16 wrong, and can leave 15 questions blank.

If you know all these numbers going into the test, you can pace yourself accordingly. You should use practice tests to teach yourself the proper pace, increasing your speed if you find that you aren't getting to answer all the questions you need to, or decreasing your pace if you find that you're rushing and making careless mistakes. If you reach your target score during preparation, give yourself a cookie or some other tasty treat and take a break for the day. But just because you hit your target score doesn't mean you should stop working altogether. In fact, you should view reaching your target score as a clue that you can do *better* than that score: set a new target to 50–

100 points above your original, and work to pick up your pace a little bit and skip fewer questions.

By working to improve in manageable increments, you can slowly work up to your top speed, integrating your new knowledge of how to take the test and the subjects the test covers without overwhelming yourself by trying to take on too much too soon. If you can handle working just a little faster without becoming careless and losing points, your score will certainly go up. If you meet your new target score again, repeat the process.

Strategies

SAT II
U.S. HISTORY
REVIEW

America Before the Europeans

Trends and Themes of the Era

- Humans first came to the Americas over a land bridge connecting Alaska to Asia more than 15,000 years ago, during an ice age.

- Over time, these nomadic hunting groups dispersed across the continent.

- As the tribes learned to farm and founded permanent settlements, they formed tribes with distinct cultural and social practices.

- Tribes adapted their ways of life to the geographical regions in which they lived.

The First Americans

About 120,000 years ago, the Earth fell into an ice age. The northern polar ice cap grew southward, water solidified into ice, and ocean levels fell. With the lowering of the oceans, hidden land was exposed, including a land bridge connecting Siberia (located in modern-day eastern Russia) and Alaska. Between 15,000 and 50,000 years ago, various small, nomadic hunting groups from Asia crossed the land bridge, becoming the first human inhabitants of the Americas.

Over the next millenia, these earliest Americans dispersed throughout much of the Western Hemisphere. As the Ice Age came to an end around 10,000 years ago and Earth's atmosphere continued to warm, the land that these groups inhabited changed drastically. Sea levels rose and melting glaciers filled the Great Lakes and Mississippi River basin with water. Glaciers receded northward, and frozen plains gave way to deciduous eastern forests, grassy central plains, and desert throughout the West. Also, the land bridge disappeared back under the body of water now known as the Bering Strait.

The descendants of the earliest Americans changed with the landscape. As Ice Age animals such as mammoths began to disappear, hunters began to prey on smaller game. The groups also began fishing more and gathering local provisions, like seeds and nuts, from the land. About 5,000 years ago, some groups began to domesticate plants. As these groups began to farm and become more efficient in their use of resources, they required less land, and many in the East and Midwest gave up their nomadic lifestyle and established small, stable communities by around 300 B.C.

The Emergence of Tribes

Once they had begun to establish permanent settlements, Native American groups began to form what are known today as tribes. Different tribes developed their own languages and social hierarchies, and distinct religious beliefs and practices. Many tribes not only invented specialized tools such as the bow and arrow, but also mastered pottery, weaving, and basketry.

Tribes in neighboring geographic areas often maintained extensive contact through trade and warfare, establishing both friendly and hostile relations. In fact, through the local contact maintained between tribes, there developed a rather extensive trade network that spanned much of the North and South American continent. Despite having such contact with one another, tribes remained distinct, each adapting its ways of life to its geographic area. Modern day anthropologists and archeologists categorize Native American tribes by culture area, which allows for such geographic trends.

Northwest Coast

Chinook, Haida, and other tribes spanned the Pacific coast from Alaska to California, living primarily off the abundant fish. The Northwest tribes built totem poles depicting supernatural creatures. They were proficient in other arts, as well.

California

Within California, tribes such as the Chumash and Pomo lived in villages of about one hundred, specializing in the processing of acorns. Acorns were one of many resources in this region that allowed these tribes to prosper.

Southwest

In the early history of the Southwest, the dominant Anasazi tribe mastered irrigation and farming. By the civilization's peak in the twelfth century, the population of some Anasazi villages topped 1,000, and the villages themselves were often marvelous cliff dwellings. A system of roads connected many of these villages in confederations, and it seems likely that Anasazi trade networks even extended into northern Mesoamerica, since some artifacts have been found in Anasazi villages that could only have been produced by the civilizations in Mexico.

Yet for some reason (drought, warfare, religious strife), tens of thousands of Anasazi people deserted their dwellings en masse around 1300, never to return. They spread throughout the Southwest, and their descendants are known as Pueblo tribes, including the Hopi and Zuni. (Meaning "village" in Spanish, Pueblo refers to both the people and the villages in which they lived). These Pueblo tribes, along with the Navajos and Apaches, who migrated from the north around the fourteenth century, farmed along rivers using advanced irrigation techniques, foraged for food, and mined turquoise for trade with Mexico.

Great Basin, Plateau

The Paiute, Shoshone, and Ute tribes made their home in the Great Basin, between the Sierra Nevada Mountains to the west and the Rockies to the east. This land, too dry for farming, gave rise to foraging bands who hunted small mammals and gathered seeds and nuts. Other tribes inhabited the Plateau—a high, flat expanse to the north of the Great Basin—and lived as food gatherers, picking berries, seeds, and roots.

Plains

The Cheyenne, Sioux, and other tribes hunted in the Great Plains, which extended from the Rocky Mountains to the Mississippi River. The Plains were largely uninhabited before the arrival of the Columbus. When Europeans brought horses and guns into the Plains, the tribes developed into powerful hunting groups.

Eastern Woodlands

The Iroquois tribes, known as the Five Nations, controlled the Northeast. The Cherokee and other tribes inhabited the Southeast; the Fox, Chee, and others lived around the Great Lakes; and the Mississippian culture dominated the Mississippi flood plains. While all these Eastern Woodlands tribes hunted, many were also skilled in agriculture, employing the "slash and burn" technique and crop rotation to manage their land for food production. These tribes are also known for their skill with crafts and their well-developed trading networks.

Of these Eastern Woodlands tribes, the Mississippian tribes, in particular, were skilled in small-scale architecture. Known as "mound builders," they built large platform mounds at the center of their towns, which served as religious temples for ceremony or burial, or as the homes of top officials. Before the age of exploration, the Mississippian centers collapsed and the inhabitants fled to establish small villages.

Mesoamerica

To the South of the current United States, in what is called Mesoamerica, some Native Americans formed rich and powerful civilizations. The Aztecs, centered in what is now Mexico City, are known for their architecture, which included stone pyramids. The Maya of Central America are also known for their architecture, as well as their advanced methods of astronomy, mathematics, calendar systems, and for developing their own form of writing. The Incas, based in Peru, built an extensive network of towns throughout the Andes.

Pre-Columbus America and the SAT II

Though the classes you take in high school might put more emphasis on this time period, there is a reason our section is so short: the SAT II barely tests it. You'll be well prepared for the test if you're familiar with: the origin of Native Americans; the connection between farming, permanent settlements, and tribes; and the characteristics of tribes in different geographical locations.

You might notice that every other chapter of this book will contain a section of terms to help you focus your study. For this time period, there simply aren't any hard terms you need to know.

The Colonial Period

Trends and Themes of the Era

- Spain dominated the early years of European exploration of the New World, with France a distant second. England did not get seriously involved in the New World until nearly a century after Columbus landed.

- After England defeated the Spanish Armada in 1588, the balance of power in the New World (and in Europe) shifted. After initial hardship in the colonies, English settlements showed the New World could bring profit and offered religious freedom. A quick buildup of colonial settlements began along the East Coast of North America and continued through the seventeeth and eighteenth centuries.

- Under its mercantilist economic policy, England created laws ensuring that its colonies existed primarily to help enrich the mother country. England did not enforce these laws too strictly, employing a policy of salutary neglect, for fear of alienating its colonists and thereby helping France's interests in the New World.

- After the 1763 French and Indian War, England no longer worried about France as a threat, but faced huge war debts. England believed the colonies should bear the brunt of the debt, since the war was for their benefit. England ended salutary neglect, to the colonist's dismay and anger.

Exploration Before Columbus

By the time Christopher Columbus landed in the Western Hemisphere in 1492, the New World had already been "discovered" more than once. First, of course, there were the Native Americans we discussed last chapter. But there is solid evidence that other Europeans made it to the Americas long before Columbus did. Around 1000 A.D., Viking Norsemen led by **Leif Ericson** sailed from Greenland across the Atlantic Ocean and set up a settlement at Newfoundland, in northeast Canada. These Vikings also explored some distance up and down the coast. This settlement, however, was short-lived. The Norsemen soon sailed back across the ocean, having had little to no affect on North America.

The Age of Exploration

Though Columbus was not the first to discover the New World, his landing in the New World in 1492 is important: it ushered in an era of unprecedented European exploration and settlement of the Americas. This period is known as the Age of Exploration.

Important Names in The Age of Exploration

Name	Country	Achievement(s)
Christopher Columbus	Spain	1492: Reached Bahamas; explored Cuba, Haiti 1493: Established Santo Domingo
John Cabot	England	1497/8: Claimed Nova Scotia, Newfoundland for England
Amerigo Vespucci	Spain Portugal	1499: Explored coast of S. America for Spain 1501: Explored coast of S. America for Portugal
Ponce de Leon	Spain	1513/21: Explored Florida
Ferdinand Magellan	Spain	1519: Began the first circumnavigation of the globe
Hernando Cortez	Spain	1519–1522: Conquered the Aztecs in Mexico
Francisco Pizarro	Spain	1530–1536: Conquered the Incas in Peru
Hernando de Soto	Spain	1539–1542: Explored coast between Mississippi River and Florida
Jacques Cartier	France	1542: Traveled St. Lawrence River to Montreal
Samuel de Champlain	France	1608–1615: Explored Great Lakes, founded Quebec, established fur trade with Native Americans
Henry Hudson	Netherlands	1609–1611: Sailed up Hudson River

During this Age, European explorers searched for trade routes, overseas wealth, and adventure. Technological innovations helped spur this exploration boom. A "maritime revolution" in Europe saw the invention of the magnetic compass as a navigational aid, the astrolabe as a device used to determine latitude, and the caravel as an unprecendentedly fast style of large vessel sailing.

The Major Players in the Age of Exploration

The individual explorers often get the glory, but for the SAT II test, it is more important that you know about the broader context: the nations that sponsored those explorers; the reasons those nations were so interested in exploring and settling the New World; and the geographical territories that these different nations claimed as their own. Don't get us wrong: familiarity with the individual explorers is helpful (that's why we gave you the chart), but you should understand the explorer's contributions within the larger context of the age.

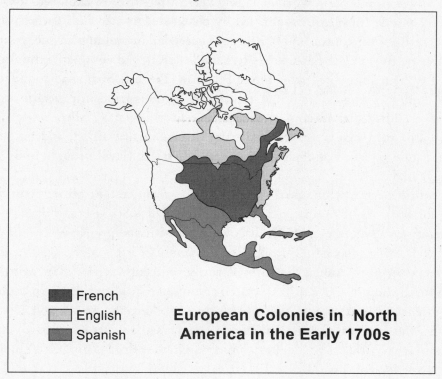

French
English
Spanish

European Colonies in North America in the Early 1700s

Spain

The Spanish monarchy began the Age of Exploration by sponsoring Christopher Columbus's attempt to reach Asia by sailing westward across the Atlantic. Columbus, of course, failed to reach Asia, instead landing on the Bahama Islands in 1492. He returned to the New World in 1493 and established the settlement of Santo Domingo as a base for further exploration. In 1493, the Pope declared that all lands west of the Azores and the Cape Verde Islands should belong to Spain, but Portugal, another great sea power, disputed the papal decree. The two countries reached a compromise with the **Treaty of Tordesillas** in 1494, which divided all future discoveries between Castile (a region of Spain) and Portugal.

The Treaty of Tordesillas reveals that both Portugal and Spain led the charge in exploring the New World. But while the Portuguese focused on navigation and geographical observation, the Spanish put their efforts into expedition and colonization.

After the Treaty of Tordesillas, Spain quickly established itself as the premier colonial power in the New World, sending wave after wave of explorers into South America. These Spanish expeditions, led by **conquistadors**, set out in search of gold, slaves, lucrative trade routes, and fame; they succeeded in building an enormous Hispanic Empire. By 1522, the Spaniard Hernando Cortez had conquered the Aztecs in Mexico; by 1536, under the leadership of Francisco Pizzaro, Spain had conquered the Incas in Peru. Conquistadors plundered the indigenous tribes for wealth and slave labor and established numerous *encomiendas*, sprawling slave-filled estates. Under Conquistador rule, many natives died from disease, malnutrition, and fatigue, and they were soon replaced on the encomiendas by African slaves brought in by Portuguese slave traders.

In North America, Spain initially proved just as dominant. Ponce de Leon claimed Florida for Spain in 1513 and Hernando de Soto led a Spanish exploration of the southeastern United States in 1539, discovering the Mississippi River. In 1565, Spain established the first successful European settlement in North America, a fortress at St. Augustine, Florida. Around the turn of the seventeenth century, Spanish settlers moved into the Southwest, establishing the colony of Santa Fe in 1610. In addition to building their own settlements, the Spanish strove to keep the British and French out of North America by attacking British and French settlements and destroying their forts. Spain saw Florida as particularly important in the effort to diminish English and French expansion southward.

France

France also played a strong role in the New World, though its efforts were mainly limited to North America. The French led the charge to find a Northwest Passage, a much hoped-for water route through which ships might be able to cross the Americas to access Asia. In three voyages between 1534 and 1542, French explorer **Jacques Cartier** traveled the St. Lawrence River to what is now Montreal. The Northwest Passage eluded him (it doesn't exist), but his explorations founded France's early dominance of the major waterways of North America. In 1562, French settlers briefly and unsuccessfully attempted to settle in North America, in what is now South Carolina. In 1564, the Spanish attacked and destroyed another French settlement near Jacksonville, Florida.

Despite its failures at settlement, France continued to be a player in North America. Most particularly, the French engaged in the highly profitable fur trade, and set up trading outposts throughout Newfoundland, Maine, and the regions further west. **Samuel de Champlain** founded the first permanent French settlement in 1608 at Quebec, and established a fur trade with the region's Native American tribes. By the end of the seventeenth century, the French controlled the major waterways of North America—the St. Lawrence River, the Great Lakes, and the Mississippi River—and, therefore, much of the land in the heart of the continent. Of all the European colonial powers, the French also enjoyed the best relationship with Native Americans.

The Netherlands

In 1609, the Dutch East India Company became interested in North American settlement when **Henry Hudson** sailed up the river that now carries his name. In 1625 the Dutch bought an island, named Manhattan, from the natives who lived there. On this island that lay near the mouth of the Hudson River, the Dutch set up a settlement, which they named New Amsterdam. This Dutch colony flourished on account of the fur trade. However, the Dutch did little to try and expand their landholdings beyond their domain around the Hudson. A European conflict between England and the Netherlands spread to the New World in 1664, during which the English took over New Amsterdam, renaming it New York. After 1664, Dutch influence waned.

England

In comparison to the other European powers that played a major role in the exploration and colonization of the New World, England got a relatively late start. True, King Henry VII of England did send explorer **John Cabot** across the Atlantic in 1497, and Cabot claimed Nova Scotia, Newfoundland, and the Grand Banks for England. But after Cabot's efforts, the English became more concerned with domestic issues and generally ceased exploring the New World. For much of the sixteenth century, England had no real presence in the New World.

English interest in the New World began to increase in the second half of the sixteenth century. Religious groups such as the Puritans, who disagreed with the practices of the Church of England, began to look at the New World as a place where they could practice their religion freely. The English monarchy was also enticed by the immense wealth it saw pouring into Spain from Mexico, South America, and the West Indies. The riches brought home by the English captain Francis Drake, and other Sea Dogs who plundered Spanish treasure ships off of Central America in the late 1570s, particularly piqued England's interest. The Spanish viewed the British as a threat to Spanish trade routes in the New World, and also opposed the Protestant English for religious reasons—Spain was fervently Catholic. The Spanish and English quickly became bitter rivals, scheming to position strategic bases throughout the New World.

England's first effort to establish a settlement in the New World ended badly. In 1584, Sir Walter Raleigh gained a royal charter to found the settlement of Roanoke, located on an island off the coast of North Carolina. The colony failed over the next six years, mostly because the settlers were incompetent to deal with the harsh realities of the New World. Still, Spain felt threatened enough (and were angry enough about contemporaneous events in Europe) to decide to severely cripple the British. In 1588, the Spanish Monarchy dispatched the great Spanish Armada to attack the British off the coast of England. Through luck and ingenuity, a fleet of outgunned English ships pulled off a major military upset and decimated the Armada. With this victory, England began to establish itself as a premier naval power, which bolstered its colonial efforts. Spain fell into a slow decline.

The struggle between Britain and Spain dragged on throughout the end of the sixteenth century, so that by 1600 the English crown and Parliament were hesitant to spend money on colonization. In place of government funding, **joint-stock companies** formed to gather funding for colonization through the sale of public stock. Along with religious groups—who saw the rise of the English Navy as a real opportunity to move to the New World—these companies were responsible for most English colonization throughout the seventeenth century.

Effects of Colonization on the Natives

Colonization had a disastrous effect on the native population. War, slavery, and starvation claimed many native lives, but disease, especially smallpox, caused the most severe population depletion. In Mexico, for example, the native population plummeted from 25 million in 1519 to 2 million by 1600. European settlement also displaced numerous tribes, setting in motion the sad fate of Native Americans throughout American history.

The Spanish, however, provided the Native Americans of the Great Plains with an unintended gift: horses. During the conquistadors' expeditions into the Southwest, some horses escaped and formed large herds on the Great Plains. Within a few generations, Native Americans in the plains region had become experts on horseback, expanding their hunting and trading capabilities, and dramatically transforming Native American culture.

The Early English Colonies

Because England got such a late start in the colonization game, they couldn't just set up their colonies wherever they wanted. Spain dominated South America, Mexico, the West Indies, the American Southwest, and Florida. The French held sway along North America's major waterways. In addition, the dense forests and occasionally hostile Native American tribes prevented English settlers from moving westward past the Appalachian Mountains. The early English settlements were therefore concentrated along the eastern coast of North America.

British colonies all fit into three types: royal, proprietary, or self-governing. Each type had its own characteristics.

- **Royal colonies** were owned by the king.

- **Proprietary colonies**, such as Pennsylvania, Maryland, and Delaware, were basically land grants from the British government. Individuals were awarded huge tracts of land that they would then supervise and govern, usually in return for political or financial favors. These colonial governors reported directly to the king.

- **Self-governing colonies**, including Rhode Island and Connecticut, formed when the king granted a charter to a joint-stock company, and the company then set up its own government independent of the crown. The king could revoke the colonial charter at any time and convert a self-governing colony into a royal colony.

There are a number of English colonies that are of particular importance, and which the SAT II test will focus on: Jamestown, Plymouth, and the Massachusetts Bay Colony.

Jamestown

Nearly twenty years after the failure of the English settlement at Roanoke, two separate joint-stock companies set out to found settlements along the Atlantic seaboard. In 1606, England's King James I authorized a charter granting land in what was then called Virginia (but stretched from modern-day Maine to North Carolina) to the Virginia Company of Plymouth and the Virginia Company of London. Colonists, considered employees of their respective companies, journeyed to America in 1607. The Virginia Company of Plymouth failed miserably, and its settlement in Sagadahoc, Maine was abandoned within two years. The Virginia Company of London was more successful, though in the New World, success was something of a relative term.

Jamestown's Early Years: Death and More Death

The 105 original Jamestown colonists were all men. In other words, Jamestown was a colony that was meant to make money, not to let people raise a family. The colonists took this ethic to heart, and focused all their efforts on getting rich quickly, neglecting to engage in any sort of agriculture. As a result, in the colony's first year, more than half of the colonists died of malnourishment and starvation (though you could also argue that they died of greed and stupidity). Only 38 colonists remained when reinforcements arrived in 1608.

Captain **John Smith**, one of the original colonists, soon emerged as a prominent leader of the community. In 1608, Smith organized work gangs to ensure the colony had food and shelter and made rules to control sanitation and hygiene. During the winter of 1608–1609, only twelve of 200 men died. Smith also excelled in Native American diplomacy, maintaining friendly ties with the nearby Powhatan Confederacy. But when Smith was wounded in 1609 and returned to England, the colony again staggered toward collapse. Of about 500 colonists in Jamestown in September 1609, 400 died by May 1610, and relations with the nearby Native Americans deteriorated badly. The first Anglo-Powhatan War erupted in 1610–1614.

Tobacco, Money, and Success

In the end, the colony of Jamestown was saved by the promise of money, though not from the source that anyone originally expected. Instead of gold or precious metals, the colony proved to be a perfect place to grow tobacco. **John Rolfe**, an Englishman who married the Powhatan leader's daughter, Pocahontas, introduced to the colony West Indian tobacco, a salable strain with many advantages over local varieties. From 1616 to 1619, Jamestown's tobacco exports grew nearly twenty-fold. Sensing the possibility for great profit, the Virginia Company dispatched money and supplies and awarded land grants to anyone able to pay for his own passage to Jamestown, or for the passage of a laborer.

The profits produced by tobacco saved Jamestown and ensured the settlement's success.

As the colony grew in size, its members began to desire a better system of government. In 1619, the colonists formed a general assembly, the **House of Burgesses**. The House of Burgesses was the first representative government in the New World, though its power was limited because the Virginia Company could still overrule its actions. Also in 1619, the first Africans were brought to Jamestown. Originally, these Africans were sold as indentured servants. By the 1640s, slavery had become more common.

The Colonial Period

> *Jamestown's House of Burgesses, formed in 1619, was America's first representative government.*

The year 1622 was a tragic one for Jamestown. High death rates from disease, the outbreak of a second war with the Powhatan tribe, a slump in tobacco prices, and fraudulent practices by local officials all conspired to transform the normal rigors of colonial life into extremely hard times. Under this strain, the joint-stock company collapsed and James I revoked its charter, making Virginia a royal colony in 1624.

Plymouth Plantation

In 1620, 102 settlers sailed across the Atlantic on the **Mayflower**, having procured a patent for settlement from the Virginia Company of London. These colonists agreed to send lumber, fish, and fur back to England for seven years before they could assume ownership of the land. Most of these settlers were **Separatists** from England, families who wanted to separate from the Anglican Church (the Church of England), and to worship as they saw fit. These Separatists had originally left England for the Netherlands to escape religious persecution. The voyage to the New World offered an even greater escape.

> *Separatists renounced the Church of England and established their own self-governing congregations. Among the Separatist groups are Pilgrims, Quakers, and Baptists. Separatists are distinct from Puritans, who originally wanted to "purify" the Anglican Church without separating from it.*

In November of 1620, the *Mayflower* landed at Plymouth Bay, outside the bounds of the British possession of Virginia. Since they had no legal right to settle there, the leaders of the **Pilgrims**, as the Separatists who came to the New World were called, insisted that all males sign the **Mayflower Compact**, which established the colony of Plymouth Plantation as a "civil body politic" under the sovereignty of James I of England. The Mayflower Compact is often described as the first example of true self-government in the New World.

> *The Mayflower Compact is often described as America's first example of true self-government.*

The Pilgrims were unprepared for the harsh New England winter, and about half of the settlers died by March 1621. Those who survived owed their lives to the aid of some English-speaking Native Americans, who taught the Pilgrims how to grow corn. In addition to the help offered by Native Americans, the Pilgrims exhibited a powerful work ethic unhindered by the greed that dominated much of Jamestown's history. Once through that first terrible winter, Plymouth quickly grew and prospered. Within a few years, the colony expanded into Cape Cod and the southeastern part of modern Massachusetts.

The Massachusetts Bay Colony

During the first half of the seventeenth century, religious and political oppression in England grew worse. In 1628, the Puritans struck a deal with the English government, under which the Puritans would leave England and settle north of the Plymouth Plantation on the condition that they would have political control of their colony. By gaining control of their charter and bringing it with them to the New World, the colonists were able to govern themselves as they saw fit, shifting the emphasis of their colony from trade to religion, and setting up a theocracy. In 1630, under the leadership of **John Winthrop,** who had been elected governor, about 900 Puritans traveled to Massachusetts. These Puritans eventually settled at the site of modern-day Boston. Winthrop set up his colony as a community based on the Bible. He saw Massachusetts Bay as being "a city upon a hill," a beacon of religious righteousness that would shine throughout the world. As happened in most settlements, the colonists were unprepared for the first winter and almost one-third of the settlers died. But by mid-1631, the colonists had put the worst behind them and the Massachusetts Bay Colony began to grow and thrive.

Government of Massachusetts Bay

Originally, the Massachusetts Bay colony was run by a General Court that allowed membership only to landholding Puritan men. After public outcry, all Puritan freemen regardless of wealth or holdings were allowed entrance. As the number of settlers increased and the General Court became too large, the settlers instituted a representative government in which two representatives from each district were elected to the General Court.

Religion and Massachusetts Bay

The Massachusetts Bay Colony operated according to a system called **congregationalism**, in which each independent church congregation served as the center of a community's political and social life. Only those individuals with good standing in the church could participate in government.

Some inhabitants of New England, however, broke with the Puritan leaders. One such dissenter was **Roger Williams**. Unlike the Puritan leadership of the colony, which believed that there must be legal separation but substantial cooperation between church and state, Roger Williams argued that total separation was the only acceptable relationship. Williams feared that without separation the state would corrupt the church. In 1635, Williams was banished from Massachusetts. He eventually established the colony of Rhode Island in 1647, where the government renounced the Church of England and allowed for religious freedom. Another dissenter was **Anne Hutchinson**, whose religious teachings were taken by some to be attacks on Puritan religious codes. Hutchinson found support in Henry Vane, who had become governor of the colony after Winthrop left office. But Winthrop staunchly opposed Hutchinson and succeeded in ousting Vane from office. In 1637, Hutchinson and her followers were banished; most of them settled in Rhode Island.

Some Massachusetts dissenters who went on to found new settlements in New England: Roger Williams (Providence, RI), Anne Hutchinson (Portsmouth, RI and Pelham Bay, NY).

The Colonial Economy: Mercantilism

Beginning around 1650, the British government pursued a policy of **mercantilism** in international trade. The mercantile theory of trade stipulated that in order to build economic strength, a nation must export more than it imported. To achieve this favorable balance of trade, the English passed regulatory laws exclusively benefiting the British economy. These laws created a trade system whereby Americans provided raw goods to Britain, and Britain used the raw goods to produce manufactured goods that were sold in European markets and back in the colonies. As the suppliers of raw goods only, the colonies could not compete with Britain in manufacturing. Through this trade scheme, English ships and merchants were always favored, excluding other countries from sharing the British Empire's wealth.

Between 1651 and 1673, the English Parliament passed four **Navigation Acts** meant to ensure the proper mercantilist trade balance. The acts declared the following:

- Only English or English colonial ships could carry cargo between imperial ports.

- Certain goods, including tobacco, rice, and furs, could not be shipped to foreign nations except through England or Scotland.

- The English Parliament would pay "bounties" to Americans who produced certain raw goods, while raising protectionist tariffs on the same goods produced in other nations.

- Americans could not compete with English manufacturers in large-scale manufacturing.

The Navigation Acts severely restricted colonial trade, to the benefit of England.

The colonists initially complained about these strictures on trade. In New England in particular, many colonists evaded the restrictions of the Navigation Acts through smuggling. But although relations between England and the colonies were often full of friction (in 1684, for example, Charles II revoked the Massachusetts Bay Colony's charter as punishment for smuggling), the two sides never came to any real conflict, since England itself did not enforce the laws vigorously. Instead, England developed a policy of **salutary neglect** toward the colonies. Salutary neglect meant that, generally, the trade laws that most hurt the colonial economy were not enforced. This policy did not simply arise from lax enforcement or the dishonesty of colonial officials; it was Britain's deliberate response to the threat of the French in North America. British officials knew that at some point they would have to clash with the French over the domination of the continent, and they needed the colonists to support them when that time came. The British did not want to alienate their much-needed allies through aggressive trade restrictions.

With the prospect of war against the French looming, the British employed salutary neglect to maintain the colonists' loyalty.

The Triangular Trade

British mercantilism manifested itself in the form of the **triangular trade**. The triangular trade routes linked the American Colonies, West Indies, Africa, and England. Each port provided shippers with a payoff and a new cargo. New England rum was shipped to Africa and traded for slaves, which were brought to the West Indies and traded for sugar and molasses, which went back to New England. Other raw goods were shipped from the colonies to England, where they were swapped for a cargo of manufactured goods.

Mercantilism and the triangular trade proved quite profitable for New England tradesmen and ship builders. But in the Southern Colonies, where the Navigation Acts vastly lowered tobacco prices, colonial economies suffered. The triangular trade also spurred a rise in the colonies' slave population and increased the merchant population, forming a class of wealthy elites that dominated both trade and politics throughout the colonies.

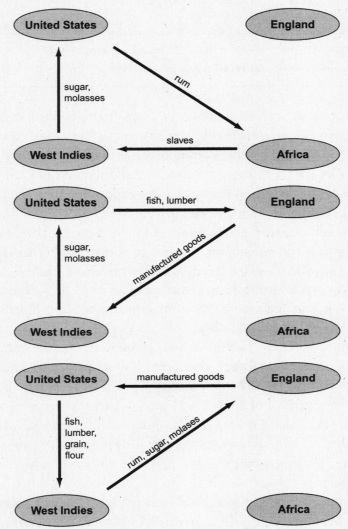

Life in Colonial America

By 1700, more than 250,000 people of European origin or descent lived within what is now the United States. These settlers covered much of the eastern seaboard. Each region of colonization was economically and socially distinct, since each area developed differently based on its geography, the nature of its immigrants, and many other factors.

The Colonial Period

The New England Colonies

The New England colonies spanned modern-day Massachusetts, New Hampshire, Maine, Connecticut, and Rhode Island. New England's economy centered on small farming, fishing, and home manufactures, as well as sea trade and shipbuilding. Boston became a center for international commerce. The region quickly expanded as immigrants streamed in and colonists produced large families.

New England economy was based on small-scale agriculture, fishing, home manufactures, shipbuilding, and trading.

Life was fairly stable for New Englanders. They generally lived 15–25 years longer than Englishmen or colonists from other regions, in part because of better diets. Individuals maintained extremely close community ties, living as they did in a homogenous Puritan society. Since Puritans believed that all followers of God should be able to read the Bible, they placed great emphasis on education. New England was likely the most literate community in the world.

Religion dominated nearly every aspect of life in New England, from politics to legal proceedings to social interaction. In order to vote or hold office, a person had to be considered a member-in-good-standing of the church. Religious dissenters were often subjected to public spectacle or, sometimes, banishment. Religious superstition also provided New England's most notorious scandal: the Salem Witch Trials of 1692 and 1693.

Starting with the Mayflower compact, and continuing when the settlers of the Massachusetts Bay Colony carried their charter with them to North America, the New England Colonies quickly established a tradition of self-government. By 1641 in Massachusetts, fifty-five percent of males could vote—a percentage far higher than that in England. Connecticut developed a similar political system, and with even more extended suffrage: all male landowners were granted the right to vote under the Fundamental Orders of Connecticut, which in 1639 became the first written constitution in the New World.

The increasing signs of self-government in the New England colonies came hand in hand with signs of resistance against the British. In 1643, colonists organized the New England Confederation as a defense against Native Americans and the encroachment of the Dutch. England saw this attempt to unite the colonies as potentially dangerous to its interests, but the Confederation remained and even worked to crush a Native American uprising in King Phillip's War (1675–1676). In the end, infighting among the colonies doomed the confederation. In 1655, four royal commissioners inspecting Massachusetts were treated rudely and advised King Charles II to revoke the colony's charter. Charles did not comply, but the incident did solidify a tradition of antagonism between New England and the mother country. In fact, in 1684, after years of increasing acrimony, James II revoked the Massachusetts Bay colony and set up the Dominion of New England, which unified all New England under one royal governor. The New England colonists hated this situation, and when the 1688 Glorious Revolution in England replaced James II with the Protestant William and Mary, the colonists forced the governor to return to England. In 1691, the Massachusetts Bay Colony charter was reinstated.

The Middle Colonies

The Middle Colonies included New York and New Jersey, and later Pennsylvania. As we mentioned earlier, England took control of New York, then called New Amsterdam, from the Dutch in 1664. The same was true for New Jersey, which was then called New Sweden. New York was made a royal province in 1685. New Jersey also became a royal province, but not until 1702. Both New York and New Jersey followed the same standard political format: each was governed by a royal governor and a general assembly. Economically, the two colonies relied on grain production, shipping, and fur trading with the local Native Americans.

In 1681, Charles II granted the last unclaimed tract of American land to **William Penn**. Penn, a Quaker, launched a "holy experiment" by founding a colony based on religious tolerance. The Quakers had long been discriminated against in both the Americas and England for their religious beliefs and their refusal to bear arms. Seeking religious freedom, many Quakers flocked to Pennsylvania, as did a host of others seeking religious tolerance, including the Mennonites, Amish, Moravians, and Baptists. Pennsylvania soon became economically prosperous, in part because of the industrious Quaker work ethic. By the 1750s, Pennsylvania's capital, Philadelphia, had become the largest city in the colonies with a population of 20,000.

The Southern Colonies

Virginia, centered in Jamestown, dominated the Southern colonies, which included the Chesapeake colonies, Maryland, and the Carolinas. The region was more religiously and ethnically diverse than the Middle or New England colonies, harboring immigrants from all over Europe, many Roman Catholics (especially in Maryland), and a large number of African slaves. In the South, families were less common and smaller than in other regions because adult men far outnumbered women. Men, after all, were needed to work on the region's massive plantations.

Plantations, which produced tobacco, rice, and indigo, influenced all aspects of life in the South. The importance of plantations limited the development of cities and a merchant class, which brought such wealth to New England. Because they needed so much labor to operate, plantations drew many immigrants to the Chesapeake region during the seventeenth century. Landowners acquired this labor through the institution of **indentured servitude**. Indentured servants were adult men, mostly white, who bound themselves to labor on plantations for a fixed number of years until they earned their freedom and, with it, a small plot of land. However, once free, indentured servants still had to struggle to survive, and great tensions arose between the freed servants and the increasingly powerful plantation owners. These tensions flared in **Bacon's Rebellion** of 1676. In this insurrection, Nathaniel Bacon, an impoverished nobleman, accused the royal governor of Virginia of failing to protect the less wealthy farmers from Native American raids. Bacon led a group of about 300 small farmers and indiscriminately attacked the Native Americans. The royal governor branded him a rebel, and Bacon then led his men to Jamestown, where he occupied, looted, and burned the city while demanding political reforms. Bacon died suddenly in 1676, and his rebellion fell with him. But Bacon's death did not eliminate the tension between rich and poor.

As tobacco plantations grew in size through the sixteenth century and demand for labor increased, slavery became the preferred labor policy in the South: it proved economically profitable and relaxed the strains that produced Bacon's Rebellion. By 1660, slavery was officially sanctioned by law. At this time, fewer than 1,000 slaves lived in Maryland and Virginia. Over the next forty years, that number grew to nearly 20,000 slaves in the region. Slavery later spread to the Carolinas and by the early eighteenth century it was so entrenched in these areas that slaves outnumbered free whites.

Black slaves were increasingly brought to the Southern colonies during the late 1600s to support an economy based on massive cash crops like tobacco, rice, and eventually cotton. By 1660, slavery was officially recognized by law.

Colonial Culture

In eighteenth-century Europe, the intellectual movement known as the **Enlightenment** arose and championed the principles of rationalism and logic, while the Scientific Revolution worked to demystify the natural world. Upper-class Americans, including many of the colonists who would eventually lead the Revolution, kept in close touch with these movements and were heavily influenced by Enlightenment ideas, such as faith in the power of human reason and skepticism toward beliefs that could not be proven by science or clear logic. Religion was a prime target for Enlightenment thinkers. The American most representative of Enlightenment ideals was **Benjamin Franklin**, who devoted his life to intellectual pursuits. Franklin published *Poor Richard's Almanac*, a collection of proverbs, in 1732. He created the American Philosophical Society in 1743.

The First Great Awakening

Not all Americans shared the Enlightenment skepticism toward religion. In fact, perhaps in response to the religious skepticism espoused by the Enlightenment, the 1730s and 1740s saw a broad movement of religious fervor called the **First Great Awakening**. During this time, revival ministers stressed the emptiness of material comfort, the corruption of human nature, and the need for immediate repentance lest individuals incur divine fury. These revivalists, such as Jonathon Edwards and the Englishman George Whitefield, stressed that believers must rely on their own conscience to achieve an inner, emotional understanding of religious truth. Jonathon Edwards gave an impassioned sermon called "Sinners in the Hands of an Angry God," in which he proclaimed that man must save himself by immediately repenting his sins.

The Great Awakening was a revival movement meant to purify religion from material distractions and renew one's personal faith in God. The movement was a reaction against the waning of religion and the spread of skepticism during the Enlightenment of the 1700s.

The Great Awakening is often credited with democratizing religion, since revivalist ministers stressed that anyone who repents can be saved by God, not just those who are prominent members of established churches. For this reason, the movement appealed to all classes and groups. Revival ministers reached out to the poor, to slaves, and to Native Americans. Because of its message, the Great Awakening divided American Protestants, pitting the revivalists, called New Lights, against the more established ministers happy with the status quo, called Old Lights. Out of this division arose many new religious congregations and sects. The schism also resulted in the formation of many universities founded to teach New Light ministers. Some of these universities are Princeton, Columbia, Brown, and Dartmouth.

Colonial Wars

By the late 1600s, the French and English had emerged as the two dominant forces in North America. The two nations jockeyed for position in Europe and the New World, resulting in occasional wars that took place simultaneously on both continents (though the wars on the two continents often had different names, and sometimes occurred over slightly different time periods). This series of wars, which ranged through the first half of the 18th century, culminated in the French and Indian War of 1754–1763.

The Path to War

In the early 1750s, Virginia, Pennsylvania, France, and the Iroquois tribe all claimed ownership of the Ohio Valley. The French began constructing forts to stave off English colonial advances and to maintain their fur trade with local Native Americans. In 1754, a young George Washington, on the orders of the Virginia governor, led about 400 Virginia militiamen against the French. He was quickly forced to surrender and lead his men home.

Following this and other skirmishes, colonial delegates gathered in Albany, New York. Benjamin Franklin submitted the **Albany Plan**, which called for the colonies to unify in the face of French and Native American threats. The Albany Plan, remarkable for its attempt to establish a unified colonial government, won the support of the delegates but was rejected by the colonies, who were not yet ready for union. British officials did not push for the union because they were wary of the powerful colonial entity it would create.

The French and Indian War

Soon after the Albany meeting, the **French and Indian War** broke out, pitting England against France and its Native American allies. This war paralleled the Seven Years War in Europe (1756–1763). England held a great advantage in men and supplies, yet in the first two years the cunning guerrilla tactics of the French and their allies resulted in numerous humiliating losses for the English. Still, under the able leadership of Prime Minister William Pitt, England righted itself and pushed France out of the Ohio Valley and into Canada. In 1759, English forces captured Quebec, effectively ending the war in North America. Under the **Treaty of Paris** (1763), Britain gained all of the land in North America east of the Mississippi.

The euphoria of victory, however, soon wore off. Because of the costs of the war, England faced tough financial straits. The English reasoned that because the colonies benefited most from the war they should be taxed to pay for England's war debt. England ended its century-long policy of salutary neglect. This change in policy sparked an escalating tension between England and its colonists that eventually led to the American Revolution.

The Writs of Assistance

The first instance of tensions between the colonies and England actually occurred in the middle of the French and Indian War. During the war, colonial traders smuggled French goods from the French West Indies in order to avoid English taxes—set by the 1733 Molasses Act—on molasses, rum, and sugar imported from non-British territories. As its war debt accumulated, England desired stricter enforcement of the Molasses Act in order to raise more revenue from the colonies. In 1760, England authorized British revenue officers to use **writs of assistance** to help them in this task. Writs of assistance served as general search warrants, allowing customs officials to enter and investigate any ship or building suspected of holding smuggled goods.

The writs of assistance proved a useful tool in fighting smuggling, allowing the British to seize and ransack many buildings and ships. However, the writs greatly angered colonists (and some people in England). In 1761, Boston merchants challenged the constitutionality of the writs before the Massachusetts Supreme Court, arguing that the writs stood "against the fundamental principles of law." Although they lost the case, the merchants and other colonists continued to protest against the writs, believing Britain had overstepped its bounds.

Colonists and many British observers were outraged at the breach of what had been considered traditional English liberties. Writs of assistance allowed officials to enter and ransack private homes and ships without proving probable cause for suspicion, a customary prerequisite for any search in England.

The Colonial Period

Revolution and Constitution

Trends and Themes of the Era

- Increased British taxation of the colonies after the French and Indian war led to tension. Colonists felt they were being taxed without representation in government. The British felt the colonists were getting the benefits of English citizenship without paying the taxes required.

- The colonies resisted British taxation and other legislation. The British responded by implementing stricter taxes and reprisals, which the colonists opposed more fiercely and violently. During this period, colonial resistance efforts became increasingly unified.

- Colonists felt the British were denying them their natural rights, as described by John Locke and other Enlightenment thinkers. As revolution became more likely, many colonists hoped to implement a government independent of the British crown and based on Enlightenment ideals.

- After the Revolution, the states reacted against their experience with the strong central government of Parliament by creating a loose federation under the Articles of Confederation. When this loose federation proved too weak, the colonists wrote the Constitution, which outlined a strong central government that, through the system of checks and balances, was still limited in scope. The Constitution represented a desire for a strong but limited government that was dedicated to preserving individual and state freedoms.

- Two debates during the writing and ratification of the Constitution highlighted issues that would generate conflicts in the newly formed United States: 1) the separate interests of northern and southern states, and the role of slavery in sectional debates; 2) the proper balance between states' rights and federal power.

British Impositions and Colonial Resistance, 1763–1770

After the **French and Indian War**, Britain was the premier colonial power in North America. The Treaty of Paris (1763) more than doubled British territories in North America and eliminated the French as a threat. While British power seemed more secure than ever, there were signs of trouble brewing in the colonies. The main problem concerned British finances. The British government had accumulated a massive debt fighting the French and Indian War, and now looked toward the American colonies to help pay it. **King George III** and his prime minister, George Grenville, noted that the colonists had benefited most from the expensive war and yet had paid very little in comparison to citizens living in England. To even this disparity, Parliament passed a series of acts (listed below) designed to secure revenue from the colonies. In addition, royal officials revoked their policy of **salutary neglect** and began to enforce the Navigation Acts, and newer taxation measures, with vigor. These policies angered many colonists, who chafed under such tight British control.

The Proclamation Line

In 1763, in efforts to keep peace with the Native Americans, the British government established the Proclamation Line barring colonial settlement west of the Allegheny Mountains in Pennsylvania. The Proclamation declared that colonists already settled in this region must remove themselves, negating colonists' claims to the West and thus inhibiting colonial expansion. This directive angered many colonists, though there was little political reaction.

The Sugar Act

In 1764, Parliament passed the **Sugar Act** to counter smuggling of foreign sugar and to establish a British monopoly in the American sugar market. The act also allowed royal officials to seize colonial cargo with little prompting or legal cause. Unlike previous acts, which had regulated trade to boost the entire British Imperial economy, the Sugar Act was designed to benefit England at the expense of the American colonists. In other words, the Sugar Act was a profit-seeking measure geared toward securing revenue *for* England *from* the colonists. The colonists felt the British were levying an unfair tax.

A major criticism of the Sugar Act was that it aimed not to regulate the economy of the British Empire but to raise revenue for the British government. This distinction became important as the colonists determined which actions of the British government warranted resistance.

The Stamp Act

As a further measure to force the colonies to help pay off the war debt, Prime Minister Grenville pushed the **Stamp Act** through Parliament in March 1765. This act required Americans to buy special watermarked paper for newspapers, playing cards, and legal documents such as wills and marriage licenses. Violators faced juryless trials in Nova Scotian vice-admiralty courts, where guilt was presumed until innocence was proven.

Like the Sugar Act, the Stamp Act was aimed at raising revenue from the colonists. As such, it elicited fierce colonial resistance. In the colonies, legal pamphlets circulated condemning the act on the grounds that it was **"taxation without representation."** Colonists believed they should not have to pay Parliamentary taxes because they did not elect any members of Parliament. They argued that they should be able to determine their own taxes independent of Parliament.

Prime Minister Grenville and his followers retorted that Americans were obliged to pay Parliamentary taxes because they shared the same status as many British males who did not have enough property to be granted the vote or who lived in certain large cities that had no seats in Parliament. He claimed that all of these people were "virtually represented" in Parliament. This theory of **virtual representation** held that the members of Parliament not only represented their specific geographical constituencies, but they also considered the well-being of all British subjects when deliberating on legislation.

Opposition to the Stamp Act

The **Stamp Act** generated the first wave of significant colonial resistance to British rule. In late May 1765, the Virginia House of Burgesses passed the **Virginia Resolves**, which denied Parliament's right to tax the colonies under the Stamp Act. Word of these resolutions spread, and by the end of the year, eight other colonial legislatures had adopted similar positions.

As dissent spread through the colonies, it quickly became more organized. Radical groups calling themselves the **Sons of Liberty** formed throughout the colonies to channel the widespread violence, often burning stamps and threatening British officials. Merchants in New York began a boycott of British goods and merchants in other cities

Revolution and Constitution

soon joined in. Representatives of nine colonial assemblies met in New York City at the **Stamp Act Congress**, where they prepared a petition asking Parliament to repeal the Stamp Act on the grounds that it violated the principle of "no taxation without representation." The congress argued that Parliament could not tax anyone outside of Great Britain and could not deny anyone a fair trial, both of which had been consequences of the Stamp Act.

The Stamp Act Congress was a major step in uniting the colonies against the British. Nine colonial delegations attended and agreed that there could be no taxation without representation.

Under strong pressure from the colonies, and with their economy slumping because of the American boycott of British goods, Parliament repealed the Stamp Act in March 1766. But, at the same time, Parliament passed the **Declaratory Act** to solidify British rule in the colonies. The Declaratory Act stated that Parliament had the power to tax and legislate for the colonies "in all cases whatsoever," denying the colonists' desire to set up their own legislature.

The Townshend Duties

In 1767, Britain's elite landowners exercised political influence to cut their taxes by one-fourth, leaving the British treasury short £500,000 from the previous year. By that time, Chancellor Charles Townshend dominated government affairs. His superior, Prime Minister William Pitt (who was the second prime minister after Grenville) had become gravely ill, and Townshend had assumed leadership of the government. Townshend proposed taxing imports into the American colonies to recover Parliament's lost revenue, and secured passage of the Revenue Act of 1767. Popularly referred to as the **Townshend Duties**, the Revenue Act taxed glass, lead, paint, paper, and tea entering the colonies. The profits from these taxes were to be used to pay the salaries of the royal governors in the colonies. In practice, however, the Townshend Duties yielded little income for the British; the taxes on tea brought in the only significant revenue.

Opposition to the Townshend Duties

While ineffective in raising revenue, the Townshend Duties proved remarkably effective in stirring up political dissent, which had lain dormant since the repeal of the Stamp Act. Protest against the taxes first took the form of intellectual and legal dissents and soon erupted in violence.

In December 1767, the colonist John Dickinson published **Letters From a Pennsylvania Farmer** in the Pennsylvania Chronicle. This series of twelve letters argued against the legality of the Townshend Duties and soon appeared in nearly every colonial newspaper. They were widely read and admired. Political opposition to the Townshend Duties spread, as colonial assemblies passed resolves denouncing the act and petitioning Parliament for its repeal.

Popular protest once again took the form of a boycott of British goods. Although the colonial boycott was only moderately successful at keeping British imports out of the colonies, it prompted many British merchants and artisans to mount a significant movement in Britain to repeal the Townshend Duties. Sailors joined the resistance by rioting against corrupt customs officials. Many customs officials exploited the ambiguous and confusing wording of the Towsnhend Act to claim that small items stored in a sailor's chest were undeclared cargo. The custom's officers then seized entire ships based on that charge. Often, they pocketed the profits. Known as "customs racketeering," this behavior amounted to little more than legalized piracy.

In 1768, 1,700 British troops landed in Boston to stem further violence, and the following year passed relatively peacefully. But tension again flared with the **Boston Massacre** in March 1770, when an unruly mob bombarded British troops with rocks and dared them to shoot. In the ensuing chaos, five colonists were killed. The Boston Massacre marked the peak of colonial opposition to the Townshend Duties.

Parliament finally relented and repealed most of the Townshend Duties in March 1770, partially because England was now led by a new prime minister, Lord North. North eliminated most of the taxes but insisted on maintaining the profitable tax on tea. In response, Americans ended the policy of general non-importation, but maintained voluntary agreements to boycott British tea. Non-consumption kept the tea tax revenues far too low to pay the royal governors, effectively nullifying what remained of the Townshend Duties.

Road to Revolution, 1770–1775

From 1770 to 1772, the British basically ignored the colonies and tension cooled substantially. However, in the fall of 1772, Lord North began preparations to pay royal governors out of customs revenue rather than let the colonial assemblies control payment. This would deny the assemblies the "power of the purse," breaking assemblies' ability to effectively check royal power by withholding, or threatening to withhold, payment. In response to this threat, **Samuel Adams** urged every Massachusetts community to appoint a committee to coordinate colony-wide measures protecting colonial rights. Within the year, approximately 250 **Committees of Correspondence** formed throughout the colonies. These committees linked political leaders of almost every colony in resistance to the British.

The Committees of Correspondence began on the community level in Massachusetts and eventually became the method by which the colonies coordinated their efforts to preserve their rights.

The Boston Tea Party

The British East India Company suffered from the American boycott of British tea. In an effort to save the company, Parliament passed the **Tea Act** in 1773, which eliminated import tariffs on tea entering England and allowed the company to sell directly to consumers rather than through merchants. These changes lowered the price of British tea to below that of smuggled tea, which the British hoped would end the boycott. Parliament planned to use the profits from tea sales to pay the salaries of the colonial royal governors, a move which, as we saw with the Townshend Duties, particularly angered colonists.

While protests of the Tea Act in the form of tea boycotts and the burning of tea cargos occurred throughout the colonies, the response in Boston was most aggressive. In December 1773, a group of colonists dressed as Native Americans dumped about $70,000 worth of the tea into Boston Harbor. This event, known as the **Boston Tea Party**, took on an epic status.

The Intolerable Acts

Parliament responded swiftly and angrily to the Tea Party with a string of legislation that came to be known as the **Intolerable Acts**. The Intolerable Acts included the four Coercive Acts of 1773 and the Quebec Act. The four Coercive Acts:

- Closed Boston Harbor to trade until the city paid for the lost tea.

- Removed certain democratic elements of the Massachusetts government, most notably by making formerly elected positions appointed by the crown.

- Restricted town meetings, requiring that their agenda be approved by the royal governor

- Declared that any royal agent charged with murder in the colonies would be tried in Britain.

- Instated the Quartering Act, forcing civilians to house and support British soldiers

The Quebec Act, unrelated to the Coercive Acts but just as offensive to the colonists, established Roman Catholicism as Quebec's official religion, gave Quebec's royal governors wide powers, and extended Quebec's borders south to the Ohio River and west to the Mississippi, thereby inhibiting westward expansion of the colonies.

Revolution and Constitution

The colonists saw the Intolerable Acts as a British plan to starve the New England colonists while reducing their ability to organize and protest. The acts not only imposed a heavy military presence in the colonies, but also, in the colonists' minds, effectively authorized the military to murder colonists with immunity. Colonists feared that once the colonies had been subdued Britain would impose the autocratic model of government outlined in the Quebec Act.

British Acts and Colonial Responses

British Act	Colonial Response(s)
Writs of Assistance, 1760	Challenged laws in Massachusetts Supreme Court, lost case (discussed in previous chapter)
Sugar Act, 1764	Weak protest by colonial legislatures
Stamp Act, 1765	Virginia Resolves, mobs, Sons of Liberty, Stamp Act Congress
Townshend Duties, 1767	*Letters from a Pennsylvania Farmer*, boycott, Boston Massacre
Tea Act, 1773	Boston Tea Party
Intolerable Acts, 1773	First Continental Congress

The First Continental Congress

In September 1774 the Committees of Correspondence of every colony except Georgia sent delegates to the **First Continental Congress**. The Congress endorsed Massachusetts' **Suffolk Resolves**, which declared that the colonies need not obey the Coercive Acts since they infringed upon basic liberties. The delegates voted for an organized boycott of British imports and sent to **King George III**'s attention a petition, which conceded that Parliament had the power to regulate commerce but objected to its arbitrary taxation and denial of fair trials to colonists. Preparing for possible British retaliation, the delegates also called upon all colonies to raise and train local militias. By the spring of 1775, colonists had established provincial congresses to enforce the decrees of the Continental Congress. These congresses rivaled the colonial governors for power.

The First Battles

In April 1775, colonial **minutemen** met and exchanged fire with British soldiers attempting to seize a supply stockpile in Concord, a town near Boston. The first confrontation came in Lexington, a town on the way to Concord. Once in Concord, the British troops faced a much larger colonial force. In the skirmish, the British lost 273 men and were driven back into Boston. The Battle of Lexington and Concord con-

Revolution and Constitution

vinced many colonists to take up arms. The next night, 20,000 New England troops began a month-long siege of the British garrison in Boston. In June of 1775, the English attacked the colonial stronghold outside Boston in the Battle of Bunker Hill. The English redcoats successfully dislodged the colonials from the hillside stronghold, but lost 1,154 men, in contrast to the just 311 colonial losses.

Attempted Reconciliation

In May 1775, as violence broke out all over New England, the **Second Continental Congress** convened in Philadelphia. Congress was split. New England delegates urged independence from Britain. Other delegates, mostly those from the Middle Colonies, wanted a more moderate course of action. The latter faction, led by John Dickinson, fervently opposed complete separation from England. In an effort to reconcile with the King, Dickinson penned the Olive Branch Petition, offering peace under the following conditions:

- A cease-fire in Boston

- The Coercive Acts be repealed

- Negotiations between the colonists and Britain commence immediately

The Olive Branch Petition reached Britain the same day as news of the Battle of Bunker Hill. King George III rejected reconciliation and declared New England to be in a state of rebellion in August 1775.

The Declaration of Independence

In June 1775, the Second Continental Congress elected **George Washington** commander in chief of the newly established American Continental Army. Meanwhile, the British forces abandoned Boston and moved to New York City, which they planned to use as a staging point for conquering New England.

In January 1776, **Thomas Paine**'s pamphlet, *Common Sense*, was published and widely distributed. Paine called for economic and political independence, and proposed that America become a new kind of nation founded on the principles of liberty. By May 1776, Rhode Island had declared its independence and New England was deep in rebellion.

In June, the Second Continental Congress adopted a resolution of independence, officially creating the United States of America. **Thomas Jefferson**'s draft of the **Declaration of Independence** was officially approved on July 4. The Declaration of Independence proclaimed a complete and irrevocable break from England, arguing that the British government had broken its contract with the colonies. It extolled the virtues of democratic self-government, and tapped into the Enlightenment ideas of John Locke and others who promoted equality, liberty, justice, and self-fulfillment.

The Revolutionary War

Note: The SAT II will not ask you specific questions about facts during the Revolutionary War, such as the names of generals or the succession of battles. It is more important to know about the events leading up to and following the war. We have included the following short summary of the war because we think it provides an important context for understanding the events preceding and following the war.

Sizing up the Competitors

After the delegates at the Second Continental Congress signed the Declaration of Independence, the two sides readied themselves for war. The numbers were heavily in Britain's favor. In 1776, 11 million people inhabited the British Isles. Only 2.5 million lived in the newly formed United Sates, and not all of the colonists favored independence.

The colonists were able to build an army about equal in size to the British forces, but while British forces were well-trained veterans, the American forces were badly funded and under-trained. The Continental Army and local militias could not compete with the Redcoats, or British troops, in pitched battles. It is for this reason that the American forces fought few major battles during the first year of the war. When they did fight, they usually lost badly. In addition, the powerful British navy patrolled the seas.

The Americans found much-needed allies in their war against Britain. In 1778, the Americans gained their most important ally when France joined the war on the American side. Within two years Spain and the Dutch Republic had also declared war against Britain. Caught in an international war, the British had to split their troops between Europe and North America. With their forces thus divided, the British relied more and more heavily on loyalists to fight in the colonies, and soon found that they had overestimated loyalist support.

Division Among the Colonists

The signing of the Declaration of Independence ignited a sharp division in the colonies between the **Whigs**, in favor of Independence, and the **Tories**, British loyalists and sympathizers. Approximately twenty percent of free Americans were Tories. Tory influence was most powerful in the Middle Colonies and in Georgia. Slaves also made up a significant number of Tory loyalists, responding to incentives offered by Britain such as freedom for any slave who fought to restore royal authority. The most prominent Whig strongholds were New England, Virginia, and South Carolina.

Revolution and Constitution

War in the North

Early in the war, George Washington's forces around New York were driven back to Pennsylvania by the superior British forces. Beginning on Christmas 1776, Washington fought back and won decisive victories at Trenton and Princeton, New Jersey. In October 1777, the Continentals won another decisive victory at the Battle of Saratoga. This victory raised the U.S. army's morale and convinced France to recognize U.S. independence and to join the war against Britain.

In early December 1777, 11,000 troops under George Washington's command marched through the snow to spend the winter at Valley Forge, Pennsylvania, where they regrouped and trained. In June 1778, these newly trained troops met the British at the Battle of Monmouth Courthouse, which lasted six hours in 100° heat. The battle ended when the Redcoats retreated, bringing victory in the North to the Americans.

War on the Frontier

The British enlisted the help of Native Americans all along the American frontier. In modern Illinois and Indiana, bands of militiamen from Kentucky and elsewhere ventured into the wilderness to combat British attempts to establish forts and to ally with Native Americans. Further east, the Americans led an attack against the pro-British Iroquois, burning some twenty villages to the ground, destroying a million bushels of corn, and forcing the Iroquois into Canada.

War in the South

In 1778, France joined the war against Britain, as did Spain and the Dutch Republic in 1779 and 1780, respectively. Finding themselves in a larger war than they'd anticipated, the British turned their attention southward because the southern ports in America provided the flexibility necessary to carry out a geographically broad conflict, and because loyalist influences were far stronger in the South than they were in the North. The British gained control of the Continental garrison at Charleston, South Carolina in May 1780. In August 1780, they crushed a group of poorly trained Continentals at Camden, South Carolina. The British troops continued to win battles between March and September 1781, though not without a significant cost to their forces.

The War Ends

Washington moved his forces from New York toward Yorktown, Virginia, where the British had established a new base. Near Yorktown, Washington joined 2,500 French troops and a small American force. In October 1781, these troops besieged the British base until the smaller British force surrendered. The British defeat crushed their troops' fighting spirit as well as public support for the war in Britain, effectively ending the war.

King George III initially refused to admit defeat, but official peace talks finally began in June 1782. The **Treaty of Paris of 1783** was signed in September 1783. In it, the British recognized American independence and defined the borders of the United States as follows: the northern border along Canada, the western border along the Mississippi, and the southern border along Spanish Florida (a line disputed by Spain). The treaty stipulated that the Continental Congress would recommend restoration of confiscated property to loyalists. Also, Britain agreed to evacuate its troops.

With the Treaty of Paris of 1783, the British recognized American independence and agreed to evacuate their troops. The United States borders were set along Canada, the Mississippi, and Spanish Florida.

A New Government for the United States

The thirteen states of the new United States of America began the process of creating state governments during the **Revolutionary War**. Rhode Island and Connecticut maintained their colonial charters while excising references to British sovereignty, but many states wrote new constitutions. State constitutions differed from traditional British constitutions in that they were written documents ratified by the people and could be amended by popular vote. These constitutions varied widely, but shared the following similarities:

- By 1784, all thirteen state constitutions contained a bill of rights outlining the civil rights and freedoms accorded citizens.

- In general, the constitutions established weak executive branches and responsive legislatures. Most called for bicameral legislatures and for appointed, rather than elected, officials.

- Most reduced property requirements for voting and otherwise increased social equality.

- Most called for no official state religion.

The Articles of Confederation

In an attempt to create a unified national government, John Dickinson brought the **Articles of Confederation** to the Continental Congress in July 1776. Congress adopted the Articles and sent copies out for ratification by state legislatures; the Articles became law in 1781.

The Articles of Confederation favored the rights of individual colonies, now called states, instead of a strong centralized system. The central government established by the Articles was virtually powerless. It consisted of a severely restricted Congress alone, with no executive branch or judicial department. Congress had no power to tax, raise troops, regulate interstate commerce, or make binding national treaties; it could only request taxes from states, not demand them, and therefore could not regulate currency or raise money for the nation. The Articles of Confederation demonstrated the colonists' dislike of centralized authority and their fear of falling under a system as potentially tyrannical as they felt the British system had been.

The Articles of Confederation set up a weak national government, which demonstrated the colonists' dislike of centralized authority and their fear of falling under a system as potentially tyrannical as they felt the British system had been.

Three major political challenges arose, testing the viability of the government created by the Articles of Confederation. The first challenge was addressing the nation's finances. After the war, the United States faced enormous debt. In 1781 and again in 1783, Congress proposed an import tax to finance the national budget and guarantee the payment of war debts, but each time, a state rejected the proposal (Rhode Island in 1781 and New York in 1783). With no power to force taxation on the states without state approval, Congress could do nothing to regulate the economy. The government was financially helpless.

The government faced the challenge of westward expansion with more success. Settlers, speculators, and state governments all pressed for expansion into the lands granted to the U.S. under the Treaty of Paris. The government attempted to control this expansion with the Land Ordinance of 1785, which outlined the protocol for settlement. A second ordinance, the **Northwest Ordinance** of 1787, forbade slavery in the territory above the Ohio River, contained a settlers' bill of rights, and defined the process through which territories could become states. In such expansion efforts, the government faced fierce opposition from the Native Americans and Spanish along the frontier. The Spanish, denying the validity of the Treaty of Paris that ended the Revolutionary War, closed the port of New Orleans to American commerce in 1784.

The third challenge to the Articles of Confederation concerned the government's ability to maintain law and order. Depression, inflation, and high taxes made life miserable for many Americans. The plight of farmers in western Massachusetts led to **Shays's Rebellion**. In August 1786, Daniel Shays, angered by high taxes and debt he could not repay, led about 2,000 men in closing the courts in three western Massachusetts counties to prevent foreclosure on farms. The actions of Shays exposed the inability of the central government to control revolt and impose order, and heightened a growing sense of panic around the nation.

For many Americans, Shays's Rebellion, along with the economic depression, revealed the shortcomings of national government under the Articles of Confederation. Congress could neither suppress revolt nor regulate inflation; it had neither policing nor financial power.

The Constitution

In September 1786, delegates from five states met at the **Annapolis Convention**. Originally concerned with interstate commerce, the delegates turned their focus to the shortcomings of the national government. They proposed a convention to consider amending the Articles of Confederation. Congress agreed, and asked the states to appoint delegates to convene in Philadelphia.

In May 1787, fifty-five delegates, representing every state except Rhode Island, met in Philadelphia. Notable delegates included George Washington, John Dickinson, **John Jay**, **Benjamin Franklin**, **Alexander Hamilton**, and **James Madison**. The delegates were convinced of the need for a stronger national government. The first question facing the delegates was whether to amend the Articles of Confederation or to create a new framework of government. The decision was made to create a new framework embodied in a new constitution, and the convention became known as the **Constitutional Convention**.

Writing the Constitution: Conflict and Resolution

The main difficulty in drafting the **Constitution** immediately became clear: achieving a balance between the needs of large and small states. James Madison presented the **Virginia Plan**, a framework of government that contained one potential solution to this problem. The plan called for a bicameral (two house) legislature with representation in both houses proportional to population. These houses of Congress would jointly name the president and federal judges. But the smaller states opposed the Virginia Plan, since representation by population would give more power to the larger states. Smaller states supported the **New Jersey Plan**, which called for a unicameral (one house) Congress in which each state would have an equal number of seats.

In June 1787, a committee assigned to resolve this conflict approved the **Connecticut Compromise**, which created a bicameral legislature where each state received an equal vote in the upper house, and representation in the lower house was proportional to population. In September 1787, the new Constitution was approved by the convention and sent to the states for ratification.

Revolution and Constitution

The Connecticut Compromise combined the Virginia Plan's suggestion of proportional representation and the New Jersey Plan's suggestion of equal representation for all states, creating the House of Representatives and the Senate as we know them today.

A second debate resolved by the Constitution concerned the representation of slave states: whether slaves should be counted as persons or as property for the purposes of representation and taxation. Northern states, where slavery was not terribly common, argued that to count slaves as members of the population would give the South an unfair advantage in the lower house, where representation was proportional to population. The solution came in the **three-fifths clause**, which allowed three-fifths of all slaves to be counted as people.

The Constitution Completed

The document that emerged from Philadelphia represented, ultimately, a balance between a number of different forces:

- The delegates' acceptance of the need to strengthen the national government and their fear of government despotism and tyranny

- The interests of the larger and smaller states

- The interests of Northern and Southern states

The government was granted the powers to set and collect taxes, to regulate interstate commerce, and to conduct diplomacy in international affairs. The national government was also given the power to invoke military action against the states. The Constitution declared all acts and treaties made by Congress to be binding on the states.

The Constitution proposed a government composed of three branches: the legislative, executive, and judicial. A system of **checks and balances,** in which each branch of the government held certain powers over the others protected against tyranny, and was the cornerstone of the new framework of government. According to the checks and balances:

- The president, the head of the executive branch, could veto acts of Congress and was responsible for appointing Supreme Court and other federal judges.

- Congress, as a joint body, was given the power to impeach, try, and remove the president or Supreme Court justices from office, if necessary. The upper house of Congress, the Senate, could ratify or reject treaties proposed by the president, and had to approve the president's cabinet appointments.

- The judicial branch, headed by the Supreme Court, had the power to interpret the laws passed by Congress.

The writers of the Constitution wanted to increase the power of the national government without debilitating the states. They reserved for state legislatures the powers to elect members of the Senate and to select delegates to the Electoral College that elected the President. Further, they stipulated that the Constitution could be amended by a vote of three-fourths of the state legislatures.

Federal government can:	State governments can:
Regulate foreign and interstate commerce	Regulate intrastate commerce
Levy taxes	Run elections
Coin money	Ratify proposed constitutional amendments
Conduct international relations	Provide education
Declare and wage war	Maintain the integrity of state borders
Raise an army and navy	Maintain police power

The centerpiece of the Constitution was the establishment of the checks and balances system, which would prevent any of the three branches of government from becoming too powerful.

The Fight For Ratification

Once approved by the Constitutional Convention in 1787, the Constitution was sent to the states for ratification. Only two-thirds (nine) of the states were needed to ratify it to put the new government into operation. Since states that did not ratify the Constitution would remain under the authority of the Articles of Confederation, the possibility existed that the United States would be divided into two countries.

The process of ratification began with two opposed and entrenched sides. The supporters of the Constitution called themselves **Federalists.** Their opponents went by the name **Anti-federalists.** The Anti-federalists claimed the Constitution granted too much power to the national government. They argued that the Constitution doomed the states to be dominated by a potentially tyrannical central government. Federalists defended the necessity of a strong national government and lauded the Constitution as the best possible framework.

The Federalists pushed ratification through eight state conventions by May 1788, though Rhode Island and North Carolina both rejected the Constitution outright.

Revolution and Constitution

Virginia and New York, states crucial to the Union in terms of population and economics, remained undecided. In June 1788, New Hampshire became the ninth state to ratify the Constitution, making the document effective as the framework of national government, and leaving Virginia and New York outside that government. Debate gripped both states. In late June 1788, Virginia finally ratified the Constitution by a narrow fifty-three percent majority. In New York, debate continued for a month until Alexander Hamilton's Federalists finally emerged victorious by a margin only slightly greater than that in Virginia.

The writings of the political leaders of this period are an important part of American history. The most notable works are collected as **The Federalist Papers**, a series of articles written by John Jay, James Madison, and Alexander Hamilton. How much influence *The Federalist Papers* actually had in the ratification of the Constitution is up for debate, but the articles do clearly explain the arguments in favor of the Constitution.

Revolution and Constitution

A New Nation

Trends and Themes of the Era

- The U.S. government began to build and define itself under George Washington.

- The differences in opinion shown in the debates over ratification of the Constitution soon spawned the development of two separate political parties. New England Federalists supported a loose interpretation of the Constitution and a strong central government. Southern Republicans supported a strict interpretation of the Constitution and a more limited central government. Enmity between the two parties deepened, until the events of the War of 1812 finally eliminated the Federalists as a significant political party.

- The U.S. made a concerted effort to stay out of European entanglements and maintain neutrality in its effort to build its national infrastructure. Often, though, the U.S. was caught in a tug-of-war between Britain and France. Eventually, British aggression and America's desire to increase its territory and prove itself as an international force led to the War of 1812.

- After the war, the U.S. enjoyed a period of optimism and general cooperation under a single political party: the Republicans. In this period, the U.S. asserted its dominance in the Western Hemisphere through the Monroe Doctrine.

- Westward expansion began in earnest after the Louisiana Purchase. The sectional tensions created by expansion, made apparent in the Missouri Compromise, illustrated the increasing role slavery and regionalism would play in the politics of the nineteenth century.

- Through various rulings, the Supreme Court established itself as a body able to declare the acts of Congress unconstitutional, and supportive of Federalist policies.

The Federalist Era Begins: George Washington as President

George Washington was elected the United States' first president, and took the oath of office on April 30, 1789. His vice president was **John Adams**.

The First Congress

The Constitution provided the new country with only a skeleton framework, which had to be elaborated upon and implemented. When Washington took office, no judiciary department existed, meaning that no laws could be enforced. Nor were there any executive posts such as attorney general or secretary of state. Also, no taxes had been set and the navy had been disbanded. During Washington's two terms as president, from 1789 to 1797, Congress developed the nation's much-needed legal, bureaucratic, and military machinery.

The first Congress under the Constitution convened in New York City in March 1789. Congress immediately set out to establish a judicial branch, develop the executive branch, set a legislative agenda, and meet the popular demand for a bill of rights. As Congress worked out the details of government bureaucracy and domestic policy, Washington focused primarily on matters of finance, diplomacy, and the military. He interacted very little with Congress. He rarely spoke publicly about policy, suggested few laws, and vetoed only two bills in all eight years of his presidency.

Creating the Courts

Congress created a court system with the **Judiciary Act of 1789**. The act established a federal district court in each state, affirmed that the Supreme Court exercised final jurisdiction in all legal matters, and set the number of Supreme Court judges at six. In 1796 the Supreme Court first asserted its power to determine the constitutionality of congressional statutes.

Building a Cabinet

The Constitution only provided the general framework of the executive branch without specifying the number and the duties of executive posts. In 1789, Congress established what came to be known as the cabinet: three executive posts (secretary of state, of war, and of treasury), as well as the office of Attorney General. Washington appointed **Thomas Jefferson** as Secretary of State, **Alexander Hamilton** as Secretary of Treasury, Henry Knox as Secretary of War, and Edmund Randolph as Attorney General.

The Bill of Rights

The Bill of Rights was a concession made by the Federalists to the Anti-federalists, who were concerned that a strong government would usurp the rights of individuals and states. James Madison led the group that drafted the first ten amendments to the Constitution, collectively known as the **Bill of Rights**, which the state legislatures ratified in December 1791. The Bill of Rights sought to enumerate certain liberties that could not be invaded by the federal government.

The Bill of Rights

1	freedom of religion, speech, press, assembly, petition
2	right to bear arms
3	soldiers shall not be quartered in any house without owner's consent
4	protection against unreasonable search and seizure
5	rights of accused persons: required indictment by grand jury; no double jeopardy; right to refuse self-incrimination; right to due process; just compensation
6	right to speedy and public trial, confrontation by witnesses, ability to call one's own witnesses
7	right to trial by jury
8	protections against excessive bail and cruel and unusual punishment
9	all rights not enumerated by the Constitution are retained by the people
10	powers not delegated to the United States are reserved to the States, or to the people

Federalists vs. Anti-federalists

The conflict between the Federalists and the Anti-federalists shaped much of the nation's early political debate and policy. The Federalists, led by Secretary of Treasury Alexander Hamilton, pushed for a strong central government, while the Anti-federalists, led by Secretary of State Thomas Jefferson, advocated states' rights over central power. Anti-federalists argued that the federal government should be limited to issues of national defense and interstate commerce, with all other powers left to the states.

A New Nation

The Anti-federalists were mainly southern and agrarian, while the Federalists were concentrated in the Northeast and represented mercantile interests.

The growing divide between Federalists and Anti-federalists revealed itself most in the debate over national finances. In 1790, Hamilton proposed that the national government assume the unpaid war debts of the states. Anti-federalists believed this plan granted the national government undue economic power over the states. Southern states particularly opposed the plan, since they had already paid off nearly all of their debts while the northern states lagged behind. Despite Southern and Anti-federalist opposition, the plan passed, in part because of a concession by the North to the South: in 1800, the nation's capital was moved from New York to a southern locale near the Potomac River, present-day Washington, D.C.

The National Bank

Even more controversial was Hamilton's proposal to establish a national bank. Hamilton claimed the **Bank of the United States** would provide a secure depository for federal revenue, issue currency and federal loans, regulate the activities of smaller banks, and extend credit to U.S. citizens. Opposing the proposal, Anti-federalists such as Thomas Jefferson feared that the creation of the bank would tie private individuals too closely to government institutions. Anti-federalists also argued that the Constitution did not explicitly give the federal government the power to grant such charters.

This latter argument came to characterize the view of **strict constructionists**, including Jefferson and **James Madison**, who believed that the national government should be confined to the powers expressly enumerated in the Constitution—nowhere did the Constitution give Congress the power to grant the bank a charter. Such a strict interpretation of the Constitution, they believed, was necessary to protect against tyranny. In opposition, Hamilton and his followers favored a loose reading of the Constitution, especially of the **elastic clause** (Article I, Section VIII), which states that Congress shall have the power "to make all laws which shall be necessary and proper for carrying into execution . . . powers vested by this Constitution in the government of the United States." For **loose constructionists** like Hamilton, this clause gave Congress the power to do anything not expressly forbidden by the Constitution, including founding a national bank. After much debate between the loose and strict constructionists, Congress approved the bank by a thin margin, granting it a 20-year charter in February 1791.

Hamilton's major proposals for national finance: national assumption of state debt; a national bank; protectionist tariffs. All of these issues pitted Federalists against Anti-Federalists, or loose constructionists against strict constructionists.

A New Nation

Tariffs

One final issue dividing Congress concerned protective tariffs. In December 1791, Hamilton proposed the passage of high protective tariffs to generate revenue for the national government and to foster industrial development in the U.S. Jefferson and Madison both opposed this protectionist economic policy, fearing that industries would become too dependent upon government aid. Many congressmen also opposed the tariff for favoring industrial and merchant interests of the North over the more rural and agrarian South. In face of this opposition, the tariff bill did not pass.

The Rise of Political Parties

The framers of the Constitution considered political parties to be self-serving factions detrimental to the good of government. However, by the end of Washington's term, the division between the strict constructionists and the loose constructionists had hardened into two distinct political parties: the loose constructionists formed the core of the **Federalist** party, while the strict constructionists comprised the core of the Democratic-Republican party—or, simply, the **Republicans**.

The birth of the Republican Party can be traced to 1793, when Jefferson resigned from Washington's cabinet in opposition to Federalist policy decisions, especially the financial decisions of Alexander Hamilton. Republicans attempted to arouse political awareness and spread criticism of Federalist decisions through a media campaign, which centered around America's first opposition newspaper, *The National Gazette*. They also founded political societies and clubs across the nation. Washington clearly allied himself with the Federalists in 1794 by accusing the Republicans of inciting the Whiskey Rebellion (discussed below). That same year, the Republicans won a slight majority in the House of Representatives, signaling the arrival of the party as a legitimate political movement.

Led by Jefferson and Madison, the Republicans aimed to limit the power of central government and to expand the rights of states and individuals. They argued that liberty could only be protected if political power rested firmly in the hands of the people and those government officials who were closest and most responsive to the people. The Federalist Party led by Washington and Hamilton, in contrast, preferred a system in which elected officials would rule without the direct influence of the people, as part of a very powerful central government. While the Federalists were concentrated in the Northeast, the Republicans had their stronghold in the South.

A New Nation

The Federalists, led by Washington and Hamilton, called for a strong central government. They represented the industrial and manufacturing interests, which were concentrated in the Northeast. The Republicans, led by Jefferson and Madison, advocated powerful state governments over centralized power, and represented the more rural and agrarian South, as well as the Western frontier.

The Whiskey Rebellion

In July 1794, frontier farmers in western Pennsylvania who produced whiskey from corn violently protested against Hamilton's 1791 excise tax on domestically produced whiskey. This revolt, which became known as the **Whiskey Rebellion**, represented the first major test of the national government's ability to enforce its laws within the states.

Whereas the earlier Shays's Rebellion exposed the central government's weakness under the Articles of Confederation, the Whiskey Rebellion revealed the new government's strength. President Washington responded decisively, leading 13,000 men into Pennsylvania to crush the rebellion. His actions demonstrated the broad reach and commitment of the national government. Many Anti-federalists condemned Washington's response, saying it was excessively oppressive and favored commercial interests over those of small-scale farmers (since commercial interests benefited most from the excise tax). Overall, the rebellion only strengthened the political power of Washington, Hamilton, and the Federalists. Many frontier farmers did, however, shift their loyalty from the Federalist to the Republican Party. The revolt also further divided the two parties.

Westward Expansion

During the 1790s, the U.S. attempted to expand its territory westward. The government devised policies for settlement and admitted three new states to the union: Vermont (1791), Kentucky (1792), and Tennessee (1796). Such expansion efforts incited opposition from Spain and Britain, both of which still owned some western territory and wanted to own more. Native Americans who inhabited much of this coveted land also resisted U.S. expansion. Military efforts in 1790 and 1791, aimed at forcing peace with the Native Americans on U.S. terms, yielded little success. The tense relations continued in stalemate until 1794, when U.S. troops routed a group of Native American warriors at the Battle of Fallen Timbers. After this defeat, 12 Native American tribes signed the **Treaty of Greenville**, which cleared the Ohio territory of tribes and opened it up to U.S. settlement.

Foreign Relations: U.S. Neutrality

Throughout his term in office, Washington worked to preserve U.S. neutrality in international relations. By keeping the U.S. out of European conflicts, he hoped to develop and enhance U.S. domestic policy and unite the nation under one strong, efficient government. Foreign affairs, however, grew increasingly difficult to ignore. The French Revolution (1789-1799) inspired opposing loyalties within the federal government. Jefferson and other Republicans sympathized with the revolutionary cause, which championed individual rights against the aristocratic government. Hamilton and other Federalists opposed it.

In 1793, when revolutionary France went to war with Britain and Spain, U.S. loyalties were again divided. Northern merchants pressed for a pro-British policy, mostly because of trade interests, while Southern planters pushed for an alliance with France. Refusing to be drawn into the war, Washington issued the **Proclamation of American Neutrality**. Although neutrality was the national policy, Southwestern settlers offered some military support to the French against the Spanish in Florida and in the Mississippi Valley, and 1,000 Americans enlisted with the French as privateers, terrorizing the British navy. The British navy retaliated by seizing more than 250 American vessels during the winter of 1794, forcing their crews into service in the Royal Navy through a policy known as "impressment." Tension flared further when Canada's royal governor denied U.S. claims to the land north of the Ohio River and encouraged the Native Americans in the region to resist expansion. War seemed almost inevitable as the British and Spanish troops began building forts on U.S. territory.

Desperate to avoid war, Washington dispatched negotiators to the warring European nations. John Jay negotiated **Jay's Treaty** (1795) with Britain, which secured the removal of British troops from American land and reopened very limited trade with the British West Indies, but he did not even address the British seizure of American ships or the "impressment" of American sailors. Although criticized by many Americans, especially Anti-federalists, for being too beneficial to Britain, Jay's Treaty did keep the U.S. out of a potentially ruinous war against a stronger and more established nation. Thomas Pinckney negotiated the **Treaty of San Lorenzo** (1795) with Spain, which granted the U.S. unrestricted access to the Mississippi River and removed Spanish troops from American land.

Washington strove to maintain U.S. neutrality in foreign affairs.

A New Nation

Washington's Farewell Address

In 1796, Washington retired from office, deciding not to run for a third term. He thereby set the precedent of presidents serving no more than two terms in office—a precedent that became law with the ratification of the Twenty-Second Amendment (1951). In his farewell address, Washington implored future generations to avoid embroilment in the affairs of other nations, and to concentrate on the creation of "efficient government" at home. He warned that the development of parties would destroy the government, fearing that special interest groups and foreign nations would come to dominate the two factions.

The Election of 1796: Divided Government

The election of 1796 was the first major political contest between Republicans and Federalists. John Adams ran as a Federalist, and Thomas Jefferson as a Republican. Republicans controlled the South, while Federalists dominated New England, New Jersey, and South Carolina. Adams won the presidency by three electoral votes. Jefferson became vice president following Constitutional protocol, which stated that the second highest vote getter would become vice president. The two rivals teamed together for what proved to be a tense and rather unproductive partnership.

Federalism Under Adams

The neutrality that George Washington worked so hard to maintain was threatened soon after Adams took office. The French saw Jay's Treaty (between the U.S. and Britain) as a signal that the U.S. supported Britain in Britain's ongoing war against France. France had delayed retribution, hoping for Jefferson to win the presidency because Jefferson, as an Anti-federalist, was sympathetic to the French. Upon his loss, France delayed no longer and began to seize American ships en route to British ports. Within one year, the French attacked more than 300 American ships and ordered that all Americans captured aboard British naval vessels be hanged.

In response to such aggression, Adams dispatched a peace commission to Paris. In what became known as the **XYZ affair**, the French foreign minister, Charles de Tallyrand, refused to meet with the commission, and instead sent three anonymous agents to deliver a bribe: Tallyrand would not negotiate with the U.S. until he received $250,000 for himself and a $12 million loan for France. In his report to Congress about the event, Adams labeled the three agents X, Y, and Z—hence the "XYZ affair." This attempt at extortion aroused public outrage among the American people, some of whom rallied for war. Citing the need for readiness should a war break out, Congress tripled the American army in 1798. In what became known as the **Quasi-war**, Congress then sent armed ships to protect Americans at sea. Although France and America never officially declared war, from 1798 to 1800, the U.S. navy seized 93 French privateers while only losing one ship.

The Alien and Sedition Acts

Riding the tide of anti-French sentiment, the Federalists overwhelmingly won the 1798 congressional elections. In an effort to protect national security, should the country enter into war with France, Congress passed a series of four measures called the **Alien and Sedition Acts** in 1798. The acts unprecedentedly asserted the power of the central government.

- The Alien Enemies Act, the first and least controversial act, defined the procedure by which, during wartime, U.S. authorities could deport a citizen of an enemy nation whom they deemed a threat to national security.

- The Alien Friends Act allowed the president to deport any citizen of any foreign nation whom he deemed a threat to the U.S., even in the absence of proof.

- The Naturalization Act changed the residency requirement for becoming a citizen of the United States from five to fourteen years.

- The Sedition Act, the final and most controversial act, forbade any individual or group to speak, write, or publish anything of a "false, scandalous and malicious" nature that brought the Congress and/or the president "into contempt or disrepute."

The Alien and Sedition Acts granted the federal government unprecedented power to infringe upon the liberty of individuals.

Of the four Sedition Acts, two—the Alien Friends Act and the Sedition Act—were set to expire near the time of the 1800 elections, so that the acts would not be used against the Federalists should they lose power. Just before the presidential election of 1800, four of the five major Republican newspapers were charged with sedition, arousing the anger of many who felt the Federalists were exploiting their political power to breach civil liberties and stifle their political opponents.

In opposition to the Alien and Sedition Acts, both Kentucky and Virginia endorsed manifestos on states' rights written anonymously by **Thomas Jefferson and James Madison**, respectively. The **Virginia and Kentucky Resolutions** (1798) declared that state legislatures could deem acts of Congress unconstitutional, on the theory that states' rights superseded federal rights. They argued that the federal government was merely a representative of the compact of states, not an overriding power, and therefore states had the final say on federal laws. In 1799, Kentucky passed a further resolution that declared states could nullify objectionable federal laws. This doctrine of states' rights and nullification would emerge again in later political crises between the North and South concerning issues of tariffs and slavery.

Jefferson's Revolution: The Beginning of Republican Rule

The election of 1800 marked the beginning of a 28-year period during which the party of Jefferson dominated national politics. The Republicans won easily in part because of the public outrage over the Federalist Alien and Sedition Acts; in many ways, the acts proved the undoing of the Federalist Party.

The election of 1800 was a protracted affair. Although the Republican ticket of Thomas Jefferson and Aaron Burr easily won the election against the Federalist team of John Adams and Charles Pickney, all of the Republican electors had voted for both Jefferson and Burr, so that both candidates earned the same number of electoral votes for president. Burr, who had been backed by the Republican Party as vice president, now had as legitimate a claim to the presidency as Jefferson did. The task of choosing the president therefore fell to the House of Representatives. After seven days and thirty-six ballots, the House chose Jefferson as president. To prevent future election deadlocks of this sort, the Twelfth Amendment, ratified in 1804, changed the election process so that candidates must be clearly listed as either running for president or vice president.

Jefferson described his victory in the election of 1800 as the "Revolution of 1800." He believed that the Republican victory over the Federalists was "as real a revolution in the principles of our government as that of 1776 was in its form." Unlike the Federalists, who had pushed for a strong central government and had favored industrial and commercial interests, the Jeffersonian Republicans aimed to limit central government in favor of states' rights and individual liberties, and favored an agrarian republic over an urban, industrialized one.

In office, Jefferson cut back on federal expenditures and federal bureaucracy. He persuaded Congress to cut almost all internal taxes, and balanced the cut with reductions in military expenditures and other government endeavors. For income, the government relied mostly on land sales and customs duties.

Midnight Judges and Judicial Review

In his last days in office, John Adams appointed a number of Federalists judges to federal court positions in efforts to mitigate the upcoming Republican rule. After the Senate confirmation hearings, during Adams's final few hours in office, Adams signed the judges' commissions—hence the name "midnight judges" or "midnight appointments." One such appointment was Federalist William Marbury as justice of the peace in the District of Columbia, but Adams had failed to deliver the commission by midnight. Jefferson's secretary of state, James Madison, refused to deliver the commission. Marbury, in response, asked the Supreme Court for a writ of mandamus to force Madison to deliver the commission and accept the appointment. In February 1803, Chief Justice John Marshall and the court denied Marbury's request, ruling that Congress had overstepped its constitutional bounds by giving the Supreme Court the authority to issue such a writ in the first place (Congress had issued such authority in the Judiciary Act of 1789). This **Marbury v. Madison** ruling was the first time that the Supreme Court declared an act of Congress to be unconstitutional.

Chief Justice John Marshall's ruling in the case of Marbury v. Madison asserted the Supreme Court's power of judicial review and marked the first time the Supreme Court declared an act of Congress unconstitutional.

The Louisiana Purchase

In 1800, France gained control of the Louisiana Territory from Spain. Fearing that the new French ruler, Napoleon, had plans of building an empire in the Americas, Jefferson sent negotiators to France in an attempt to purchase the territory. The envoy found that Napoleon had abandoned his plan for a colonial empire, in part because a massive slave revolt in Haiti, led by Toussaint L'Ouverture, had severely depleted Napoleon's forces. Napoleon thus agreed to sell all of the Louisiana territory in order to finance French efforts in the war in Europe. After some negotiation, the price was set at $15 million in April 1803. With the **Louisiana Purchase**, the U.S. gained an enormous, uncharted piece of land, almost doubling the country's size for the price of thirteen and a half cents per acre.

The Louisiana Purchase nearly doubled the size of the U.S. and eliminated the French (and remnant Spanish) control of New Orleans and the Mississippi River.

A New Nation

Jefferson, always a **strict constructionist**, feared that the purchase would be deemed unconstitutional because the Constitution did not explicitly grant such purchasing and expansionist powers to the federal government. He personally drafted a constitutional amendment authorizing the national government to acquire new lands. He was eventually convinced by fellow Republicans, however, to drop the amendment and directly submit the purchase treaty to the Senate to prevent Napoleon from recanting his sale offer. The Senate speedily ratified the purchase. Thus Jefferson, in spite of his overall aims to restrict the central government's power, initiated a dramatic expansion of federal powers by backing the purchase.

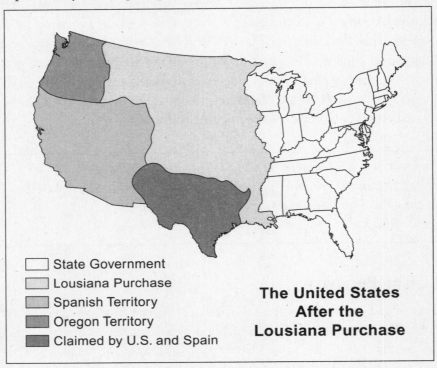

State Government
Lousiana Purchase
Spanish Territory
Oregon Territory
Claimed by U.S. and Spain

**The United States
After the
Lousiana Purchase**

Westward Exploration

Even before the Louisiana Purchase, Jefferson was fascinated with the undiscovered frontier. He envisioned the U.S. as an agrarian republic, not an industrial powerhouse, and therefore sought to open up new farming along the vast and fertile frontier. Once the Louisiana Purchase was negotiated, Jefferson commissioned teams of explorers, including Meriwether Lewis, who was a captain in the army, and Lieutenant William Clark, to map out the new territory. In 1804, **Lewis and Clark** set off from St. Louis with 45 soldiers. In the Dakotas, they met **Sacajawea**, an Indian woman who proved indispensable as a guide. The group reached the Pacific Ocean in 1805 and landed back at St. Louis in 1806, having traveled nearly 3,000 miles in two and a half years. The success of the Lewis and Clark expedition inspired increasing exploration and settlement of the new territory.

Tension Overseas: The Embargo Act

In 1803, as part of the Napoleonic Wars, France and Britain resumed war against each other. Trading with both nations and clinging to neutrality, the U.S. soon found itself drawn into the battle, because the French and British took aggressive measures that violated U.S. neutrality rights. The French policy, known as the Continental System, subjected to seizure any ship that first stopped in a British port. Through a series of countermeasures known as Orders in Council, Britain blockaded French-controlled ports in Europe. The British also began searching American ships for goods from the French West Indies and threatening American crews with impressment into the Royal Navy.

Anglo-American tensions peaked in the **Chesapeake-Leopard affair** in 1807, when the British frigate *HMS Leopard* opened fired on the American frigate *USS Chesapeake* off the Chesapeake Bay, after its request to board had been denied. When the British finally did board, they hanged four crew members and sailed away. Outraged, Jefferson banned all British warships from American waters. Congress then passed the **Embargo Act** of 1807, which prohibited any ship from leaving a U.S. port for a foreign port, effectively ending both exportation and importation. Jefferson and Congress hoped that such a measure would so damage the British and French economies that the countries would be forced to honor U.S. neutrality. Yet such peaceable coercion failed: the Embargo Act hurt the U.S. economy more than England's or France's.

James Madison and the War of 1812

Jefferson retired from office after serving two terms, solidifying the two-term limit precedent that Washington had set. **James Madison**, Jefferson's Secretary of State, won the election of 1808 and became president on March 4, 1809. He immediately confronted the nation's deteriorating foreign relations.

Under Madison, Congress first replaced the Embargo Act with the **Non-Intercourse Act**, which prevented trade with Britain and France only, thereby opening up all other foreign markets. But because the British and French were the largest and most powerful traders in the world, the Non-Intercourse Act did little to stimulate the struggling U.S. economy. In 1810, Congress substituted Macon's Bill No. 2 for the Non-Intercourse Act, as a ploy for either Britain or France to lift trade restrictions. Macon's Bill No. 2 resumed open trade with both Britain and France and stated that if either nation repealed its restrictions on neutral shipping, the United States would instate an embargo against the other nation. Napoleon seized this opportunity and repealed French restrictions, provoking an American declaration of non-intercourse with Britain. Despite Napoleon's promise, the French continued to seize American ships.

The War Hawks

As it became clear that peaceable coercion would not ease the hostilities, Madison faced increasing pressure from **War Hawks** within Congress. These southerners and westerners, led by South Carolina's **John C. Calhoun** and Kentucky's **Henry Clay**, resented the post-embargo recession that had plagued southern and western regions from 1808 to 1810, and advocated war rather than disgraceful terms of peace. They also hoped that, through war, the U.S. would win some western and southwestern territories, annex Canada in order to eliminate the British and Native American threat along the frontier, and open up new lands to settlement.

The War Hawks feared that the British were recruiting Native Americans along the Canadian border to fight American settlers. Heightening these fears, a Shawnee chief, **Tecumseh,** and his brother "The Prophet" attempted to unite a number of tribes in Ohio and Indiana under an anti-white government. In response, future president William Henry Harrison, then governor of the Indiana Territory, crushed the Shawnees in the 1811 **Battle of Tippecanoe**, though his own forces also suffered heavy losses. Almost 30 years later, Harrison would run for president on his popularity as an Indian fighter, using the campaign slogan, "Tippecanoe and Tyler too!" (John Tyler ran as his vice president.) Although the Battle of Tippecanoe represented an American victory over the Shawnees, it did not end the threat of Anglo-Indian alliance—Tecumseh and the Shawnees later allied with British troops during the War of 1812.

The War of 1812

Note: The SAT II rarely asks specific questions about war facts, such as the names of battles and generals. It is more important to know what caused the war and how it ended.

In June 1812, convinced of the inevitability of war against Britain, Madison sent a message to Congress enumerating British violations of U.S. neutrality rights, including the presence of British ships in American waters and the impressment of American sailors. In a conciliatory measure, Britain repealed the Orders in Council, its aggressive naval policy, but it was too late. Congress had already passed a declaration of war, and the War Hawks pushed for full engagement.

The American forces, however, were outmatched by British forces, in part because the Republicans had drastically cut military expenditures and programs, leaving the U.S. forces seriously underfunded and under-trained. Nonetheless, the war ended in stalemate, mainly because the British were also occupied with events in Europe. The signing of the **Treaty of Ghent** in December 1814 ended the war and restored the status quo. The treaty did not mention free trade or sailor's rights.

Two weeks after the signing of Treaty of Ghent, but before news of the treaty had reached America, American troops won a decisive victory in the **Battle of New Orleans**.

General **Andrew Jackson**'s troops defended the city, killing more than 2,000 British troops while losing only thirteen men. The timing of the Battle of New Orleans inspired the popular misconception that the U.S. had won the war and had forced the British to surrender and sign the treaty. Even without officially "winning" the war, the U.S. did succeed in protecting itself against one of the world's premier powers, for which reason the War of 1812 has been called the "second war of independence."

The Hartford Convention

In 1814, during the later stages of the War of 1812, a group of disillusioned Federalists met at the **Hartford Convention**, where the New England-based party enumerated its complaints against the ruling Republican Party. Some Federalists called for New England's secession, but cooler heads prevailed and called for a resolution summarizing New England's grievances, both general and those specifically relating to the War of 1812. These complaints included the charge that Republicans were neglecting the needs of New England industry and commerce. The war, and its accompanying trade restrictions in particular, hurt New England because of the region's concentration of seaboard manufacturers and merchants. The group at the Hartford Convention also drafted seven constitutional amendments meant to politically strengthen the Northeast, including an amendment to abolish the three-fifths clause, to change the policy by which Congress declared war, and to set a maximum time limit for trade embargoes.

The Federalists had hoped to deliver their resolution to Madison as the U.S. struggled on in a deadlocked war and anti-war sentiment ran high. They arrived in Washington, D.C., however, just as news spread of the victory at New Orleans and the signing of the Treaty of Ghent. The perceived war victory and the restoration of peace stripped the Federalists of their central complaints and made them look like traitors and secessionists. Many Federalists who had attended the convention were forever stigmatized as disloyal Americans, crippling their political careers. The embarrassment of the Hartford Convention marked the end of the Federalist Party as a prominent influence in national politics.

American Nationalism and the Spirit of Cooperation

The perceived American victory in the War of 1812 ushered in an era of nationalism and cooperation. On a cultural level, the war yielded a number of important symbols of national pride and cooperative spirit, including the "The Star Spangled Banner," which a young American, Francis Scott Key, composed while observing the British attack on Fort McHenry. Another patriotic element emerging from the war was the popular term "White House" for the presidential mansion (after the British burned Washington, D.C., in battle, the presidential mansion was covered in whitewash to conceal the stains).

A New Nation

Influenced by the postwar spirit, Madison presented a nationalist policy program. With the Federalists no longer posing a political threat to Republican leadership after the debacle of the Hartford Convention, Madison proposed a number of policies that Republicans might earlier have avoided, since the policies, which increased the power of the central government, were rather Federalist in nature. In 1816, Madison signed the bill to charter the **Second Bank of the United States**, pushed through a moderate tariff bill in order to protect America's growing industries, and urged federal funding for internal improvements, including a national system of roads and canals. In Congress, **Henry Clay** fleshed out these nationalist economic policies in his **American System**, a policy program aimed at economic self-sufficiency.

Nationalist proposals under Madison included the charter for the Second Bank of the United States, protectionist tariffs, and federal funding for internal improvements.

Monroe and The Era of Good Feelings

The demise of the Federalist Party was confirmed in the 1816 presidential election, which **James Monroe** won easily. Monroe was the first clear representative of the one-party system under the Republicans. His term in office became known as the **Era of Good Feelings,** in part because of the political cooperation stemming from one-party politics, and in part because of America's high morale after its perceived victory in the War of 1812. This unifying nationalist spirit peaked in the election of 1820, which Monroe won, 231 votes to his opponent **John Quincy Adams**'s one.

Monroe rarely departed from James Madison's nationalistic program. He supported federal funding for internal improvements, though he hesitated to authorize direct federal involvement, and he raised protective tariffs to spur American manufacturing.

The Transportation Revolution Begins

In 1817, ten years after the invention of the steamboat, New York began construction of the **Erie Canal**, the first major canal project in the United States. Upon its completion in 1825, the canal stretched 363 miles, from Albany to Buffalo, much farther than any other American or European canal. A system of canals soon developed around the nation, linking waterways from the Northeast to the frontier West. At the same time, the U.S. government invested in the National Road, which by 1818 stretched from Cumberland, Maryland, to Wheeling, Virginia. Added to this national road were systems of privately owned toll roads around each major U.S. city, which served as the foundation for the growing national road system.

Economic Boom and Bust

Postwar economic prosperity enhanced the political optimism in the United States. The economy dramatically expanded as a result of a postwar borrowing and buying frenzy. Banks lent money with little or no collateral to businessmen seeking to buy land, build factories, and develop industries. The high protective tariff of 1816 promoted further domestic development. Accompanying this expansion was the steady rise of **inflation**, the increase of paper money and credit leading to higher prices and less valuable currency.

In 1818, the global demand for American goods declined, in part because Europe had recovered from the devastation of the Napoleonic Wars. As a result of the decline in trade, the U.S. economy began to collapse and banks began contracting their lending practices. Many state banks folded and many borrowers declared bankruptcy. In what became known as the **panic of 1819**, land values fell 50 to 75 percent, rich land speculators lost fortunes, and homesteaders became mired in debt. The depression lasted roughly three years.

The Transcontinental Treaty

Spain and the U.S. long debated whether or not the Louisiana Purchase included western Florida. In 1819, the matter was settled when Spain agreed to the Adams-Onís Treaty, also known as the **Transcontinental Treaty**. By the terms of this treaty, Spain ceded eastern Florida to the United States, renounced all claims to western Florida, and agreed to a southern border of the United States west of the Mississippi River extending all the way to the Pacific Ocean, thereby recognizing U.S. claims to the Oregon Territory. This treaty gave the United States its first legitimate claim to the west coast.

The Missouri Compromise

Despite its name, the Era of Good Feelings was not all cooperation and goodwill. The period also saw political controversy between the North and South. Westward expansion spawned sectional conflict, as the North and South feuded about whether western territories should be slave-holding or free.

In 1819 the Union consisted of eleven free states and eleven slave states. But the application for statehood by the territory of Missouri threatened to upset this balance. Congress fell into heated debate, until James Tallmadge, Jr. of New York proposed a resolution. He proposed an amendment to the bill for Missouri's admission that would prohibit the further introduction of slaves into Missouri and mandate the emancipation at age twenty-five of slaves' offspring born after the state was admitted to the Union. The House approved the bill with the **Tallmadge Amendment**, but the Senate struck the amendment from the bill.

A New Nation

The application of Maine for statehood allowed the Senate to escape its deadlock and agree on the terms of the **Missouri Compromise**. Maine was to be admitted as a free state and Missouri as a slave state, but in the remainder of the Louisiana Territory, slavery would be prohibited north of 36°30' latitude (the southern border of Missouri). However, the compromise rapidly disintegrated when Missouri submitted a draft constitution that prohibited free blacks from entering the state. Northern opposition blocked Missouri from statehood until 1821, when **Henry Clay** designed a new agreement that prohibited Missouri from discriminating against citizens of other states, including blacks with citizenship. The Compromise cooled tensions between the North and South, but only temporarily. Sectional conflict would only increase in the years to come.

Elements of the Missouri Compromise, in its final form: Maine admitted as a free state; Missouri admitted as a slave state; slavery prohibited in the Louisiana Territory north of 36°30'; Missouri prohibited from discriminating against black citizens of other states.

The Monroe Doctrine

During James Monroe's presidency, several revolutions against Spanish rule flared up in South and Central America and ousted the colonial governments. New leaders such as Simon Bolivar established independent regimes. The U.S., having itself broken away from colonial rule, officially recognized these new countries, and established lucrative trading relations with many of them. Fearing that European governments would intervene and try to reassert colonial dominance, Secretary of State John Quincy Adams composed the **Monroe Doctrine**, which Monroe revealed in 1823. This doctrine declared American dominance in the Western Hemisphere and warned against European interference in the Americas. It consisted of three principles:

- Unless American interests were involved, the United States would stay out of European wars.

- The "American continents", including both North and South America, were not subject to any further colonization by European powers.

- The United States would construe any attempt at European colonization in the New World as an "unfriendly act."

Although the U.S. had little military power to back up its claims, the declaration nonetheless had immense symbolic importance, since the U.S. was declaring itself a world power equal to the great European nations.

The Monroe Doctrine asserted U.S. preeminence in the affairs of the Americas, a position that has informed American foreign relations ever since.

The Marshall Court

John Marshall was appointed Chief Justice of the Supreme Court in 1801, and remained in office until he died in 1835. Under his leadership, the court became as powerful a government force as Congress and the president. A staunch Federalist, Marshall delivered decisions that strengthened the central government at the expense of states' rights, and he upheld a broad reading of the Constitution. Despite the death of the Federalist Party in the early 1800s, Marshall continued to exert a strong Federalist influence on government. His rulings elicited resistance from the Republican leadership and sparked political controversy in an age otherwise known for its spirit of cooperation. The Supreme Court rulings exposed latent dissent within the American government concerning issues of government authority, state versus federal rights, and the regulation of trade.

Marshall's first significant decision came in the 1803 case of ***Marbury v. Madison***, discussed earlier. This ruling established the principle of **judicial review**, the Supreme Court's power to rule an act of Congress unconstitutional. The Court did not again invoke this power until the ***Dred Scott*** case, 54 years later.

In 1819, the Supreme Court delivered two controversial decisions on the issue of state versus federal rights. In ***Dartmouth College v. Woodward*** (1819), Marshall ruled that New Hampshire could not convert Dartmouth College into a state university because the college's charter, issued by Britain before the American Revolution, qualified as a contract, and the Constitution forbids states to interfere with contracts. A month later, Marshall delivered an even more momentous decision in ***McCulloch v. Maryland*** (1819), which questioned whether Maryland could tax the Second Bank of the United States. Marshall argued that the federal government's power must be considered supreme within its sphere, and that states did not have the power to interfere with the exercise of federal powers. He therefore deemed the Maryland tax unconstitutional. Republicans, long-standing advocates of states' rights, were outraged by these two rulings, since they stripped state governments of the necessary power to impose the will of their people on corporations operating within their borders.

The case of ***Gibbons v. Ogden*** (1824) concerned the issue of interstate commerce. The case involved a New York state steamboat franchise that had been granted a monopoly by the state legislature to run passenger ships between New York and New Jersey. This state license conflicted with a federal license, granted to another boat operator, to run the same steamboat route. Marshall ruled in favor of the federal license, arguing that a state cannot interfere with Congress's right to regulate interstate commerce. Marshall thus interpreted "commerce" broadly to include all forms of business, not just the exchange of goods—an interpretation that would prove crucial to the drafting and constitutional defense of the Civil Rights Act of 1964, with which Congress prohibited discrimination in public accommodations. As they had with Marshall's earlier rulings, Republicans condemned this ruling as too antagonistic toward states' rights.

Chief Justice Marshall issued significant rulings on judicial review, federal vesus state power, the sanctity of contracts, and congressional control of interstate commerce. He transformed the Court into a formidable government force, equal to Congress and the president.

The Age of Jackson

Trends and Themes of the Era

- Cracks based on regional differences began to appear in the Republican Party, resulting in a split into two parties: Democratic and Republican.

- Coupled with lowered voting restrictions, the two-party system ushered in a newly democratic age, marked by more election choice and increased voter turnout. Andrew Jackson, the first man from the West to win the presidency, won in large part on his appeal to the "common man." Politics began to be increasingly swayed by the public, rather than by the elites.

- The Nullification Crisis revealed deep regional differences in economic needs and attitudes about states' rights versus federal power. The Nullification Crisis introduced the possibility of state secession from the Union.

- Jackson turned the presidency into a vastly more powerful office, using the presidential veto to assert his political and legislative will and more deeply embedding the government in party politics.

Return of the Two-Party System: 1824–1828

From 1800 to 1824, the Republican Party faced little political opposition and fostered a spirit of political unity and cooperation. The election of 1824, however, marked a return to factional politics.

In the 1820s, voter participation rose dramatically. By 1820, most states had eliminated wealth-based voting requirements, so that all free white males could vote. In some northern states, free black men could vote as well. The voting procedure also changed: secret written ballots replaced voting aloud, which stopped social superiors from influencing their inferiors at polling time. In addition, many appointive offices became elective, and the process by which state legislatures chose Electoral College electors largely gave way to popular selection of electors. A democratic and egalitarian spirit filled the nation, prompting many historians to call the 1820s "the age of the common man." Women and most blacks, however, were still barred from political involvement.

During the 1820s, the U.S. electorate expanded, increasing popular participation in politics.

The Election of 1824: First Modern Election

Greater popular involvement in politics, along with in-party fighting, fragmented the Republican Party. Before the election of 1824, party leaders chose a single presidential candidate to represent the party in a centralized nomination system known as the **congressional caucus**. In the election of 1824, however, many states allowed their citizens to vote directly for presidential candidates, so that instead of one candidate representing the Republicans, five Republican candidates emerged to compete for the presidency. These candidates highlighted the divisions within American society and within the crumbling Republican coalition. **John Quincy Adams** was New England's choice for president (and John Adams' son). **John C. Calhoun** and William Crawford vied for the South's support, and **Henry Clay** and **Andrew Jackson** came out of the West, the former appealing to merchants and manufacturers and the latter to more rural groups. The Republican Party leaders in the congressional caucus chose Crawford as the party's official candidate, but it was clear that the caucus no longer spoke for the party as a whole. Because of the demise of the congressional caucus system, the 1824 election is called the first modern election: it was the first election in which party leaders no longer had exclusive control over the nomination process.

Andrew Jackson won more popular and electoral votes than any other candidate, but he did not win a majority, so the election was thrown into the House of Representatives. Clay, the Speaker of the House, backed Adams for the presidency and helped ensure Adams's victory. In return, Adams rewarded Clay by making him secretary of state. Jackson and Jackson's supporters saw this backroom deal-making as a political conspiracy and denounced it as a "**corrupt bargain**."

The Age of Jackson

Adams in Office

Adams' presidency proved unproductive, in large part because of an uncooperative Congress. Unlike Adams, who advocated a loose reading of the Constitution, most in Congress were strict constructionists, favoring states' rights over central power. Congress thus rejected all of Adams's proposals for federally funded internal improvements, a national system of roads and canals, higher tariffs, and federal schools. The consideration that Adams was unpleasant and refused to engage in political maneuvering—trading favors and distributing patronage—did not win him any support, either.

The Democratic Party

The factions within the Republican Party that arose in 1824 became the foundation of a new political party. Jackson's supporters, led by **Martin Van Buren** and **John C. Calhoun** (who was also Adams' vice president), rallied together and formed what became known as the **Democratic Party**. Angered over Jackson's loss in 1824, Democrats chose to nominate Jackson for president in 1828. The opposition, now known as the **National Republicans**, supported Adams for re-election.

Democrats portrayed Jackson as a hero of the common man and states' rights, and Adams as an aloof aristocrat. This campaign tactic worked. Jackson swept 56 percent of the popular vote. Just as important, the election returns revealed the nation's growing sectionalism: Adams won much of the New England vote, while Jackson carried the South and Southwest.

The new two-party system reflected a sectional split within the United States. The South and West supported Jackson's Democrats, while the North sided with Adams and the National Republicans.

Jackson as President

Andrew Jackson came to Washington in 1829, intending to rule according to the will of the people and not the Washington select. A strong presence in the White House, he exerted stringent control over his administration and was the first president to use the veto power extensively. He took a heavy hand with Congress and other government departments. He also broke with many traditions, and in doing so, set new ones that continue to affect American politics.

The Kitchen Cabinet and Spoils System

Past presidents had used the cabinet as a policy forum, selecting men of different backgrounds to represent the varied allegiances and interests of the country. Jackson, by contrast, surrounded himself with only his political allies and close friends from Tennessee. Because cabinet members were all Jackson supporters and often had questionable political skill, opponents dubbed Jackson's advisors the "**Kitchen Cabinet**."

For all government appointments, Jackson favored a rotation of office known as the **spoils system**, whereby the winning party (in this case, Jackson's Democrats) would remove officeholders belonging to the opposing party and fill the open position with its own supporters—"to the victor belongs the spoils." Jackson reasoned that ordinary party members could fill government positions as well as any trained officials.

Nullification Crisis

The first and most important crisis Jackson faced while in office was the **Nullification Crisis**. Congress had raised protective tariffs steadily over the previous decade: in 1816, in 1824, and again, most extremely, in 1828, a year before Jackson's presidency. These tariffs protected Western farming interests, New England manufacturers, and Pennsylvania miners, but they hurt farmers in the South. Southern politicians grew so angry at the imbalance that they named the 1828 tariff the "**Tariff of Abominations**." South Carolina reacted particularly strongly, flying its flags at half-mast when the 1828 bill was passed, and threatening to boycott New England's manufactured goods.

Led by John C. Calhoun, a South Carolina native, the state denounced the tariff as unconstitutional on the argument that Congress could only levy tariffs that raised revenue for common purposes, not tariffs that protected regional interests. Calhoun argued that federal laws must benefit all equally in order to be constitutional, and urged southern states to nullify, or void, the tariffs within their own borders. Calhoun's justification for nullification, published in his *South Carolina Exposition and Protest* (1828), were largely derived from Jefferson and Madison's arguments in the Virginia and Kentucky Resolutions (1798). Calhoun, like Jefferson and Madison, argued that the states were sovereign over the central government, and therefore the states should have the final authority to judge the constitutionality of laws affecting their regions. Calhoun saw the Constitution as a compact of states, not an overriding federal power, which meant that all powers that the Constitution did not explicitly delegate to the federal government fell, without question, to the states.

Jackson came into office in 1829, after the publication of Calhoun's protest. Southern interests hoped that Jackson would modify the "Tariff of Abominations," especially since Calhoun served as Jackson's vice president. Although Jackson did push through a modified, milder tariff in 1832, the changes did little to satisfy many southerners. By 1832, Calhoun had grown so enraged over the tariff bills that he resigned from office and returned home to South Carolina; he and Jackson had permanently split over the issue. In November 1832, the South Carolina legislature approved Calhoun's Ordinance of Nullification, which nullified the tariffs of 1828 and 1832 and ordered state officials to stop collecting duties at South Carolina's ports. The state threatened to secede if the national government intervened to force tax collection.

Jackson responded swiftly and decisively, denouncing the nullifiers and sending arms to loyal Unionists in South Carolina. The following March, Jackson signed the two-part **Compromise of 1833**. The tariff of 1833 provided for a gradual lowering of duties over the next decade. The second measure, the **Force Bill**, authorized the president to use the U.S. Army and Navy, if necessary, to force the collection of customs duties in South Carolina. South Carolina at first nullified the Force Bill, but under threat of force, reconsidered and rescinded its previous nullifications.

The Nullification Crisis was precipitated by a series of tariffs that hurt the Southern economy. Drawing on Madison and Jefferson's Kentucky and Virginia Resolutions, Calhoun urged Southern states to nullify the tariffs within their own borders, arguing that states' rights were supreme and advancing a compact theory of the Union: that is, the Union as a compact of states only, not an overriding central power. The Crisis was averted by the Compromise of 1833.

Indian Removal Act

Jackson was determined to secure Native American lands for U.S. settlement. The **Indian Removal Act**, passed in 1830, granted Jackson the funds and the authority to move Native Americans to assigned lands in the West, using as much force as necessary. U.S. officials began aggressively clearing out the Cherokee tribe from the Southwest, and Georgia took control of the formerly Cherokee territory.

In 1832, the Supreme Court under Chief Justice John Marshall delivered a ruling against Cherokee removal. In *Worcester v. Georgia*, the Court ruled that the Cherokee comprised a "domestic dependent nation" with a right to freedom from molestation. Jackson opposed the ruling and proceeded with removal, supposedly commenting in defiance, "John Marshall has made his decision; now let him enforce it." Without the president enforcing its decision, the Supreme Court could not protect the Cherokees, and the aggressive Cherokee removal continued unabated. Between 1835 and 1838, the U.S. army forced bands of Cherokees to move west on a journey known as the **Trail of Tears**. Nearly one quarter of the tribe died on the journey.

The Age of Jackson

> *Cherokees staggered along the Trail of Tears from Georgia to Oklahoma*
> *between 1835 and 1838. Between 2,000 and 4,000 of the 16,000*
> *migrating Cherokees died from the harsh conditions.*

Opposition to the Bank

In 1816, the **Second Bank of the United States** received a twenty-year charter from Congress. In 1832, four years before the charter expired, the Bank sought a recharter of the Bank. Congress approved the charter, but Jackson issued the **Bank veto**, denouncing the Bank as a privileged monopoly, unfriendly to the interests of the West. After easily winning reelection in 1832, Jackson effectively destroyed the Bank by removing its federal deposits and placing the money in state banks. Jackson's critics called these banks "pet banks" because they seemed to be chosen based solely on their allegiance to the Democratic Party. In 1836, Jackson further enhanced the power of state banks by signing the Deposit Act, which increased the number of state banks serving as depositories and loosened federal control over the banking system. Despite these changes, Jackson did not succeed in fundamentally altering either the banking system or the use of paper money.

> *Jackson's war on the Bank succeeded in ending the life of the Second*
> *Bank of the United States but failed to fundamentally change the*
> *banking system or stem the inflation caused by the state banks' extension*
> *of credit.*

The Rise of the Whig Party

During Andrew Jackson's second term in office, leaders of the National Republican Party and other opponents of Jackson allied to form the **Whig Party**. Led by Henry Clay, **Daniel Webster**, and John C. Calhoun (who had split from Jackson and the Democratic Party over tariffs and nullification), the Whig Party comprised all different factions—Southern Republicans, Northern Democrats, and social reformers—who united in their hatred of Jackson, whom many considered so tyrannical that they called him "King Andrew I." Whigs opposed both Jackson's strong-armed political tactics and his policies. Southern Whigs opposed Jackson's handling of protective tariffs and the Nullification Crisis, among other issues, while Northern Democrats defected to the Whigs in part because of Jackson's anti-business stance. (Jackson cultivated his image as "friend to the common man" and grew increasingly hostile toward business and merchant interest, and more generally, toward all factions representing elite, privileged Americans.)

By the election of 1836, the Whigs had become a national party with widespread popularity. On the strength of Jackson's common appeal, however, the Democrats maintained their hold on the presidency. In the election, Jackson's chosen successor, Martin Van Buren, defeated William Henry Harrison and three other Whig candidates.

The Whig Party continued to grow in popularity, though, and in 1840 won the presidential election behind William Henry Harrison. The party, however, lost its national prominence soon thereafter. United in their dislike of Jackson, the Whigs were irreconcilably divided on other major issues, most notably slavery and protective tariffs. Southern Republican Whigs could never wholly ally with Northern Democratic Whigs on such matters. The Whig alliance began to disintegrate and, by the 1850s, had disappeared from the political scene.

Van Buren in Office

Martin Van Buren was called the "Crown Prince" to Jackson's "King Andrew I" because he had been Jackson's hand-picked successor and had won the 1936 election largely because of Jackson's support. Unable to escape from the shadow of his charismatic predecessor, Van Buren ruled mostly in obscurity, simply continuing the Jacksonian tradition.

The Panic of 1837

Van Buren assumed office in the midst of a severe economic depression. During 1835 and 1836, Andrew Jackson's policy of removing federal deposits from the Second Bank of the United States and placing them in state banks promoted an economy of speculative buying, risky lending, and unregulated banking practices. Prices increased and land sales multiplied rapidly from 1835 to 1837. In an attempt to stabilize the currency, Jackson issued the **Specie Circular** in 1836, which required that land payments be made in gold and silver rather than in paper money or in credit. This move caused prices to drop and left speculators with enormous debts. Many banks failed and the economy fell into a depression called the **panic of 1837**. Unemployment spread and wages dropped by one-third between 1836 and 1842.

Van Buren spent his time in office trying to solve the nation's economic woes. He called for the creation of an Independent Treasury, which would hold public funds in reserve and prevent excessive lending by state banks, thereby guarding against inflation. Van Buren and his Democrat supporters hailed the **Independent Treasury Bill**, signed in 1840, as a second Declaration of Independence, using it as a rallying call to battle against the entire banking system. In Louisiana and Arkansas, Democrats succeeded in prohibiting banks altogether. By 1840, the Democrats had firmly established themselves as an anti-bank party.

Jacksonian Legacies

Andrew Jackson forever changed the face of American government by promoting a more egalitarian political climate. To extend politics to the so-called "common man," he fought for a system in which all groups had a voice in government (excluding slaves, women, and Native Americans). He questioned the ascendancy of the business community and championed the rights of small farmers, empowering them to meet economic elites on an even playing field. Known as "the age of the common man," the Jacksonian Age thus witnessed a rise in popular politics and in overall political involvement.

In summary, legacies of Jackson's years in office include:

- A return to the **two-party system**, which remains with us today. This system aroused public political participation to a point never before seen in American history, in part because the public had a clear-cut choice between two distinct political agendas. Party competition forced both parties to clearly define their positions on major issues and to remain responsive to the popular will.

- **Heightened voter turnout**. The number of American voters jumped from 1.5 million in 1836 to 2.4 million in 1840—the greatest proportional jump between elections in American history. (Even in losing the election of 1840, Van Buren received 400,000 more popular votes than any presidential candidate before him.) The jump in voting resulted from the rise in the number of eligible voters and the number of voters who chose to vote. Eighty percent of eligible white males voted in 1840, as opposed to less than 60 percent in the three previous elections.

- The development of a **strong executive**. Jackson was the first president to use the veto power extensively to express his political will, and he controlled his cabinet closely to ensure that the executive department was united in pursuing its goals. Jackson revolutionized the presidency by setting an example of strength that nearly every president has followed.

The Age of Jackson

Cultural Trends: 1781–Mid-1800s

Chapter Contents

DURING THE FIRST HALF OF THE NINETEENTH CENTURY, Americans worked hard to carve out a national identity in religion and culture, as well as in politics. This chapter covers the trends of the first 60 years of the United States, which is why we don't include a trends and themes list.

Religion

Since the Revolution, America had become increasingly secular. Educated Americans, in particular, came to embrace the doctrines of the **Enlightenment**, which favored logic and reason over piety. Partly as a reaction against this growing rationalism, the Second Great Awakening emerged in the 1800s and caused a resurgence of religious faith.

Enlightenment Critique of Religion

Influenced by the Enlightenment ideals of logic and reason, many Americans began to question certain elements of the Christian faith, embracing new rational views on religion. Proponents of **rationalism** held that religious beliefs should not simply be accepted, but should instead be acquired through investigation and reflection. For most rationalists, the existence of God was proven most prominently by the orderly workings of nature, which hinted at a rational creator. The most extreme rationalists, called **Deists**, argued that where the Bible conflicted with reason, it should be ignored. These Deists, including Benjamin Franklin and Thomas Jefferson, believed that a rational God, like a celestial clockmaker, had created a perfect universe and then stepped back to let it operate according to natural laws.

The ideas of the Enlightenment led Americans to seek more rational religious ideas. These Americans criticized traditional religion and looked to science and logic for proof of their religious beliefs.

Along with Deism, other rationalist challenges arose to traditional religion, including Universalism and Unitarianism. Universalism held that science and reason ensured that all souls would eternally progress toward salvation, regardless of the adoption of any specific creed. Between 1794 and 1807, **Thomas Paine** published his Universalist book, **The *Age of Reason***, which objected to all organized religion. Many critics condemned this book as a defense of Atheism. The other new creed, Unitarianism, opposed the Christian doctrine of the trinity (the belief that God exists in three equal and eternal parts: God the Father, God the Son, and God the Holy Spirit). Unitarianism gained a small following of religious liberals during the late eighteenth century, and grew throughout the early nineteenth century to emerge as a separate denomination with its own churches.

The Second Great Awakening

About seventy years after the First Great Awakening, the **Second Great Awakening** emerged during the early 1800s, partly as a backlash against the spread of rationalism, and partly in response to calls for an organized religion more accessible to the common man. As in the First Great Awakening, revivalist ministers during the Second Great Awakening urged followers to reach a personal, emotional understanding of God. Women, blacks, and Native Americans participated heavily in the revival meetings.

The revivals began in Connecticut in 1790. Unlike the revivals during the First Great Awakening, which were emotionally raucous and neared hysteria, these revivals were often calmer and quieter, as gatherers respectfully observed believers in prayer. In New England, these revivals spawned a movement to educate and reform America. Social activists, inspired by their renewed religious spirit, founded all sorts of evangelical and reform groups: the American Bible Society (1816), the Society for the Promotion of Temperance, abolition groups, and groups urging educational reform and women's rights.

Religious fervor quickly spread to the West, where revivals more closely resembled the earlier, more animated revivals. In Kentucky and Tennessee, **camp meetings** were rowdy gatherings filled with dancing, singing, and shouting. The Methodists, who emphasized that religion was a matter of the heart rather an issue of logic, came to dominate frontier revivals. By 1845, Methodism was the most popular denomination of Protestantism in the U.S.

While the Second Great Awakening made great strides toward converting a secularized American public, it was not without critics. Some claimed the revivals encouraged more lust than salvation. Unitarians criticized the emotional displays of the revivals and argued that goodness sprang from gradual character building, not sudden emotional conversion.

Transcendentalism and Literature

Along with the Second Great Awakening, other religious reform movements arose in the nineteenth century to challenge rationalism. One such movement was **transcendentalism**, which emerged during the 1830s. Transcendentalists argued that knowledge did not come exclusively through the intellect, but also through the senses, intuition, and sudden insight. They believed that concepts such as God, freedom, and absolute truth were inborn and could be accessed through inner experience and emotional openness.

Two prominent transcendentalists were the authors Ralph Waldo Emerson and Henry David Thoreau, whose works emphasized spontaneous and vivid expression of emotion rather than logic and analysis. In his essays "Nature" and "Self-Reliance," **Ralph Waldo Emerson** claimed that all people were capable of seeing the truth if they relied on their inner selves and trusted their hearts. In *Walden*, **Henry David Thoreau** recounted his two years spent living in a cabin in the woods away from civilization and materialism. He advocated living a simple life according to one's conscience, not according to society's repressive codes.

Mormonism

The Church of Jesus Christ of Latter-Day Saints, also known as **Mormonism**, was the most controversial challenge to traditional religion. Its founder, **Joseph Smith**, claimed that God and Jesus Christ appeared to him and directed him to a buried book of revelation. The Book of Mormon, similar in form and style to the Bible, tells of the descendents of a sixth century B.C. prophet whose family founded a civilization in South America. Violent religious persecution forced Mormons to move steadily westward in search of land upon which to establish a perfect spiritual community. After Smith's murder in Illinois, a new leader, Brigham Young, led the Mormons to present-day Utah, where they have since prospered.

Social Reform

The 1820s and 1830s saw a great rise in popular politics, as free white males achieved universal suffrage. Women, blacks, and Native Americans, however, remained excluded from the political process and were often neglected by politicians. In protest, these marginalized groups and their sympathizers organized reform movements to heighten public awareness and to influence social and political policy. Many reformers believed that they were doing God's work, and the Second Great Awakening did much to encourage them in their missions.

These reform movements, like many issues of the day, quickly became sectional in nature. New England and Midwestern areas settled by New Englanders were most likely to be reformist. Southerners, by contrast, actively opposed the abolition of slavery, pursued temperance and school reform only halfheartedly, and largely ignored women's rights.

Abolitionism

Perhaps the most prominent and controversial reform movement of the period was abolitionism, the anti-slave movement. Although abolitionism had attracted many followers in the revolutionary period, the movement lagged during the early 1800s. By the 1830s, the spirit of abolitionism surged, especially in the Northeast. In 1831, **William Lloyd Garrison** launched an abolitionist newspaper, **The Liberator**, earning himself a reputation as the most radical white abolitionist. Whereas past abolitionists had suggested blacks be shipped back to Africa, Garrison worked in conjunction with prominent black abolitionists, including **Fredrick Douglass**, to demand equal civil rights for blacks. Garrison's battle cry was "immediate emancipation," but he recognized that it would take years to convince enough Americans to oppose slavery. To spread the abolition fervor, he founded the New England Anti-Slavery Society in 1832 and the American Anti-Slavery Society in 1833. By 1840, these organizations had spawned more than 1,500 local chapters. Even so, abolitionists were a small minority in the United States in the 1830s and 1840s, often subjected to jeering and physical violence.

William Lloyd Garrison's newspaper, The Liberator, *spoke for the most extreme abolitionists. Along with Frederick Douglass, Garrison called for emancipation of slaves and full civil rights for blacks.*

Opposed to abolitionism, Southern congressmen succeeded in pushing the **gag rule** through Congress in 1836. This rule tabled all abolitionist petitions in Congress and thereby served as a preemptive strike against all anti-slavery discussions. The gag rule was not repealed until 1844, under increased pressure from Northern abolitionists and others concerned with the restriction of the right to petition granted by the Constitution.

Women's Rights

The position of American women in the early 1800s was legally and socially inferior to men. Women could not vote and, if married, could not own property or retain their own earnings. The reform movements of the 1830s, specifically abolition and temperance, gave women a chance to get involved in the public arena. Women reformers soon began to agitate not just for temperance and abolition, but also for women's rights. Activists such as Angelina and Sarah Grimké, **Elizabeth Cady Stanton**, and **Lucretia Mott** argued that men and women are created equal and should be treated as such under the law. These advocates allied with abolitionist William Lloyd Garrison, also an ardent feminist, merging the powers of the abolition and the women's rights movements. Other advocates of both causes include Sojourner Truth and Frederick Douglass.

In 1848, Mott and Stanton organized a women's rights convention in Seneca Falls, New York. The **Seneca Falls Convention** issued a Declaration of Sentiments, modeled on the Declaration of Independence, that stated that all men and women are created equal. The Declaration and other reformist strategies, however, effected little change. While some states passed Married Women's Property Acts to allow married women to retain their property, women would have to wait until 1920 to gain the vote.

Public Schools

The movement to reform public schools began in rural areas, where one-room schoolhouses provided only minimal education. School reformers hoped to improve education so that children would become responsible citizens sharing common cultural values. Extending the right to vote to all free males no doubt helped galvanize the movement, since politicians began fearing the affects of an illiterate, ill-educated electorate.

In 1837, **Horace Mann** of Massachusetts became secretary of that state's board of education. He reformed the school system by increasing state spending on schools, lengthening the school year, dividing the students into grades, and introducing standardized textbooks. Much of the North reformed its schools along the lines dictated by Horace Mann, and free public schools spread throughout the region. The South, however, made little progress in public education, partly owing to its low population density and a general indifference toward progressive reforms.

Temperance

The production and consumption of alcohol in the United States rose markedly in the early 1800s. The temperance movement emerged as a backlash against the rising popularity of drink. Founded in 1826, the American Temperance Society advocated total abstinence from alcohol. Many advocates saw drinking as an immoral and/or irreligious practice that caused poverty or mental instability. Others saw it as a male indulgence that harmed women and children who often suffered abuse at drunkards' hands. During the 1830s, an increasing number of workingmen joined the movement in concern over the ill effects of alcohol on job performance. By 1835, about 5,000 temperance societies were affiliated with the American Temperance Society. Owing largely to this association's impact, consumption of liquor began to decrease in the late 1830s and early 1840s, and many states passed restrictions or bans on the sale of alcohol.

Prisons, Poorhouses, and Asylums

Beginning in the 1820s, social activists pressed for prison reform. These reformers argued that prisons, instead of simply confining criminals, should provide them with instruction, order, and discipline, so that they would be rehabilitated rather than just punished. Believing crime was largely the result of childhood neglect and trauma, prison reformers hoped that such instruction would counteract the effects of a poor upbringing and effectively purge criminals of their violent and immoral tendencies.

Further rehabilitative efforts were directed at the poor and the insane. To combat poverty, almshouses were built for poor invalids. Workhouses were built for the able-bodied poor in the hopes that a regimented environment would turn them into productive citizens. Until the early 1840s, the insane were confined in these poorhouses or in prisons, living in miserable conditions that often exacerbated their illnesses. In 1843, **Dorothea Dix**, a Massachusetts schoolteacher, described to the state legislature the conditions of the insane in prison and encouraged the construction of insane asylums to better rehabilitate the mentally ill. In the following years, asylums opened throughout the United States.

Utopian Communities

The most extreme reform movement in the United States during the first half of the 1800s was the utopian movement, founded on the belief that humans could live perfectly in small experimental societies. Though **utopian communities** varied in their philosophies, most were designed and founded by intellectuals as alternatives to the competitive economy. Utopian communities aimed to perfect social relationships; reform the institutions of marriage and private property; and balance political, occupational, and religious influences. Most utopian communities did not last beyond the early 1850s, but one, the Oneida community in New York, survived from 1848 to 1881.

The North and South Diverge

In the 80 years between the American Revolution and the Civil War, the North and South developed along distinct and opposing lines—economically, politically, and culturally. While the North became an industrial and manufacturing powerhouse deeply affected by social reform movements like abolitionism and women's rights, the South became a cotton kingdom, founded on slavery, whose inhabitants generally abstained from or opposed such reformist tendencies.

Manufacturing in the North

Manufacturing first took hold in New England. The region's poor soil made large-scale farming unprofitable, and its extensive waterways and steady influx of immigrants favored the development of manufacturing—the waterways supplied power for mills and facilitated trade, while the immigrants comprised a nearly inexhaustible labor supply. Small New England mills gave way to larger, more productive ones, and the expansion of foreign markets allowed the factory system to blossom. Factories became the center of planned towns designed to accommodate the needs of the factory owners and workers.

Cotton and Slavery in the South

The South took a very different economic course than the North. After the Revolution, when tobacco income plummeted, cotton reinvigorated the stagnant southern economy. The widespread use of the **cotton gin**, invented by Eli Whitney in 1793, made cotton plantations efficient and profitable. The demand for cotton also grew because of the developing textile industries in the North and in Britain. Cotton plantations spread across the South, and by 1850, the southern U.S. grew more than 80 percent of the world's cotton.

As the cotton-based economy boomed so did slavery, since slaves were needed to man the large-scale and labor-intensive plantations. Although Congress banned the importation of slaves in 1808, the smuggling of slaves continued until the 1850s, and the southern slave population doubled between 1810 and 1830. Three-quarters of these slaves worked on cotton plantations, while the remainder worked a variety of skilled and unskilled jobs. The rise in slavery led to the development of a slave culture, and also to an increasing, though generally unfounded, fear of slave revolts. Various slave uprisings did occasionally erupt, though—most notably, Nat Turner's Rebellion in Virginia in 1831.

The South became a veritable "Cotton Kingdom," remaining rural and agrarian while the North became industrialized. Rich plantation owners saw little reason to spend their capital on unsure industrial projects when cash crops brought in a large fixed income.

The Blossoming of American Literature

During the early 1800s, American literature began to separate itself from its British roots. **Washington Irving** and **James Fennimore Cooper** helped carve out the early territory of American literature, using distinctly American literary themes. Washington Irving achieved international acclaim, writing often satirical accounts of life in colonial New York. Two of his most famous stories are "Rip Van Winkle" and "The Legend of Sleepy Hollow." James Fennimore Cooper, the author of *The Pioneers* (1823) and *The Last of the Mohicans* (1826), is credited with creating the first western hero. In "The American Scholar" (1837), Ralph Waldo Emerson lauded such American literary advances and urged American authors to continue setting their own course.

Nathaniel Hawthorne, **Herman Melville**, and **Edgar Allen Poe** emerged in the late 1840s and early 1850s as prominent writers of fiction. They portrayed individuals as conflicted and obsessive, proud and guilt-ridden. In *The Scarlet Letter*, published in 1850, Hawthorne explores the moral dilemmas of an adulterous Puritan minister. Melville's *Moby-Dick* (1851) portrays a sea captain's tortured obsession. Poe's macabre short stories, including "The Tell-Tale Heart" (1843) and "The Raven" (1844), examine depravity and moral corruption.

Prominent essayists and poets also emerged during the 1840s and 1850s. Two of the most renowned essayists were the Transcendentalists Ralph Waldo Emerson and Henry David Thoreau (discussed in the Transcendentalism section), who favored emotion and intuition over pure logic. The poet **Walt Whitman**, a follower of Emerson, celebrated America for producing a new type of democratic man uncorrupted by European vice in his compilation of poems, *Leaves of Grass*, published in 1855.

Westward Expansion and Sectional Strife

Trends and Themes of the Era

- In the first half of the nineteenth century, the United States and its citizens were moved by a belief in manifest destiny, which held that it was the right and fate of the United States to cover the continent.

- Technology, specifically in the form of the railroad, dramatically accelerated expansion.

- Expansion intensified the sectional tension between the North and South by bringing to the forefront the issue of the extension of slavery into the West. Brief compromises relieved the tension from time to time, but no compromise was able to resolve the fundamental differences between the North and South.

Westward Expansion
and Sectional Strife

Settling the West

In the mid-1800s, Americans surged westward past the Mississippi River, the previously drawn boundary of the frontier. As settlers migrated toward the Pacific coast in their overloaded wagons, the West became the fastest growing area of the country. Despite fierce resistance from Native Americans, Mexicans, and the British, Americans eventually claimed the entire region west of the Mississippi. Westward expansion did not come without a cost, however—a cost to settlers, to Native Americans, and even to the integrity of the Union.

Manifest Destiny

Fueling the expansion westward was the popular belief that it was America's **manifest destiny** to expand through Texas, toward the Pacific coast. In 1845, a New York journalist wrote of "our manifest destiny to overspread and to possess the whole of our continent which Providence has given us for the development of the great experiment of liberty." This notion of manifest destiny tapped into America's nationalist spirit, which had been growing since the War of 1812, and echoed Protestant beliefs that America was a "called nation"—that is, chosen by God as a haven from which Protestants could spread their faith.

Texas and the Mexican War

During the 1820s, Americans streamed into Texas, then a Mexican territory, often receiving land grants from the Mexican government. Mexico gave these grants in the hopes of promoting the region's trade and development. By 1830, about 7,000 Americans lived in Texas, outnumbering Hispanic settlers two to one and alarming the Mexican government. In 1834, rebel Texan leaders, most of them American, declared their independence from the Mexican dictatorship. After two years of fighting, Texas became an independent republic, although the Mexican government refused to officially acknowledge its independence.

Because most Texan settlers were American, the question immediately arose of Texas's potential statehood. President **John Tyler**, who became president in 1841 after William Henry Harrison died in office, favored the annexation of Texas and its admission to the Union. In 1844, Democrat **James K. Polk** won the presidential election on a slogan of expansion, "Re-annex Texas and re-occupy Oregon." One month into his presidency, Congress voted to annex Texas. In 1845, Texas was admitted in the Union as the twenty-eighth state. Mexico, however, had never officially recognized Texan independence, and threatened war over U.S. annexation.

War finally erupted a year later over the new state's borders: the U.S. argued that the southern Texas border lay along the Rio Grande River, while Mexico insisted that the border lay much further north. After trying unsuccessfully to buy the New Mexican and Californian territories from Mexico, the U.S. found a pretense to declare war against Mexico in 1846, when Mexican troops crossed the Rio Grande. The **Mexican War** ranged throughout Texas, New Mexico, and California, and into the Mexican interior, finally ending in U.S. victory. With the **Treaty of Guadalupe Hidalgo**, signed in February 1848, Mexico ceded Texas, New Mexico, and California to the U.S. for $15 million. (Note that this ceded territory encompassed present-day Arizona, Nevada, California, Utah, and parts of New Mexico, Colorado, and Wyoming). The treaty secured the West for American settlement, and American land now stretched continuously from the Atlantic to the Pacific Ocean.

The Treaty of Guadalupe Hidalgo granted the U.S. claims to Texas, New Mexico, and California.

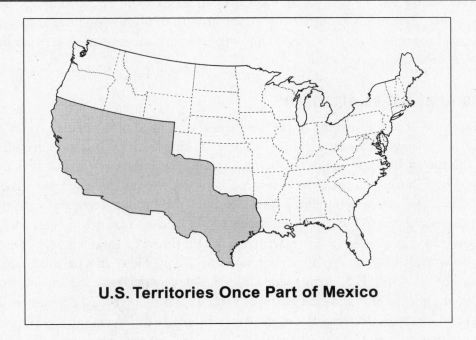

U.S. Territories Once Part of Mexico

Oregon

The second half of Polk's campaign slogan, "Re-annex Mexico and re-occupy Oregon," referred to territory in the Northwest jointly held by the U.S. and Great Britain. This territory included present-day Oregon, Washington, and Idaho; parts of Montana and Wyoming; and much of western Canada. Expansionists pressured Congress to annex the entire Oregon territory, as indicated by their motto, "Fifty-four-forty or fight" (the numbers indicated the region's latitude and longitude). Northerners also pushed for acquisition, since the admission of Oregon, a free state, would balance the admission of slave-holding Texas. President Polk, however, despite his expansionist aims, could not commit to acquiring the territory. Already caught up in border disputes with Mexico, he did not wish to engage in further conflict, and instead proposed a compromise with Britain. By this 1846 compromise, the U.S. and Britain divided the Oregon territory along the forty-ninth parallel. South of this line lay the U.S.–owned Oregon territory, and north lay the British-owned Washington territories. Oregon was admitted as a state in 1859.

California Gold Rush

In January 1848, an American carpenter struck gold in California's Sierra Nevada Mountains. As news of this discovery drifted east, a gold rush began, drawing thousands to the West Coast in search of their fortunes. Including Mexicans, Europeans, and Americans from the East Coast, California attracted about 100,000 immigrants in a single year. This influx of settlers led to the growth of numerous cities and mining towns, and pressure grew for California to organize its own government, either independent of the Union or as a state.

Removal of Native Americans

A central aspect of the opening of the West was the removal of the Native Americans who already occupied the land. Removal started during Andrew Jackson's presidency with the **Indian Removal Act** of 1830, which authorized the president to force the removal of Midwestern tribes to reservations in Oklahoma and elsewhere. By the early 1860s, the U.S. government had systematized this "Indian territory" into small reservations and, in 1867 set aside two large tracts of land—one north of Nebraska and one south of Kansas—for tribal resettlement. The threat of force convinced many tribes to comply with resettlement. But some tribes, the Sioux in particular, fiercely resisted. In 1874, the U.S. Army sent Colonel **George Armstrong Custer** into South Dakota to fight the Sioux. At the Battle of Little Bighorn, in 1876, the Sioux crushed Custer and his men. After this defeat, the Army adopted a different tactic by launching a war of attrition, persistently harassing the Sioux and gradually weakening their will to resist. U.S. forces finally vanquished the Sioux in the Battle of Wounded Knee in 1890. Over the next decade, the Sioux relocated to reservations.

Not all Americans supported such aggressive removal tactics, however. Helen Hunt Jackson's *A Century of Dishonor*, published in 1881, attempted to raise public awareness of the Native American plight. Some hoped to "save" the Native Americans through religion, or to "civilize" them by teaching them white ways. Other humanitarians suggested that the best approach would be to fully integrate the tribes into white society.

These latter concerns were expressed in the 1887 **Dawes Severalty Act** (or simply the Dawes Act), which called for the breakup of the reservation system and the treatment of Native Americans as individuals rather than as tribes. Congressman Henry Dawes believed that private land ownership would help Native Americans become "civilized" and assimilated. Under the act, formally communal land from the reservations was distributed to individuals in 160-acre allotments, and these individuals were guaranteed U.S. citizenship after twenty-five years. The surplus land that remained of the reservations after these allotments had been made was sold to white settlers and land speculators. In practice, much of the land parceled out to Native Americans also wound up in white hands after poverty forced many Native Americans to sell their plots and become literally homeless. As a result, many Native Americans were left destitute and dependent on federal aid to survive. Though passed with good intent, in practice, the Dawes Act had disastrous effects: it disintegrated tribal communities and deprived Native Americans of millions of acres of land—in the process, clearing the way for American settlement.

Another factor impairing the Native American way of life was the mass slaughter of buffalo. Many Plains tribes depended on buffalo for food, leather, and other material needs. By the 1870s, however, the buffalo population neared extinction, as white hunters killed 9 million buffalo between 1872 and 1875. American hunters often killed the animals solely for their hide, leaving the carcass to rot, while Army generals killed the buffalo in deliberate attempts to drive Native Americans off of desired lands.

The Homestead Act and the Transcontinental Railroad

To promote settlement of the West, Congress passed the **Homestead Act** in 1862, which offered 160 acres to anyone who would cultivate and improve the land. Much of this western land, however, was ill-suited to farming, so ranchers and railroad builders ended up owning most it.

Another way Congress spurred settlement was by extending the railroad network into the West. In 1862, Congress passed the Pacific Railway Act, which chartered the Union Pacific Railroad company and authorized the building of the **transcontinental railroad**. While the Union Pacific Railroad Company built tracks westward from Iowa, the Central Pacific Railroad Company built tracks eastward from California. The two tracks converged on May 10, 1869 in Promontory, Utah. This historic moment marked the completion of the first transcontinental railroad, and by 1884, there were four such lines. Whereas just fifty years earlier it had taken pioneers many grueling months to cross the nation, Americans could now travel from coast to coast in a week's time. Railroads attracted many new settlers to the newly accessible West by offering free transportation and long-term loans to travelers.

Effects of Expansion: Sectional Tension Intensified

The expansion of the U.S. into the West reopened a controversy that had been temporarily settled by the 1821 **Missouri Compromise**: the balance of slave-holding versus free lands. Regional passions flared as the nation debated the extension of slavery into the new territories. In 1844, Congress repealed the 1836 **gag rule**, which had suppressed all debates on slavery, and disputed the status of the newly acquired territories. Texas naturally entered the Union as a slave state in 1845 because the territory was already slave-holding when it sought admission. But the other lands ceded by Mexico—including California and New Mexico—were not yet slave-holding, so Northern and Southern interests rallied to recruit these lands to their side.

In 1846, Democratic congressman David Wilmot attempted to preempt the debates that would erupt when the U.S. gained additional western lands by proposing the **Wilmot Proviso**, which stipulated that slavery be prohibited in any territory gained from Mexico. With strong support from the North, the proviso passed through the House of Representatives but stalled in the Senate, where it was repeatedly reintroduced without success. The issue sparked intense sectional debate. In the debates, four main arguments emerged.

- Antislavery Northerners cited the **Northwest Ordinance** of 1787, which forbade slavery north of the Ohio River, as proof that the founding fathers opposed the extension of slavery, and therefore that America should add no new slave states.

- Southerners, led by John C. Calhoun, argued that all lands acquired from Mexico should become slave-holding.

- Moderates, including President Polk, suggested that the 36°30' line from the Missouri Compromise be extended into the Western territory, so that all territory north of the line would be free, and all territory south of the line would be slave-holding.

- Others suggested the system of **popular sovereignty**, in which the settlers themselves, through their local governments, would decide whether their regions should be slave-holding or free.

Before the 1848 election, antislavery advocates united to form the **Free-Soil Party** and nominated Martin Van Buren for president. The Free-Soil Party consisted of antislavery **Whigs**, members of the abolitionist Liberty Party, and a faction of **Democratic Party** (known as the Barnburners) that supported the Wilmot Proviso. Although the Free-Soil Party did not win any electoral votes, it did earn ten percent of the national popular vote. Van Buren lost the election to Whig candidate **Zachary Taylor**.

The Compromise of 1850

Although he held slaves himself, President Taylor opposed the extension of slavery into the territories of California and New Mexico. In 1849, California requested admission as a free state, which frightened the South because the admission of another free state into the Union would make slave-holding interests a minority in Congress. Southern Congressmen tried to block California's admission. With the national government in gridlock, **Henry Clay** stepped forward in May 1850 to present a compromise, much as he had thirty years earlier when Missouri sought statehood. Clay's 1850 proposals included five points:

- California would be admitted as a free state.

- The remainder of the Mexican cession would be divided into two separate territories, New Mexico and Utah, and these territories would decide by popular sovereignty whether to be slave-holding or free.

- Texas would cede its claim to parts of the New Mexico territory, and, in exchange, the government would cover Texas's $10 million war debt.

- The slave trade would be abolished in the District of Columbia, but slavery itself would continue.

- Congress would strengthen the **Fugitive Slave Act** by requiring citizens of any state, slave or free, to assist in the capture and return of runaway slaves.

Clay's proposal threw Congress into an eight-month discussion known as the "**Great Debate**." Proponents of each side—the North and the South—each criticized Clay's compromise for being too lenient on the other. Most prominent among the debaters were Clay, **Daniel Webster**, and **John C. Calhoun**. Eventually, the bill passed. Two events in particular facilitated its passage: first, when President Taylor died in July 1850, Vice President Millard Fillmore took over and adopted a pro-compromise position. Second, **Stephen A. Douglas** took over for Henry Clay as speaker of the house and divided the compromise bill up into separate components, each of which passed. Together, the separate bills became known as the **Compromise of 1850**.

The Compromise of 1850 called for: the admission of California as a free state; the strengthening of the Fugitive Slave Law; popular sovereignty in Utah and New Mexico concerning the question of slavery; the abolition of the slave trade in D.C.; and the federal assumption of Texas's debt.

Compromise Undermined: A Divided Nation

During the Great Debate, one particular point of contention was the strengthening of the **Fugitive Slave Act**. The Fugitive Slave Act denied alleged fugitives the right to a trial and did not allow them to testify in their own defense. It further granted court-appointed commissioners greater payment if they ruled in favor of the slaveholder. In addition, the law authorized federal marshals and southern posses to enter the North and target runaway slaves who had escaped decades earlier. The Fugitive Slave Act reminded Northerners of their complicity with the institution of slavery.

Some Northerners worked vigorously to undermine the Fugitive Slave Act, whether through legal tactics, organized social protest, or violent resistance. During the 1850s, nine Northern states passed **personal liberty laws** to counteract the Fugitive Slave Act. These state laws guaranteed all alleged fugitives the right to a trial by jury and to a lawyer, and they prohibited state jails from holding alleged fugitives. In terms of social resistance, Northern Vigilance Committees worked hard to protect escaped slaves, at times in conjunction with the **Underground Railroad**—a network of safe houses and escorts throughout the North that helped escaped slaves to freedom. A former slave herself, **Harriet Tubman** was instrumental in forming this network, for which reason she is sometimes referred to as a "Moses" to her people (in the Bible, Moses led the Israelites to freedom). Less systematic resistance came in the form of violent protest. In 1854, a Boston mob broke into a courthouse and killed a guard, in a failed attempt to free a fugitive slave.

Unjust provisions of the Fugitive Slave Act prompted Northerners to resist its enforcement through violent protest, clandestine efforts to aid escaped slaves, and legal tactics such as personal liberty laws.

Such strong-armed resistance against the Fugitive Slave Act revealed that Northern abolitionist sentiment was rising. No event did more to encourage Northern abolitionism and sympathy for runaway slaves than the 1852 publication of **Uncle Tom's Cabin**, written by **Harriet Beecher Stowe.** Stowe portrayed the institution of slavery in a horrifying light, telling the story of a black slave who is torn from his family, sold from place to place, and eventually whipped to death. Three hundred thousand copies of *Uncle Tom's Cabin* were sold in 1852, and 1.2 million had been sold by the summer of 1853. Dramatized versions of the story were produced at playhouses throughout the North, attracting audience members from all segments of society.

Election of 1852

As a symptom of the national division, the Whig party disintegrated during the 1850s along North and South lines, and its presidential candidate in 1852 fared badly. The Free Soil Party's candidate also won little support. The winner was Democratic nominee **Franklin Pierce**.

Compromise Collapses

Franklin Pierce, a Democrat, won the election of 1852. Pierce sought to avoid the controversial slave issue and instead focused on territorially expanding into Mexico and Cuba and on opening up international trade. However, he could not keep the slavery issue at bay for long. Beginning with the **Kansas-Nebraska Act** of 1854, the tenuous stalemate provided by the Compromise of 1850 was destroyed. Regional passions soon exploded into violence that foreshadowed the coming Civil War.

The Kansas-Nebraska Act

In January 1854, Senator Stephen A. Douglas of Illinois proposed a bill to organize Nebraska (part of the Louisiana Purchase) as a territory, in order to facilitate the building of a transcontinental railroad along a northern route from Chicago to the West. Because the Nebraska Territory lay above the 36°30' line, set by the Missouri Compromise to disallow slavery, Nebraska would automatically become a candidate for admission as a free state. Southerners therefore planned to oppose the bill unless Douglas made some concessions.

To ensure passage of the bill, Douglas yielded to Southerners who desired to void the **Missouri Compromise**'s 36°30' line. He inserted in his Nebraska bill an explicit repeal of the Missouri Compromise so that no territory would be automatically designated non-slaveholding. As an alternative, the bill declared that the slavery issue in the Nebraska region would be decided by popular sovereignty, thus extending the Compromise of 1850's concept of popular sovereignty to territories outside New Mexico and Utah. Douglas further divided the Nebraska Territory into two parts: Nebraska to the west of Iowa, and Kansas to the west of Missouri. Many assumed that this meant Kansas would be reserved for slavery and Nebraska for free soil. With these concessions attached, the bill passed through Congress and became law in May 1854.

Westward Expansion and Sectional Strife

The Kansas-Nebraska Act effectively nullified the Missouri Compromise and opened up the Nebraska and Kansas territories to popular sovereignty.

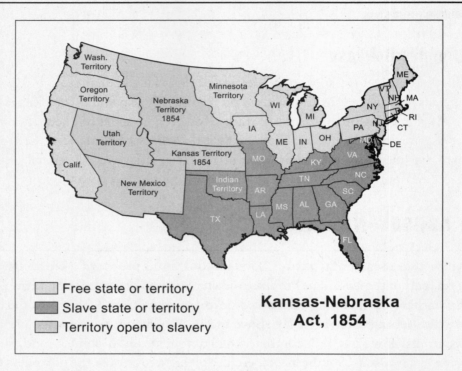

Kansas-Nebraska Act, 1854

The Kansas-Nebraska Act, however, did not stave off sectional conflict. Because Nebraska was likely to prohibit slavery, as a territory above the 36°30' line, Kansas became a battleground for sectional interests. Both Northern abolitionist groups and Southern interests rushed into the territory to try to control the local elections. In March 1855, during the first election of the territorial legislature, thousands of pro-slavery inhabitants of Western Missouri crossed into Kansas to tilt the vote in favor of slaveholding interests. Because of the election fraud perpetrated by these "border ruffians," a pro-slavery government swept into power. This new government immediately ousted antislavery legislators and set up a pro-slavery constitution known as the Lecompton Constitution.

In opposition to the new legislature, abolitionist **John Brown** led a massacre of five men at a pro-slavery camp, setting off an outbreak of violence. More than 200 people died in the ensuing months of violence, earning the territory the nickname **Bleeding Kansas**. Three years later, in 1859, Brown led an even larger antislavery revolt in Virginia, when he attempted to seize federal arsenal at **Harpers Ferry** in order to arm a massive slave uprising. His raid was unsuccessful, however, and he was caught and hanged.

Westward Expansion and Sectional Strife

The *Dred Scott* Decision

Distraught by the violence of Bleeding Kansas, President **James Buchanan**, who was elected in 1856, sought a judicial resolution to the issue of slavery's extension. A case he saw as potentially providing such a resolution was that of Dred Scott, in which Scott, a Missouri slave, sued for his freedom on the basis that his owner had taken him to live in a free state (Illinois), and later a free territory (Wisconsin). In March 1857, Chief Justice **Roger B. Taney** delivered the majority opinion on *Dred Scott v. Sandford*.

To begin his ruling, Taney stated that Scott, as a slave, had no right to sue in federal court, and further claimed that no black, whether slave or free, could become a citizen of the United States. Slaves were property only, according to Taney, and would remain property even if they resided in free territory. Furthermore, Taney ruled that Congress could not forbid slavery in any U.S. territory because doing so would violate the Fifth Amendment's protection of property, including slaves, from being taken away without due process. This decision rendered the Missouri Compromise unconstitutional (though the Compromise had already been effectively nullified by the Kansas-Nebraska Act). Taney further suggested that the Compromise of 1850 and the Kansas-Nebraska Act were unconstitutional, since they enforced popular sovereignty, which allowed territorial governments to prohibit slavery and therefore violated the Fifth Amendment as interpreted by the Court. Though Buchanan initially had hoped that the *Dred Scott* ruling might resolve the debates about extending slavery, it actually aggravated sectional tensions. Northerners harshly condemned the ruling, while Southerners celebrated it.

The Dred Scott *decision ruled the Missouri Compromise unconstitutional, and affirmed the status of slaves as simple property. Further, the decision cast serious doubt upon the legality of the Compromise of 1850.*

The New Politics of Sectionalism

The Whig Party, which was an anti-Jackson alliance between Southern Republicans and Northern Democrats, disintegrated in the 1850s over the increasingly contentious issue of slavery. In its place, the **Republican Party** arose as the chief political opposition to the Democrats. The Republican Party crystallized in opposition to slavery, while the Democrats supported the institution.

From Whigs to Republicans

The Kansas-Nebraska Act ruined the **Whig Party** by dividing its Southern pro-slavery and Northern antislavery components. The fractures ran so deep that even Northern Whigs were divided, between antislavery "Conscience Whigs" and conservatives who supported the Compromise of 1850. This split forced many antislavery Whigs to look for a political alternative less muddied by internal conflict.

One alternative was the American Party, which became known as the **Know-Nothings** because the members met secretly and refused to identify themselves. This party was a nativist organization (basically foreign-hating) that spread anti-German, anti-Irish, and anti-Catholic propaganda. Most members also favored temperance and opposed slavery. It seemed the Know-Nothings would form the primary opposition party to the Democrats until, in 1855, they also succumbed to sectional conflict when the party's Southern branch made acceptance of the Kansas-Nebraska Act part of the Know-Nothing platform. The Know-Nothing party found itself weakened and near ruin.

In its place, the **Republican Party** emerged as the premier antislavery coalition. The Republicans originally formed in the North between 1854 and 1855, as Northern Democrats, antislavery Whigs, and former Free Soil party members united to oppose the Democratic Party. Although all Republicans disapproved of the Kansas-Nebraska Act, some Republicans merely wanted to restore the Missouri Compromise. Others were middleground free-soilers, and still others were adamant abolitionists. Nevertheless, opposition to slavery's extension united these disparate groups.

The Whig Party disintegrated during the mid-1850s, throwing Northern Whigs into the Know-Nothing Party and the Republican Party. By 1856, the Republican Party had risen to national prominence as the main opposition to the Democrats.

Republicans and Democrats Face Off: Lincoln-Douglas Debates

In the 1858 midterm elections, Republicans and Democrats faced off for the first time. The most visible of these battles took place in Illinois, where prominent Democratic Senator Stephen A. Douglas faced a reelection challenge in the form of Republican **Abraham Lincoln**. This campaign pitted the Republican Party's rising star, Lincoln, against the Democratic Party's leading Senator. In a series of seven debates known as the **Lincoln-Douglas Debates**, Douglas advocated popular sovereignty while Lincoln espoused the free-soil argument.

Douglas painted a picture of his opponent as an abolitionist and an advocate of racial equality and racial mixing, positions that were still very unpopular at the time. Lincoln countered that he was not an abolitionist—that he simply opposed the *extension* of slavery into the territories, but did not aim to abolish slavery where it already existed, in the South. He further claimed, "I am not, nor ever have been in favor of bringing about the social and political equality of the white and black man." In attack of his opponent, Lincoln challenged that Douglas's belief in popular sovereignty, in particular his "**Freeport Doctrine**," was incompatible with the *Dred Scott* decision. In this doctrine, Douglas stated that territorial governments could effectively forbid slavery by refusing to enact slave codes, even though the *Dred Scott* decision had explicitly deprived Congress of the authority to restrict slavery in the territories.

In the end, neither candidate emerged from the debates as the clear victor. Although Douglas won the Senate seat, he alienated Southern supporters by encouraging disobedience of the *Dred Scott* decision with his Freeport Doctrine. Lincoln, meanwhile, lost the election, but emerged with national prominence as a spokesman for antislavery interests.

Republican Ascendancy: The Election of 1860

In 1860, Buchanan announced he would not run for reelection. The Democratic Party ruptured over whom to nominate in Buchanan's place. While Northern Democrats defended the doctrine of popular sovereignty and nominated Stephen Douglas for president, Southern Democrats opposed popular sovereignty in favor of the *Dred Scott* decision—which provided absolute protection of slavery in all territories—and nominated vice president John Breckenridge for president. Southern moderates from the lower South walked out of the Democratic Convention and formed their own party, the Constitutional Party, which nominated John C. Bell for president. These three candidates faced Republican nominee Abraham Lincoln.

Lincoln emerged with a majority of the electoral votes, 180 in total. He carried all eighteen free states, but had not even appeared on the ballots of a number of slave states, and in 10 slave states, had not received a single popular vote. Lincoln's election so alienated the South that secession seemed imminent. While South Carolina had threatened earlier to secede from the Union over the Tariff of Abominations in 1828, the current threat was much more dire.

In the election of 1860, Republican Abraham Lincoln defeated three challengers representing the country's varying pro-slavery political positions—Northern Democrats, Southern Democrats, and Southern moderates.

Civil War and Reconstruction

Trends and Themes of the Era

- After Lincoln's election, sectional differences over slavery and the question of states' rights versus federal power erupted in the Civil War.

- After the war, Lincoln favored a mild Reconstruction of the South, though Congress was dominated by Radical Republicans who favored a harsher reconstruction plan in order to punish the South for secession and for slavery. After Lincoln's assassination, Congress overwhelmed Andrew Johnson, who had taken over as president, and instituted punitive Reconstruction policies.

- Blacks in the South, freed during the Civil War, gained considerable rights during radical Reconstruction. Through both legal and illegal means, Southerners fought against the granting of these rights. After the failure of radical Reconstruction, Southerners used the Supreme Court's *Plessy v. Ferguson* decision to institutionalize segregation and the discrimination of blacks.

Toward War

Abraham Lincoln's victory in the election of 1860 began a chain of events that pushed the nation rapidly toward civil war.

Secession

During the 1860 election, some Southerners threatened secession pending Lincoln's victory, even though he promised that while he would forbid the extension of slavery into the territories, he would not interfere with slavery in the South. In December 1860, soon after Lincoln's victory, a special South Carolina convention voted unanimously for secession. By February 1861, six more Southern states followed suit: Alabama, Mississippi, Florida, Georgia, Louisiana, and Texas. Delegates from all seven states met to establish the **Confederate States of America,** and they chose **Jefferson Davis** as the Confederacy's first president.

Lincoln refused to recognize the confederacy and declared the secession "legally void." Although he personally favored the gradual emancipation of slaves with compensation given to slave owners, as president, he strove to preserve the Union first and foremost, by whatever means necessary—even if that meant freeing no slaves at all. He once said, "If I could save the Union without freeing *any* slaves I would do it, and if I could save the Union by freeing *all* the slaves I would do it." Lincoln hoped that loyal Unionists in the South would help him overturn secession.

However, the nation's rift only widened in the early months of Lincoln's presidency. In April 1861, Confederate troops opened fire on the federal army base at **Fort Sumter**, forcing federal troops to surrender. Lincoln proclaimed the Lower South in rebellion and called for an army to suppress the insurrection. The threat of incoming federal troops prompted Virginia, Arkansas, Tennessee, and North Carolina to secede and join the Confederacy. Maryland, Delaware, Kentucky, and Missouri, all slave states, remained in the Union.

Civil War and Reconstruction

The Confederate attack on federal troops at Fort Sumter sparked the
secession of the Upper South and the commitment of the North to war.

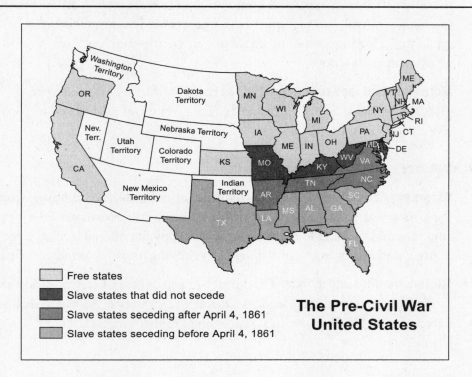

**The Pre-Civil War
United States**

☐ Free states

■ Slave states that did not secede

▨ Slave states seceding after April 4, 1861

▨ Slave states seceding before April 4, 1861

Mobilizing for War

Each side predicted an early victory for itself. While the North seemed favored to win
the war, given its larger and better-equipped army, the South also had some distinct
military advantages.

The Union's advantages over the South:

- **Population size:** The North had a population of 22 million (23 states) versus
  the South's 9 million (11 states). Northern forces totaled 2,100,000,
  compared to the South's paltry 800,000.

- **Greater wartime funding:** Both the North and South sold war bonds, but the
  North also instituted an income tax and had more effective tax collection.
  The Northern economy also fared better during the war, suffering only
  moderate inflation, while the Southern economy collapsed from severe
  inflation (prices in the South rose more than 300 percent annually).

- **More advanced industry:** The North held more than ninety percent of the nation's industrial plants and could easily produce heavy artillery weapons. The North also had seventy percent of the nation's railroad tracks and could therefore effectively transport arms and food to distant troops. The South, on the other hand, had to import arms until it could build an industrial base, could not afford supplies, and could not efficiently ship food and equipment to its troops.

- **More abundant food resources:** Northern agriculture was geared toward grain, whereas the South specialized in the growing of inedible cash crops like cotton, tobacco, and indigo.

The Confederacy's advantages over the North:

- **Geography:** The Confederacy was fighting for independence at home, while the Union was entering enemy territory. Whereas the North would have to ship men and supplies long distances and occupy conquered territory, the South could maintain an arc of defense by moving its men around very little.

- **Military tradition and morale:** The South had a stronger military tradition and more experienced military leaders. During the war, fewer Southern troops defected than Northern troops, suggesting a higher morale among Confederate forces.

The Civil War

The Civil War began more as a battle over the preservation of the Union than as a battle over slavery. Many felt that the real issue at stake was the question of states' rights versus federal power—whether states could secede from the Union in protest against federal policy, regardless of whether that policy concerned slavery or another issue, such as tariffs. Slavery was therefore considered the catalyst for the nation's rupture, but not the primary cause. It was not until Lincoln's Emancipation Proclamation that slavery emerged as the central issue at stake.

In the East, the Union Army aimed to capture the Confederate capital of Richmond, Virginia. Most of the early battles ended in stalemate, with both sides suffering devastating losses. After a Southern victory in June 1862, Confederate general **Robert E. Lee** led his forces on a powerful march northward from Virginia, aiming to break Union lines. What followed, in September 17, 1862, was the bloodiest single-day battle in the Civil War: the **Battle of Antietam**, in which more than 8,000 men died on the field and 18,000 were wounded. Though a strategic draw, the battle proved a Union victory in that Lee halted his Confederate advance northward. Lincoln responded to this victory by issuing the **Emancipation Proclamation**.

General Lee struck northward into Pennsylvania in July 1863, but was again blocked by a strong Union defense. In the three-day **Battle of Gettysburg**, 90,000 Union soldiers battled 75,000 Confederates and secured a Union victory. The losses were ruinous to both sides: a total of 7,000 soldiers died on the field and 40,000 were wounded. Although fighting would continue for more than a year after the Battle of Gettysburg, the battle proved a decisive victory for the Union, and the war thereafter tilted in the Union's favor. Later that year, Lincoln delivered his famed **Gettysburg Address**, in which he portrayed the war as a test of democracy's strength.

In the West, the Union experienced successes much earlier on. Led by General **Ulysses S. Grant**, the Union secured control of the Mississippi River and moved southward. At the Battle of Shiloh, in April 1862, Grant's troops were ambushed by Confederates, but Grant proved victorious. Both sides suffered heavy losses, as nearly one-third of the 77,000 men involved were killed.

The Emancipation Proclamation

Early in the war, Union officials were uncertain how to treat Southern slaves who fled to the North or were captured by the army. Lincoln was cautious in his approach to this matter, since the Union contained four slave states and many pro-slavery Democrats. He vaguely supported the policy of confiscation, in which slaves who had worked for the Confederate military were considered captives of war and put to work for the Union Army. Each Union loss in the war, however, made emancipation a more attractive recourse, since slave labor drove the Southern economy and allowed the Confederacy to devote more white men to war. Lincoln eventually came to favor emancipation, and only awaited the right moment to announce his decision.

After the Union victory at Antietam in September 1862, Lincoln issued the Preliminary Emancipation Proclamation, declaring all slaves under rebel control free as of January 1, 1863. The final **Emancipation Proclamation** was issued on January 1. In practice, the Proclamation freed very few slaves because it did not affect the slave states within the Union or the parts of the Confederacy under Union control. But as a political move, it proved decisive and brilliant. The proclamation mobilized the support of European liberals (Great Britain and France had outlawed slavery earlier in the century), and it appeased the **Radical Republicans** in Congress. Abolishing slavery thus became one of the Union's primary objectives for war, along with preserving the Union.

Civil War and Reconstruction

The Emancipation Proclamation freed all slaves under rebel control on January 1, 1863. Though the practical effect of the proclamation on Southern slaves was slight, it proved a brilliant political move.

Black Soldiers

The Emancipation Proclamation did significantly affect the war by bolstering the Union's forces. After the Proclamation, the Union began to enlist black soldiers in conquered areas of the South. In all, almost 200,000 blacks enlisted. By the end of the war, black soldiers comprised almost one-tenth of Union Army. Although blacks were paid less than whites and assigned to less desirable posts, their military service was as an important symbol of black citizenship.

Union Victory

In early 1864, Lincoln appointed General Ulysses S. Grant commander of all Union armies. The string of Union victories that followed that summer, especially General William T. Sherman's victories in Georgia, helped Lincoln win reelection in 1864. Union forces continued to rout the Confederate Army after Lincoln's reelection, destroying much of Georgia and South Carolina in what is known as **Sherman's March to Sea**: Sherman and his troops first burned Atlanta, and then marched toward the coast, demolishing everything in their way, including railroads and factories. Sherman estimated that his forces ruined $100 million worth of property.

One month after Sherman's forces conquered Charleston, South Carolina, Grant took the Confederacy capital in Richmond, Virginia. Robert E. Lee's forces officially surrendered to Grant on April 9, 1865. One month later, Confederacy President Jefferson Davis was captured in Georgia.

Reconstruction

More Americans died in the Civil War than in any other conflict before or since. The war was particularly disastrous for the South, where one in twenty white men were killed or wounded, and the land lay in ruins. After the Union victory, the nation faced the complex tasks of reintegrating the damaged South into the Union and helping heal the nation's wounds.

Presidential Reconstruction under Lincoln

Unlike the **Radical Republicans** in Congress who wanted to severely punish the Confederate states, Lincoln proposed a more forgiving and flexible plan for Reconstruction. In December 1863, before the war had ended, Lincoln issued the Proclamation of Amnesty and Reconstruction, also known as the **"ten percent plan**," which offered pardon to any former Confederates who would take an oath to support the Constitution. This pardon was not extended to officers in the Confederate armed forces above certain ranks, or to those who had resigned Union government posts to aid in the rebellion. In each state, when one-tenth of the voting population had taken the oath of loyalty to the Union and established a new government, Lincoln would recognize that government.

> *Lincoln's plan for Reconstruction, known as the "ten percent plan," allowed a state to reenter the Union when ten percent of its voters pledged allegiance to the Union.*

Radical Republicans in Congress denounced the plan for being too lenient on the South and for not securing any rights for freed slaves. Moreover, these Republicans believed that Congress, not the president, should dictate the terms by which the nation would reunite. In July 1864, Congress proposed its own plan for Reconstruction by passing the **Wade-Davis Bill**, which declared that each Confederate state would be run by a military governor. After half of each state's eligible voters took an oath of allegiance to the Union, a state convention could be called to overturn secession and outlaw slavery. Lincoln, however, vetoed the bill by leaving it unsigned for more than ten days after the adjournment of Congress. Reconstruction thus stalled, with Congress and the president in deadlock over the terms of the Confederate states' readmission.

> *Radical Republicans opposed Lincoln's "ten percent plan," and instead proposed a more stringent and punitive plan calling for military rule of the South.*

The Radical Republicans in Congress did succeed in dictating some terms of Reconstruction. To help former slaves adjust to their new lives, Congress established the **Freedmen's Bureau**, which offered education, employment, economic relief, and legal aid to freed slaves. The Freedmen's Bureau helped build hospitals and supervised the founding of black schools throughout the South, including Howard, Atlanta, and Fisk Universities (founded 1866-1867). Along with establishing the Freedmen's Bureau,

Civil War and Reconstruction

Civiil War and
Reconstruction

Congress passed the **Thirteenth Amendment**, which abolished slavery. The Amendment was ratified by the necessary number of states, twenty-seven, in December 1865, though Lincoln did not live to see that day.

In April 1865, soon after Lee's surrender, Lincoln was assassinated by John Wilkes Booth, an actor and supporter of the Confederacy. Vice President **Andrew Johnson** became president.

Presidential Reconstruction Under Johnson

A Southern Democrat who opposed secession, Johnson had been added to the presidential ticket in 1864 to broaden Lincoln's support. When Johnson became president, Congress was in recess, so Johnson forged ahead with a slight modification of Lincoln's Reconstruction plan without facing any opposition from Congress.

Under Johnson's plan, nearly all Southerners would be pardoned who took an oath of allegiance to the Union, with the exception of high-ranking Confederate officials and powerful plantation owners, who would be forever barred from government. His plan further required reconstructed state governments to denounce secession and ratify the Thirteenth Amendment. In practice, however, Johnson's Reconstruction plan was far weaker than it sounded. He pardoned many powerful ex-Confederates and allowed reconstructed Southern governments to be dominated by pro-slavery forces—by Confederate army officers, plantation owners, and former government officials.

Governed by these Confederate forces, many of the "reconstructed" Southern governments refused to ratify the Thirteenth Amendment and further enforced **black codes** in an attempt to create a subjugated black workforce. Most states outlawed interracial marriage and jury service by blacks, and banned blacks from the right to testify against whites. Most codes also imposed a curfew on blacks and limited their access to public institutions. South Carolina further required licenses for blacks wishing to enter nonagricultural employment. When Radical Republicans attacked the black codes, Johnson defended the codes along with his overall plan for reconstruction.

Andrew Johnson presented a weak plan for Reconstruction, liberally pardoning ex-Confederates and allowing reconstructed governments to be dominated by pro-slavery forces, which passed black codes to keep the freedmen subjugated.

Congressional Reconstruction

Congress reconvened in December 1865 and immediately expressed displeasure with Johnson's Reconstruction plan. Radical Republicans, led by Senator Charles Sumner and Representative Thaddeus Stevens, set out to dismantle Johnson's Reconstruction plan and to dictate Reconstruction on Congress's own terms. They called for black voting rights, confiscation of Confederate estates, and military occupation of the South.

Congress then passed two bills by overriding Johnson's veto: the Civil Rights Act, which granted blacks full citizenship and civil rights, and an act to extend the life of the Freedmen's Bureau. Johnson's attempt to veto these two bills prompted many moderates to ally themselves with the Radicals against his plan.

To give the Civil Rights Act constitutional protection, Congress passed the **Fourteenth Amendment** in 1866, which declared all persons born or naturalized in the United States to be citizens of their states and of the nation, and prohibited states from denying citizens equal protection and due process of the law. Congress thus reversed the *Dred Scott* decision, which had denied blacks citizenship. Not surprisingly, Johnson opposed the amendment and every Southern state except Tennessee rejected it, leaving the radicals without enough support to ratify the amendment.

After overwhelmingly winning the 1866 Congressional election, Radicals gained the power they needed to push for passage of the Fourteenth Amendment and military occupation of the South. With a two-thirds majority in the House and a four-fifths majority in the Senate, Republicans charged ahead with Reconstruction on their own terms. In March 1867, Congress passed the **Reconstruction Act of 1867** over Johnson's veto, which invalidated state governments formed under presidential Reconstruction and imposed martial law on the ex-Confederate states. Only Tennessee, which had ratified the Fourteenth Amendment, escaped invalidation and military subjugation. The other ten states were reorganized into five military districts run by Union generals. The act also expedited passage of the Fourteenth Amendment by requiring that Southern states ratify the Fourteenth Amendment in order to be eligible for readmission into the Union. In June 1868, seven ex-Confederate states voted to ratify the amendment, and the amendment finally passed.

Under the stringent terms of congressional Reconstruction, ratification of the Fourteenth Amendment was made a condition of readmission to the Union.

Impeachment Crisis

In March 1867, the same month Congress passed the Reconstruction Act, Congress passed two bills to limit President Johnson's authority. The Tenure of Office Act prohibited the president from removing civil officers without Senate approval, while the Command of the Army Act prevented the president from issuing military orders except through the commanding general, **Ulysses S. Grant** (who could not be removed without the Senate's approval). In August 1867, with Congress out of session, Johnson suspended Secretary of War Edwin Stanton and replaced him with Grant. Republicans in Congress refused to approve Johnson's change, and called for impeachment on the grounds that Johnson had violated the Tenure of Office Act. In truth, Johnson's violation served as a mere excuse for Congress to launch impeachment proceedings; Congress's real motivation was to remove a president hostile to Congressional Reconstruction.

Johnson's impeachment trial began in March 1868 and lasted nearly three months. In May, Johnson escaped impeachment by one vote. Although impeachment failed, Johnson was left effectively powerless. His acquittal set a precedent against impeachment based on political rivalry, lasting until the Clinton impeachment crisis of the late 1990's.

Congressional Reconstruction Continues

The **Fifteenth Amendment**, proposed in 1869 and passed in 1870, guaranteed the right to vote to any citizen regardless of race, color, or previous condition of servitude. The amendment aimed to promote black suffrage in the South, and to guarantee it in the North and West. (Much of the North had not yet extended suffrage to blacks, even though the South had been required to do so by Congress). The last Southern states awaiting readmission—Texas, Mississippi, and Virginia—were required to ratify the new amendment as a precondition for readmission.

Working to undermine the Fifteenth Amendment was the **Ku Klux Klan** (KKK), founded in 1866 in Tennessee and operating in all Southern states by 1868. The Klan conducted raids to intimidate black voters as part of its campaign to assert white supremacy in the South. Along with these raids, the Klan orchestrated lynchings and floggings of blacks. In May 1870, to counter the Klan's impairment of black suffrage and to bolster the Fifteenth Amendment, Congress passed the **Enforcement Acts of 1870 and 1871**, which protected black voters. Congress also passed the Ku Klux Klan Act in 1871 to authorize the president to use federal troops and emergency measures to overthrow the Klan. Although incidences of vigilantism declined, the Klan maintained a strong presence in many areas.

Reconstructed Governments in the New South

Because of the enfranchisement of blacks, the disfranchisement of ex-Confederates, and the influx of Northern opportunists, the Republican Party dominated Reconstruction governments in the South. All Southern Reconstruction constitutions guaranteed universal male suffrage, and Louisiana and South Carolina even opened public schools to blacks. To fund these schools and other new social programs, state governments raised state taxes and accumulated exorbitant debt.

Opponents of Reconstruction accused these new governments of being unsound and corrupt—and, indeed, many involved in these new governments did take bribes and exchanged favors for votes. Democrats called the Southern moderates who cooperated with Republicans **scalawags**, and labeled the Northern opportunists **carpetbaggers** (an unsavory title meant to suggest that the Northerners came to the South just to gain easy political power and wealth through bribes). Led by Democratic politicians, the Ku Klux Klan attacked and even murdered many of these "scalawags," "carpetbaggers," and other political leaders.

Reconstruction Wanes

During the 1870s, the Radical Republicans lost influence in Congress, as two key leaders, Charles Sumner and Thaddeus Stevens, died, and many others turned moderate. The Radicals' demise, along with reports of corruption in "reconstructed" governments, sapped Northerners' enthusiasm for Reconstruction. At the same time, economic panic and political scandal diverted the nation's attention. Another factor contributing to the end of Reconstruction were the rulings of the Supreme Court. In a series of decisions, the Court reversed many of the trends the Radicals had begun.

The Supreme Court Repudiates Reconstruction

In a series of cases in the 1860s and 1870s, the Supreme Court established a narrow reading of the Fourteenth and Fifteenth Amendments. The Court ruled that the Fourteenth Amendment only protected the rights of national citizenship, not state citizenship, and therefore allowed for a number of restrictions on state voting privileges. In the years following this decision, many Southern states imposed literacy tests, poll taxes, property requirements, and grandfather clauses (which allowed only those men to vote whose grandfathers had voted) in an effort to limit voting among blacks. Since many blacks were poor and uneducated, and their grandfathers had not voted, they could not pass these new voting requirements. The Court also limited the scope of the Fifteenth Amendment, ruling that the amendment did not confer the right of suffrage upon anyone, but merely prohibited the barring of suffrage based on race, color, or previous condition of servitude. Since the Enforcement Acts of 1870 and 1871 served to reinforce the Fifteenth Amendment, the Court declared key parts of the acts invalid.

Corruption and Dissent in the Grant Administration

In 1868, the Union Civil War hero **Ulysses S. Grant** defeated the Democratic candidate for president, Horatio Seymour. Grant's two terms in office were laden with scandal, including the 1869 "Black Friday" scandal, the 1875 "Whiskey Ring," and the 1876 "Belknap scandal." In "Black Friday," Grant's brother-in-law conspired with two powerful industrialists to corner the gold market; in the "Whiskey Ring," Grant's personal secretary was proven to have taken bribes from a group of distillers seeking to evade millions of dollars in taxes; and in the "Belknap scandal," Grant's secretary of war, William E. Belknap, was impeached for accepting bribes to sell Native American trading posts in Oklahoma. The widespread corruption in Grant's administration weakened the Republican Party and diverted the nation's attention from Reconstruction.

Approaching the election of 1872, dissident Republicans split off from the party in protest of Grant's corruption and formed a new political party called the **Liberal Republicans**. Liberal Republicans opposed corruption and favored sectional harmony. The new party joined with the Democrats and nominated Horace Greeley for president. Greeley, though a determined campaigner, lost convincingly to Grant. Despite Grant's victory, the division in the Republican Party was a clear sign of the loss of momentum for Congressional Reconstruction.

The division of the Republican Party during the election of 1872 demonstrated the weakening of support for Reconstruction. The solid core in Congress, which had pushed Reconstruction measures through, disintegrated in the wake of the Grant administration's corruption.

The Panic of 1873

In Grant's second term in office, the nation faced serious economic woes. As a result of over-expansion by railroad builders and businessmen, the nation's economy collapsed, in what is known as the **panic of 1873.** The stock market crashed, the largest bank in the nation failed—as did many smaller banks and firms—and 25 percent of railroads shut down. This economic panic, coupled with Grant's many political scandals, distracted the nation from Reconstruction.

The End of Reconstruction

The 1872 split in the Republican Party hastened the collapse of Republican rule in the South. Moderates in Congress pushed through Amnesty Acts allowing almost all ex-Confederate officials to return to politics and hold office. Using tactics such as promising tax cuts and engaging in outright violence and intimidation, Democrats took control of one state after another. Some Republicans gave up and moved back North, while others defected to the Democratic Party. By 1877, Democrats gained enough votes to win state elections in every one of the former Confederate states.

Democrats called their return to power **Redemption**. Once under Democratic control, every state in the South cut expenses, ended social programs, and revised their tax systems to grant relief to landowners. Many blacks migrated northward to escape the discriminatory policies of the Redeemed South. In 1879, 4,000 blacks from Mississippi and Louisiana alone reached Kansas to settle on land outside the grasp of southern Democrats.

In the 1876 election, Republicans nominated the moderate Rutherford B. Hayes, and Democrats nominated Samuel J. Tilden, for president. Although Tilden won the popular vote, Republicans challenged the election returns from South Carolina, Florida, and Louisiana. Republicans still controlled the political machinery in these states, and threw out enough votes to ensure Hayes's victory. To prevent Democrats from obstructing Hayes's path to the White House, Republicans promised that in return for the Presidency, Hayes would remove federal troops from South Carolina and Louisiana. After he assumed office, Hayes abided by this so-called **Hayes-Tilden Compromise**, and removed federal troops from the last two occupied states in the South. By January 1877, Democrats had won control of all Southern state governments and Redemption was complete. Southern governments, under Democratic rule, reimposed laws severely restricting black suffrage and civil rights. Reconstruction was officially over.

Reconstruction died in January 1877, after the Hayes-Tilden Compromise removed troops from the last two occupied states in the South and allowed Democrats in those states to take control of the legislature.

Society in the South After Reconstruction

While blacks gained freedom in the South, they hardly gained equality. Despite the Radical Republicans' efforts at Reconstruction, many blacks in the South struggled with poverty, illiteracy, and unemployment. As Reconstruction waned, the condition of freedmen only worsened. The Freedmen's Bureau closed, voting restrictions such as poll taxes and literacy tests proliferated, and racist violence spread. Discrimination in the South further intensified with the passage of **Jim Crow laws** in the 1880s. Jim Crow laws segregated many public accommodations such as trains, steamboats, streetcars, and schools, and restricted or forbade black access to other facilities, like theaters and restaurants. The Supreme Court upheld such segregation in its *Plessy v. Ferguson* decision (1896), which declared all "separate but equal" facilities to be constitutional. This decision cleared the way for decades of demoralizing discrimination against blacks.

Destitute and unemployed, many blacks moved to cities in search of work. As a result of this migration, the population of urban blacks in the South increased by seventy-five percent in the late 1800s. Other freedmen tried to establish farms of their own, but, lacking resources and equipment, were forced to rent out land as tenant farmers under the **sharecropping system**. By the end of the 1860s, the sharecropping system had replaced slave-filled plantations as the driving force behind the Southern economy. Under this system, freedmen and poor whites rented out plots of land from plantation owners. In exchange for use of the land, shelter, and farming equipment, these laborers, known as sharecroppers, would give the landowner up to one half of their crop yield. The system basically ensured that the sharecropper could never raise enough money to gain real financial independence.

Industrial Revolution

Trends and Themes of the Era

- Big Business, first in the form of massive corporations and then in even larger trusts, built up monopolies over markets and made astronomical profits. Big Business drove industrialization and helped foster the belief in America as the land of opportunity, where anyone who worked hard could get rich. It also, however, generated a vast imbalance between the rich and the poor.

- The government at first followed a hands-off policy with Big Business. As business abuses increased, state governments and then the Federal government passed a spate of regulatory legislation. True regulation of business would not begin until the early twentieth century, however.

- Industrialism attracted rural Americans and many European immigrants to cities in the United States. As a result, the U.S. shifted from an agrarian to an urban country. Immigration became a key ingredient in the success of industrialism, since immigrants were willing to work as cheap labor.

- Politics were dominated by local political parties, called Machines, rather than individuals. Politics and politicians were often corrupt, complicit with Big Business interests. Beginning with the Pendleton Act in the 1880s, the government began to try to clean itself up.

- Technology, in the form of railroads and other innovations that increased efficiency and communication, helped drive industrialism. Increased industrialism, in turn, created the wealth and impetus that drove the need for better technology. Technology became essential to American economic success.

Big Business in the Industrial Age

Business ruled during the years after the Civil War. Just before the Civil War, Congress passed legislation allowing businesses to form corporations without a charter from the U.S. government. After the Civil War, these corporations came to dominate much of American business, and, in the process, to define American life.

The era of Big Business began when entrepreneurs in search of profits consolidated their businesses into massive corporations, which were so large that they could force out competition and gain control of a market. Control of a market allowed a corporation to set prices for a product at whatever level it wanted, and thereby to amass incredible fortunes. These corporations, and the businessmen who ran them, became exceedingly wealthy and powerful, often at the expense of the many poor workers throughout the U.S. Some of the most powerful corporations were **John D. Rockefeller**'s Standard Oil Company, **Andrew Carnegie**'s Carnegie Steel, Cornelius Vanderbilt's New York Central Railroad System, and **J.P. Morgan**'s banking house, J.P. Morgan & Company. These corporations dominated almost all aspects of their respective industries: by 1879, for example, Rockefeller controlled ninety percent of the country's oil refining capacity. Much of the public saw the leaders of big business as **"robber barons"** who exploited workers in order to amass vast fortunes.

In 1882, Rockefeller further solidified this control by establishing a monopoly or **trust**, which centralized control of a number of oil-related companies under one board of trustees. As a result, Rockefeller owned nearly the entire oil business in the United States, and he could set prices at will. Companies in other industries quickly imitated this trust model and used their broad market control to push prices higher.

Trusts integrated control of many companies, both horizontally by combining similar companies, and vertically by combining companies involved in all stages of production. Trusts were used to gain control of markets and force out competition.

The Government and Big Business

In the early years of the Industrial Revolution, the government maintained a hands-off attitude toward business. The government, and much of the nation, believed in the principles of **laissez-faire** economics, which dictated that the economic market should run freely without government interference. According to the theory, free, unregulated markets led to competition, which in turn led to fair prices of goods for consumers. The government did not want to interfere in the free market.

Industrial Revolution

The plight of the poor during this time was minimized by the tenets of **Social Darwinism**, which became popular in the late 1800s. Social Darwinism adapted Charles Darwin's theory of evolution—"survival of the fittest"—to the business world, arguing that competition was necessary to foster the healthiest economy (just as competition in the natural world was necessary to foster the healthiest, or fittest, species). By this reasoning, government should not protect the poor because the poor were weak and unfit, and therefore imperiled the nation's financial health. The rich, meanwhile, were the strong, hard working citizens who bettered the nation, and, as such, should not be subject to government regulation. Prominent Social Darwinists included Herbert Spencer and Andrew Carnegie, whose essay promoting free market economy, "The Gospel of Wealth," was published in 1889.

The Move Toward Regulation

By the 1880s, however, it was beginning to become clear that markets were *not* free. Corporations had grown so big and powerful that they controlled markets entirely, forcing smaller businesses out of business and setting the prices of goods at extremely high rates. The actions of the robber barons, and in particular the corrupt officials of the railraods, led to public outcry. Consumers grew enraged over the high prices that monopolies had set, while small businesses demanded protection from being squeezed out of the market. Railroad monopolies were overcharging small-time customers, especially farmers, while giving rebates to powerful politicians and favored clients.

State legislatures tried to limit the abuses of the railroads by issuing maximum rate laws, which set a ceiling on the prices a railroad could charge. Congress struck these laws down, claiming they were unconstitutional. But as public anger continued to grow over the practices of corporations, the federal government began to change its tune. In 1887, Congress passed the **Interstate Commerce Act** to try to stop railroads from price discrimination. Also, beginning in 1888, legislative committees in Congress began to investigate and expose the business practices of the robber barons.

Two years later, Congress passed the **Sherman Antitrust Act**, which outlawed trusts and any other contracts that restrained free trade. Though this act eventually became extremely important in regulating business, in its early years it was rarely enforced. In fact, the act was so loosely phrased that it sometimes had the opposite of its intended effect: instead of regulating business monopolies, it regulated the labor unions that challenged these monopolies. In the 1890s, courts invoked the Sherman Antitrust Act to restrain laborers' right to strike, ruling that strikes violated the act's prohibition against "a conspiracy in restraint of trade." Big business thus benefited from the judiciary's (in particular the Supreme Court's) pro-business stance and its unwillingness to restrict commercial behavior. It was not until the early 1900s that government began to enforce the Sherman Antitrust regulatory policies in full.

Industrial Revolution

Industrial Revolution

The Growth of Unions

Although labor unions began forming in the early 1800s, they did not gain any significant membership base or bargaining power until the 1860s and 1870s. The harsh, even hazardous, working conditions arising from industrialization drove laborers to organize into unions. One of the first major unions was the **Knights of Labor**, founded in 1869. The Knights demanded equal pay for women, an end to child labor, and a progressive income tax, among other reforms. The union claimed a substantial membership, including women, blacks, and immigrants. In 1885, the group staged a successful strike against railroad "robber baron" Jay Gould. The strike so severely crippled Gould's operation that he had no choice but to fold. On the strength of this victory, the Knights' membership and political power grew. The Knights successfully supported a number of politicians for election and forced laws favorable to workers through Congress.

The Knights' power waned, however, after the leadership lost control of the local chapters and a series of unauthorized strikes grew violent. The bloody **Haymarket riot** in Chicago in 1886 sounded the union's death knell. The riot, intended to protest police cruelty against strikers, got out of hand when one member of the Knights of Labor threw a bomb, killing a police officer. In the resultant chaos, nine people were killed and close to sixty injured. Prominent leaders of the Knights of Labor were convicted of inciting the riot, and public support for the union plummeted.

To salvage the labor movement, craft laborers who had been members of the Knights of Labor broke off and formed the **American Federation of Labor** (AFL). Whereas the Knights of Labor had boasted an open membership policy and sweeping labor goals, the AFL catered exclusively to skilled laborers and focused on smaller, more practical issues: increasing wages, reducing hours, and imposing safety measures. **Samuel Gompers**, the AFL's leader from 1886 to 1924, proved a master tactician who united many labor groups in a federation of trade unions.

More radical labor organizations also emerged, most notably the **Industrial Workers of the World**, nicknamed the Wobblies, founded in 1905. More famous for their militant anticapitalism than for being large or influential, the Wobblies never grew to more than 30,000 members before fading away in about 1920.

Between 1880 and 1905, union activity in the the United States led to well over 35,000 strikes. As evidenced by the Haymarket riot, these demonstrations at times erupted in violence. This violence alienated much of the American public and the popular support for unions plunged, and employers were free to exact severe retribution on striking workers. As a result, strikes proved largely ineffective at advancing the labor cause.

Major strikes and outbreaks of labor-related violence during the later nineteenth century tended to impair the labor cause instead of advance it. Public sympathy for unions plummeted, companies imposed anti-union hiring policies, and the Supreme Court authorized the use of injunctions against strikers.

In addition to the Haymarket riot, some of the more notable strikes include:

- The **railroad strike** followed the onset of a national economic recession in 1877. Railroad workers for nearly every rail line struck, provoking widespread violence and requiring federal troops to subdue the angry mobs. The strike prompted many employers to get tough on labor by imposing an antiunion policy: they required workers to sign contracts barring them from striking or joining a union. Some employers even hired private detectives to root out labor agitators and private armies to suppress strikes.

- Workers staged the 1892 **Homestead strike** against Carnegie Steel Company to protest a pay cut and seventy-hour workweek. Ten workers were killed in the riot. Federal troops were called in to suppress the violence, and non-union workers were hired to break the strike.

- In the 1894 **Pullman strike**, **Eugene Debs** led thousands of workers in a strike against the Pullman Palace Car Company after wages were slashed. The courts ruled that the strikers violated the Sherman Antitrust Act and issued an injunction against them. When the strikers refused to obey the injunction, Debs was arrested and federal troops marched in to crush the strike. In the ensuing frenzy, thirteen died and fifty-three were injured. The Supreme Court later upheld the use of injunctions against labor unions, giving businesses a powerful new weapon to suppress strikes. Organized labor began to fade in strength, and did not resurge until the 1930s.

Industrialization, Urbanization, and Immigration

Business and industrialization centered on the cities. The ever increasing number of factories created an intense need for labor, convincing people in rural areas to move to the city, and convincing immigrants from Europe to come to the United States. As a result, the United States transformed from an agrarian to an urban nation, and the demographics of the country shifted dramatically.

Industrial Revolution

Industrial Revolution

Immigration

Roughly 10 million European immigrants settled in the U.S. between 1860 and 1890. Nearly all of these immigrants were from northern and western Europe, which was the traditional point of origin for European immigrants to the United States. During the 1890s, though, new immigrants began to come to the United States: Greeks, Slavs, Armenians, and Jews from various countries. Most of these "new" European immigrants settled in the Northeast, dominated by Irish and Italians, and the Midwest, dominated by Germans. While the West also experienced an influx of European immigrants, it mostly attracted immigrants from China. Lured by the prospect of earning money by working on the expanding western railroad system, many Chinese immigrants settled in California.

Many immigrants found the transition to American life difficult, in spite of their efforts to ease the transition by founding churches and charity organizations. Often poor, immigrants lived in dirty, crowded conditions and worked unskilled jobs in potentially dangerous factories. More than 500,000 injuries to workers were reported each year in the 1880s and 1890s. Immigrants, especially "new" immigrants, also faced extreme discrimination in the workplace from native workers who resented the immigrants' willingness to accept lower wages and work in worse conditions. In the presidential election of 1880, both major party platforms included anti-immigration measures, and in 1882 Congress passed the **Chinese Exclusion Act**, placing a ten-year ban on Chinese immigration.

The Development of Urban Life

The growth of U.S. cities gave rise to a number of features of urban life not before seen in American history. One such feature was the spread of **tenements**, which were narrow four- or five-story buildings with few windows, limited plumbing and electricity, and tiny rooms often packed with people, mostly blacks and immigrants. Tenements were the main housing available in slums and ghettos, the segregated communities into which blacks and immigrants were forced by poverty, prejudice, even law. These ghettos fostered disease, high infant mortality, and horrific levels of pollution, and were often the site of interracial and ethnic strife.

While tenements housed the poor, plush areas arose to house the rich. During the 1870s and 1880s, the cities' rich inhabitants moved outside the city center to escape the overcrowded conditions. Developments sprung up around many of the major cities, their cleanliness and preservation of green spaces a sharp contrast to the cities they abutted. Electric streetcars, commuter trains, and trolleys ferried these inhabitants to and from their city jobs.

Machine Politics

Local politics during this era were marked by **machine politics**, so called because the system and the party, rather than individuals, held power. In virtually every region of the U.S., local officials, or "machines," controlled voter loyalty by distributing political and economic benefits such as offices, jobs, and city contracts. "Machines" were presided over by "party bosses," professional politicians who dominated city government. These bosses often controlled the jobs of thousands of city workers and influenced the activities of schools, hospitals, and other city-run services. Machine politics often thrived on corruption, which contributed to the system's collapse around the turn of the twentieth century.

U.S. Presidents

The presidents of this period were generally weak, pro-business, and never served more than one term in office (with the exception of Grover Cleveland, who served two nonconsecutive terms). None of these presidents are terribly important in terms of the test, though it is helpful to have a general sense of the politics of the nation during the period. We have included a quick overview of each administration so you can keep track of all the political turnover.

- James Garfield, elected in 1880, was fatally shot four months after taking office.

- Chester Arthur, Garfield's vice president, served as president from 1881 to 1885. Congress, spurred on by Arthur's reputation as a corrupt politician and a supporter of machine politics, passed the **Pendleton Act** in efforts to create a meritocratic and professional civil service.

- Grover Cleveland served as president from 1885 to 1889. He pushed for a reduction of tariffs, and, in 1887, he signed the Interstate Commerce Act into law.

- Benjamin Harrison was president from 1889 to 1893. A pro-business Republican, he supported high protective tariffs, and brought about a severe economic depression beginning in 1893.

- Grover Cleveland won a second term from 1893 to 1897. He is the only President to serve two terms out of sequence. His second term was dominated by efforts to deal with the economic depression that started in 1893, under Benjamin Harrison.

The Struggles of Farmers

Farmers found themselves on the bottom rungs of the economic ladder after the Civil War. They struggled to pay off mounting debts as land prices rose but crop prices plummeted. Struggling farmers demanded help from state and federal governments. When this relief did not come, Midwestern farmers banded together to form the **Grange** in 1867. By 1875, the Grange had more than 800,000 members. The Grange offered farmers education and fellowship through biweekly social functions, at which farmers shared their grievances and discussed agricultural and political reforms. To increase farm profits, Grangers negotiated deals with machinery companies and set up cooperatives and grain storage facilities. They also fought against railroad companies for hiking prices for short-distance shipment. The efforts of the Grange played a big role in the passage of the 1887 Interstate Commerce Act.

By 1880, the Grange had faded and was replaced by the **Farmers' Alliance**. Beginning as a local phenomenon in Texas in the late 1870s, alliances spread throughout the South and Northwest, and by 1890, boasted a membership of 1.5 million nationwide. The alliances proved to be powerful political forces. Alliance-supported candidates did well throughout the Great Plains and South in the elections of 1890. In 1892 Alliance members were central actors in the founding of the People's Party of the United States, or **Populist Party**, discussed below.

Political Activism: Farmers and Labor Unite

The Populist Party, founded by members of the Farmer's Alliance, also drew support from urban laborers. The Populist Party supported policies that would create inflation, making debts easier to pay off and raising crop prices. The party's candidate in the 1892 election did not do well.

However, the **panic of 1893** gave the Populists new life. In the three years after 1893, unemployment soared, worker strikes spread, and support for the Populist Party grew. Already opposed to President Cleveland, the Populists were further enraged by Cleveland's deals with J.P. Morgan and other powerful industrialists to bail out the U.S. government: the bankers lent $62 million to the government in return for U.S. bonds. The Populists portrayed Cleveland as a pro-business Republican who neglected the poor, and they began rallying for the next election.

In the 1896 election, the Populists joined with the Democratic Party in supporting **William Jennings Bryan**. Republicans backed **William McKinley**, who ran on a pro-business platform and supported high protective tariffs. Six years earlier, as a Representative in Congress, McKinley had engineered the passage of the **McKinley Tariff** (1890), a protective tariff that raised the price of imports by nearly fifty percent. By doing so, he gained the support of business interests. Boosted by this business backing and the enormous contributions from the industrialists J.P. Morgan and John D. Rockefeller, McKinley won the election against Bryan.

During McKinley's two terms as president, the depression eased and prosperity began to return. This prosperity, combined with Bryan's defeat, killed the Populist Party and sent the Democratic Party back to its minority position in the South.

The Social Response to Industrialization

Industrialization had far-reaching effects on American society. Social reform movements sprung up around the country to address the needs of the new industrial society, and American authors used literature to comment on the changes they saw occurring.

The Socioeconomic Divide

While poor urbanites lived in crowded tenements and worked at grueling and often unsafe jobs, a few men amassed wealth beyond these city-dwellers' imaginations. Social theories were developed to justify the growing gap between rich and poor:

- **Social Darwinism**, discussed above. Yale professor William Graham Sumner's 1883 book, *What Social Classes Owe to Each Other*, argued that social programs to help the poor worked against nature and sapped the hardworking individual of his due reward. In an 1889 essay, "The Gospel of Wealth," **Andrew Carnegie** applied Charles Darwin's theories to human society, stating that free-market economics and governmental noninterference provided a forum where survival of the fittest could play out.

- The **Gospel of Success** centered on the claim that any man could achieve wealth through hard work. **Horatio Alger** wrote fictional tales of hard-working young men going from "rags to riches" based solely on their ambition and determination.

Andrew Carnegie and Horatio Alger, among others, tried to justify the gap between rich and poor by arguing that hard work could make any man wealthy and that programs to help the poor went against the natural process of evolution as played out in human society.

These justifications for the growing gap between rich and poor did not go unchallenged. Henry George's book *Progress and Poverty* (1879) urged that the government use tax income to fund social programs for the poor, while Lester Frank Ward's

Dynamic Sociology (1883) also argued that government power be harnessed for social aid. In 1890, Jacob Riis exposed the conditions of immigrants in New York City tenements in *How the Other Half Lives*, and in 1899, Thorsten Veblen's *Theory of the Leisure Class* attacked the "conspicuous consumption" of the affluent.

Many other works directly criticized the capitalist system. In an 1888 book entitled *Looking Backward From 2000 to 1887*, Edward Bellamy conceived of a socialist utopia in which the government controlled all means of production and distribution. Bellamy's moderate socialism accompanied a rise in American interest in Marxism, which condemned the capitalists' exploitation of the working class and foretold revolution. Marxism, however, never gained a significant following in the U.S., perhaps because other means, short of revolution, eventually emerged to address poverty and exploitation.

Addressing Poverty

In the late nineteenth century, most middle-class reformers believed that poverty arose from lax morals and the lack of self-discipline. They therefore focused their relief efforts on improving morality rather than addressing the cripplingly low wages and unhealthy working and living conditions of the poor. Among their aims, reformers sought to "Americanize" poor immigrants and rid them of customs deemed offensive or impractical. Their programs mostly targeted children, whom they believed to be the most malleable. Organizations like the **Young Men's Christian Association**, and later the Young Women's Christian Association (YMCA, YWCA), provided housing and recreational activities for urban children. Imported from England in 1880, the **Salvation Army** provided food, shelter, and employment to the urban poor while preaching temperance and morality. The New York Charity Organization Society operated similarly, promoting morality and self-sufficiency.

In the 1880s, a new generation of social workers, led by **Jane Addams**, argued that providing education and opportunity was more important than preaching morality. In 1889, Addams and a friend established **Hull House** in Chicago, where they lived and worked among the poor immigrants they aimed to help. Addams set up a kindergarten, a day nursery, and an employment bureau for the poor.

Women in the Industrial Revolution

Middle-class women in the industrial age became involved in a wider sphere beyond the home. Women joined the labor force in record numbers and also became active in social reform movements. Women were especially prominent in the temperance movement, primarily through the **Woman's Christian Temperance Union** (WTCU). Other issues included prison reform, labor arbitration, and public health concerns. As social activism among women increased, so did their desire for the right to vote.

Industrial Revolution

Despite this fervor, women only slowly gained social and political power. Their most significant gains came in the area of education, as a number of higher learning institutions went coed or created separate schools for women. By 1900, more than 70 percent of colleges admitted women. Feminine empowerment was also seen in feminist literature such as ***The Awakening***, by Kate Chopin, published in 1899.

Works of Fiction

Social commentary of a subtler sort emerged in the works of fiction produced by American authors during the period of industrialization. Realism replaced romanticism as the genre of choice for American authors. Henry James, an expatriate who left America for Europe in 1875, wrote about the psychological experience of being an American in Europe in books like *Daisy Miller* (1879) and *The Portrait of a Lady* (1881). Other authors hit much closer to home, commenting on the era of industrialization around them. No author was better known for this than **Mark Twain**, whose 1873 satirical novel, *The Gilded Age* (cowritten with Charles Dudley Warner), described the Industrial Revolution as a period that looked like gold on the outside but on the inside was hollow. Twain, like other authors, described an America full of urban poverty, political crookedness, and class tensions. These elements, especially class and racial tensions, are present in his most famous works, *The Adventures of Tom Sawyer* (1876) and *The Adventures of Huckleberry Finn* (1884), in which he uses the perspective of two young boys to expose ignorance and hatred in American society.

Industrial Revolution

The Age of Imperialism

Trends and Themes of the Era

- American industrialization created a need for foreign markets in which to sell manufactured goods and from which to buy raw materials.

- Early efforts to find foreign markets involved economic expansionism, which focused on opening markets through investment rather than military involvement. Under President McKinley, near the end of the nineteenth century, the United States wanted to increase its exposure to foreign markets and shifted to a more military and imperialist policy.

- Victory in the Spanish-American War gave the U.S. an empire, and also marked the ascendance of the U.S. as a world power.

Expansionism

In the 1860s and early 1870s, the U.S. focused primarily on domestic issues: Reconstruction, settlement of the American West, and industrialization. Apart from acquiring Alaska from Russia in 1867, the U.S. achieved little in the area of foreign expansion. But as the American factory system developed and industrial output soared, the nation began to look abroad with new interest, because, as a rising industrial power, the U.S. needed to find foreign markets in which to sell its manufactured products and from which to acquire raw goods. Initially, the policy that the U.S. pursued to meet its growing economic needs was one of expansionism rather than imperialism. Instead of imposing a military presence and colonial government—as many European countries were doing in Africa and throughout the globe—the U.S. aimed to advance its interests through investments and business transactions. American businesses began opening up production sites and markets in Latin America and elsewhere.

McKinley and Imperialism

William McKinley, elected president in 1896, advanced a much more aggressive foreign policy. McKinley was extremely pro-business, and instead of simply developing commercial markets abroad, McKinley supported military intervention and U.S. acquisition of foreign lands.

The Spanish-American War

Nationalist rebels in Cuba had been resisting Spanish rule since 1895. Americans became increasingly sympathetic to the rebels' cause primarily because of sensationalist news reports about Spanish brutality. Embroiled in a vicious circulation war, New York newspapers—especially the *New York Journal*, owend by **William Randolph Hearst**, and the *New York World*, owned by **Joseph Pulitzer**—exaggerated and even invented accounts of atrocities committed by the Spanish military against the rebels. These inflammatory journalistic practices, called **yellow journalism**, convinced much of the American public to side with the rebels, and to call for government action against Spain. In April 1898, McKinley and the country in general got the opening they desired. A U.S. ship, the *Maine*, exploded in Havana. The cause of the explosion was unknown, but the Spaniards were blamed. McKinley sent a war message to Congress and was authorized to use force in the interest of Cuban independence.

The **Spanish-American War** lasted only two months. Before the war, Spain, a long-established imperial power, had been feared as a formidable enemy. But Spanish strength had been overestimated, and the U.S. easily crushed the Spanish forces. One of the most famous battles was the U.S. capture of San Juan Hill in Cuba, an attack led by **Theodore Roosevelt**, who headed the volunteer Rough Riders unit. America's easy victory in the war established the U.S. as a significant presence on the world stage, and signified Spain's demise as a military powerhouse.

With the **Treaty of Paris**, which ended the war in December 1898, Cuba achieved independence and Spain ceded the Philippines, Guam, and Puerto Rico to the U.S. for a payment of $20 million. America's decisive war victory, coupled with the nation's economic prosperity, led to an overwhelming reelection win for McKinley in 1900. The victory also encouraged the government to further demonstrate American strength abroad.

The Spanish-American War lasted only two months and ended in a decisive victory for the United States, encouraging the government to further demonstrate its strength abroad.

The Legacy of Victory: Increasing Imperialism

Victory in the Spanish-American War left the U.S. with new decisions to make. By the end of 1898, the U.S. had acquired a number of new island territories: Guam, Puerto Rico, and the Philippines, ceded to the U.S. in the Treaty of Paris; Cuba, which the U.S. Army had governed for four years; and Hawaii, which the U.S. annexed in 1898 independent of the Spanish-American War. In establishing U.S. governing policies abroad, Congress faced two pressing questions: first, how to grant Cuban independence in a way that would also protect American interests on the island; and second, whether to annex the Philippines or grant the small country independence.

Cuba

In 1901, the **Platt Amendment** enumerated the conditions for the U.S. Army's withdrawal from Cuban soil. The amendment required Cuba to vow to make no treaty with a foreign power, to limit its independence, and reserved for the U.S.:

- The right to intervene in Cuba when it saw fit.

- The right to maintain a naval base in Cuba, at Guantánamo Bay.

Though the Cubans did not like these severe restrictions on Cuban sovereignty, they did accept the amendment. The U.S. held wide powers over Cuba for more than thirty years, and maintains its military base to this day.

The Age of Imperialism

The Philippines

In the Senate, proponents of expansionism won the debate about the Philippines. Influenced by business interests who saw the Philippines as a valuable gateway to China, the Senate voted to annex the country rather than give it independence. Filipino rebels resisted U.S. rule by attacking the U.S. base of operations and setting off two years of fighting that finally ended with a U.S. victory. The Philippines remained a part of the United States until 1946, when the U.S. granted it independence.

The U.S. in China

The U.S. government aimed to promote U.S. business and open trade markets in China. China's Manchu Dynasty was weak and particularly vulnerable to foreign intervention, as evidenced by the **spheres of influence** that other nations—Russia, Germany, France, England, and Japan—had succeeded in carving out. These nations had each secured exclusive trading rights to certain key ports in China, so that entire regions, or spheres, were blocked to U.S. business. In 1899, as a way to open up all "exclusive" ports to American business, Secretary of State John Hay proclaimed an **Open Door policy** in China, which meant that no favoritism would be awarded at Chinese ports. European countries, however, refused to endorse this policy. In the following years, Hay continued working to secure advantages for U.S. firms as part of his policy of economic expansionism, which sought not to control new territory but rather to open new markets.

The Open Door policy was invoked to combat European spheres of influence in China and aid U.S. businesses in Chinese markets.

The extreme influence that European nations and the United States exerted in China angered many Chinese. This anger exploded in 1899 in the form of the **Boxer Rebellion.** In this revolt, an antiforeign secret society calling itself the Harmonious Righteous Fists, known as the Boxers to westerners, killed thousands of foreigners and Chinese Christians and captured Beijing (Peking) in 1900. The U.S. sent 2,500 troops as part of an international force that marched on Beijing and drove out the Boxers. By helping dispel the Boxer threat, the U.S. secured some bargaining power in the settlement that followed. Hay demanded that an Open Door policy be implemented in all of China, and other powers agreed. The Boxer Rebellion further weakened the Chinese government. Following the end of the uprising, the U.S. government committed itself to propping up China's government in the interest of maintaining open markets for the U.S. in the Far East.

Anti-imperialism

Not all Americans supported American imperialism. In November 1898, after the fighting had ended in the Spanish-American War but before any treaty had been signed, an organization known as the **Anti-Imperialist League** arose in the U.S. The league opposed American expansion and foreign involvement on the grounds that the U.S. had no right to force its will upon others and also because such involvement would likely incite further conflict. The group had many illustrious members, including the writer Mark Twain and the philosopher William James. In 1899 the anti-imperialists had nearly succeeded in preventing the Senate from ratifying the expansionist Treaty of Paris. This time, howeverm the forces of imperialism won out, and the Anti-Imperialist League lost whatever strength it might have had.

Assassination of McKinley

In September 1901, President McKinley was shot by an anarchist named Leon Czolgosz. Vice President **Theodore Roosevelt** became president, and continued to implement an aggressive foreign policy. His presidency marked the beginning of the Progressive Era.

The Age of Imperialism

The Progressive Era

Trends and Themes of the Era

- Backlash against the excesses and corruption of the big business Industrial Revolution led to a fervor for reform. Reform stretched across economic, environmental, social, and racial lines.

- In foreign affairs through the first half of the Progressive Era, the U.S. continued to assert its power internationally through military and economic means, particularly in the Western Hemisphere. Woodrow Wilson shifted this aggressive interventionist policy to a more idealistic one, but the outbreak of World War I interrupted his plans.

Agitation for Reform

Theodore Roosevelt's assumption of the presidency in 1901 coincided with the beginning of what became known as the Progressive Era, which lasted roughly until 1917. These years were marked by progressivism, a fervent reform impulse in America promoting social justice and democracy. This movement arose partly in response to the ill effects of industrialization: urban poverty and ruthless business policy, including the exploitation of workers and the overuse of resources. Progressives agitated for far-reaching reform in politics, business, poverty relief, and conservation. Progressives represented a diverse base: farmers, laborers, small-business owners, and many of America's elite, including esteemed authors, philosophers, and statesmen. On a crusade to rout out corruption in all areas of life, Progressives saw themselves as enhancing the welfare of the entire nation.

Novelists and Muckrakers

Novelists and journalists helped spread the progressive spirit through the nation by exposing the political corruption and corporate immorality that had been the norm during the Industrial Revolution. Known as **"muckrakers,"** a term coined by Roosevelt to describe their journalistic tactics of "raking the filth" in search of wrongs, these authors and journalists wrote searing accounts of corporate and political evils. Their writings moved the public to demand reform. Among the most notable muckraking exposés:

- Ida Tarbell's *History of Standard Oil* (1904) exposed the ruthless and exploitative practices of Rockefeller's oil company.

- **Upton Sinclair**'s *The Jungle* (1906) exposed the inhumane working environment and unsanitary conditions in meatpacking plants.

- Lincoln Steffens's *The Shame of the Cities* (1904) explored political corruption in local governments.

Through their writings, muckrakers such as Upton Sinclair exposed the dark side of industrialization during the early 1900s, leading to public calls for reform.

Local Government Reform

Political reform on the local level actually began to spread through American cities in the late 1890s, when municipal and state governments passed a slew of progressive laws. These laws included labor laws that established the eight-hour workday and workers' compensation and restricted child labor. Local governments also attacked private monopolies in gas, water, and electricity by regulating rates and weakening the companies' political power. Some states, including Wisconsin and California, reformed the statewide election system by developing the direct primary, in which party members rather than the party leadership selected candidates for office.

Social Control: Morality, Immigration, and Eugenics

Many Progressives saw it as their duty to "clean up" American society and morality. Early attempts at moral reform included censorship of movies and attempts to end prostitution. Moral reform peaked with the prohibition movement, which sought the legal abolition of alcohol. This movement, led by the Anti-Saloon League, gained momentum through the Progressive Era and in 1919 finally succeeded in pushing the Eighteenth Amendment through Congress. This amendment outlawed the manufacture, transport, and sale of alcoholic beverages (and will be covered in the next chapter).

The social reform movement included another, more menacing side. Many reformers, seeing social problems as most prevalent in poor immigrant communities, sought to end immigration. Knowing that immigrants were seldom literate, Congress passed bills requiring literacy tests as a condition for entry to the U.S. in 1896, 1913, 1915, and 1917. The first three were defeated by presidential vetoes, but Congress passed the 1917 bill over the president's veto.

By far the darkest side of progressive reform was the **eugenics** movement, centered on the premise that genetic manipulation could reform American society. Many eugenicists hoped to turn the U.S. into an exclusively white and Protestant nation. In 1904, the Carnegie Foundation established a eugenics research center that was dominated by racist, anti-Semitic, and anti-immigrant ideology. Such ideology led to calls from some circles for ethnic segregation and the sterilization of "less fit" ethnic groups.

Though many social reformers interested in social control focused on the traditional targets of morality and temperance, some reformers advocated more extreme measures such as immigration restriction and the use of eugenics to eliminate what they saw as undesirable racial elements.

Black Rights

During the Progressive Era, those fighting for the rights of black Americans were torn between two charismatic and intelligent leaders. **Booker T. Washington** advocated patience, arguing that blacks must first acquire vocational skills and prove their economic worth before hoping to be treated equally. In 1881, Washington had founded what would become Tuskegee University in his efforts to implement this plan. Many northern blacks, however, rejected Washington's philosophy in favor of the more radical ideas presented by **W.E.B. Du Bois**, who demanded immediate equal treatment for blacks and their equal access to *all* intellectual opportunities, not just vocational training.

The two main black leaders of the Progressive Era were Booker T. Washington and W.E.B. Du Bois. The former advocated patience and the development of vocational skills. The latter demanded immediate change in the condition of American blacks.

In 1909, a group of blacks led by W.E.B. Du Bois joined with a group of white reformers to form the **National Association for the Advancement of Colored People** (NAACP), which called for an end to racial discrimination. The NAACP, along with groups like the National Urban League, attacked **Jim Crow laws** in the South and the 1896 Supreme Court decision in ***Plessy v. Ferguson***. These organized efforts led to few actual political or social gains, but they did begin laying the foundation for the future.

Feminism

Female suffrage, the granting of the right to vote to women, was the primary feminist cause of the Progressive Era. In its early stages, this movement was led by **Susan B. Anthony**, who retired as president of the National American Woman Suffrage Association (NAWSA) in 1900. During the early 1900s, the NAWSA served as the point of central control for nationwide grassroots groups that lobbied legislators, held small rallies, and distributed literature. Other suffragists were more aggressive, staging demonstrations and picketing the White House. Nevertheless, women would have to wait until after World War I for the Nineteenth Amendment, which granted them suffrage in 1920.

Women were active beyond the suffrage movement, supporting campaigns for building playgrounds and nurseries, improving conditions for women workers, equalizing women's wages with those of men, and banning child labor. Feminists also actively pushed for women's education and birth control.

Theodore Roosevelt's Square Deal

Theodore Roosevelt became president in September 1901 after the assassination of William McKinley. Although he had been vice president under McKinley, Roosevelt did not share McKinley's conservative, pro-business policies. Instead, as president, Roosevelt advanced aggressive political reforms, including the heavy regulation of business. Known as the "trust-buster," Roosevelt was the first president to successfully invoke the **Sherman Antitrust Act** against monopolies and continued to restrict businesses throughout his presidency. His reforms reached far beyond business, as well. He greatly influenced economic, environmental, and international affairs. His platform became known as the **"Square Deal"** because he vowed not to favor any group of Americans but to be fair to all.

Relations with Labor and Corporations

Roosevelt was committed to addressing the problems of labor and corporate activity. Unlike his predecessors, Roosevelt defended the right of labor to organize, and eschewed the use of federal troops to put down strikes. In 1902, he intervened in a United Mine Workers Strike and helped labor get management to agree to binding arbitration. The arbitrators awarded the miners a wage increase and a shortened workday.

Roosevelt also worked to restrict the power of big business by breaking up a monopoly. In his administration's first trust-busting case, his attorney general filed suit against the Northern Securities Company, a railroad holding company, for violating the Sherman Antitrust Act, which had not been successfully used against monopolies since its passage in 1890. After this case, though, the Act became an extremely important tool for government regulation of corporations. In 1904, the Supreme Court ordered that the Northern Securities Company be dissolved, a decision that launched a series of antitrust suits. In all, the Roosevelt administration filed forty-three trust-busting suits.

After winning reelection in 1904, Roosevelt traded sporadic bursts of trust-busting for more permanent regulation. He successfully negotiated the passage of the Hepburn Act in 1906, which empowered the **Interstate Commerce Commission** (ICC), previously a weak agency, to set maximum railroad rates and inspect railroad companies' financial records.

> *Roosevelt, unlike his Republican predecessors in office, was not pro-business. He aggressively enforced the Sherman Antitrust Act and empowered the Interstate Commerce Commission, both key elements in his "Square Deal."*

Protecting Consumers and Conserving the Environment

Responding to the muckrakers' exposés on the unsanitary conditions in food plants and the dangerous ingredients in foods and medicines, Roosevelt endorsed the **Pure Food and Drug Act** and the **Meat Inspection Act**, both passed in 1906. The first act prohibited the sale of adulterated or inaccurately labeled foods and medicines, and the second established federal regulations for meatpackers and a system of inspection.

The early twentieth century also saw a rise in concern for the wilderness. Those who supported conservation and protection of wilderness sites were called preservationists. Preservationists were often in conflict with business interests who saw the wilderness in terms of resources and space for commercial and residential development. Roosevelt was at heart a preservationist, but understood the need for compromise. He achieved this compromise through his conservation program, which provided for the regulated use of the nation's wilderness. Roosevelt designated 200 million acres as national forests, mineral reserves, and potential waterpower sites, and added five national parks and eighteen national monuments to the list of protected lands. In 1908 Roosevelt created the **National Conservation Commission** to inventory the nation's resources and manage their use more efficiently.

Conservationism was a hallmark of Roosevelt's presidency. He protected land through the creation of national parks and monuments, and advocated the responsible use of the nation's resources by establishing the National Conservation Commission.

Aggressive Foreign Policy: "Big Stick" Diplomacy

Roosevelt summed up his approach to foreign policy in a single sentence: "Speak softly and carry a **big stick**." Having become president shortly after the American victory in the Spanish-American War, Roosevelt was confident in America's status as a major power. He thus adopted an aggressive diplomatic approach.

Roosevelt's most notable achievement in foreign policy was the building of the **Panama Canal**, an artificial waterway stretching through the isthmus of Panama, which was then part of Colombia. Since the canal connected the Atlantic and Pacific oceans and vastly shortened shipping routes, Roosevelt saw its creation as vitally important to American economic and maritime interests. When the Colombian government first rejected America's offer to lease the land and build the canal for over $10 million, Roosevelt helped engineer a revolution in the isthmus. The revolution erupted in 1903, and the new Panamanian government that took power proved to be much more cooperative with the U.S. The new government granted the U.S. permanent possession of the ten-mile-wide strip of land across Panama on the same financial terms rejected earlier by Colombia. Construction on the canal began in 1906, and it opened in 1914.

Roosevelt's intervention in Panama was indicative of his entire attitude toward Latin America, where he asserted the **Roosevelt Corollary to the Monroe Doctrine**. In 1904, with several European nations poised to invade the Dominican Republic, Roosevelt declared that the United States and not Europe should dominate Latin America, and that although the U.S. had no expansionist intentions, any "chronic wrongdoing" by a Latin American nation would justify U.S. intervention as a global policeman. (Remember that the Monroe Doctrine had warned Europeans not to intervene in Latin America; the Roosevelt Corollary maintained this warning, and asserted that the U.S. alone could intervene.) During Roosevelt's presidency, the U.S. invoked the Roosevelt Corollary repeatedly as justification for its involvement in the affairs of the Dominican Republic, Haiti, Venezuela, Nicaragua, and Cuba.

The Roosevelt Corollary to the Monroe Doctrine asserted the right of the U.S. government to intervene in the affairs of Latin American countries while maintaining the warning that European powers should stay out of Latin America.

Roosevelt also involved himself in the affairs of Asia after the **Russo-Japanese War** broke out in 1904. Concerned about maintaining the balance of power between nations, Roosevelt invited delegates from Russia and Japan to the U.S. for a peace conference in 1905 that resulted in the signing of a treaty. Roosevelt received the Nobel Peace Prize for his actions. Partially in an effort to discourage further trouble in Asia, Roosevelt sent sixteen gleaming new white battleships—the Great White Fleet—to Asian ports and elsewhere around the world.

Taft in the White House

In the election of 1908, Roosevelt's hand picked successor, **William Howard Taft**, won by a large margin on a conservative platform. Taft, however, could not match Roosevelt's popularity or legislative success. Although he continued Roosevelt's progressive reform programs, his pace was more gradual, and he even lent his support to some conservative pro-business policies. His policies divided the Republican Party into progressive and conservative factions.

Reform Under Taft

Taft supported corporate regulation, and even strengthened the Interstate Commerce Commission's powers and extended its authority to the telephone and telegraph industries. He surpassed the Roosevelt administration in trust-busting. He prosecuted ninety cases to Roosevelt's forty-three. These cases, however, did not achieve the same level of publicity or impact as those under Roosevelt, and so Taft was generally considered a less avid trust-buster.

Additional reform under Taft centered on two amendments to the Constitution, both ratified after he exited office. In 1913, the **Sixteenth Amendment** granted Congress the authority to tax income. After the amendment passed, Congress quickly established a graduated income tax with a maximum tax rate of seven percent. The **Seventeenth Amendment**, also ratified in 1913, provided for direct election of U.S. senators by the people rather than their selection by state legislatures. This amendment was one part of a general movement for government reform, under which the public took an increasingly powerful and direct role in electing officials.

"Dollar Diplomacy"

In foreign affairs, Taft moved away from Roosevelt's "big stick" policies toward what became known as "**dollar diplomacy**." Aiming to avoid military intervention, Taft argued that the influx of American investment abroad, as well as the advancement of American economic interests, would promote stability. Dollar diplomacy failed in China, where European and Japanese economic interests squeezed American businesses out, and it proved only marginally more successful elsewhere. In 1912, Taft resorted to "big stick" policies in Nicaragua when he sent in marines to suppress a revolt.

Republicans Divided

Taft alienated the progressive members of his party by supporting the Payne-Alrdich Act, raising protective tariff rates—a move supported by conservative pro-business interests. He further outraged progressives by supporting the ultra-conservative speaker of the house, Joseph Cannon, and the ultra-conservative secretary of the interior, Richard A. Ballinger, who reversed Roosevelt's conservation efforts by, among other things, selling off several million acres of public land in Alaska to bankers interested in mining the land for coal. Angered by Taft's lack of enthusiasm for reform, Roosevelt himself campaigned for progressive candidates in the 1910 midterm election. Roosevelt advocated increasing regulation for business and even went so far as to suggest that the popular vote be used to overturn Supreme Court decisions. Roosevelt's defection from the party split the Republican Party in half entering the election of 1912.

> *Taft's support for the Payne-Aldrich Act and other conservative moves precipitated a split within the Republican Party approaching the election of 1912.*

The Election of 1912

In 1912, Roosevelt declared his intention to run against Taft for the Republican nomination. When Taft supporters blocked Roosevelt's nomination at the Republican Convention, Roosevelt and his supporters broke with the Republican Party and formed the Progressive Party, nicknamed the **Bull Moose Party**. Roosevelt and Taft entered the election against Socialist Eugene Debs and Democrat **Woodrow Wilson**. The Bull Moose Party proved to be the most successful third party in American history, with Roosevelt winning over 27 percent of the popular vote to Taft's 23 percent. Yet with the Republican vote split, Democrat Wilson captured the presidency, winning forty-two percent of the vote.

> *Woodrow Wilson won the election of 1912 partially owing to the split in the Republican Party, which ruined both Roosevelt and Taft's chances for the presidency.*

Wilson in Office: The Revival of Progressivism

Once in office, Wilson pushed a more aggressive progressive agenda than either of his two predecessors. He lowered tariffs and championed corporate regulation and banking reform, among other policies.

Lowering Tariffs

Wilson's first legislative action was to lower the tariff. In 1913, he sponsored the **Underwood Tariff**, which cut tariffs substantially. It was the nation's first reduction in tariffs since before the civil war. Also in 1913, Wilson helped launch an investigation into the possibly corrupt relations between pro-tariff lobbyists and certain senators.

The Federal Reserve System

Wilson and his supporters sought to create a centralized bank system under public control, which would be able to stabilize the economy in times of panic. After months of bargaining, Congress passed the **Federal Reserve Act** in 1913. This act established a network of regional Federal Reserve banks under partially private and partially public control. The Federal Reserve Board was created to oversee the entire network and national fiscal policy. Although weak at first, the "Fed" would become a powerful force in American economics.

Wilson's most notable legislative achievement was the 1913 passage of the Federal Reserve Act, establishing the system of Federal Reserve banks still in use today.

Business Regulation

Wilson pushed two important regulatory measures through Congress in 1914. First, the **Federal Trade Commission Act** created a five-member agency to investigate suspected violations of interstate trade regulations and to issue "cease and desist" orders should it find corporations guilty of unfair practices. Secondly, the **Clayton Antitrust Act** improved upon the vague **Sherman Antitrust Act** by enumerating a series of illegal business practices. The Wilson administration initiated antitrust suits against almost one hundred corporations.

Labor and Farm Reform

Wilson strongly supported worker's rights. Under his administration, Congress passed a series of labor laws designed to ban child labor, shorten workdays, and, in the Workmen's Compensation Act, provide injury protection to federal employees. Wilson also supported reforms benefiting farmers, such as low-interest loan programs.

"New Freedom" in Foreign Policy

Wilson rejected the big stick and dollar diplomacy approaches to foreign policy in favor of "**new freedom**," an idealistic foreign policy aimed at morality in international affairs. He pledged never to seek territorial expansion by conquest, and instead focused on advancing capitalism and democracy throughout the world. To signal his rejection of the old methods, Wilson withdrew American partnership from a loan consortium in China in 1913. Between 1913 and 1917, he tried with varying success to help foster democracy and stability in Mexico.

In 1914, world war erupted across Europe. In line with the peaceful foreign policy he had followed since 1912, Wilson was determined not to get involved in the war. In 1914, soon after the war's outbreak, Wilson issued a statement of neutrality designed to keep the U.S. out of the conflict. In 1916, Wilson was reelected in large part on the slogan, "He kept us out of war."

World War I

Trends and Themes of the Era

- Although the U.S. wanted to stay neutral in the war, it could not. U.S. involvement in the war helped turn the tide in favor of the Allies. If the Spanish-American War had left any doubt, World War I firmly established the U.S. as a dominant world power.

- Woodrow Wilson saw the war as an opportunity to end all future wars. He wanted to make peace through a liberal and merciful peace settlement. The ravaged European victors and many members of Congress, though, rejected his aims. His proposed League of Nations was not even supported by his own country.

- The war effort brought blacks and women into the workforce in record numbers. It also prompted the migration of nearly 500,000 blacks from the South to the North. Women's work in the war effort had a direct result in their achieving the right to vote with the Nineteenth Amendment.

- Progressivism continued throughount the war, and secured its last great success with the passage of the prohibition of alcohol in the Eighteenth Amendment.

Proclaimed Neutrality

World War I pitted the **Allies** (Great Britain, Russia, France, and later Italy) against the **Central Powers** (Germany and Austria-Hungary). In August 1914, Wilson proclaimed U.S. neutrality, and urged the public to remain neutral in opinion as well. The American public, however, was partial to the Allies: though most Americans were glad to be remote from the war, strong emotional, historic, and economic ties to Great Britain and France meant great public sympathy for the Allied cause. While American investment in the Central Powers nations dwindled between 1914 and 1917, it surged in the Allied nations. American sources provided weapons, food, and funding to the Allies equal to nearly one hundred times that provided to the Central Powers. Wilson himself seemed to favor an Allied victory, in part because he saw a victory by Germany and its autocratic ruler, Kaiser Wilhelm, as antagonistic to his vision of a world order based on liberalism, democracy, and capitalism. Nonetheless, he clung to neutrality.

After 1914, it became increasingly clear that American neutrality would be difficult to maintain. British naval vessels seized American ships headed for German ports and filled the North Sea with mines, despite American protests. In 1915, Germany announced a **U-boat** blockade of the Allies' ports and, in the ensuing months, killed a number of Americans in torpedo attacks on British vessels and one U.S. tanker. On May 7, 1915, a U-boat sank the British ocean liner *Lusitania*, killing close to 1,200 people, including 128 Americans. This event provoked an anti-German backlash in American public opinion, and prompted Wilson to call for a major military buildup. Congress passed the **National Defense Act** in 1916, which called for the buildup of military forces in anticipation of war, a policy known as "preparedness."

After the *Lusitania* incident, Germany stopped attacking passenger ships for a few months. But in August 1915, Germany resumed attacks, sinking both British and French vessels. In 1916, when Wilson threatened to break diplomatic relations after one such attack, Germany responded with the *Sussex* **Pledge**, promising not to attack merchant ships without warning. This pledge eased the strain on U.S. neutrality for the remainder of 1916.

In 1916, Wilson was reelected on the slogan, "He kept us out of war," a tribute to his maintenance of American neutrality. Wilson and the Democrats portrayed the Republican Party as the party of war and uncertainty.

The U.S. Enters the War

In early January 1917, Wilson called for "peace without victory," meaning he wanted the European powers to come to peace without pursuing military means to their bloody ends. By late January, however, this hope for peace seemed impossible after

Germany proclaimed the resumption of unrestricted submarine warfare: Germany vowed to sink all ships, belligerent or neutral, in a wide zone around the Allies. In response, Wilson cut diplomatic relations with Germany. In the next few months, five U.S. ships were sunk. In the meantime, British intelligence intercepted the **Zimmerman Telegram**. Sent from the German foreign secretary to the German ambassador to Mexico, the Zimmerman Telegram suggested that Mexico enter the war against the U.S. in return for a German pledge to aid in the restoration of Mexico's former territories of Texas, Arizona, and New Mexico. Germany also promised to help Japan if Japan went to war against the U.S. The telegram's aggressive tactics, as well as the sinking of U.S. ships, convinced Wilson to break U.S. neutrality and call for war.

Germany's resumption of unrestricted submarine warfare and the interception of the Zimmerman Telegram convinced Wilson to break from his insistence upon neutrality and call for war.

In April 1917, the U.S. declared war on Germany. Wilson, who had been elected six months earlier on the slogan, "He kept us out of war," now charged into the war, proclaiming it necessary "to make the world safe for democracy."

Raising an Army

At the time the U.S. passed the declaration of war against Germany, the U.S. Army included 120,000 enlisted men and 80,000 National Guardsmen. In 1917, Congress passed the **Selective Service Act**, which required all men from age 21 to 30 to register for military duty. By November 1918, some three million men had been drafted. About 11,000 women served in the navy, and a few hundred more joined the marines. Women were invaluable in the noncombat positions open to them during the war. More than 250,000 black Americans served in the war, but racism was strong in the military, and black troops were segregated from white troops, given menial positions, and excluded altogether by the marines.

Fighting the War

American involvement in World War I lasted from the summer of 1917 to the armistice that ended the war in November 1918—just over one year. American involvement helped boost the Allies to victory: American troops overran heavily fortified German trenches and reinvigorated the British and French war efforts. At the war's end, the American death toll exceeded 110,000. At home, the outbreak of the Spanish influenza claimed over 500,000 lives in 1918—the worst single U.S. epidemic in history.

World War I

Making Peace

Even before the armistice (or truce) in November 1918, complex negotiations for peace had begun. Achieving international peace was an arduous and complex process.

Wilson's Fourteen Points

From the beginning of World War I, Wilson had hoped for a peace settlement promoting America's democratic ideals. He saw the Allied victory as a victory over autocratic government (Germany was an autocracy), and therefore as an opportunity to advance democracy and liberalism worldwide. In a 1918 speech to Congress, Wilson summarized American goals for the terms of peace after the war in what became known as the **Fourteen Points**:

- Eight points dealt with the territorial reorganization of Europe, aimed at granting self-determination to nations formerly under the control of the Austro-Hungarian and Ottoman empires.

- One point advocated the settlement of colonial disputes with due consideration given to the colonized peoples, as well as to the colonial powers.

- Five points broadly laid out Wilson's plan for a new world order. Wilson proposed unrestricted sea travel, free trade, arms reductions, an end to secret treaties, and, most importantly, "a general association of nations" to protect peace and resolve conflicts.

Republicans in Congress opposed the plan, and no Allies fully endorsed it—some lent cautious support, others disdained it. Many Americans, however, agreed with and supported Wilson's plans, and the Fourteen Points became a rallying issue for the U.S. war effort.

Wilson's Fourteen Points, enumerated in January 1918, set forth U.S. aims in World War I. The most important point called for "a general association of nations" to preserve international peace.

The Treaty of Versailles

Wilson decided to head the negotiation team himself at the Versailles Peace Conference, and offended Republicans by appointing just one Republican to the peace commission. The commission arrived in Europe in 1918 full of optimism, but this optimism faded quickly after the conference began. The delegates from the Allied Powers (France, Britain, and Italy) fiercely resisted Wilson's attempts at a liberal settlement. They represented bitter, war-torn nations bent on destroying the Central Powers. Instead of negotiating a peace with the Central Powers, they aimed to impose penalties, and made vindictive demands.

The **Treaty of Versailles**, signed in June 1919, was quite harsh toward the Germans. Germany was disarmed, forced to admit sole blame for the war, and required to pay massive reparations to the Allies. Land reorganization ceded one-eighth of Germany's territory to other nations, and set the stage for French occupation of the west bank of the Rhine (which lasted 15 years). Wilson did succeed in achieving autonomy for Poland, the Baltic states, Czechoslovakia and Yugoslavia, but overall did little to salvage his liberal aims. Harsh measures instilled the German people with a spirit of resentment that would resurface in the 1930s and play a part in World War II. The treaty also offended Russia, since portions were clearly designed to weaken Russian influence.

Wilson's one clear victory at Versailles was the acceptance of his plan for a **League of Nations**. The League of Nations was the embodiment of Wilson's dream of a supranational organization whose purpose was to preserve peace and resolve conflicts. It soon became clear, however, that though the League was the brainchild of the U.S. president, even U.S. membership in this League was uncertain.

Major elements of the Treaty of Versailles: Germany assumed blame for war, was required to pay massive reparations; German territory distributed; League of Nations formed.

Battle over the League of Nations

In 1919, Wilson presented the Treaty of Versailles to the Senate for ratification. Wilson had already alienated much of the Senate, which was predominantly Republican, by failing to take a leading Republican with him on his negotiation team to Versailles. Given this political antagonism, the Senate opposed many of Wilson's peace efforts. Thirty-nine senators signed a letter rejecting the League of Nations, primarily because of its requirement that members protect the "territorial integrity" and "political independence" of other member states. Ten to fifteen senators, known as "irreconcilables," refused to consider joining the League altogether, while a group of about thirty-five "reservationists," led by **Henry Cabot Lodge**, pledged to ratify the treaty only with major revisions. Wilson, however, refused to compromise, and the treaty was rejected. The U.S. would not enter the League of Nations.

World War I

The opposition of "irreconcilables" to joining the League of Nations and Wilson and the Democrats' refusal to compromise with "reservationists" ensured that the Treaty of Versailles would not be ratified and the U.S. would not join the League of Nations.

The U.S. after the War

World War I stimulated growth in the U.S. economy. The entrance of women and blacks into the workforce added more than one million to the ranks of working Americans, and factory output increased tremendously. After the war, the boom continued, in part because there was great demand for American goods from war-torn European countries.

The war also affected the demographics of the country. It is estimated that 500,000 southern blacks moved north during the war, most of them settling in cities to work industrial jobs. As urban black populations increased, so did racial strife. In 1917, a white mob in Illinois lit black homes on fire and shot the fleeing inhabitants, killing nearly forty. Weeks later, the NAACP organized a silent march down Fifth Avenue in New York to protest racial violence. The end of the war did not mean the end of racial tension. In 1919, eighty-three blacks were victims of lynching. That year, race riots exploded in twenty-five cities, most notably Chicago, where a thirteen-day riot in July left fifteen whites and twenty-three blacks dead, hundreds injured, and more than a thousand homeless.

Red Scare

After World War I, anti-German hysteria turned into anti-Russian hysteria in response to the Bolshevik revolution of 1917, which brought a communist regime to power. Although fewer than 100,000 Americans were members of the nation's communist parties, many Americans feared that communist influence went deeper, and had infiltrated the working class, immigrant communities and labor unions.

In 1919, Attorney General A. Mitchell Palmer assigned **J. Edgar Hoover** to head a new Intelligence Division to root out subversives. Hoover arrested hundreds of suspected radicals and deported many "undesirable" aliens, especially those of Eastern European background. In 1920, in a coordinated operation, police and federal marshals raided the homes of suspected radicals and the headquarters of radical organizations in thirty-two cities. These **Palmer Raids** resulted in more than 4,000 arrests, 550 deportations, and uncountable violations of civil rights.

The central event of the postwar Red Scare, the Palmer Raids of January 2, 1920, resulted in more than 4,000 arrests and more than 550 deportations of suspected radicals.

The End of the Progressive Agenda

World War I slowed the advance of progressive reform but did not stop it. Progressive forces continued to operate during the war, pressing for further domestic reform. One prominent movement was the drive for prohibition. During the war, prohibition forces pointed to the German names of America's breweries and argued that German beer would undermine American morality. Prohibitionists therefore presented the **Eighteenth Amendment**, which prohibited the manufacture, transport, or sale of alcohol, as a war measure. This Amendment was passed in 1917 and ratified in 1919.

The woman suffrage movement made great strides during the war, largely because of the important role women played on the home front, filling men's jobs and promoting the war effort. Congress passed the **Nineteenth Amendment**, which granted women the vote, in 1919, and the states ratified the Amendment in 1920. Despite this major advance, however, women were forced to vacate their jobs when men returned from war and resume their traditional societal roles. Women would have to wait for advances in social status that met the legal advances they made in 1920.

Opposition to the War

Many American citizens of widely differing backgrounds refused to support the war. Some were German immigrants, some were members of pacifist religions, and others simply objected to the war on moral and intellectual grounds. Antiwar writings increased as journalists dissected and criticized pro-war reasoning. Intellectuals condemned the war in political magazines, while socialist publications denounced the war as a contest for global market dominance. As the war began, the government did all it could to counter, and even quiet, these criticisms.

Concerned by the antiwar campaigns, Wilson and his advisers worked hard to promote the war. His administration enlisted the help of famous movie stars to urge Americans to aid the war effort and conducted government bond drives to finance the war. In 1917, the federal government established the Committee on Public Information. This committee functioned primarily as a propaganda agency that discredited all critics of the government and set up guidelines for self-censorship. The committee also enlisted the help of artists, journalists, and authors to publicize the war through speeches, posters, articles, and films. These pro-war efforts helped generate and intensify the public's mistrust, even hatred, of Germany and the Central Powers.

World War I

The patriotic—but often intolerant—sentiments inspired by such propaganda spilled over into public policy as well. The **Espionage Act**, passed in 1917, enumerated a vague list of anti-war activities warranting fines or imprisonment. The 1918 **Sedition Amendment** to the Espionage Act provided for punishment of anyone using "disloyal, profane, scurrilous, or abusive language" in regard to the government, flag, or military. Government officials invoked these measures to suppress dissent and justify the arrest of roughly 1,500 people during the war. **Eugene Debs**, a prominent socialist and five-time presidential candidate, was imprisoned in 1918 for denouncing the government's aggressive tactics under the Sedition Amendment (he was released in 1921). The Espionage Act was also used to bar a number of periodicals from circulation by mail. The Supreme Court upheld these laws when they were challenged until well after the war had ended, most notably in *Schenk v. U.S.* (1919), in which the Court ruled that speech could be restricted when free speech presented a "clear and present danger."

The Espionage Act and the Sedition Amendment were used to stamp out anti-war ideology and activism during World War I.

The Roaring Twenties

Trends and Themes of the Era

- America turned away from the ideals of progressivism. Even the prohibition amendment was not always strictly enforced. Republicans regained the presidency and ushered in a new era of pro-business policies.

- Government policies, progress in technology, and a new consumer society produced a booming economy. Radio helped transform the U.S. into a single national market, and a mass popular culture developed based largely on the consumption of luxury items. To take full advantage of the profits to be made, businesses merged and grew ever larger.

- Tired from the war and disillusioned by Wilson's failure with the League of Nations, America entered a period of isolationism. The U.S. aimed to stay out of European affairs and severely limited immigration. New immigrants were often subject to suspicion and hatred.

- The younger generation rebelled against traditional morals. College students took to drinking and throwing wild parties. Women became more forward in dress and behavior. Premarital sex became less taboo. The two symbols of this new, looser social behavior were jazz and the "flapper."

Republicans and a "Return to Normalcy"

In the early 1920s, weary from fighting a world war and disillusioned by the failure of Wilson's plans to create a new world order, Americans sought stability. Popular support for Republicans grew, since Republicans promised a "return to normalcy." Republicans ceased to promise progressive reforms and instead aimed to settle into traditional patterns of government. In 1920, after eight years under a progressive Democrat, Americans elected a conservative Republican as president, the first of the decade's three Republican presidents. Big business and advocates of isolationism reaped the benefits of Republican rule.

Warren G. Harding won the election of 1920 by a landslide on the promise of a "return to normalcy"—which, for Republicans in the 1920s, meant a return to big business. In addition to its pro-business stance, Harding's administration was known primarily for its corruption, exposed fully after Harding's death in office in 1923. Many officials were forced from office, and some narrowly escaped prison time. The most prominent scandal, the **Teapot Dome scandal**, involved secretary of the interior Albert B. Fall secretly leasing government oil reserves to two businessmen and accepting about $400,000 in return.

Harding's vice president, **Calvin Coolidge**, became president upon Harding's death in 1923 and was then elected himself in 1924. In contrast to his predecessor, Coolidge ran a relatively scandal-free White House. Staunchly pro-business, Coolidge opposed government regulation of, or interference with, the economy.

Herbert Hoover, the third Republican president of the decade, rode the tide of economic prosperity to victory in 1928. He took a slightly different stance toward big business than had his predecessors. Hoover thought that capitalism produced social obligations but believed in voluntarism rather than government coercion as the method of fulfilling these obligations. Hoover urged and persuaded industry reform, but refused to institutionalize reform in law. This reliance on voluntarism would hurt him as prosperity began to fade.

Pro-Business Policies

The Republican presidents of the 1920s—Harding, Coolidge, and Hoover—reversed the Progressive Era trend of regulating big business and lowering tariffs. Instead, Republican policies generally gave corporations free rein, raised protective tariffs, and cut taxes for the wealthy. Big business and wealthy businessmen especially benefited from the following policies:

The Roaring Twenties

- The Supreme Court overturned a number of measures designed to regulate the activities of big business. The Court declared boycotts by labor unconstitutional and authorized the use of antitrust laws against unions.

- The Fordney-McCumber Tariff of 1922 and the **Smoot-Hawley Tariff** of 1930 were two of six major tariffs passed that hiked rates to all-time highs. These tariffs protected American companies from international competition.

- Andrew Mellon, treasury secretary from 1921 to 1932, persuaded Congress to lower income tax rates for the wealthy.

The Republican presidents of the 1920s reversed the Progressive Era trend of corporate regulation. Progressive trust-busting gave way to an era of big business.

A Decade of Prosperity

Following a postwar recession from mid-1920 to the end of 1921, the economy picked up again and remained strong until the end of the decade. This prosperity, combined with tax cuts for the rich, led to a rising consumer culture.

The very nature of consumerism changed during this period, as new products filled the market. The automobile first became popular outside wealthy circles in the 1920s. Electrical appliances grew rapidly in popularity as electricity reached almost two-thirds of American homes by the mid-1920s. Refrigerators, washing machines, and vacuum cleaners flew off the shelves. The incredible speed and vast reach of the newly invented radio created a national market and spurred advertising to unprecedented levels.

One effect of prosperity was the consolidation of big business and banks. By the decade's end, more than 1,000 companies per year were being swallowed up by mergers. A few corporations, such as Ford and Chrysler in automobiles and General Electric in electricity and electric appliances, dominated major industries. Industry leaders became immensely popular public figures.

Rising Productivity

New technologies allowed corporations to meet public demand by increasing productivity. Henry Ford installed the **assembly line** process in his automobile plants, maximizing outputs by allowing workers to stay in one place and master one repeated task. New developments in management methods increased efficiency by departmentaliz-

The Roaring Twenties

ing varied business concerns and creating a class of professional managers. Installment buying and credit programs allowed consumers to buy expensive goods they could not afford to purchase with one payment.

During the 1920s, industry benefited from the consolidation of large firms, assembly line manufacturing, professional management, and installment buying and credit programs.

Labor and Agriculture

The 1920s ushered in a new era for workers. To increase productivity, some employers raised the wages of skilled workers without the prodding of labor unions. Partially in response, union membership declined during the 1920s. Manufacturers' associations praised the non-union workplace, and companies made concessions to workers in attempts to stave off union formations.

This industrial boom left agriculture largely behind. Crop prices fell rapidly between 1919 and 1921 and remained low during the 1920s. Republicans, who did not believe in government intervention in the economy, were reluctant to help.

Isolationism

The Republican-dominated government of the 1920s advocated a spirit of isolationism, which meant retreating from global affairs. The U.S. refused to join both the League of Nations and the World Court established by the League. In 1928, the U.S. and France (and later, sixty other nations) signed the Kellogg-Briand Pact, which called for the outlawing of war and an end to aggression. This pact, however strong in theory, provided no enforcement mechanism.

Despite its isolationism, the U.S. did become involved in international affairs over the issue of war debts and reparations. The Allies had borrowed significantly from the U.S. during World War I and could not pay back this debt. Meanwhile, Germany owed reparations to the Allies but also could not pay. The **Dawes Plan**, devised by American banker Charles G. Dawes in 1924, scaled back U.S. demands for debt payments and reparations and established a cycle of U.S. loans that provided Germany with funds for reparations to the Allies, thus funding Allied debt payments to the U.S.

Immigration in the 1920s

A prominent expression of American isolationism was immigration restriction. Not only did isolationists oppose U.S. involvement in European affairs, they also opposed the flood of European immigrants coming to the U.S. Between 1900 and 1915, more than 13 million immigrants came to the U.S., many of them from eastern and southern Europe and many either Catholic or Jewish, to the general dismay of the Protestant American public. Many Americans viewed these immigrants as a threat to American religious and social values, as well as to economic opportunities (because immigrants competed for jobs). In 1921, Congress set a quota of 350,000 for annual immigration. In 1924, the **National Origins Act** cut that number to 164,000 and restricted immigration from any one nation to two percent of the number of people in the U.S. of that national origin in 1890. This standard curtailed immigration from southern and eastern Europe and excluded Asians entirely.

Anti-immigrant sentiment peaked in the **Sacco-Vanzetti case** of 1921. Sacco and Vanzetti were two Italian immigrants charged with an April 1920 murder in Massachusetts. They were anarchists as well as immigrants, arousing frank hatred from the media and the judge in their case, who sentenced them to death. The case against Sacco and Vanzetti was circumstantial and poorly argued (although evidence now suggests that they were in fact guilty). The case was significant for its demonstration of nativist and conservative forces in America.

Culture in the 1920s: Loosening Social Structure

According to one journalist in 1920, Americans were "weary of being noble" after a decade of intense progressive reform, morality, and self-righteousness. The 1920s saw a restless culture, spearheaded by America's youth rebelling against the moral restrictions of past generations.

The Sexual Revolution

During the 1920s, some Americans—especially young college students—challenged traditional notions of proper behavior. Buoyed by the decade's prosperity, young people threw raucous parties, drank illegal liquor, and danced new, sexually suggestive steps at jazz clubs. One of the staple symbols of this decade was the **flapper**, a name given to the fashionable, pleasure-seeking young women of the time. The archetypal flapper look was tomboyish and flamboyant: short bobbed hair; knee-length, fringed skirts; long, draping necklaces; and rolled stockings. Although few women actually fit this image, it was used widely in journalism and advertising to represent the rebelliousness of the period. The traditional bastions of American morality lamented these developments, and especially criticized the new dances and college students' proclivity for drinking and smoking. These critics, however, soon found themselves facing much larger opposition as the older generations began to adopt some of the socially liberated practices of their children.

The Roaring Twenties

With new social thinking and activities came new social conventions. Most prominently, among the youth of the 1920s, sex became far less taboo than it had been previously. Sex was more openly discussed and premarital sex more common. Such activity led naturally to the promotion of birth control, though it was still widely illegal. The **sexual revolution** brought with it changing ideas about women. Female sexuality was less suppressed, skirt hems were worn higher, and makeup became more common.

It is important to note that although the Roaring '20s and its attendant characters and events came to symbolize the decade, these stereotypes fit only a small segment of society. Traditional values, especially outside the cities, were not discarded completely, or even much changed.

Prohibition

The **Eighteenth Amendment**, which made it illegal to manufacture, sell, or transport alcoholic beverages, went into effect in January 1920. Enforcement of prohibition, however, was sporadic and underfunded and faced opposition in many states and cities, especially northern cities, where many prohibition laws were repealed. Given this lax enforcement, many Americans viewed prohibition as something of a joke. **Bootleggers** smuggled liquor from the West Indies and Canada, while **speakeasies** in every city provided alcohol illegally. Organized crime controlled the distribution of alcohol in major American cities, and gangsters such as Al Capone made a fortune while law enforcement officials often looked the other way. Capone's income in 1927 was reportedly over $1 million, while the average American's income was below $2,500. Prohibition fueled much debate within the United States until its repeal in 1933.

The Jazz Age and the Harlem Renaissance

The 1920s saw the flowering of African American culture in the arts. In music, black culture expressed itself through jazz, an improvisational and spontaneous musical form derived in part from slave songs and African spirituals. Jazz first emerged in the early 1900s in New Orleans then spread to Chicago, New York City, and elsewhere. The 1920s is often called the **Jazz Age** because jazz flourished and gained widespread appeal during the decade. The improvisational character of the music was often associated with the "loose" morals and relaxed social codes of the time. Among the famous jazz performers of the period were Louis Armstrong, Bessie Smith, and Duke Ellington.

The flowering of black literature in the Northeast, especially in Harlem in New York City, was known as the **Harlem Renaissance**. Black artists explored the African American perspective through poetry and novels. One of the most famous authors of the time was the poet Langston Hughes, who published "The Weary Blues," in 1926. Harlem was the site of social activity as well as intellectual activity, because prominent and wealthy blacks hosted extravagant gatherings for Harlem Renaissance figures.

The Roaring Twenties

The "Lost Generation"

One reason it is difficult to separate stereotypes about the 1920s from reality is the attention paid to these stereotypes by American authors and the media. The author who best represented this trend was **F. Scott Fitzgerald**, who wrote extensively about the rebellious youth of the Jazz Age in stories and novels such as *This Side of Paradise*, published in 1920, and *The Great Gatsby*, published in 1925. In *The Great Gatsby*, his most famous novel, Fitzgerald criticized the superficiality and material excess of America's post-war culture, portraying prosperity gone wrong in wealthy New York society.

Many other literary figures rose alongside Fitzgerald to dissect American postwar society. Several notables, including Sinclair Lewis, attacked America's prevalent Protestant, middle-class, conformist morality. Lewis's satirical critique, *Babbitt*, was published in 1922. **H.L. Mencken** was the journalistic counterpart to the alienated novelists, using political satire in his magazine, *American Mercury*, to attack the political leaders of the day and the American "booboisie," as he called the middle class.

Disgusted with the American life they saw as overly material and spiritually void, many writers during this period lived in Europe, including Ezra Pound, Gertrude Stein, and **Ernest Hemingway**. The most famous expatriate, Hemingway produced *The Sun Also Rises* in 1926 and *A Farewell to Arms* in 1929, both reflecting the horror and futility of World War I. The self-imposed exile of these writers from America is one reason they were nicknamed "the lost generation."

Entertainment and Popular Culture

The 1920s saw the growth of popular recreation, in part because of high wages and increased leisure time. Just as automobiles were mass-produced, so was recreation during the 1920s. Mass-circulations magazines like *Reader's Digest* and *Time* (established 1923) enjoyed enormous success. Radio also first rose to prominence as a source of news and entertainment during the 1920s: NBC was founded in 1926 and CBS a year later. Movies were the most popular leisure attraction of the times, making stars out of Charlie Chaplin, Rudolph Valentino, Gloria Swanson, and Mary Pickford. In 1927, with *The Jazz Singer*, movies began to include sound, and 1928 saw the first animated sound film, *Steamboat Willy*. Professional sports gained a new popularity, as well. Baseball star Babe Ruth enjoyed massive fame, as did boxers such as Jack Dempsey. College sports rose to national attention, as demonstrated by the fame of the Notre Dame football team's "four horsemen." The 1920s also saw the emergence of nonsporting national heroes like Charles Lindbergh, who made the first solo nonstop flight across the Atlantic in May 1927.

The Roaring Twenties

Social Tension in a Decade of Prosperity

The prosperity and leisure of the 1920s hid serious social tensions. In the political realm, such tensions exposed themselves in isolationism and anti-immigration policies. Elsewhere in American society, social tensions centered on questions of race, religion, and fundamentalism.

The Garvey Movement and African Americans

Many blacks, unhappy with the continued slow pace of social advancement, in the 1920s turned to **Marcus Garvey** and the **United Negro Improvement Association** (UNIA), which Garvey had moved from Jamaica to the U.S. in 1916. Garvey glorified black culture and founded a chain of UNIA businesses to promote black economic cooperation. Garvey urged American blacks to return to Africa and establish an independent nation. The Garvey movement attracted many followers, with the UNIA claiming 80,000 members, but was sharply criticized by the **National Association for the Advancement of Colored People** (NAACP) for being too radical. In 1923, Marcus Garvey was found guilty of fraud, and in 1927 he was deported to Jamaica. The UNIA could not survive without his leadership, but it left an important legacy as a prominent African American mass movement.

The NAACP was a more conservative force for social reform. Led by **W.E.B. Du Bois**, the NAACP called for integration and equal treatment for blacks. In part because of migration of blacks northward during World War I, membership in the NAACP grew markedly during the early 1920s. Still, lynchings continued in the South, and racist Americans gained influence through organizations such as the Ku Klux Klan.

The Ku Klux Klan

Nativism and intolerance during the 1920s was seen most prominently in the resurgence of the **Ku Klux Klan** (KKK) in 1915. The Klan organized a wildly successful membership drive in 1920, with estimates of new recruits as high as five million. Instead of just targeting blacks for attack, as the earlier Klan had done, the new Klan expanded its target to include all non-Protestants. By calling for "100 percent Americanism," the Klan capitalized on middle-class Protestant dismay at changing social and economic conditions in America. The Klan took root throughout the South, where it mostly targeted blacks, and in parts of the West and Midwest, where Catholics and Jews bore the brunt of Klan intimidation and murder. In some states, the Klan even exerted dominant political, as well as social, force. The Klan collapsed in 1925 after the widespread corruption of Klan leadership was exposed. Membership faded quickly, but the Klan would return after World War II as a significant force.

The Scopes Monkey Trial

During the late nineteenth and early twentieth centuries, science challenged the infallibility of religious doctrine. Liberal Protestants accepted the majority of scientific findings and sought to integrate these findings into their religion, but more conservative Protestants refused this strategy. This refusal was known as **fundamentalism**. Fundamentalists insisted on the divine inspiration and truth of every word in the Bible, and focused in the early 1920s on refuting the theory of evolution. Articulated by Charles Darwin in 1895, evolution contradicted biblical accounts of the creation of man. **William Jennings Bryan**, former presidential candidate and secretary of state, led a movement to ban schools from teaching evolution. In 1925, the Tennessee legislature did just that, prompting the **American Civil Liberties Union** (ACLU) to offer to defend any teacher willing to challenge this law. John T. Scopes accepted this offer, broke the law, and was arrested, bringing the issue to court. In the famed **Scopes Monkey Trial**, Bryan aided the prosecution, and Chicago lawyer **Clarence Darrow** defended Scopes. The judge would not allow expert testimony, leaving the matter basically up to debate between Darrow and Bryan. In cross-examination, Darrow made a fool of Bryan, exposing the latter's lack of scientific knowledge. Although Scopes was found guilty, the nation at large, paying close attention to the trial, generally considered the anti-fundamentalist forces to have won the argument.

The Roaring Twenties

The Great Depression and the New Deal

Trends and Themes of the Era

- The frenzied speculation and mergers of the booming economy in the 1920s led to the horrendous depression of the 1930s.

- Under President Franklin Delano Roosevelt, the government committed itself to unprecedented levels of regulation and control over the national economy. These policies of the New Deal made FDR and the Democrats extremely popular and also changed American government forever. After the New Deal, American citizens came to see one role of the government as offering a safety net, not just an opportunity to succeed.

- FDR's policies changed the demographics of the political parties. His support for blacks, the poor, and labor unions won him and the Democrats support from those groups—a support base that remains in place today. Up until that time, blacks tended to voted for Republicans (Republicans had been the antislavery party during the Civil War and Reconstruction). FDR's policies also lost Democrats their traditional support from the white South, which shifted to the Republicans.

- The depression, a worldwide phenomenon, created the circumstances that allowed for Fascists to rise to power in Germany and Italy.

The Crash

During the Roaring Twenties, the United States basked in unprecedented prosperity. Levels of investment, often speculative investments, grew to new heights. The economy, however, could not support such unchecked growth. On Thursday, October 24, 1929, dubbed **Black Thursday**, the stock market crashed. When trading closed, the Dow Jones Industrial Average had fallen nine percent. Despite the crash, reports remained optimistic. New York banks united to buy up $30 million worth of stock in efforts to stabilize the market, and President **Herbert Hoover** announced that recovery was expected. But the situation only became bleaker during the next week. On October 29, known as "Black Tuesday," the Dow dropped over 17 percent, confirming the permanency of the crash. By mid-November, market losses topped $30 billion.

Results of the Crash

As a result of the crash, the national economy fell into the worst depression in its history. Banks closed their doors in record numbers, and more than 30,000 businesses failed in 1932 alone. Unemployment reached an unheard of high of 25 percent in 1933, and hovered between 15 and 20 percent for most of the 1930s. Small towns and villages were hit the hardest, as were unskilled workers and minorities. Abject poverty spread. Children suffered from inadequate nutrition and healthcare, and starvation became an everyday occurrence. The refrain of a popular song during the period was, "Brother, can you spare a dime?"

Hoover's Response

During the first few months of depression, Herbert Hoover was optimistic about the prospects of recovery, believing that the economy would rebound by itself. But, as the depression continued into 1930, he was forced to take action.

Hoover's most notable foray into trade regulation was his advocacy of the **Smoot-Hawley Tariff** in 1930. The tariff was designed to protect the nation's farmers but did not have its intended effect: it hurt farmers more than it helped them and further intensified the national depression. Other steps that Hoover took to help farmers included overseeing the activity of the Federal Farm Board, which administered loans to farmers, and creating the Grain Stabilization Corporation, which bought wheat at high prices in attempts to drive prices up.

Hoover's principal attempts to address the depression's effects on agriculture included the Smoot-Hawley Tariff and the Grain Stabilization Corporation.

To help businesses, Hoover authorized $2 billion in funding for the creation of the **Reconstruction Finance Corporation** (RFC). The RFC was intended to loan money to large, stable institutions such as banks, railroads, and insurance firms. The RFC authorized almost $2 billion in loans in 1932. In July 1932, Hoover authorized the RFC to spend an additional $2 billion on state and local public works projects. These actions, however, were largely ineffective at countering the Depression.

To spur business recovery, Hoover created the Reconstruction Finance Corporation, which loaned money to companies attempting to rebuild after the market crash. It did little to help the market recover.

The onset of the Great Depression left many Americans without jobs, without homes, and without hope. In an effort to address these problems, Hoover established the **Emergency Committee for Employment** in 1930 to coordinate the efforts of private agencies to provide unemployment relief but granted the committee limited resources. He remained firmly opposed to the use of federal funds for public works programs, preferring private charity to public relief.

But Hoover's efforts did little to spur the economy or redress unemployment. The consummate symbol of Hoover's failure was the **Hooverville**. Hoovervilles, or communities of homeless Americans living in shanties and makeshift shacks, sprang up around many U.S. cities and served as stark reminders of the Depression's terrible toll.

The Election of 1932

As the Depression worsened, public calls for aggressive government intervention intensified. The people wanted their president to be a hero and representative of the people rather than an aloof bureaucrat—a departure from the do-nothing presidents of the 1920s and from Hoover's restrained approach in the early 1930s. **Franklin Delano Roosevelt** promised to answer this call. In 1932, FDR won the election handily against Hoover, who many believed had done too little, too late in fighting the Depression. Democrats also controlled both houses of Congress.

Roosevelt's New Deal

FDR came to office convinced of the economic theories of John Maynard Keynes, who argued that government spending could revive a faltering economy. FDR's New Deal embodied this strategy.

The First Hundred Days and the First New Deal

In his inauguration speech of 1933, FDR pledged to devote his presidency to helping the poor and promoting recovery, claiming, "the only thing we have to fear is fear itself." During the **first hundred days** of his presidency, FDR set forth his plan for national recovery, known as the **New Deal**. The New Deal ushered in an unprecedented era of government intervention in the economy.

The first problem FDR faced during the early months of 1933 was a rash of bank closures in thirty-eight states. In response, he called for a bank holiday, during which he met with the heads of many suffering banks and developed the **Emergency Banking Relief Act**, passed March 9. This act provided a framework under which banks could reopen with federal support. Other important reforms of the "first hundred days" include:

- On March 31, Congress passed the Unemployment Relief Act, which created the **Civilian Conservation Corps** (CCC), a program to employ the destitute in conservation and other productive work.

- May 12 saw the passage of the Agricultural Adjustment Act, creating the **Agricultural Adjustment Administration** (AAA) to manage federal aid to farmers and control production. The AAA controlled the production of crops, and thus prices, by offering subsidies to farmers who produced under set quotas. The same day, the **Federal Emergency Relief Act** (FERA) was passed, appropriating $500 million to support state and local treasuries that had run dry.

- On May 18 a bill was passed creating the **Tennessee Valley Authority** (TVA), a plan to develop energy production sites and conserve resources in the Tennessee Valley.

- On May 27, the **Federal Securities Act** was passed in efforts to improve corporate honesty about stocks and other securities, prefacing the creation of the Securities Exchange Commission (SEC) in 1934.

- On June 16, the National Industrial Recovery Act was passed, creating the **National Recovery Administration** (NRA) to manage the recovery of industry and finance. The NRA established regulations for fair competition that bound industry during the entire New Deal. The National Industrial Recovery Act also created the **Public Works Administration** (PWA), which spent over $4 million on projects designed to employ the jobless and infuse the economy with money.

- June 16 also saw the passage of the Banking Act of 1933, creating the **Federal Deposit Insurance Corporation** (FDIC) to back individuals' bank deposits with federal funds.

After June 16, Congress recessed, officially ending the "first hundred days" of reform which created the framework for heavy government involvement to help bring the U.S. out of the depression.

FDR's first hundred days in office saw unprecedented government intervention in the economy, industry, and agriculture. Democrats in Congress, at FDR's behest, passed measures creating a massive structure of agencies under executive control.

Legislation and Agencies of the First New Deal

Emergency Banking Relief Act	ended the bank panic, provided banks with federal support
Civilian Conservation Corps (CCC)	employed more than two million young men from 1933 to 1941
Agricultural Adjustment Administration (AAA)	regulated farm production, helped raise farm income
Federal Emergency Relief Act (FERA)	funded state and local treasuries
Tennessee Valley Authority (TVA)	helped develop and preserve the resources of the Tennessee Valley
Federal Securities Act	regulated the stock market
Federal Deposit Insurance Corporation (FDIC)	backed individuals' bank deposits with federal funds
National Recovery Administration (NRA)	regulated business by establishing fair codes of competition
Public Works Administration (PWA)	employed jobless men and women from all fields (industrial workers, artists, teachers)
Civil Works Administration (CWA)	provided short-term projects for the unemployed

Challenges to the New Deal

After the first hundred days, continued economic distress and mounting opposition to FDR's programs cast doubt upon the New Deal. The first sign that the New Deal was in danger was trouble with the NRA. Opposition to the NRA came to a head in 1935, when the conservative Supreme Court declared the agency unconstitutional, claiming the NRA gave the executive branch regulatory powers that belonged exclusively to Congress. This decision began a series of court decisions that overturned key elements of the New Deal.

The efforts of the AAA, combined with a severe drought in the American heartland, effected a drop in farm production, prompting a rise in farm prices. However, while the AAA did much to help large landowners and commercial farmers, it did little for landless laborers and tenant farmers who populated the rural Midwest. This large group of dispossessed farmers made up the majority of those who participated in the western migration from the **dust bowl** to California in search of land and employment. As the plight of the dust bowl poor became more widely recognized, questions arose about the effectiveness of the AAA. In 1936, the Supreme Court ruled the AAA unconstitutional, claiming it enforced illegal taxation.

Another source of criticism was the conservative **American Liberty League**, composed of elites who claimed that the New Deal restricted democratically guaranteed freedoms to earn and save money and acquire property. Other challenges to the New Deal arose from those appealing to the discontented lower and middle classes, including Father Charles Coughlin and **Huey Long**, who argued that the New Deal was not going far enough in alleviating poverty. The most famous political opposition movement of the Great Depression years, Long's Share Our Wealth program, pressed for far greater income redistribution and benefits for the poor.

These challenges passed, at least in part, with the midterm elections of 1934. Despite a vocal minority of dissenters, FDR remained a popular president because of his efforts at relief, his charismatic leadership, and his connection with the citizens symbolized by his frequent **fireside chats**, radio broadcasts that he used to rally the support of the people and to offer assurances of economic recovery. FDR's popularity and public confidence in the New Deal resulted in a resounding approval of the Democratic program in the elections of 1934. Democrats gained seats in both the House and Senate.

The Second New Deal

Reassured by the overwhelming Democratic victory in the midterm elections of 1934, FDR laid out his plans for the **Second New Deal** in the January 1935 State of The Union Address. He outlined six ways in which the administration would renew and intensify the efforts begun under the first New Deal. These plans included an enlarged unemployment relief program, assistance to the rural poor, support for organized labor, social welfare benefits for the elderly and disadvantaged, strict regulation of business and finance, and heavier taxes on the wealthy.

In April 1935, Congress passed the Emergency Relief Appropriation Act. This act granted FDR $5 billion to use on whatever programs he chose. The majority of that funding went to the **Works Progress Administration** (WPA). Over eight years, the WPA pumped $11 billion into the economy and supported the unemployed of all backgrounds, from industrial engineers to authors and artists. Unemployment fell over five percent from 1935 to 1937, partially due to the WPA's efforts.

To regulate the economy, FDR empowered the **Federal Reserve Board** to exert tighter control over the money supply, and called for strict enforcement of the Securities Exchange Act of 1934, which required that a detailed and truthful prospectus be publicized for each company issuing stock on the U.S. market.

One of the most lasting achievements of the Second New Deal was the creation of **Social Security** benefits for the elderly through the Social Security Act of 1935. This act, passed largely in response to the elderly rights movement, exemplified the New Deal focus on social services.

The best known achievement of the Second New Deal is the passage of the Social Security Act of 1935, which created the modern Social Security program.

Support for organized labor was another major feature of the Second New Deal. The government supported unionization and collective bargaining with the 1935 **National Labor Relations Act**, popularly known as the **Wagner Act**, which provided a framework for collective bargaining. The Wagner Act granted workers the right to join unions and engage in bargaining, and forbid employers from interfering with, or discriminating against, union rights.

Under the government's favorable treatment of labor, unions gained membership, power, and political influence, often lending their support to the Democratic Party — an alliance that remains in place today. Strikes were a common occurrence throughout the 1930s, and workers increasingly won concessions. In 1935, the Committee for Industrial Organization formed within the American Federation of Labor (AFL), eventually becoming the independent **Congress of Industrial Organizations** (CIO) in 1938. In less than two years, the CIO claimed more than four million members. The AFL and CIO were the nation's most dominant and successful unions throughout the late 1930s and 1940s, and in 1955 merged to form the AFL-CIO.

The New Deal Changes Party Alignments

FDR's landslide victory in the 1936 election confirmed his and his party's success in becoming the representatives of the downtrodden and disadvantaged. Farmers appreciated FDR's consistent efforts to forge an effective agricultural plan. Urban voters and organized labor, a great source of funding for FDR's 1936 campaign, valued his support of union rights and his efforts to cope with rampant unemployment. Many women recognized that FDR's programs attacked the concept of inequality and appreciated that he had appointed the first female cabinet member, Frances Perkins, as Secretary of Labor. Black Americans, as the group most devastated by unemployment, had benefited extensively from New Deal measures. Black support gradually shifted toward FDR and the Democratic Party away from Republican Party, which had consistently won the black vote since the late 1800s (remember that Lincoln and those in Congress favoring emancipation had been Republican).

The election of 1936 saw the rise of a new Democratic coalition, including farmers, urban workers, women, and blacks. This coalition helped FDR win the 1936 election by a landslide.

FDR's presidency and the New Deal thus brought about a realignment of the Democratic and Republican parties. As Democrats won the support of blacks, urban workers, and farmers, they lost the support of the white South, a traditional Democratic stronghold. The Republican Party, meanwhile, lost its long-held black vote.

Legislation and Agencies of the Second New Deal

Resettlement Administration	relocated and otherwise assisted the rural poor
Works Progress Administration (WPA)	employed workers of all fields, from industry to art (the PWA became a subdivision of the WPA)
National Labor Relations Act (Wagner Act)	guaranteed labor's right to organize in unions and collectively bargain
Social Security Act	created social security, or benefits for the elderly and the disabled
Revenue Act	raised personal income taxes for those in the highest tax bracket

New Deal Fades

The stage seemed set for FDR's continued success in pushing through the New Deal, but he faced a host of political challenges that hindered his efforts. The first element in the downturn was his involvement in the **Court Packing scheme**. Early in 1937, Roosevelt proposed a court-reform bill allowing the President to appoint an additional Supreme Court Justice for each current justice over the age of seventy. FDR claimed that the bill addressed concerns about the justices' workload, but it was clear that the proposal was meant to dilute the power of the conservative justices of the Supreme Court who had been hostile to New Deal legislation (they had ruled that the AAA and NRA were unconstitutional, among other decisions). The Senate vetoed the scheme in July 1937. Several justices retired shortly after or announced their intention to do so, and the Supreme Court presented less resistance during the final years of the Second New Deal than it had during earlier years, but the Court Packing scheme was a blemish on Roosevelt's record.

A more direct factor in the decline of the Second New Deal was the inability of FDR's programs to revive the economy. In August of 1937, the nation plunged into the 1937 recession, also known as the "Roosevelt Depression." By early 1938 unemployment had again risen above 20 percent.

The final obstacle to the extension of the Second New Deal came from within Congress, where critics of FDR were growing in power. A conservative coalition legislated cuts in relief programs and blocked further legislation proposed by New Deal supporters. As a result, FDR proposed few new reform measures during his second term in office. That he proposed no new domestic programs in his January 1939 State of the Union address signaled the end of the New Deal.

The New Deal had effectively ended by 1939, owing, in part, to the embarrassing Court Packing scheme, the 1937 recession, and growing congressional opposition.

Popular Culture and Literature During the Depression

The 1930s saw the marked growth of mass culture as citizens sought diversion from their troubles. Most popular culture centered on escapist themes and/or humor. In film, comedies were the most highly attended of all genres. The Marx Brothers became huge stars, often appearing in farcical productions depicting get-rich-quick schemes. Radio shows also became immensely popular during this period, so much so that the

1930s is often called the Golden Age of Radio. Magazines similarly provided popular diversion. *Life* magazine began publication during the 1930s, filling its pages with pictures of spectacular scenes and glorified personalities.

Literary work of the 1930s focused on the rejection of the notion of progress and a desire to return to an earlier age of purity and simplicity. **John Steinbeck**'s 1939 novel, *The Grapes of Wrath*, glorified a simple, rural way of life. Jack Conroy's *The Disinherited*, a 1933 chronicle of an average industrial worker's life in the Depression Era, conveyed disillusionment and cynicism. William Faulkner also emerged as an important American writer, examining Southern life in novels such as *A Light in August*, published in 1932, and *Absalom! Absalom!,* published in 1936.

Disillusioned with capitalism, many intellectuals and writers, including Langston Hughes, John Dos Passos, and **Ernest Hemingway,** formed allegiances, direct and indirect, to the Communist Party. Along with other intellectuals, these writers joined the **Popular Front**, a political group active in aiding the leftist forces in the Spanish Civil War against fascist powers. Hemingway's 1940 novel, *For Whom the Bell Tolls*, portrays the life of an American soldier fighting in the Spanish Civil War against a fascist dictatorship.

The Great Depression in an International Context

It is important to note that the Great Depression was a worldwide phenomenon. Though struggling Americans mostly focused on domestic matters during this period, the U.S. did not exist in a vacuum and faced an array of international challenges.

By the early 1930s, nearly every nation of the world had sunk into depression. One of the most significant political responses in Europe was the rise of fascism. Fascism emerged most notably in Italy and Germany, under the leadership of **Benito Mussolini** and **Adolf Hitler**, respectively. Spain endured a civil war from 1936 to 1939, in which fascist forces under **Francisco Franco** defeated the leftist republicans, ushering in thirty-six years of fascist rule.

One international response to the Great Depression was the rise of fascism in Germany under Hitler, Italy under Mussolini, and Spain under Franco.

U.S. International Relations in a Depression Era

During the 1930s, FDR pursued a primarily isolationist course, concentrating on domestic programs. In 1933 he announced the **"Good Neighbor"** policy toward Latin America, in which he stated that no nation, including the U.S., had a right to interfere in the affairs of any other nation.

World War II

Trends and Themes of the Era

- The strict terms of the Treaty of Versailles, which ended World War I, and the depression of the 1930s created the terms under which fascism and extreme nationalism arose in Germany and Italy. The expansionist designs of these fascist regimes started World War II.

- During the years before the war began and in its first two years, the U.S. maintained its isolationist policies. As the war continued, though, American sympathies increasingly moved toward the Allies. American isolationism shifted first to indirect involvement and then to full involvement after Japan bombed Pearl Harbor on December 7, 1941.

- The war effort brought the American economy out of the Great Depression. Socially, blacks and women played large roles in the war effort.

- As the war neared its end, relations between the United States and the USSR became increasingly hostile. The discussions between the Allies about how to divide and rebuild Europe after Germany fell were also an occasion for the U.S. and the USSR to jockey for power. The endgame of World War II was in many ways the beginning of the Cold War.

- When the U.S. dropped atomic bombs on the Japanese cities of Hiroshima and Nagasaki, it changed the nature of war. A country now had the capacity to destroy vast regions with a single bomb. The dropping of the bomb presaged the arms race between the U.S. and the USSR that was such a dominating aspect of the Cold War.

The Road to War in Europe

Many people of the 1920s and 1930s referred to World War I as the "war to end all wars." But the vindictive terms of the Versailles Treaty that ended World War I, in concert with the international depression of the 1930s, actually created the circumstances that led to World War II. In Germany, the harshly punitive Treaty of Versailles provoked intense bitterness and resentment. These feelings of anger and despair paved the way for the charismatic demagogue **Adolph Hitler** to take power in Germany and install a fascist regime in 1933. Eleven years earlier, a fascist regime had risen to power in Italy under **Benito Mussolini**. These two fascist governments combined their extreme nationalist rhetoric with an aggressive desire to expand.

In October 1935, Italian forces invaded Ethiopia, gaining control of the African nation by May 1936. Also in 1935, Hitler announced plans for German troops to reoccupy the Rhineland, which had been demilitarized by the Treaty of Versailles. Troops marched into the Rhineland unopposed in March 1936. Germany and Italy formed an alliance, the Rome-Berlin Axis, in October 1936. In March 1938, Austria joined this alliance when Hitler announced the *Anschluss*, a union between Germany and Austria, and German forces marched into Vienna. When Hitler declared his intention to take the Czech Sudetenland by force if necessary, British and French leaders acceded to his demands, signing the **Munich Pact** in September 1938, which granted the Sudetenland to Germany in an attempt to appease Hitler and avoid war.

During the 1930s, Britain and France responded to fascist aggression largely with inaction, hoping that Germany would cease its expansionary actions on its own. The two powers attempted to appease Hitler with the September 1938 Munich Pact.

Germany, however, did not cease its expansionary actions: German troops invaded Czechoslovakia in March 1939 and Poland in September 1939. Two days after the invasion of Poland, Britain and France declared war on Germany, honoring their treaty with Poland.

The United States and the War

In the mid-1930s, mired in the Depression, the U.S. focused on its own problems. Isolationism and antiwar sentiments ran high. A series of **Neutrality Acts**, passed between 1935 and 1937, reflected these isolationist currents. The acts made arms sales to warring countries illegal and forbade American citizens to travel aboard the ships of belligerent nations. President **Franklin Delano Roosevelt** supported the neutrality acts only half-heartedly but found it impossible to fight the will of the majority and urge U.S. involvement in international affairs. FDR did succeed in helping to defeat the 1938 proposal for a constitutional amendment, the Ludlow Amendment, which would have required a national referendum on any declaration of war not sparked by a direct attack.

American isolationism before World War II led to the passage of a series of Neutrality Acts between 1935 and 1937, and to the proposal for a constitutional amendment requiring a national referendum on any declaration of war not provoked by direct attack.

In this atmosphere of isolationism, American response to the rise of fascist states in Germany and Italy was limited and weak. During most of the 1930s, few Americans saw Adolph Hitler and Benito Mussolini as dangerous. FDR urged negotiations with Hitler, but never openly advocated military action before the late 1930s. In 1937, he suggested a plan to "quarantine" the aggressor nations in Europe, but when this plan received little public support, he backed down.

The only sign of wavering in America's isolationism during the early and mid-1930s was its involvement in China. In 1931, Japan invaded the Chinese province of Manchuria and in 1937 began launching attacks on the remainder of China as part of its aim to build an Asian empire. Alarmed that Japan's aggressive expansionism might threaten U.S. holdings in the Pacific, if not the U.S. itself, the U.S. refused to recognize the Japanese government in Manchuria. In 1937, the U.S. extended loans to China and urged a boycott of Japanese silk.

Waning Isolationism

American public opinion began to turn against the fascist powers during the late 1930s, mostly in response to the publicized brutality of Hitler's Nazis toward German Jews and other groups. Nonetheless, many Americans continued to push for neutrality and for immigration restriction, in part because roughly 60,000 Jewish refugees fled to the U.S. between 1933 and 1938.

In early 1939, FDR asked Congress to appropriate funds for a military buildup and an increased production of military material. In September 1939, FDR succeeded in pushing Congress to revise the **Neutrality Acts** to allow warring nations to purchase arms from the U.S. as long as they paid in cash and carried the arms away on their own ships. This **cash-and-carry** provision appealed to a nation that was increasingly committed to aiding the **Allied** war effort but did not want to get directly involved in the war.

Opposition to war continued to fade as Hitler's troops invaded and conquered Denmark and Norway in April 1940, Belgium and the Netherlands in May, and France in June, followed by the **Battle of Britain** throughout the summer and fall, in which German planes bombed British cities.

Early support for the Allies could be seen in the cash-and-carry policy, which allowed warring nations to purchase American arms only if they paid in cash and carried the arms away on their own ships.

In this atmosphere of growing alarm, FDR decided to run for an unprecedented third term in office. (**George Washington** had established the convention that no president serve more than two terms in office, which every president until FDR had followed.) During his 1940 campaign, Roosevelt appointed a Council of National Defense to oversee defense production, appointed Republican Henry Stimson secretary of war, and approved a peacetime draft by signing the **Selective Service and Training Act**. Although he approved the draft, FDR pledged never to "send an American boy to fight in a European war." Isolationists opposed to FDR's reelection sponsored the **Committee to Defend America First**, urging neutrality and claiming that the U.S. could stand alone regardless of Hitler's advances in Europe. FDR won reelection in spite of the committee's efforts.

End to Isolationism and Entry into War

After winning reelection, FDR felt confident in stepping up American aid to the Allies. He pushed for passage of the **Lend-Lease Act** in March 1941, which allowed the president to lend or lease supplies to any nation deemed "vital to the defense of the United States," such as Britain. FDR extended lend-lease aid to the Soviet Union after Germany invaded in November 1941. The U.S. also helped the Allies by tracking German submarines and warning the British of their location, and by convoying British ships carrying lend-lease supplies—that is, surrounding British ships with U.S. Navy vessels ordered to attack any menacing vessel.

In August 1941, FDR met with British Prime Minister **Winston Churchill** on a British ship off Newfoundland. The two discussed military strategy and issued the **Atlantic Charter**, which outlined their ideal postwar world: among other provisions, it called for disarmament and freedom of the seas. In response to a German attack against a U.S. destroyer, Roosevelt issued the **shoot-on-sight order** in September 1941, which authorized American naval patrols to fire on all Axis ships (see below) found between the U.S. and Iceland. After American destroyers were twice attacked in October, Congress authorized the arming of merchant ships.

The final provocation for American entry into the war came from Japan, which had joined the Rome-Berlin-Tokyo **Axis** in September 1940 by signing the **Tripartite Pact**. Japan's desires to build an East Asian empire had alarmed the U.S. since Japan's invasion of China in 1931. In September 1940, Japanese forces continued their invasion into French Indochina. The U.S. responded to this invasion as it had to other invasions in the past: it added items to a lengthy list of embargoed Japanese goods, and eventually froze all trade with Japan. In 1941, U.S. intelligence became aware of plans for a Japanese attack and sent out warnings to commanders of U.S. bases in the Pacific, but most American officials did not believe that the threat was immediate. These officials were proved wrong on December 7, 1941, when, in an attempt to destroy American sea power in the Pacific, Japanese planes bombed the U.S. base at **Pearl Harbor**. The Japanese destroyed nearly 200 aircraft, eight battleships, three cruisers, and three destroyers. Almost 2,400 Americans died. On December 8, the Senate voted unanimously in favor of FDR's request for a declaration of war on Japan. The House passed the declaration over only one dissenting vote. On December 11, Germany and Italy joined Japan in war against the U.S.

The Japanese attacked Pearl Harbor on December 7, 1941, and the U.S. declared war against Japan on December 8. On December 11, Germany and Italy declared war on the U.S., completing the entry of the U.S. into World War II.

On January 1, 1942, representatives of 26 nations signed the **Declaration of the United Nations**, pledging support for the Atlantic Charter and vowing not to make separate peace agreements with the Axis powers.

The War at Home

Although the U.S. had begun preparing for war during the summer of 1940, war production comprised only 15 percent of the nation's industrial output in 1941, and U.S. armed forces were seriously understaffed and undersupplied. During the next four years, war production on the home front churned into high gear.

Expanding the Military

In 1942, FDR created the **Joint Chiefs of Staff** to oversee America's rapidly expanding military. By the end of the war, more than 15 million men had served in the U.S. armed forces. About 350,000 women served as well, most in the Women's Army Corps (WAC) and Women Accepted for Voluntary Emergency Service in the navy (WAVES). The air force, a minor corps at the outset of the war, grew substantially and gained a measure of autonomy during the war. The Joint Chiefs also established the **Office of Strategic Services** (OSS) to assess the enemy's assets and liabilities, conduct espionage, and gather information to be used in strategic planning.

Boosting Production

The U.S. mobilized industry to assist in the war effort. The **War Production Board**, created in 1942, oversaw the production of thousands of planes, tanks, and artillery pieces required for the war. The War Production Board allocated scarce resources and shifted production from civilian to military items by offering incentives for firms to produce military goods. The last new civilian car was produced in the U.S. in 1942, after which plants were redesigned to produce tanks, planes, weapons, and munitions. By the end of the war, the U.S. had built about 300,000 aircraft, 85,000 tanks, 375,000 artillery pieces, 2.5 million machine guns, and 90,000 sea ships—more war material than the four Axis powers, combined, had produced. This feat was accomplished through substantial investment of capital and the development of new, highly efficient manufacturing techniques.

During World War II, American industry shifted from producing civilian goods to military goods under the supervision of the War Production Board. Due to this shift in production, heavy investment, and new, efficient techniques, the U.S. produced more war material than all of the Axis powers combined.

War Economy

The federal budget multiplied tenfold between 1940 and 1945. U.S. expenditures during World War II totaled nearly twice the amount spent by the U.S. government in its previous 150 years of existence. Spending on war production precipitated a shift in American income distribution, with the share of national income allocated to the richest Americans decreasing and that allocated to the middle class doubling. The **Revenue Act of 1942**, passed to help pay for the war, increased taxes for the wealthiest Americans.

War spending, accompanied by the draft, ended the high rates of unemployment which had not rebounded from from the Great Depression. Organized labor grew strong and wealthy during World War II, with union membership growing by about sixty percent. Although most unions abided by a no-strike policy, unions secured new benefits (such as fewer hours and better health plans) for their members, partially as a concession from the **National War Labor Board**, which limited wage increases to avoid inflation. Union power suffered a setback when a series of coal miners' strikes provoked Congress to pass the **Smith-Connolly War Labor Disputes Act** in June 1943, which limited the right to strike in key industries and allowed the president to take control of any firm beset by strikes.

The Office of Price Administration waged a battle against inflation and the overuse of resources. The OPA oversaw a rationing program designed to curb new purchases and conserve materials, in particular gas, sugar, coffee, butter, and meat. The American people largely complied with these efforts by forsaking many goods—for example, implementing "meatless Tuesdays"—and by planting "victory gardens" and conducting collection drives to gather materials for recycling. Another tactic aimed at financing the war was the sale of war bonds.

The Office of Price Administration oversaw a rationing program with which most Americans cooperated, giving up many goods and otherwise doing their part to support the war effort.

Controlling Information and Advertising the War

FDR relied on the **Office of Censorship** and the **Office of War Information** to regulate the communications of American citizens. The former, created shortly after the U.S. entry into the war, examined all letters sent overseas and worked with media firms to control information broadcast to the people. The latter, formed in June 1942, employed artists, writers, and advertisers to shape public opinion by explaining the reasons for U.S. entry in the war and by portraying the enemy as barbaric and cruel.

One important aspect of war advertising was the effort to encourage women to actively participate in the war effort. During World War II, even more so than in World War I, women were strongly encouraged to enter the workforce to replace men at war and aid in the production of war materials. The image of **Rosie the Riveter**, a muscle-bound woman with a rivet gun, was pervasive and effective. Increasing numbers of women entered the workforce to perform all sorts of jobs. The roles women played in the armed forces helped create new respect for the working woman. Women, however, were paid far less than working men, and traditional notions of gender roles still prevailed throughout the war.

> *During World War II, women were encouraged to enter the workforce, and women aiding in the war effort were glorified. Although traditional notions about gender roles still remained intact, female participation in the war was an important step toward greater respect for women in the U.S.*

Japanese Internment

During World War II, the U.S. government rounded up more than 110,000 Japanese immigrants and U.S.-born Japanese-Americans and sent them to relocation centers guarded by military police. Military leaders, West Coast farmers, and others rationalized this policy as necessary to prevent acts of sabotage and espionage in support of Japan. In 1942, FDR authorized this relocation in Executive Order 9066, and in 1944 the Supreme Court upheld the constitutionality of the order in *Korematsu v. U.S.* In 1988, Congress voted to pay reparations of $20,000 to every internee still living.

Reelection and Succession

FDR ran for reelection once again in 1944, in the midst of World War II, with moderate Democrat **Harry S. Truman** as his running mate. FDR won an unprecedented fourth term, though by his narrowest margin ever. Shortly after Roosevelt's fourth term began, he died of a cerebral hemorrhage in April 1945, leaving Truman to oversee the war effort.

Winning the War

While the home front buzzed busily in support of the war effort, U.S. armed forces faced a two-front battle, in Europe and the Pacific.

Drive to Victory in Europe

The Allies and the United States agreed to focus on victory in Europe before turning to Japan. European involvement for U.S. troops began in 1942 with Operation Torch, a North African campaign in which more than 100,000 Allied troops under American general **Dwight D. Eisenhower** forced a Vichy (or German-controlled) France surrender in Tunisia. In the summer of 1943, Allied troops conquered Sicily and forced Mussolini's overthrow. In 1944, Soviet troops, who had succeeded in pushing the Nazis out of the Soviet Union, advanced toward Germany and liberated Poland, Romania, Bulgaria, and Yugoslavia from German rule.

In 1944, the U.S. launched a front against the Germans in France in the form of **Operation Overlord**. This operation centered on the June 6, 1944 "D-Day" invasion of Normandy, in which American, British, and Canadian forces under Eisenhower (now the supreme allied commander in Europe) undertook a massive land, sea, and air assault. Despite heavy resistance and many casualties, the Allies pressed on. By the end of the summer they had liberated Belgium, Luxembourg, and most of France.

In December 1944, Hitler sent the last of his reserves to attack the oncoming Allied troops in Belgium and Luxembourg. The reserves penetrated the Allies' line but were forced back in late December and early January. The **Battle of the Bulge** ended with Allied victory in January 1945, despite heavy Allied losses—55,000 Allied troops were killed and another 18,000 taken prisoner.

By the end of April, Berlin was encircled by American, British, and Soviet troops. Germany surrendered unconditionally on May 8, 1945. American citizens celebrated the Allied victory in Europe but mourned the loss of more than six million Jews and several million others who had died in the concentration camps discovered by Allied forces invading Germany. The Nazi-driven persecution and extermination of European Jews, which lasted from 1933 until the end of the war in 1945, is called the **Holocaust**.

War in the Pacific

In 1942, American and Japanese forces clashed at various strategic locations, including the Philippines, the Coral Sea (northeast of Australia), and the Solomon Islands. Late in 1943, Americans took a two-pronged offensive, as the army under General **Douglas MacArthur** "leapfrogged" from island to island on a path north from Australia, and the navy island-hopped toward Japan from the Central Pacific. Securing U.S. control of these Japanese islands put Tokyo, Japan's capital city, within range for U.S. bombers. In the summer of 1944, U.S. forces destroyed the imperial fleet, wiping out Japan's naval power. With their armed forces in shambles and Japanese cities being bombed daily, Japanese leaders still refused to surrender.

The Atomic Bombs

The final push to victory in Japan began in 1945, when American troops won long, bloody battles on the islands of Iwo Jima and Okinawa from February to June, losing about 65,000 men between the two battles. Despite these American victories and the daily bombing of Tokyo, Japanese officials refused to consider surrender.

In the U.S., a secret project to develop an atomic bomb had been in progress since 1941. In July 1945, the **Manhattan Project** and its director, **J. Robert Oppenheimer,** successfully detonated an atomic bomb in the desert in New Mexico. This was the first successful detonation of an atomic bomb in history.

While meeting with Soviet Premier **Joseph Stalin** and British Prime Minister **Winston Churchill** at the **Potsdam Conference**, Truman issued a secret order to drop an atomic bomb if Japan did not surrender by August 3. In late July 1945, Truman warned Japan to surrender immediately or face "prompt and utter destruction." Japan rejected this threat, and on August 6, 1945, an American B-29 bomber, the *Enola Gay*, dropped an atomic bomb on the Japanese city of **Hiroshima**, killing more than 70,000 and injuring another 70,000, many fatally. Three days later, a bomb was dropped on **Nagasaki**, killing 40,000 and injuring 60,000. On August 14, 1945, Japan surrendered.

Atomic bombs were dropped on Hiroshima and Nagasaki on August 6 and August 9, 1945, killing more than 110,000 in the blasts and injuring many more who died soon thereafter. This destruction prompted Japan to surrender on August 14, ending World War II.

Although Truman claimed the use of the atomic bombs was necessary to end the war quickly with minimal loss of American life, his motives have been questioned. Some believe racism toward the Japanese inspired the bombs' use, and some claim that Truman could have forced Japan's surrender simply by demonstrating the bombs' effect on an abandoned island. Others argue that the bombs were used mainly to intimidate Joseph Stalin and to prevent the Soviet Union, which declared war on Japan on August 8, 1945, from claiming a share in victory over Japan. Truman would thereby gain a diplomatic edge over the communist Soviets.

Negotiating a Postwar World Order

Even while the war was proceeding, the Allies met to settle the details of the postwar world order. Their diplomatic agreements, and disagreements, reached far beyond the war's end.

The Tehran Conference

FDR and Churchill arrived at Tehran, Iran to meet Stalin at the **Tehran Conference** in 1943. At this first meeting of the Big Three, the Allies planned the 1944 assault on France and agreed to divide Germany into zones of occupation after the war. They also agreed to establish a new international peacekeeping organization, the **United Nations**.

The Yalta Conference

In February 1945, the Big Three met again in the Soviet city of Yalta. Stalin, whose troops had overrun Eastern Europe, had the most bargaining power at the **Yalta Conference**, leaving the other Allies with much to request but little leverage with which to force Stalin's hand. Stalin did agree to declare war against Japan soon after Germany surrendered and approved plans for a United Nations conference in San Francisco in April 1945. Discussion of reparations, large payments that Stalin demanded from Germany which Roosevelt and Churchill opposed, was postponed.

The Potsdam Conference

After FDR's death and the end of the war in Europe, Harry Truman, new British Prime Minister Clement Atlee, and Stalin met at the **Potsdam Conference** in Germany from July 17 to August 2, 1945. Little was accomplished diplomatically, as relations between the Americans and Soviets grew increasingly chilly, but the three leaders did agree to demilitarize Germany and agreed upon the concept of war crimes trials. The Potsdam Agreement divided Germany into four zones, administrated by the Soviet Union, France, Britain, and the U.S., and established joint administration of Berlin, which lay well within the Soviet zone. This arrangement proved to be a recipe for conflict in later years.

War Crime Trials at Nuremberg

The **Nuremberg Trials** of Nazi war criminals began in Nuremberg, Germany, in 1945. Prosecutors charged twenty-four Germans with an assortment of crimes, including waging aggressive war, extermination of ethnic and religious groups, and murder and mistreatment of prisoners and inhabitants of occupied territories. The tribunal heard testimony and saw documentation chronicling the "crimes against humanity" perpetrated by the Nazis against European Jews and others. The Nuremberg Tribunal concluded that though not explicitly stated in international law, the instigation of aggressive war was a crime and that the defendants' claim that they were "just following orders" was unsound because the opportunity for moral choice always existed. Twelve defendants were sentenced to death and seven others to prison sentences of varying length. After this first trial, twelve more trials were held, with about 185 Germans indicted. Only thirty-five were acquitted. The rest were sentenced to death or prison.

World War II

The Postwar Settlement in Asia

After Japan surrendered on September 2, 1945, American forces under General **Douglas MacArthur** occupied the country. MacArthur rigidly suppressed Japanese nationalism, held war crimes trials, and imposed democratic norms on the Japanese government. Under MacArthur's supervision, which lasted until the end of occupation in 1952, Japan became an economically powerful democracy.

Another element of the postwar settlement in Asia was the division of Korea at the thirty-eighth parallel, an agreement reached between the Soviet Union and the U.S. shortly before the end of the war as part of the Japanese surrender. The Soviets occupied North Korea and the U.S. occupied South Korea, each supporting governments antagonistic toward each other. This antagonism would erupt in the Korean War in 1950.

The United Nations

In April 1945, the **United Nations** Conference on International Organization met in San Francisco. Delegates from fifty countries outlined their aims for global peace and collective security. In their charter, they created a General Assembly to make policy and a Security Council to settle disputes. In October 1945, the UN officially came into being, with fifty-one founding members.

The 1950s: Cold War, Civil Rights, and Social Trends

Chapter Contents

Trends and Themes of the Era

- The U.S. and the USSR emerged from World War II as the two sole superpowers in the world. The two quickly became enemies and rivals, battling in politics, technology, and military power. The arms race, in which each nation developed an arsenal of nuclear weapons that could destroy the other numerous times over, was a defining fact and metaphor of the conflict. Neither side wanted to face destruction, however, which is what made the Cold War cold: though crisis after crisis loomed, the two sides avoided direct conflict. Policies of containing communism influenced virtually all U.S. foreign policy decisions.

- Fear of communist subversion of the U.S. government led to intense domestic anticommunist fervor. Communists and suspected communists were closely watched, vilified, blacklisted, and in one case tried and executed. Domestic anticommunism reached its peak in the mid-1950s with the rise of Senator Joseph McCarthy, and waned after he lost influence and power. But fear of communism remained a part of American culture for decades to follow.

- Bolstered by the landmark 1954 Supreme Court decision in *Brown v. Board of Education*, the civil rights movement began to come into its own. Following an ethic of nonviolence, blacks in the South began to win their first battles for equality.

- 1950s postwar prosperity helped propel the creation of suburbs and the popularization of the automobile, which in turn caused the decline of cities as wealthy whites left urban areas for suburban ones. Prosperity also led to a baby boom and the promotion of conservative values. In the late 1950s, artists began to rebel against this conservativism.

The Cold War Begins

After the close of World War II, a new and very different conflict rose to the forefront of American national attention: the Cold War. The Cold War pitted the communist Soviet Union against the capitalist U.S. and its Western Allies. While there was little actual violence, both sides considered the conflict to be severe and threatening. President **Harry S. Truman**, who had succeeded Franklin Roosevelt as president after the latter's death in April 1945, thus found himself in an increasingly difficult and complex battle against communism. **Dwight D. Eisenhower**, who succeeded Truman as president in 1952, inherited this battle.

Origins of the Cold War and the Iron Curtain

After Germany's defeat in World War II, the leaders of the Allied countries met at a series of conferences to shape the postwar world. Crucial among these was the Potsdam Conference in 1945, at which the Allies divided Germany into four zones, controlled by France, Britain, the U.S., and the USSR. Berlin, deep in the Soviet zone, was also divided into four zones. Also at Potsdam, Truman informed **Joseph Stalin** that U.S. scientists had successfully detonated an atomic bomb, an achievement presaging the nuclear arms race that developed between the two countries.

In the late 1940s, the U.S. and USSR emerged as supreme among the nations of the world. The former wartime allies soon became bitter enemies. Both superpowers rushed to establish **spheres of influence** in Europe. Stalin wished to establish a buffer region of pro-Soviet states in Eastern Europe in order to avoid the recurrence of invasions such as those undertaken by Germany during the war. The Red Army established **puppet governments** in Bulgaria, Hungary, and Romania, adding to the ranks of independently established pro-Soviet governments in Albania and Yugoslavia. In 1945, Stalin disregarded the Yalta Declaration of Liberated Europe and disallowed free elections in Poland, which had served as a gateway to the Soviet Union for German invaders. In early March 1946, the former British prime minister **Winston Churchill** gave a speech at Westminster College in Missouri, coining the phrase the **"iron curtain"** to describe the USSR's division of Eastern Europe from the West.

The term "iron curtain" was coined by Winston Churchill to describe the division of Europe imposed by the USSR.

The United States and the Cold War

A combination of political, economic, and moral considerations led the U.S. government to oppose Soviet dominance of Eastern Europe. President Truman took a strong stance against the Soviet territorial advances, advocating a policy of **containment**. Under this policy, the U.S. would not attempt change the post–World War II situation in Europe, but it would work to prevent further Soviet expansion through peaceful or military means.

Atomic Arms Race

Nuclear weapons played a central role in the possibility of military engagement between the U.S. and the USSR. In 1946, Truman proposed a plan to the United Nations to require the USSR to cease construction on any atomic weaponry, saying that only then would the U.S. destroy its growing arsenal. The Soviets rejected this plan and both sides rushed to develop weapons of mass destruction. In 1946, the federal government established the **Atomic Energy Commission** to oversee the development of nuclear energy and arms. The battle for nuclear dominance was characteristic of the Cold War, in which few battles were ever waged face to face.

In September 1949, the USSR detonated its first atomic bomb. This development, combined with the establishment of a communist regime in China (see page 211), inspired a new and fiercer anticommunism in the U.S. government, expressed in its decision to more than triple the defense budget and to mount a furious campaign to develop a hydrogen bomb. The drive for the hydrogen bomb succeeded in the November 1952 detonation of an H-bomb in the Marshall Islands. But the American advantage was short-lived. In July 1953, the Russians detonated their own H-bomb.

The Truman Doctrine and the Marshall Plan

Early in 1947, allies in Western Europe asked the U.S. to help fund the effort to prevent the rise of communist governments in Greece and Turkey. The economies and governments of Western Europe were nearing collapse. In March 1947, Truman asked a joint session of Congress to authorize military assistance to Turkey and Greece, depicting

The 1950s

the issue as one of liberty versus oppression, and proclaimed that the U.S. would support people anywhere in the world facing "attempted subjugation by armed minorities or by outside pressures." This proclamation, known as the **Truman Doctrine**, committed the U.S. to a role as global policeman.

The financial counterpart to the Truman Doctrine was the **Marshall Plan**, under which the U.S. pledged a great deal of financial assistance to Europe, specifically to stimulate European postwar recovery, and to provide relief for the hungry, homeless, and desperate. Truman and his secretary of state George C. Marshall hoped this plan would eliminate the devastation and political instability that communists had exploited in the past in order to set up communist puppet governments. The Marshall Plan was intended to strengthen European states against possible communist threats. As expected, the USSR rejected such aid because of its accompanying conditions of U.S. influence and control. By 1952, Congress had appropriated some $17 billion for Marshall Plan aid. In that time, the Western European economy largely recovered.

The Truman Doctrine proclaimed that America would aid people anywhere in the world subjected to "attempted subjugation by armed minorities or by outside pressures." The Marshall Plan was the financial counterpart to this doctrine, providing for economic aid to rebuild an unstable Europe.

The Berlin Blockade

France, Britain, and the United States gradually united their three zones of occupation within Germany and announced their intention to create a West German Republic in 1948. In opposition to such a republic—which would have included West Berlin, far within the Soviet zone—Stalin established the **Berlin Blockade** in June 1948, cutting off all rail and highway access to Berlin from the west. Choosing not to abandon Berlin, nor to use military force, Truman ordered an airlift, called "Operation Vittles," to supply West Berlin. The airlift continued until May 1949, when the USSR lifted the blockade. Immediately after the demise of the blockade, Western forces pulled out of Germany and approved the creation of the Federal Republic of Germany, or West Germany. The USSR responded by creating the German Democratic Republic, or East Germany.

NATO and the Warsaw Pact

The heightened fear of conflict produced by the Berlin Blockade helped convince Western Europe of the need for a security alliance. In April 1949, ten Western European nations, Canada, and the U.S. established the **North Atlantic Treaty Organization** (NATO), and declared that an attack against any member of the alliance would be seen as an attack against all—a policy known as collective security. In July, the U.S. officially joined NATO, and Congress authorized $1.3 billion for military aid to NATO countries. The USSR responded by establishing a rival alliance, the **Warsaw Pact**, in 1955.

The Korean War: Containment in Asia

In Asia, as in Europe, Truman tried to contain the spread of communism. The U.S. denied the USSR any hand in the postwar reconstruction of Japan and occupied Japan until 1952, at which point the U.S. officially exited but left troops behind on American military bases. In China, the U.S. spent almost $3 billion in a failed effort to support Chinese nationalists under Chiang Kai-shek against **Mao Zedong**'s communists. In 1949, the communists achieved victory and established the People's Republic of China (PRC). The nationalists fled to Taiwan, where they established their own government to rival the PRC. Asia, much like Germany, became the site of division between contending camps, communist and noncommunist.

The Cold War conflict in Asia erupted into outright war in June 1950, when troops from Soviet-supported North Korea invaded South Korea. Without asking for a declaration of war, Truman committed U.S. troops as part of a United Nations "police action." In actuality, the **Korean War** was carried out by predominantly American forces under the command of General **Douglas MacArthur**. By late September, MacArthur's troops had forced the North Koreans back past the thirty-eighth parallel, the dividing line between North and South Korea. Truman authorized an offensive drive across this divide and toward China, but MacArthur was repelled by Chinese forces in November. Fighting stabilized around the previous border, and in the spring of 1951 Truman sought to scale back the war effort and negotiate peace, despite MacArthur's proposals for bombing attacks north of the Yalu River in China. After a month of publicly denouncing the administration's policy of restraint, MacArthur was relieved from duty in April 1951. Limited fighting would continue until June 1953, when an armistice basically restored the prewar border between North and South. The U.S. had lost almost 55,000 lives.

Eisenhower and the Cold War

Even though the threat of direct confrontation seemed to be waning by the early 1950s, the Cold War was by no means near an end. Secretary of State John Foster Dulles committed the U.S. to mutual defense pacts with forty-three nations. World War II hero Eisenhower won the election of 1952. Convinced that a large nuclear arsenal would deter the Soviets from rash action, Eisenhower advocated cuts in the army and navy to provide funding for the construction of nuclear weapons and the planes that dropped them. This **"New Look"** emphasized massive retaliation rather than ground force involvement in countries threatened by Soviet influence. This form of retaliatory defense was articulated in the U.S. military doctrine **Mutual Assured Destruction** (MAD). Developed in the early 1960s, MAD promised that whoever launched a nuclear attack would be immediately counterattacked, resulting in total nuclear devastation on both sides.

The focus on massive retaliation, however, did not detract from interest in the extension of each superpower's spheres of influence. The focus of the Cold War now turned toward the Third World, where proxy wars were waged by local groups backed by the two powers. The U.S. **Central Intelligence Agency** (CIA), which grew rapidly throughout Eisenhower's time in office, spearheaded U.S. efforts in these proxy wars by providing covert assistance to those opposing Soviet-backed forces. In 1953, the CIA helped to restore the deposed Shah of Iran to power, securing an American ally along the Soviet border. Also in 1953, the CIA intervened in elections in the Philippines. In 1954, it backed a military coup in Guatemala. One marked example of the CIA's failure came in early 1959, when Cuba became a communist state led by Fidel Castro.

During the 1950s, the Cold War's focus turned to the Third World, where the U.S. and USSR often backed rival groups in civil conflicts. The CIA spearheaded U.S. activity, engaging in covert operations to aid U.S.-supported groups.

Threats to Stability: Vietnam and the Middle East

The CIA's most important activities in the 1950s occurred in Vietnam. Truman and later Eisenhower provided American aid to the French, who battled the communist nationalist Vietminh for control of the former French colony. In May 1954, the French surrendered. At a conference in Geneva in July, Vietnam was divided at the seventeenth parallel, pending possible reunification through free elections. Eisenhower, however, refused to sign the Geneva Peace Accords on account of his **"domino theory,"** which stated that should Vietnam fall to Soviet control—as would likely happen if elections reunified the country because the communist forces were dominant—all of Asia would soon follow. The CIA thus helped to install Ngo Dinh Diem as president of South Vietnam and helped him block the elections that would have reunified Vietnam. Diem's control was tenuous at best, however, and in 1960, the National Liberation Front of South Vietnam, backed by North Vietnam, formed in opposition to Diem. Eisenhower sent funds and advisers to aid Diem, committing the U.S. to involvement in a potentially volatile situation.

Perhaps the greatest crisis faced by the Eisenhower administration sprang up in the Middle East. In 1954, Gamal Abdel Nasser came to power in Egypt and nationalized the **Suez Canal**, which had previously been foreign-owned. Israel, Britain, and France subsequently attacked Egypt in October 1956. Eisenhower, enraged at his allies for acting without consulting him, condemned their actions and prepared for potential war. Finally, Britain, Israel, and France agreed to pull out of Egypt in November 1956. In January 1957, Eisenhower announced that the U.S. would increase its involvement in the Middle East to oppose Soviet aggression by sending military aid and troops if necessary. This **"Eisenhower Doctrine"** justified the deployment of 14,000 marines to Lebanon in July 1958 to promote stability.

The Eisenhower Doctrine, elucidated after the Suez Canal crisis, committed the U.S. to military involvement in the Middle East when necessary to counter communist advances.

The Space Race

The struggle for nuclear dominance begot a battle between the superpowers to exhibit technological prowess in all fields. In October 1957 the USSR launched a space satellite, *Sputnik*. The U.S. countered, launching *Explorer I* in January 1958. Still, American concern over technological competitiveness lingered, spurring the 1958 creation of the National Aeronautics and Space Administration (NASA).

Fighting Communism at Home

While Truman and Eisenhower both sought to contain communism in Europe and Asia, their administrations also presided over efforts to rid the U.S. itself of communist elements.

Investigating Loyalty

The American Communist Party had peaked in strength during World War II and had been linked to covert operations designed to aid the Soviet Union. Such espionage was known to have involved individuals within the federal government. In March 1947, Truman issued an executive order establishing the Federal Employee Loyalty Program, which became so powerful that it often abridged the rights of officials in its search for disloyalty. Employees who criticized American policy were subject to humiliating investigations. By 1956, this program had led to more than 2,500 dismissals and 12,000 resignations from official posts.

The 1950s

As Cold War fears grew, much of the nation became convinced that communists within the country were working on a large scale to subvert the American government. Thirty-nine states passed antisubversion laws and loyalty programs. Any criticism of the government was likely to meet with investigation and denouncement. In 1947, the **House Un-American Activities Committee** (HUAC) led a series of highly publicized hearings, in which witnesses were forced into confessions, or, if they refused to confess, faced restrictions of their rights. HUAC attacked a number of prominent screenwriters and directors, prompting Hollywood to establish an unofficial blacklist that prevented any questionable individuals from getting work. During the presidential campaign of 1948, Truman sought to demonstrate his stance against communism by prosecuting eleven leaders of the Communist Party under the 1940 **Smith Act**, which prohibited any conspiracy from overthrowing the government. Unions shrank from public action lest they be labeled communist. The Communist Party itself began to fade in strength, with membership falling to about 25,000. But some government officials nevertheless asserted that the communist threat was everywhere.

The Hiss and Rosenberg Cases

In 1948, Whittaker Chambers, a senior editor at *Time* magazine and a former Soviet spy, named **Alger Hiss** as an underground member of the Communist Party. Hiss, a graduate of Harvard Law School who had worked within the federal government for years, denied Chambers's claims in court. In January 1950, Hiss was convicted of perjury and sentenced to five years imprisonment, emboldening conservatives and raising questions about the past activities of many Democrats in government.

In February 1950, Klaus Fuchs, a scientist involved in the Manhattan Project, was arrested for passing information on nuclear weapons development to the Soviets during World War II. This arrest led to the implication of Harry Gold, David Greenglass, and most notably, **the Rosenbergs**, Ethel and Julius. The Rosenbergs claimed they were the victims of anti-Semitism and were targeted for their leftist beliefs. In March 1951 they were convicted and sentenced to death. They were executed in June 1953.

McCarthyism

Anticommunism reached its peak in the U.S. with the rise of **McCarthyism**. In 1950, Senator Joseph McCarthy claimed to have a list of 205 people known to be members of the Communist Party who were still working in the State Department. McCarthy continued to make such speeches, though he reduced the number of names on his list and modified the allegations to merely "bad risks." Although a Senate committee called these accusations a hoax, McCarthy continued his rhetoric. Republicans in the Senate soon came to support McCarthy, if only for the political benefits to be gained from attacks on liberals. McCarthy's appeal grew steadily throughout the nation, until the Democrats feared that to oppose him would mean certain humiliation and charges of disloyalty. In 1950, in the spirit of McCarthyism, Congress passed the McCarran Internal Security Act, which stated that organizations the attorney general deemed communist had to register with the Department of Justice and provide member lists and financial statements. The act also barred communists from working in defense plants, and allowed the government to deport any alien suspected of subversion.

The anticommunism of the late 1940s and early 1950s took its most radical form in McCarthyism. Joseph McCarthy led an anticommunist witch-hunt designed to root out subversive elements in American government and society.

In 1954, at the height of his powers, McCarthy accused the military of being a haven for spies. The army countered by accusing McCarthy of using his power to secure preferential treatment for a member of his staff who had been drafted. In televised congressional hearings on these matters, McCarthy behaved poorly—he appeared aggressive and bullying—and thereby turned public opinion against him. The Senate voted to censure McCarthy in December 1954, with support from Eisenhower. The fall of McCarthy lessened the fervor of anticommunism, though it did not wipe out fears of subversion.

Domestic Policies of Truman and Eisenhower

Inflation plagued America's postwar economy, as food prices rose over fifteen percent in 1946. At the same time, American workers were demanding higher pay and strikes were rampant across the country. The railroad system shut down completely in the spring of 1946. Truman intervened in the strikes and, in so doing, alienated many working-class interest groups. As a result, Democrats fared badly in the midterm election of 1946, and Republicans gained control of Congress for the first time since 1928.

Truman struggled to push his liberal initiatives through a Republican-controlled Congress. In his aims to extend FDR's New Deal, Truman did gain passage of the Employment Act of 1946, which committed the government to stimulating economic growth, but only through significant compromise: Congress stripped the bill of many of its more important elements, such as the stated goal of providing full employment. This opposition set the tone for many of Truman's efforts to create a social safety net for Americans. Congress blocked Truman's attempts to provide for public housing, the expansion of Social Security, and a higher minimum wage, among other elements derived from the New Deal.

> *Truman's domestic policy attempted to extend FDR's New Deal. After Republicans gained control of Congress in 1946, Truman's policies were largely rejected.*

The Election of 1948 and the Fair Deal

The Republican Congress passed tax cuts for the rich and kept the minimum wage down in attempts to dismantle the New Deal. Union activities were restricted, most prominently by the **Taft-Hartley Act** of 1947, which banned certain practices and allowed the president to call for an eighty-day cooling off period to delay strikes thought to pose risks to national safety. Truman vetoed the measure, and though his veto was overridden, his actions roused the support of organized labor, a group crucial to his election bid in 1948. In efforts to maintain the support of this and other groups central to FDR's New Deal coalition, Truman proposed many liberal reforms aimed at winning the labor, Catholic, Jewish, black, farm, and immigrant vote. He was moderately successful in this endeavor, and though many pundits assumed he would lose the election to Republican candidate Thomas Dewey, he pulled through a narrow victory.

Truman saw this victory as a mandate for liberalism and unveiled a new program, which he called the **Fair Deal**, in 1949. Congress now proved more cooperative and passed bills to increase the minimum wage, expand Social Security, and construct low-income housing. But as America entered a period of postwar prosperity and became increasingly interested in international affairs, the Fair Deal lost steam.

The Election of 1952 and Eisenhower

Truman decided not to run again for president in 1952, so the Democrats nominated Adlai Stevenson to run against Republican candidate **Dwight D. Eisenhower**. A moderate and a World War II hero, Eisenhower chose as his running mate **Richard Nixon**, a more conservative Republican and a fervent anticommunist. Eisenhower's choice captured the spirit of the ultra-conservative anticommunism of the period and helped push him to a decisive Republican victory in the election of 1952.

Eisenhower called his philosophy of government "**dynamic conservatism**." He set a moderate, corporate-oriented course for his administration, staffing his cabinet largely with business executives. He was determined to work with the Democratic Party rather than against it and at times opposed proposals made by more conservative members of his own party. Ike, as Eisenhower was known, advocated a strong effort by the government to stimulate the economy. Faced with depressions in 1953 and 1957, he went against the tendency of his party by increasing spending rather than trying to maintain a balanced budget. He cooperated with the Democratic Congress in expanding Social Security benefits and raising the minimum wage. In 1956, Eisenhower supported the Interstate Highway Act, the most expensive public works program in American history. His success in boosting prosperity and pleasing many different factions while keeping the U.S. out of war resulted in his landslide victory in the election of 1956.

Civil Rights Under Truman and Eisenhower

As the Cold War raged during the late 1940s and 1950s, great changes occurred in American society, especially concerning civil rights. The civil rights movement gathered strength and momentum during the postwar years.

Truman and Civil Rights

In efforts to preserve the support of southern whites, Truman at first avoided issues of civil rights for blacks. But he could not stay removed for long. In 1947, the Presidential Committee on Civil Rights, created a year earlier, produced a report, **To Secure These Rights**, calling for the elimination of segregation. In 1948, Truman endorsed the findings of the report and called for an end to racial discrimination in federal hiring practices. He also issued an executive order to end segregation in the military, an initiative that would be completed by Eisenhower. Although these moves cost Truman the support of many southern whites, the increased support of black voters made up for the political loss.

Eisenhower and the Civil Rights Acts

Eisenhower backed the Civil Rights Act of 1957 and the Civil Rights Act of 1960. The former created a permanent Civil Rights Commission, as well as a Civil Rights Division within the Justice Department aimed at combating efforts to deny blacks the vote. The latter granted the federal courts the authority to register black voters.

Brown v. Board of Education

The fight for civil rights took a major leap forward in May 1954, when the Supreme Court, under the leadership of liberal Chief Justice **Earl Warren**, handed down one of the most famous decisions in American judicial history. In the case of **Brown v. Board of Education of Topeka**, the Court overturned the 1896 *Plessy v. Ferguson* decision and ruled that segregation of schools was unconstitutional, arguing that separate schools are inherently unequal. The Court demanded that the states desegregate immediately. Eisenhower ordered the desegregation of Washington, D.C., schools but at first refused to force southern states to comply with the Court's ruling. Encouraged by

The 1950s

this lack of federal backing, southern state governments engaged in "massive resistance" by choosing not to desegregate schools and by denying funding to districts that attempted desegregation. The resistance to integration was so fierce in Arkansas that Eisenhower dispatched federal troops to Little Rock to force desegregation of public schools there.

The Supreme Court's decision in Brown v. Board of Education *overturned the "separate but equal" doctrine established by* Plessy v. Ferguson *in 1896. In 1957, federal troops were called into Little Rock, Arkansas, to enforce integration of public schools.*

The Civil Rights Movement Takes Shape

Amid the conflict over *Brown v. Board of Education of Topeka*, a strong civil rights movement began taking shape in the South. In December 1955 in Montgomery, Alabama, a black woman named **Rosa Parks** was arrested for refusing to give her bus seat to a white man. Led by a minister, **Martin Luther King Jr.**, Montgomery blacks organized a boycott of the bus system. Despite violent attacks on black leaders, the boycott continued, reducing bus revenue by over 60 percent. In 1956, the Supreme Court upheld a lower court's decision outlawing segregation on buses.

The success of the Montgomery bus boycott inspired civil rights leaders to adopt Martin Luther King Jr.'s philosophy of nonviolent civil disobedience. To direct his followers in a campaign against segregation and discrimination, King and other black ministers established the **Southern Christian Leadership Conference** (SCLC) in 1957. The SCLC soon found an ally in the Student Nonviolent Coordinating Committee (SNCC), which formed after a number of sit-ins at places of business that discriminated against blacks.

The civil rights movement gained strength by employing the doctrine of nonviolent civil disobedience during the 1950s. Led by Martin Luther King Jr. and the Southern Christian Leadership Conference, southern blacks staged direct acts of defiance against segregation.

Social Trends of the 1950s

The decade following World War II was characterized by affluence in much of American society, giving rise to high levels of consumption and a boom in population. Beneath this widespread prosperity, however, lay deepening poverty for some Americans, and the gap between the rich and poor widened.

Automation and Consolidation

Eisenhower's support for government spending greatly stimulated economic growth during the 1950s. Defense spending, which accounted for half of the federal budget, spurred industrial growth and funded scientific and technological advances. The nation's first nuclear power plant opened in 1957, and the chemical and electronics industries both boomed. Industrial plants and American homes alike became automated, with electrical devices performing tasks formerly left to humans. Fossil fuel consumption skyrocketed as a result of increased electricity use. With gas prices low, the automobile industry upped production. The first electric computer was built in 1945, and computer production advanced rapidly throughout the 1950s.

Boosted by the production benefits of automation, big business flourished, until less than one half of a percent of American corporations controlled more than half of the nation's corporate wealth. These massive corporations crushed and absorbed their competition and formed conglomerates to link companies in different industries. Agriculture mirrored big industry. Technology drastically cut the amount of work needed to successfully grow crops, and many farmers moved to the cities as rich farm companies consolidated family farms, fertilized them with new chemicals, and harvested crops with new machinery.

Advances in science and technology decreased the amount of labor necessary for industry and agriculture to be financially successful and led to consolidation of industry and agriculture into large corporations.

Unions responded to the consolidation of business by consolidating as well. In 1955, the American Federation of Labor and the Congress of Industrial Organizations merged to form the **AFL-CIO.** Prosperity meant high wages and few labor complaints, depriving unions of the high-profile status they enjoyed in 1930s and 1940s. Also weakening unions was the decrease in blue-collar workers because of the rise of automation and the accompanying increase in white-collar jobs—office employees, managers, salespersons. This loss of blue-collar workers stripped the labor movement of its core influence and contributed to the sharp decline in union membership during the 1950s.

Results of Prosperity: Suburbanization, the Baby Boom, Religion, and Conservatism

Prosperous American consumers went on a spending spree in the 1950s. The automobile industry benefited markedly from this surge in spending: Americans bought nearly 60 million cars during the 1950s. The resulting increase in mobility contributed to the rise of motels, fast-food restaurants, gas stations, and, most notably, suburbs. Areas once considered too far from jobs in urban centers were now accessible and desirable, and middle-class and wealthy Americans began to flee the poverty and congestion of the cities for outlying areas. Suburbs offered a clean, homogeneous, child-friendly, and safe environment. The American suburban population nearly doubled during the 1950s.

Prosperity and mobility provided by the automobile during the 1950s led middle-class and wealthy Americans to move to suburbs around the nation's great cities.

Prosperity led Americans to have more children and start families earlier. The birth rate grew steadily from 1950 to its peak in 1957; at the same time, advances in science and medecine led to lower infant mortality rates and longer life expectancy. The U.S. population accordingly grew from about 150 million to about 180 million during the 1950s. The **baby boom**, as this explosion was called, was both the product of and a cause for conservative views about the family, and especially about the place of women in American society. Dr. Benjamin Spock, author of the wildly successful *Baby and Child Care* (1946), suggested that mothers devote themselves to the full-time care of their children. Popular culture depicted marriage and feminine domesticity as a primary goal for American women, and the education system reinforced this portrayal. This revival of domesticity as a social value was accompanied by a revival of religion in the U.S. Religious messages began to creep into popular culture as religious leaders became famous faces. It was during the 1950s that Congress added the words "under God" to the Pledge of Allegiance.

The Less Fortunate

Though 1950s prosperity benefited many Americans, it also obscured widespread poverty. While some Americans became extravagantly rich, others became desperately poor. More than one-fifth of the nation lived below the poverty line: some in desolate rural conditions as migrant workers, others in the crowded and dirty slums of American cities. As wealthy whites moved to the suburbs, cities exhausted their funds attempting to provide social services to an increasing number of poor urbanites, most of whom were minorities. Historically black and immigrant in population, the urban poor now included an increasing number of Hispanic-Americans and Native Americans, who migrated to the cities when unable to find work in rural areas. The needs of these disadvantaged groups went largely unanswered, and the condition of cities deteriorated rapidly.

American Culture: Television, Rock and Roll, and the Beats

Television grew rapidly as the medium of choice for Americans. By the 1960s, over 90 percent of American households owned at least one television. Television brought a message of conformity and consumerism to the American people. Programs fed Americans a steady diet of cookie-cutter idealizations of American life filled with racial and gender stereotypes. Commercials became pervasive, at times dominating the programs themselves. Television produced many of the period's heroes and fads, such as the Davy Crockett coonskin cap and the hula hoop.

Television dominated American culture during the 1950s, presenting a cookie-cutter, stereotyped image of the contented, prosperous American family.

Despite the widespread conformity of the period, some elements of culture rebelled. One source of rebellion was rock and roll, which rose to prominence in the 1950s. No one epitomized rock and roll during the 1950s more than **Elvis Presley**, who produced 14 consecutive records between 1956 and 1958 that each sold over a million copies. Elvis's sexual innuendo and hip gyrations shocked many middle-class parents but captured the attention of their children. Another voice of rebellion came in painting. Artists like Jackson Pollock eschewed traditional techniques and pursued Abstract Expressionism by, among other methods, flinging paint and other materials across huge canvases.

In the realm of literature, the spirit of rebellion was embodied in **"the Beats,"** a group of nonconformists led by writers such as Allan Ginsberg, the author of the long poem *Howl* (1956), and Jack Kerouac, the author of *On the Road* (1957). These authors rejected uniform middle-class culture and sought to overturn the sexual and social conservatism of the period. The Beats eventually won favor among college-age Americans, who joined together in protests against the death penalty, nuclear weaponry, racial segregation, and other facets of American life that went largely unquestioned throughout the 1950s. This burgeoning youth movement would explode in the 1960s.

The 1960s

Trends and Themes of the Era

- Democrats, who held the presidency in the 1960s, tried to bring about the liberal social reforms that were the hallmarks of their party's philosophy.

- Led by Dr. Martin Luther King Jr., the civil rights movement achieved its greatest successes, culminating in the 1964 Civil Rights Act and the 1965 Voting Rights Act. The civil rights movement gained massive public support and helped convince the nation of the power of social action.

- The Cold War continued throughout the decade, and nearly erupted in nuclear war during the Cuban Missile Crisis in 1962. Cold War anxieties and concerns over Soviet domination in Asia led to the buildup of American forces in Vietnam and the Vietnam War.

- In the tradition of social action built during the civil rights movement and in response to U.S. involvement in a foreign war that took over 50,000 American lives and seemed unwinnable, a vocal minority of Americans formed the antiwar movement. Supporters and critics of the war often opposed each other bitterly.

- The 1960s was a time of dramatic social engagement and action. In addition to the civil rights and antiwar movements, a powerful women's rights movement also took root.

Domestic Politics in the 1960s

In 1961, Democrats gained control of the White House and kept it until 1969. Democratic leadership meant that domestic politics revolved around liberal reforms. John F. Kennedy grappled with congressional opposition to his plan for a New Frontier until his assassination in 1963, when Lyndon B. Johnson took office and pushed his predecessor's proposed reforms through Congress under the umbrella of what he called the Great Society.

The JFK Administration and the New Frontier at Home

John F. Kennedy, who won the presidency over Richard Nixon in 1960, promised a **"New Frontier"** for America, encompassing reform at home and victory in the Cold War. To accomplish these goals, he assembled a group of young technocrats and politically savvy advisers, termed "the best and the brightest" by historian David Halberstam. Robert McNamara, the president of Ford Motor Company, served as secretary of defense. McGeorge Bundy, a dean of Harvard University, was special assistant for national-security affairs, and the president's brother Robert Kennedy filled the post of attorney general. JFK carefully crafted his image as a young, intelligent, and vibrant leader.

Despite JFK's reputation, he was unable to push much reform through Congress, where he faced an opposing coalition of Republicans and southern Democrats. After a string of early legislative failures, Kennedy backed off from his reform program. His plans for increased federal aid to education, urban renewal, and government-provided medical care went unrealized. Kennedy's primary achievements at home were the raising of the minimum wage and the 1961 establishment of the **Peace Corps**, a program created to send volunteer teachers, health workers, and engineers to Third World countries.

Despite JFK's image as a dynamic and successful leader, he was unable to push his plans for social welfare reform through Congress, where he faced an opposing coalition of Republicans and southern Democrats.

An important aspect of JFK's domestic record arose near the end of his time as president. Rachel Carson's publication of **Silent Spring** in 1962, which exposed the environmental hazards of the pesticide DDT, touched off a broad movement to push environmental measures through Congress. In 1963, this effort spurred the passage of the Clean Air Act to regulate factory and automobile emissions. This act, along with the 1960 Clean Water Act, marked the beginning of a period during which the federal government became increasingly invested in environmental matters.

On November 22, 1963, JFK's presidency abruptly ended when he was assassinated by Lee Harvey Oswald in Dallas, Texas. Kennedy's vice president, **Lyndon B. Johnson**, was sworn in as president aboard Air Force One.

LBJ and the Great Society

Following the death of JFK, Lyndon B. Johnson backed his predecessor's failed program of reform, calling for the passage of tax cuts and civil rights bills as a memorial to the slain president. In 1964, Johnson's skillful backroom bargaining achieved just that: the passage of both a tax cut and the **Civil Rights Act**, which outlawed segregation in public accommodations, gave the government broader powers to enforce desegregation in schools, and established the Equal Employment Opportunity Commission to prevent job discrimination. A year later, Johnson pushed through the **Voting Rights Act**, which authorized federal examiners to register qualified voters and to suspend literacy tests in voting districts where fewer than half of the minority population of voting age was registered. The bill's passage resulted in an explosion in black enfranchisement. The number of registered black voters doubled in many areas.

Along with furthering civil rights, Johnson mounted a "war on poverty" by pushing for a wide array of social legislation. In 1964, Congress passed the **Economic Opportunity Act**, which provided young Americans with job training and created a volunteer network devoted to social work and education in poor areas. The 1965 **Medical Care Act** created Medicare and Medicaid, providing senior citizens with Medical insurance and welfare recipients with free health care.

These reform programs became a part of what Johnson called the **Great Society**, a vision of the future that included an end to poverty, improvements in health-care, protection for the environment, and racial equality. The Great Society, however, never fully emerged. The program's failure was due partially to poor design and partially to the enormity of the task LBJ had set for himself. Primarily, though, the Great Society was undermined by a shift in the federal government's focus from domestic to foreign policy in response to the worsening situation in Vietnam (see page 229).

LBJ's Great Society program sought to end poverty, provide health care to all, increase spending on education, and achieve racial equality. However, as foreign relations became increasingly pressing, the Great Society was left unattained.

The 1960s

The Supreme Court under Warren

During the 1960s, the Supreme Court, under the liberal chief justice **Earl Warren**, delivered a number of significant decisions that earned the admiration of many and the enmity of many others. In 1962, *Baker v. Carr* granted federal courts jurisdiction over state apportionment systems to assure that all citizens' votes were granted equal weight. The decision in *Engel v. Vitale* that same year prohibited prayer in public schools. The 1963 decision in *Gideon v. Wainwright* obliged the states to provide indigent defendants in felony cases with public defenders. The 1966 decision in *Miranda v. Arizona* required police to make suspects aware of their rights to remain silent and to have an attorney present during questioning, the so-called Miranda rights. In 1967, *Loving v. Virginia* declared laws against interracial marriage unconstitutional. That same year, **Thurgood Marshall** was appointed to the Supreme Court, making him the first African-American to receive such an honor.

Civil Rights in a Turbulent Decade

During the 1960s, the civil rights movement built upon its achievements of the previous decade. Activists worked to counter discrimination, segregation, inequality of opportunity, and social problems particular to blacks.

Civil Rights in the Kennedy Years

JFK came to office wary of becoming entangled in the complex issue of civil rights. He did not stay removed for long, however. In the spring of 1961, the Congress of Racial Equality held a **freedom ride** through the Deep South to protest illegal segregation in interstate transportation. After whites in Alabama assaulted the freedom riders, Kennedy sent federal marshals to protect them. In the fall of 1962, Kennedy again sent federal marshals to the South to enforce civil rights, when students and angry white citizens attempted to prevent a black man, James Meredith, from attending the University of Mississippi.

In 1963, **Martin Luther King Jr.** led a series of peaceful demonstrations in Alabama that police nonetheless attacked. These attacks, along with other high-profile abuses of civil rights, prompted Kennedy to propose a comprehensive civil rights bill to Congress. In support of this legislation, a quarter of a million Americans gathered in Washington, D.C., in August 1963. It was at this "March on Washington" that Martin Luther King Jr. gave his famous "I have a dream" speech, outlining an idealistic view of what America could be. Despite this demonstration and King's eloquence, Republicans in Congress blocked the civil rights bill.

In support of JFK's civil rights bill, some 250,000 Americans converged on Washington, D.C., in August 1963, where they listened to Martin Luther King Jr.'s "I have a dream" speech.

Civil Rights under Johnson

Civil rights advocates had cause for optimism during Lyndon B. Johnson's early years as president, since Johnson's Great Society program aimed to achieve racial equality. In 1964, Johnson pushed the Civil Rights Act through Congress, which outlawed discrimination in public facilities (discussed in *LBJ and the Great Society,* page 225). Civil Right activists, however, demanded more—in particular, an end to black disenfranchisement. In 1965, Martin Luther King Jr. and the **Southern Christian Leadership Conference** organized a mass protest against black disenfranchisement. The demonstration, which took place in Birmingham, Alabama, elicited a violent police reaction. The police attacks were caught on television and cemented national sympathies behind the Civil Rights movement. This national response culminated in the Voting Rights Act, signed in August 1965, which protected and encouraged black enfranchisement (also discussed on page 225). By 1968, one million blacks were registered in the Deep South, and many black representatives had been elected to office.

The Voting Rights Act was a major achievement of the civil rights movement in the 1960s. It authorized the federal government to institute measures designed to encourage black enfranchisement.

The Black Power Movement

Martin Luther King, Jr. and his nonviolent strategies of resistance were supported by the majority of civil rights activists, both black and white. But not all supporters of the rights of blacks in the United States believed in nonviolence. The **Black Power** movement expressed the outrage felt by many African-Americans. The movement began with the teachings of **Malcolm X**, who became a prominent spokesman for black rights after joining the Nation of Islam. Rejecting the goal of integration, Malcolm X taught American blacks that they should be proud of their blackness and remain separate from white society. Instead of nonviolence, he favored armed self-defense. In 1965, amid signs that he might be softening his stance and just after publicly breaking from the Nation of Islam, Malcolm X was assassinated. Nonetheless, he remained a powerful voice among African-Americans, his influence preserved through his teachings and his autobiography, published the year of his death.

The 1960s

Malcolm X preached violent resistance and separation from white society to African-Americans until his death in 1965.

After Malcolm X's death, the mantle of Black Power was carried on by **Stokely Carmichael**, the leader of the Student Nonviolent Coordinating Committee who came to reject nonviolence in favor of violent resistance. In 1966, Carmichael's influence led to the founding of the **Black Panthers** by Huey Newton and Bobby Seale. The Panthers carried firearms and at times engaged in violent confrontations with police.

The slogan "Black Power," however, did not apply exclusively to radical groups such as the Black Panthers; it also applied to more moderate groups who worked to reaffirm black culture as distinct from white culture and valuable in its own way. Off-shoots of the Black Power movement included "Native American Power" and "Chicano Power," movements that sought to assert the value of ethnic heritage and to counter oppression from mainstream white society.

Assassination

On April 4, 1968, Martin Luther King Jr., the most prominent black leader of the period, was shot and killed in Memphis, Tennessee, by white racist James Earl Ray. Blacks responded by taking to the streets in anger in more than 100 U.S. cities, causing enormous property damage and social chaos. The riots led to 46 deaths, over 3,000 injuries, and 27,000 arrests. The effect of King's death on the civil rights movement and on America cannot be measured.

The Cold War Continues

During Kennedy's and Johnson's presidencies, tensions remained high with the USSR. These tensions peaked most notably in Berlin, Cuba, and Vietnam.

The Berlin Wall

In 1961, the USSR completed construction of the **Berlin Wall,** which physically separated East and West Berlin and was patrolled by East German guards. The wall was meant to prevent the exodus of talented and intelligent East Germans to West Germany, but it also came to symbolize the division of the entire world into two carefully guarded Cold War spheres.

The Cold War in Cuba

After **Fidel Castro** and the Cuban communists overthrew the Cuban government in 1959, the island nation became a subject of much anxiety to the U.S., since it represented an extension of the Soviet sphere of influence close to American territory. In 1961, JFK authorized a plan, drawn up by the Eisenhower administration, to send 1,500 Cuban exiles, trained and armed by the U.S., back to Cuba to spark an insurrection. The **Bay of Pigs Invasion**, as this operation was known, took place in April 1961, and resulted in an embarrassing defeat for the returning exiles and the United States.

The focus of the Cold War turned toward Cuba once again in 1962, when Americans discovered Soviet missile bases under construction in Cuba. In what became known as the **Cuban Missile Crisis,** JFK vowed to quarantine Cuba with a naval blockade to prevent the shipment of more missiles and to dismantle the existing missile bases by force if the USSR did not do so. Some 250,000 troops gathered in Florida to prepare to invade Cuba, and U.S. naval forces readied themselves to intercept Russian freighters en route. U.S.-USSR relations became tenser than ever. Nuclear war seemed very possible: U.S. B-52s carrying nuclear weapons remained constantly airborne, ready to strike. After several days, Soviet Premier Khrushchev recalled the Russian freighters and sent Kennedy a message that he would dismantle the Cuban missiles in exchange for a U.S. promise never to invade Cuba. Kennedy accepted the compromise. The Cuban Missile Crisis has been viewed as the defining moment of JFK's presidency.

The discovery of Soviet missile sites in Cuba in 1962 led to a standoff between the U.S. and the USSR. The Cuban Missile Crisis led the world's two superpowers closer to nuclear war than had any other Cold War episode.

In July 1963, the U.S. and USSR signed the **Limited Test-Ban Treaty**, which prohibited undersea and atmospheric testing of nuclear weaponry. This effort at easing tensions would later be known as **détente**.

Vietnam and the Vietnam War

Vietnam, divided at the seventeenth parallel between communist North Vietnam and U.S.-dominated South Vietnam, concerned Kennedy from the very beginning of his presidency. He believed in Eisenhower's **"domino theory,"** which held that when one nation fell under Soviet domination, others in the region would soon follow. In efforts to stave off communist advances, Kennedy boosted the number of U.S. forces in South Vietnam to 16,000 by 1963. These forces aimed to protect the South Vietnamese from the pro-communist National Liberation Front, called the **Vietcong**.

The 1960s

Less than a month later, JFK was assassinated and Lyndon Johnson took over the presidency and the oversight of American operations in Vietnam. In August 1964, two American destroyers allegedly clashed with North Vietnamese patrol boats in the Gulf of Tonkin, off North Vietnam. Johnson announced that Americans had been attacked without cause and ordered air strikes. Congress passed the **Gulf of Tonkin Resolution** in August 1964, which authorized the escalation of American troops' involvement in Vietnam. Nearly equivalent to a declaration of war, this resolution allowed Johnson to act as he saw fit in Vietnam. In 1965, Johnson ordered "Operation Rolling Thunder," which launched continuous bombing of North Vietnam. This plan, however, failed to force North Vietnam to negotiate, and did not stop the flow of soldiers and supplies to communist forces in the South.

Since bombing was ineffective, Johnson decided in March 1965 to commit ground forces to the struggle. By the end of 1967, nearly 500,000 U.S. troops were stationed in Vietnam. The enemy these soldiers faced—the North Vietnamese Army and the Vietcong—used untraditional guerrilla methods of warfare and were well supplied, well reinforced, and determined to fight until the U.S. moved out of Vietnam. The war became a guerrilla battle with little geographil indication of success or failure.

The American public began to gauge success through casualty figures. In January 1968, the North Vietnamese Army and the Vietcong launched a massive offensive, known as the **Tet Offensive**. Though American troops repelled the offensive after about a month of fighting, many thousands of Americans were killed, and the enemy managed to breach many areas thought to be secure. Following the Tet Offensive, the American public began to believe that victory in Vietnam would be impossible. The growing antiwar movement gained immense strength and support, and Johnson's approval ratings plummeted. During the 1968 presidential campaign, Johnson halted the sustained bombing of North Vietnam and announced that he would not seek reelection. The increasingly unpopular war would be placed in the hands of his successor.

The Tet Offensive was a major turning point in the Vietnam War. Though a tactical defeat for the pro-communist forces, thousands of American deaths and the scope of the offensive convinced many Americans of the impossibility of victory.

Protesting the Vietnam War

Opposition to the Vietnam War began on college campuses around the nation. In 1965, the first "teach-in" was held at the University of Michigan to discuss U.S. actions. In 1966, after a wave of military draft calls, mass protests erupted on college campuses.

Many clergy, intellectuals, politicians, and others joined students in voicing opposition to the war. These critics denounced American involvement in an essentially Vietnamese war, claiming there was no way to win without great cost and loss of life, and noted that the war was fought predominantly by poor Americans. Television coverage of the war further intensified antiwar sentiments, as Americans saw firsthand the brutal devastation involved.

Although a majority of Americans still supported the war, those who opposed it did so fervently, and the nation became sharply polarized between the two sides. At times, this polarization yielded violence, as when antiwar protesters clashed with police outside the Democratic National Convention in 1968.

The Vietnam War sharply divided the American people into antagonistic pro-war and antiwar camps. Student movements, criticism from respected American luminaries, and televised atrocities all contributed to antiwar sentiments.

Further Social Activism in the 1960s

Encouraged by the success of the antiwar and civil rights movements during the 1960s, many groups launched their own movements to redress perceived wrongs in American government and society.

The Youth Movement

Many reform movements during the 1960s sprang from the college-age population. College attendance soared during the decade, and college campuses became centers for protest movements. While it must be noted that the majority of college students did not engage in such protests, the minority that did was both significant and vocal. Leading the youth movement was the **Students for a Democratic Society** (SDS), a group founded in 1962. The SDS aimed to create a "New Left" in the U.S. in order to mobilize support for leftist goals throughout the nation. Students sat-in, marched, and rallied to end mandatory ROTC programs, halt military research, address racism, and most prominently, to express their disgust with the Vietnam War. The antiwar cause inspired huge rallies, draft-card burning, and harassment of anyone connected to the military.

Notable student protests included a mass demonstration at Columbia University in the spring of 1968, which resulted in a temporary shutdown of the school, and the fall 1969 **March Against Death**, in which about 300,000 people marched in a long, cir-

The 1960s

cling path through Washington, D.C., for 40 hours straight, each holding a candle and the name of a soldier killed or a village destroyed in Vietnam.

The youth movement began to fade following a series of violent crackdowns on protesters. In the most infamous, on May 4, 1970, students at Kent State University in Ohio who were protesting **Richard Nixon**'s expansion of the Vietnam War into Cambodia were met by armed National Guardsmen and inundated with tear gas. Then a panicking troop of guardsmen fired into the crowd, killing four and wounding nine; two of the dead had not even been a part of the demonstration. Events like this sapped the student movement of its zeal, and college campuses grew steadily quieter.

Women's Liberation

The feminist movement, which had grown somewhat dormant in the 1950s, reawakened in the U.S. during the 1960s. The most prominent symbol of this resurgence was the 1963 publication of Betty Friedan's *The Feminine Mystique*, which urged women to break free from the domestic role and seek "something more." JFK created the Presidential Commission on the Status of Women, which issued a report in 1963 detailing the inequalities between men and women in the American workforce. The **Civil Rights Act** of 1964 prohibited sexual as well as racial discrimination in hiring practices. The **National Organization for Women** (NOW) formed in 1966 to lobby Congress, file lawsuits, and publicize the feminist cause. By 1970, more than forty percent of all women worked outside the home.

Spurred on by the publication of Betty Friedan's The Feminist Mystique, *the feminist movement reawakened in the 1960s. Organizations like NOW pushed for change at the national level to promote equality.*

Many women involved in the liberation movement had gained experience in the antiwar or civil rights movements and dedicated the same tactics to the feminist cause. They encouraged women to meet in small groups to discuss their problems and met in larger groups to burn bras and beauty items seen as demeaning. They founded health centers geared toward women and advocated abortion education. In 1970, the **Women's Strike for Equality** saw tens of thousands of women nationwide hold demonstrations to demand the right to equal employment and legal abortions. Pro-choice activists gained a major success in 1973, when the Supreme Court legalized abortion in the landmark decision *Roe v. Wade*.

1970s-2000

Trends and Themes of the Era

- The Cold War varied in intensity during this 30-year period. Nevertheless, it dominated foreign policy throughout the era and influenced domestic policy, as well. The Cold War ended in 1989 with the fall of the Soviet Union.

- After the fall of the Soviet Union, the world stage changed dramatically. U.S. interests ceased to be so easily defined, because there was no longer a huge entity to oppose. As the sole superpower, the U.S. debated about but ultimately maintained its role as an international policeman.

- Domestically, the United States underwent cycles of economic boom and bust, and shifted between Republican and Democratic presidents.

Richard Nixon in Office

Richard Nixon was elected president in 1968. His conservatism appealed to a nation weary from a tumultuous decade of social activism and political reform. Nixon opposed racial integration, denounced the liberal Supreme Court, and promised a return to order, stability, and decency in America. In office, he scaled back progressive reforms, eventually pulled U.S. troops out of Vietnam, and focused on **détente** between the U.S. and its Cold War enemies. Despite all these activities, Nixon is best remembered for the **Watergate** scandal that ended his presidency.

In the election of 1968, Nixon portrayed himself as the representative of the "**silent majority**," a label he used to designate American citizens who had grown tired of progressive reforms, student protests, and racial integration of schools. However, to the Republicans' dismay, Democrats in Congress blocked many of Nixon's conservative efforts and succeeded in pushing through progressive reforms, including bills to extend social welfare programs and protect the environment. One of the most telling signs that the 1960s' spirit of liberalism and youth activism still held strong was the Woodstock Festival, a three-day music festival attended by thousands of young liberal Americans in August 1969.

Although many of Nixon's conservative initiatives failed in Congress, including his attempt to hold off the integration of Mississippi schools and his opposition to the extension of the Voting Rights Act of 1965, his efforts did succeed in winning the support of the white South. This support proved key to Nixon's crushing defeat of ultra-liberal Democrat George McGovern in the election of 1972.

Vietnamization of the Vietnam War and Détente

The Vietnam War was perhaps the most pressing issue Nixon faced upon coming to office. The war, now widely opposed by the American public, was sapping the nation of military strength and economic resources. Nixon and his top adviser on foreign affairs, National Security Adviser and later Secretary of State **Henry Kissinger**, devised three main strategies to "Vietnamize" (or "de-Americanize") the Vietnam War. First, he gradually pulled American ground troops out of Vietnam, reducing the U.S. forces from about 500,000 in 1968 to about 30,000 in 1972. As a corollary to these efforts, he announced the **Nixon Doctrine**, which pledged a change in the U.S. role in the Third World from military protector to helpful partner. His second tactic to Vietnamize the war was to send Kissinger to North Vietnam to negotiate a treaty. Third, he authorized a massive bombing campaign in March 1969, which targeted North Vietnamese supply routes throughout Cambodia and Laos. (The Kent State protests covered in the last chapter were in response to the bombing in Cambodia.)

The **Paris Accords**, signed in January 1973, finally settled the terms of U.S. withdrawal, ending the war between the U.S. and North Vietnam but leaving the conflict between North and South Vietnam unresolved. The last American troops left South Vietnam in March 1973. By the time U.S. involvement ended, 58,000 Americans had died, 300,000 had been wounded, and conditions in Vietnam were as unstable and war-torn as ever. The war in Vietnam continued until 1975, when North Vietnam won control of the entire country.

U.S. participation in the Vietnam War effectively ended in January 1973 with the signing of the Paris Accords.

The gradual reduction of U.S. troops in Vietnam was an integral part of Nixon's plan to achieve **détente**, an easing of tensions between the U.S. and its Cold War enemies. In April 1971, the communist People's Republic of China hosted the U.S. table-tennis team, and in February 1972 Nixon himself visited China for a highly publicized tour and meetings with **Mao Zedong**, China's leader. Though official diplomatic relations between the two nations were not established until 1979, this visit resulted in greatly improved communication between the two nations.

In May 1972, Nixon went to Moscow, where he signed the first **Strategic Arms Limitation Treaty** (SALT I). SALT I limited each of the superpowers to 200 antiballistic missiles and set quotas for intercontinental and submarine missiles. Though largely symbolic, the agreement sparked hope for cooperation between the two powers.

Watergate

Nixon's presidency ended with the **Watergate** scandal. During the 1972 presidential campaign, Nixon created the Committee to Re-elect the President (CREEP). In June 1972, burglars later found to be employed by CREEP were caught breaking into Democratic National Committee headquarters in the Watergate office complex in Washington, DC, to plant bugs. A massive cover-up effort began, with Nixon vowing that no one in his administration was involved in the break-in. Attempts to destroy paperwork and bribe key individuals were gradually exposed, most prominently in a series of articles in the *Washington Post*. Reporters Carl Bernstein and Bob Woodward unmasked the Nixon administration's corruption and attempted cover-up, having received much of their information from an unnamed informant known as **Deep Throat**. Top officials from Nixon's administration resigned, including Vice President Spiro Agnew.

In July 1974, the House Judiciary Committee adopted an article of impeachment charging Nixon with obstructing justice. In August, Nixon turned over tapes of con-

The 1970s-2000

versations proving his involvement in the cover-up and resigned as president before impeachment proceedings began. **Gerald Ford** assumed the presidency (Ford had been appointed vice president following Agnew's resignation). Coming on the heels of the Vietnam War, the Watergate scandal inflamed the American public's mistrust of—and antagonism toward—the national government.

Facing impeachment because of his involvement in the Watergate cover-up, Nixon resigned as president on August 9, 1974.

Gerald Ford as President

Gerald Ford served as little more than a caretaker in the White House until the election of 1976. Though he received bad press after pardoning Nixon in September 1974, Ford's presidency was unblemished by scandal. However, economic crisis tarnished his time in office.

Ford proved more conservative than Nixon in his domestic politics. He vetoed measures aimed at social welfare, environmental protection, and civil rights. A Democratic Congress overrode most of these vetoes. Ford's woes increased with the Arab **oil embargo**, in effect from October 1973 to March 1974, which devastated the U.S. economy. Rising oil prices sparked enormous inflation, which hit twelve percent in 1974. In October of that year, Ford initiated the "Whip Inflation Now" program (WIN), but instead of reversing inflation and stabilizing the economy, his efforts threw the economy into a recession, with unemployment reaching eleven percent in 1975.

In 1975, Ford and Soviet Premier Leonid Brezhnev, along with the leaders of thirty-one other states, signed the **Helsinki Accords**, which solidified European boundaries and promised to respect human rights and the freedom to travel.

Jimmy Carter: Washington Outsider in the White House

Jimmy Carter, a Democrat, was elected president in a narrow victory over Gerald Ford in 1976. A former governor of Georgia, Carter presented himself as a political outsider, uncorrupted by Washington. His presidency was favorably marked by a commitment to morality, but scarred by economic crisis, incomplete domestic programs, and some foreign policy crises.

Carter successfully supported a tax cut and the creation of a public works program, which helped reduce unemployment to five percent by late 1978. However, Carter failed to push many of his other economic programs through Congress. By the end of Carter's term, unemployment was again over seven percent, and inflation hovered around twelve percent.

The economy was further hurt in 1979 by the decade's second energy shortage, provoked by OPEC's (the Organization of Petroleum Exporting Countries) hike in oil prices. In efforts to promote conservation and responsible energy use, Carter had created the Department of Energy in 1977, proposed taxes on fossil-fuel use, and supported research on alternative energy sources. The most substantive result of these actions was a weak energy bill passed in 1978.

Foreign Affairs: A Mixed Record

Carter is best known for his foreign relations dealings. He supported human rights around the world, working to unveil and halt abuses. Carter also worked to improve relations with nations previously hostile toward the U.S. In 1977, he negotiated a treaty with Panama to transfer the Panama Canal back to the Panamanians in 1999, and officially recognized the People's Republic of China in 1979.

In June 1979, Carter and Leonid Brezhnev signed SALT II (Strategic Arms Limitation Treaty), but the Senate was hesitant to ratify the treaty. Hopes for ratification were dashed in January 1980 when Soviet troops invaded Afghanistan. Carter reacted with a series of anti-Soviet measures, including a boycott of the 1980 Summer Olympics in Moscow. Growing increasingly hostile toward the USSR, Carter effectively destroyed détente.

Carter's biggest success and biggest challenge in foreign affairs arose from the Middle East. In September 1978, Carter invited Israel's leader, Menachem Begin, and Egypt's leader, Anwar el-Sadat, to Camp David, where they worked out a draft of a treaty between the two warring countries. The **Camp David Accords** were signed by the two leaders at the White House in March 1979, but quickly fell apart when Sadat was assassinated by Islamic fundamentalists in 1981.

Adding to this tension, in January 1979 the Shah of Iran, a U.S. ally, fled his country to escape a revolution. In November 1979, when Carter admitted the shah to the U.S., Iranian students stormed the U.S. embassy in Tehran, taking more than fifty Americans hostage. A risky rescue effort in April 1980 failed, and the crisis continued through the end of Carter's presidency. Carter's inability to resolve the Iran hostage crisis was a major blemish on his presidency.

The 1970s–2000

Conservatism Resurgent: Ronald Reagan and the 1980s

Ronald Reagan, a Republican, won the election of 1980 by promising to end the "tax and spend" policies of his liberal predecessors and to revive the patriotism needed to win the Cold War. These two goals would dominate his presidency.

Reaganomics

Ronald Reagan's economic program, dubbed **Reaganomics**, was founded on the belief that a capitalist system free from taxation and government involvement would be most productive, and that the prosperity of a rich upper class would "trickle down" to the poor. He pushed a three-year, 25 percent tax cut through Congress in 1981, as well as a $40 billion cut in federal spending on school lunches, student loans, and public transportation, among other services.

To curb inflation, the Federal Reserve Board hiked interest rates in 1981, plunging the country into a severe recession. Unemployment soared to 10 percent, and because of Reagan's cut in social spending the impoverished found themselves without social programs. Along with unemployment, trade and federal deficits skyrocketed (the federal deficit rose because the government offset its cuts in social spending with huge increases in military spending). Recession, however, gave way to a rebound in early 1983, when inflation stabilized and consumers began to spend in great amounts.

From 1983 to 1987, the economy boomed, spurred by speculation in the stock market. The bubble burst, however, on October 19, 1987, when 20 percent of the stock market's value was lost, the largest single-day decline in history. The crash exposed the economic problems concealed by the four boom years: a high trade deficit and the widening gap between rich and poor. These problems were still unresolved when the economy began to recover in 1988.

The "Evil Empire"

Reagan began issuing anti-Soviet statements soon after coming to the White House, referring to the USSR as the "evil empire." His administration's central Cold War strategy was military buildup. The Pentagon's budget nearly doubled during Reagan's first term in office, paralleling an increase in nuclear weapons and alarming the nation about a seeming increase in the likelihood of nuclear war. In March 1983, responding to vast domestic protest of nuclear weapons proliferation, Reagan proposed an anti-ballistic missile defense system known as the Strategic Defense Initiative (SDI), or "Star Wars." Though "Star Wars" never came close to completion, because technology lagged behind the program's defensive aims, some historians argue that the massive arms buildup proved to be the ultimate Cold War defense system by forcing the USSR to spend itself into demise in the late 1980s. Other historians counter that internal elements had more to do with the Soviet Union's eventual collapse.

The Reagan administration's enmity for the Soviets and all Soviet allies led it into a scandal known as the **Iran-Contra affair**. In 1982, the CIA organized a force of 10,000 men in Nicaragua, who called themselves "Contras," to fight against the Sandinista regime, which had military ties to the Soviet Union and Cuba. Reagan hoped to establish a democratic government in Nicaragua friendly to the United States, but Congress voted to ban aid to the Contras. The administration, however, maintained secret support, organized from within the White House by **Oliver North**, a member of the National Security Council. A series of 1987 investigations uncovered the government's machinations: the U.S. had been selling arms to the anti-American government in Iran and using profits from these sales to secretly finance the Contras in Nicaragua. Although there was no evidence that Reagan himself had known of the plan, the Iran-Contra scandal rekindled the American public's distrust of the U.S. government.

In 1987, investigations revealed that the Reagan administration had been selling arms to anti-American forces in Iran and using the profits to finance the Contras in Nicaragua, an act specifically prohibited by Congress.

The Bush Administration

George Bush, Reagan's vice president, won the presidency in 1988. Bush faced a crumbling Soviet Union, extreme tension in the Middle East and the Persian Gulf, and a huge budget deficit. In addition, a recession began in 1990 and lasted until 1992, sapping tax income for the government and leading to a cut in social programs.

The End of the Cold War

Under **Mikhail Gorbachev**, the Soviet leader who assumed power in 1985, the USSR became a less aggressive world power and more amenable to reform. On November 9, 1989, the **Berlin Wall** was torn down amid much euphoria, signifying the end of the Cold War. In August 1991, Bush and Gorbachev agreed to reduce their nuclear arsenals by one quarter. With the USSR tottering on the brink of economic collapse, hard-line Communists attempted to oust Mikhail Gorbachev to prevent the collapse of the Soviet Union. Their efforts, however, were blocked by **Boris Yeltsin**, the president of the new Russian federation, who led the drive to dissolve the USSR. Yeltsin and the leaders of the other Soviet republics soon declared an end to the USSR, forcing Gorbachev to resign.

> *In November 1989, the Berlin Wall was torn down, symbolizing an end to the Cold War.*

After the fall of the USSR, U.S. foreign relations radically transformed around the globe as the Bush administration extended economic support to the former Soviet republics and revoked its support from governments favored only for their opposition to leftist forces. China remained staunchly communist, however, and relations with China soured when in 1989 the Chinese army violently crushed a pro-democracy protest in **Tiananmen Square**.

The Gulf War

Led by **Saddam Hussein**, Iraq invaded its tiny neighbor, Kuwait, in August 1990. President Bush rallied the U.S. Congress and people, as well as the United Nations, in support of a counterattack to force the Iraqis out. In January 1991, the **Gulf War** began with an air assault on Iraqi troops, supply lines, and communications bases in Baghdad. The military campaign, led by Army General H. Norman Schwartzkopf, was called "Operation Desert Storm." The American people watched the attacks on TV in carefully edited clips. In late February, U.S. ground troops began an attack on Kuwait City, driving out the Iraqis stationed there in under a week. Victory was achieved with only 148 American deaths. More than 100,000 Iraqis, military and civilian, died.

The Environment

One important area of domestic politics for George Bush was the environment. In March 1989, the *Exxon Valdez* oil tanker ran aground, spilling over 10 million gallons of crude oil into the waters of Alaska's Prince William Sound. The spill galvanized environmentalists and provoked a worldwide initiative to clean up the environment. Bush cooperated with the Democratic Congress to pass the Clean Air Act in 1990. At other times, though, the Bush administration clashed with environmentalists, advocating fossil-fuel extraction in Alaska, avoiding international environmental treaties, and even ridiculing environmentalists.

The 1990s and President Clinton

Bill Clinton won the presidency in 1992 in a three-way campaign with Bush and **Ross Perot**, who ran on the Independent ticket. Clinton's presidency included some notable successes, despite Congressional gridlock and scandals calling his morality into question.

Legislative Struggles

Bill Clinton struggled to push his domestic reform package through an antagonistic Congress, which was controlled by conservatives after the midterm elections of 1994. His most notable failure came in the realm of health-care, when Congress blocked his efforts to create a national health-care system. Clinton did manage to push an anti-crime bill and a welfare reform bill through Congress, but both were modified from his proposals and represented exceptions to the trend of his administration's legislative defeats. Political divisiveness over the budget peaked in late 1995, when the Republican Congress twice shut down the government because it could not agree on a budget. The shutdown hurt the Republicans' public image, however, and boosted Clinton's. In this newly supportive atmosphere, Clinton was able to revise the welfare system and increase the minimum wage.

Economic and Foreign Policy

Perhaps the most important achievements of Bill Clinton's presidency were the balancing of the federal budget and a return to economic prosperity. Clinton's economic policies at home were mirrored by efforts to strengthen the U.S. economy through integration in the global economy. In November 1993, the House passed the **North American Free Trade Agreement** (NAFTA), eliminating most trade barriers with Mexico and Canada. During Clinton's eight years in office the United States experienced the most powerful economic expansion in the history of the United States.

Impeachment

Clinton was harangued throughout his first campaign for president and his time in office by accusations and rumors of sexual misconduct. The accusations came to a head in August 1998, when Clinton testified in front of a grand jury that he had not engaged in inappropriate sexual relations with Monica Lewinsky, a White House intern. Later, he was forced to admit that he had. In December 1998, the House of Representatives approved articles of impeachment for perjury and obstruction of justice. Clinton became only the second president to be impeached, the first being Andrew Johnson in 1868. In February 1999, the Senate defeated both articles of impeachment. Clinton remained in office, but the scandal overshadowed the rest of his presidency. Many pundits believe that Clinton's scandals helped pave the way for the victory of Republican George W. Bush in the heavily disputed 2000 presidential election.

The 1970s-2000

Glossary

John Adams   America's second president, Adams served from 1797 to 1801. A Federalist, he supported a powerful centralized government. His most notable actions in office were the undertaking of the Quasi-war with France and the passage of the Alien and Sedition Acts.

John Quincy Adams   As James Monroe's Secretary of State, John Quincy Adams worked to clarify the borders of the nation and devised the Monroe Doctrine. As president from 1825 to 1829, Adams proved a less adroit politician. Facing opposition from Congress and refusing to engage in political maneuvering to win support, Adams served a rather unproductive term as president. He failed to push any of his proposals through Congress.

Samuel Adams   Samuel Adams played a key role in the defense of colonial rights. He had been a leader of the Sons of Liberty and suggested the formation of the Committees of Correspondence. Adams played a crucial role in spreading the principle of colonial rights throughout New England and is credited with provoking the Boston Tea Party.

Jane Addams   Addams was a reformer and pacifist best known for her founding of Hull House, an early settlement house, in 1889. Hull House provided various educational and cultural activities for poor immigrants.

The Age of Reason   Thomas Paine's *The Age of Reason* was published in three parts between 1794 and 1807. A critique of organized religion, the book was widely criticized as a defense of Atheism. Paine's argument is a prime example of the rationalist approach to religion inspired by Enlightenment ideals.

Agricultural Adjustment Administration (AAA)   Created in 1933 as part of FDR's New Deal, the AAA controlled the production of crops, and thus prices, by offering subsidies to farmers who produced under set quotas. The Supreme Court declared the AAA unconstitutional in 1936.

Albany Plan   Benjamin Franklin submitted the Albany Plan at the 1754 gathering of colonial delgates in Albany, New York. The plan called for the colonies to unify in the face of French and Native American threats—a Plan of Union for the colonies. Although the delegates in Albany approved the plan, the colonies rejected it for fear of losing too much power. The Crown did not support the plan, either, as it was wary of too much cooperation between the colonies.

Horatio Alger   Horatio Alger wrote popular novels during the Industrial Revolution that told of young men who, with a lot of hard work and a bit of good luck, went from being paupers to rich industrialists. These "rags to riches" tales suggested that anyone could become the next Andrew Carnegie if only he worked hard enough.

Alien and Sedition Acts   The 1798 Alien and Sedition Acts gave the federal government unprecedented power to infringe upon the liberty of individuals. While the Federalists claimed these acts were essential for national security, Republicans countered that they were politically motivated and served only to deny Americans their guaranteed rights to fair trials and free speech. The Alien and Sedition Acts were the undoing of the Federalist Party, as Republican Thomas Jefferson won the presidency in 1800 based largely on popular dissatisfaction with the acts.

Allies   The Allies in World War I consisted of Great Britain, France, and Italy. The Allies were pitted against the Central Powers of Germany and Austria-Hungary. In 1917, the U.S. joined the war on the Allies' side. In World War II, the Allies included Great Britain, the Soviet Union, the U.S., and France, though Germany occupied most of France during the war.

American Civil Liberties Union (ACLU)   The American Civil Liberties Union, founded in 1920, sought (and still seeks) to protect the civil liberties of individuals throughout the U.S., often by bringing "test cases" to court in order to challenge questionable laws. In 1925, the ACLU challenged a Christian fundamentalist law in the Scopes Monkey Trial.

American Federation of Labor (AFL)   Founded in 1886, the AFL sought to organize craft unions in a federation in which the individual unions maintained some autonomy. The structure of the AFL differed from that of the Knights of Labor, which aimed to absorb individual unions. Samuel Gompers was the AFL's founding leader.

American System   Henry Clay's brainchild, the American System proposed a series of measures, including tariffs and federal support for internal improvements, geared toward achieving national economic self-sufficiency. In the late 1820s and 1830s, the National Republican Party wholly backed the American System while the Democrats opposed it.

Annapolis Convention   Originally planning to discuss the promotion of interstate commerce, delegates from five states met at Annapolis in September 1786 and ended up suggesting a convention to amend the Articles of Confederation.

Susan B. Anthony   Susan B. Anthony was a leading member of the women's suffrage movement. She served as president of the National American Woman Suffrage Association from 1892 until 1900.

Anti-Imperialist League   The Anti-Imperialist League argued against American imperialism in the late 1890s. Its members included such luminaries as William James, Andrew Carnegie, and Mark Twain.

Anti-federalists   Anti-federalists rose up as the opponents of the Constitution during the period of ratification. They opposed the Constitution's powerful centralized government, arguing that the Constitution gave the federal government too much political, economic, and military control. They instead advocated a decentralized governmental structure that granted most power to the states.

Anti-Saloon League   The Anti-Saloon League, founded in 1895, spearheaded the prohibition movement during the Progressive Era.

Articles of Confederation   Adopted in 1777 during the Revolutionary War, the Articles established the United States of America. The Articles granted very limited powers to the central government, reserving most powers for the individual states. The result was a weak, poorly defined national state that couldn't adequately govern the country's finances or maintain internal stability. The Articles were replaced by the Constitution in 1789.

Glossary

Assembly line   Industrialist Henry Ford installed the first assembly line when developing his Model T car around 1910 and perfected its use in the 1920s. Assembly line manufacturing helped maximize worker output by allowing workers to remain in one place and master one repetitive action. It became a widespread production method during the 1920s and 1930s.

Atlantic Charter   On August 9, 1941, FDR met with British Prime Minister Winston Churchill on a British ship off Newfoundland. The two discussed military strategy and issued the Atlantic Charter on August 14, which outlined their ideal postwar world. The Atlantic Charter condemned military aggression, asserted the right to national self-determination, and advocated disarmament.

Atomic Energy Commission   After World War II, the Atomic Energy Commission worked on developing more effective ways of using nuclear material such as uranium in order to mass-produce nuclear weapons.

The *Awakening*   Kate Chopin's 1899 novel reflects the changing role of women during this period. *The Awakening* portrays a married woman who defies social convention first by falling in love with another man, and then by committing suicide when she finds that his views on women are as oppressive as her husband's.

Axis powers   The Axis powers of World War II included Germany and Italy, and later Japan. The three powers signed the Tripartite Pact in September 1940.

Baby boom   The term "baby boom" refers to the decade of the 1950s, when the U.S. population swelled from 150 million to 180 million.

Bacon's Rebellion   In 1676, Nathaniel Bacon, a Virginia planter, led a group of 300 settlers in a war against the local Native Americans. When Virginia's royal governor questioned Bacon's actions, Bacon and his men burned and looted Jamestown. Bacon's rebellion manifested the increasing hostility between the poor and the wealthy in the Chesapeake region.

Bank of the United States   The Bank of the United States was chartered in 1791, as a controversial part of Alexander Hamilton's Federalist economic program.

Bank veto   The bank veto refers to Andrew Jackson's 1832 veto of the bill providing for a renewed charter for the Second Bank of the United States. The veto marked the beginning of Jackson's five-year battle against the national bank.

Battle of Antietam   The Battle of Antietam made September 17, 1862 the single bloodiest day of the Civil War, resulting in some 25,000 casualties. Although Union forces failed to defeat Lee's Confederate forces, they did succeed in halting Lee's advance through Northern soil at Maryland.

Battle of Britain   Conducted during the summer and fall of 1940, the Battle of Britain was a period of continuous bombing of London by the German air force, in preparation for a German amphibious assault. Hitler hoped the bombing would destroy British industry and morale, but the British successfully staved off the German invasion.

Battle of the Bulge   Lasting from December 16, 1944, to January 16, 1945, the Battle of the Bulge was the final German offensive in the West, as Hitler amassed his last reserves against Allied troops in France. Germany made a substantial bulge in the Allied front line, but the Allies were able to recover and repel the Germans, clearing the way for an Allied march toward Berlin.

Battle of Gettysburg   Gettysburg, Pennsylvania was the site of the largest battle of the Civil War. Widely considered to be the turning point of the war, the battle marked the Union's first major victory in the East. The three-day campaign, from July 1 to 4, 1863, resulted in an unprecedented 51,000 total casualties.

Battle of Tippecanoe   Led by future president William Henry Harrison, U.S. forces defeated Shawnee forces in the Battle of Tippecanoe in 1811. The U.S. victory lessened the Native American threat in Ohio and Indiana.

Bay of Pigs Invasion   The Bay of Pigs Invasion, in April 1961, was a failed attempt by U.S.-backed Cuban exiles to invade Cuba and overthrow Fidel Castro's communist government.

The Beats   A major American literary movement of the 1950s, the Beats were a group of nonconformists led by writers such as Allan Ginsberg, the author of *Howl* (1956), and Jack Kerouac, who penned *On the Road* (1957). These authors rejected uniform middle-class culture and sought to overturn the sexual and social conservatism of the period.

Berlin Blockade   In June 1948, the Soviets attempted to cut off Western access to Berlin by blockading all road and rail routes to the city 90 miles inside East Germany. In response, the U.S. began an airlift of supplies to the city, a campaign known as "Operation Vittles." The blockade lasted until May 1949.

Glossary

Berlin Wall   The USSR completed construction of the Berlin Wall in August 1961, aiming to prevent East Berliners from fleeing to West Berlin. The wall made concrete the political split of Berlin between the communist and authoritian East and the capitalist and democratic West. The wall was torn down on November 9, 1989 amid much celebration, setting the stage for the reunification of Germany and signifying the end of the Cold War.

Big stick   "Big stick" diplomacy refers to the foreign relations policies of Theodore Roosevelt, who summed up his aggressive stance toward international affairs with the phrase, "Speak softly and carry a big stick."

Black Panthers   Organized in 1966 in Oakland, California, the Black Panthers stressed a program of black pride, economic self-sufficiency, and armed resistance to white oppression.

Black Power   Black Power was the term for the more militant faction of Civil Rights groups that sprang up in the late 1960s. These groups stressed forceful resistance to white oppression and advocated separation from white society rather than integration.

Bill of Rights   Although the Anti-federalists were not able to block the ratification of the Constitution, they did ensure that the Bill of Rights would be created to protect individuals from government interference and possible tyranny. The Bill of Rights, drafted by a group led by James Madison, consisted of the first ten amendments to the Constitution, which guaranteed the civil rights of American citizens.

Black codes   All Southern state governments established under Andrew Johnson's plan for presidential Reconstruction enacted black codes, which granted the freedmen some basic rights but also enforced heavy civil restrictions based on race.

Black Thursday   The Great Depression had a distinct starting point in the United States. It began on Thursday, October 24, 1929—"Black Thursday"—when daystock traders fell into a selling panic, moving more than 12 million shares through the market. The market dropped in value by an astounding nine percent, beginning the snowball effect that destroyed the stock market and led the economy to ruin.

Bleeding Kansas   "Bleeding Kansas" was the popular name for the Kansas Territory during 1856, when violence broke out between representatives of the free-state government in Topeka and the fraudulently elected pro-slavery government in Lecompton. Bleeding Kansas represented a major setback for the doctrine of popular sovereignty, as the doctrine failed to provide a clear resolution to the question of slavery's expansion in Kansas.

Bootleggers   Bootleggers smuggled alcohol into the United States during the Prohibition Era (1920–1933), often from Canada or the West Indies.

Boston Massacre   In March 1770, a crowd of colonists protested against Boston customs agents and the Townsend Duties. Violence flared and five colonists were killed.

Boston Tea Party   Boston patriots organized the Boston Tea Party in protest against the 1773 Tea Act, which allowed Britain to use the profits from selling tea to pay the salaries of royal governors (who had, until then, been dependent upon the colonial assemblies for their salaries). In December 1773, Samuel Adams gathered Boston residents and warned them of the consequences of the Tea Act. Following the meeting, approximately fifty young men dressed as Mohawk Indians boarded the ships and dumped the cargo into the harbor.

Boxer Rebellion   In 1899, antiforeign sentiment in China erupted in the Boxer Rebellion. A group of zealous Chinese nationalists terrorized foreigners and Chinese Christians, capturing Beijing (Peking) in June 1900 and threatening European and American interests in Chinese markets. The United States committed 2,500 men to an international force that crushed the rebellion in August 1900.

John Brown   John Brown was a religious zealot and an extreme abolitionist who believed God had ordained him to end slavery. In 1856, he led an attack against pro-slavery government officials in Kansas, killing five and sparking months of violence that earned the territory the name "Bleeding Kansas." In 1859, he led twenty-one men in seizing a federal arsenal in Harper's Ferry, Virginia, in a failed attempt to incite a slave rebellion. He was caught and hanged.

Brown v. Board of Education of Topeka   A landmark Supreme Court decision, *Brown v. Board of Education of Topeka* (1954) reversed the "separate but equal" doctrine that had been established in the 1896 *Plessy v. Ferguson* decision to justify segregation laws. The Court ruled that separate facilities were inherently unequal and ordered public schools to desegregate nationwide. This decision was characteristic of the Supreme Court rulings under liberal Chief Justice Earl Warren.

Glossary

William Jennings Bryan   William Jennings Bryan was the Democratic candidate for president in 1896 whose goal of "free silver" (unlimited coinage of silver) won him the support of the Populist Party. Though a gifted orator, Bryan lost the election to Republican William McKinley. He ran again for president and lost in 1900. In the 1920s, Bryan made his mark as a leader of the fundamentalist cause and the key witness in the Scopes Monkey Trial.

James Buchanan   James Buchanan, a moderate Democrat with support from both the North and South, served as president of the United States from 1857 to 1861. He could not stem the tide of sectional conflict that eventually erupted inthe Civil War.

Bull Moose Party   The Bull Moose Party was the nickname of the Progressive Republican Party, led by Theodore Roosevelt in the 1912 election. The Bull Moose Party had the best showing of any third party in the history of the United States. The emergence of the Bull Moose Party dramatically weakened the Republican Party and allowed Democratic nominee Woodrow Wilson to win the election decisively with only forty-two percent of the popular vote.

George Bush   George Bush, a Republican, served as president of the United States from 1989 to 1993. His term in office was marked by economic recession and U.S. involvement in the Gulf War.

John Cabot   John Cabot explored the northeast coast of North America in 1497 and 1498, claiming Nova Scotia, Newfoundland, and the Grand Banks for England.

John C. Calhoun   John C. Calhoun was involved in politics throughout the Era of Good Feelings and the Age of Jackson. Calhoun served as James Monroe's secretary of war, as John Quincy Adams's vice president, and then as Andrew Jackson's vice president (during Jackson's first term only). A firm believer in states' rights, Calhoun clashed with Jackson over many issues, most notably nullification.

Camp meetings   During the Second Great Awakening, religious revivals on the frontier took the form of camp meetings, at which hundreds or even thousands of people, members of various denominations, met to hear speeches on repentance and sing hymns.

Camp David Accords   A major accomplishment of the Carter presidency, the Camp David Accords were signed by Israel's leader, Menachem Begin, and Egypt's leader, Anwar el-Sadat, on March 26, 1979. The treaty, however, fell apart when Sadat was assassinated by Islamic fundamentalists in 1981.

Stokely Carmichael   Once a prominent member of the Student Nonviolent Coordinating Committee, Carmichael abandoned his nonviolent leanings and became a leader of the Black Nationalist movement in 1966. He coined the phrase "Black Power."

Andrew Carnegie   Carnegie, a Scottish immigrant, came to own what in 1900 was the world's largest corporation, Carnegie Steel. In addition to being an entrepreneur and industrialist, Carnegie was a philanthropist who donated more than $300 million to charity during his lifetime.

Carpetbaggers   Southern white Democrats gave the nickname "carpetbaggers" to northerners who moved South during Reconstruction in search of political and economic opportunity. These northern opportunists purportedly had left home so quickly and took so little with them that they were able to carry all their belongings in rough suitcases made from carpeting materials.

Jimmy Carter   Jimmy Carter, a Democrat, served as president of the United States from 1977 to 1981. Carter is best known for his commitment to morality and for advancing the human rights cause. During his term in office, he faced an oil crisis, a weak economy, and severe tension in the Middle East.

Jacques Cartier   A French sailor who explored the St. Lawrence River region between 1534 and 1542, Cartier searched for a Northwest Passage, a waterway through which ships could cross the Americas and access Asia. He found no such passage but opened the region up to future exploration and colonization by the French.

Cash-and-carry   In September 1939, FDR persuaded Congress to pass a new, amended Neutrality Act, which allowed warring nations to purchase arms from the U.S. as long as they paid in cash and carried the arms away on their own ships. This cash-and-carry program allowed the U.S. to aid the Allies but stay officially out of the war.

Fidel Castro   Castro, a communist revolutionary, ousted a rightist regime in Cuba in 1959 and established the communist regime that remains in power to this day.

Central Intelligence Agency   The CIA is primarily concerned with international espionage and information gathering. In the 1950s, the organization became heavily involved in many civil struggles in the Third World, supporting groups likely to cooperate with the U.S. rather than the USSR.

Central Powers   The Central Powers, Germany and Austria-Hungary, fought against the Allies—Great Britain, France, and Italy—in World War I. In 1917, the U.S. joined the war effort against the Central Powers.

Glossary

A Century of Dishonor   Written by Helen Hunt Jackson and published in 1881, *A Century of Dishonor* attempted to raise public awareness of the harsh and dishonorable treatment of Native Americans at the hands of the United States.

Samuel de Champlain   Samuel de Champlain, a Frenchman, explored the Great Lakes and established the first French colony in North America at Quebec in 1608.

Checks and balances   The Constitution set forth a government composed of three branches: the legislative, executive, and judicial. Each branch was given certain powers over the others to ensure that no one branch gained a dangerous amount of power. This system, known as checks and balances, represented the solution to the problem of how to empower the central government while also protecting against corruption and despotism.

Chesapeake-Leopard affair   This event represented the peak of British defiance of American neutrality at sea. In June 1807, the British naval frigate *HMS Leopard* opened fire on the American naval frigate *USS Chesapeake*, killing three men and wounding twenty. The British naval officers then boarded the American ship, seized four men who had deserted the Royal Navy, hanged them from a yardarm, and sailed away. Outraged, Thomas Jefferson responded with the Embargo Act in an attempt to force Britain to respect American neutrality rights.

Chinese Exclusion Act   In 1882, amid a wave of anti-immigrant sentiment among American workers, Congress passed the Chinese Exclusion Act. The act banned Chinese immigration for ten years.

Winston Churchill   Churchill served as prime minister of England from 1940 to 1945. Churchill was known for his inspirational speeches and zealous pursuit of war victory. Together, he, FDR and Stalin formed the Big Three who were instrumental in mapping out the post-war world order. In 1946, Churchill coined the term "iron curtain" to describe the USSR's division of eastern Europe from the West.

Civil Rights Act   A landmark law, the Civil Rights Act of 1964 outlawed discrimination in education, employment, and all public accommodations.

Civil Works Administration (CWA)   FDR created the Civil Works Administration (CWA) to cope with the added economic difficulties brought on by the cold winter months of 1933. The CWA spent approximately $1 billion on short-term projects for the unemployed but was abolished in the spring of that year.

Civilian Conservation Corps (CCC)   The CCC, created in 1933 as part of FDR's New Deal, pumped money into the economy by employing the destitute in conservation and other projects.

Henry Clay   Henry Clay had a vast impact on the politics of the Era of Good Feelings and the Age of Jackson. He engineered and championed the American System, a program aimed at economic self-sufficiency for the nation. As speaker of the house during Monroe's term in office, he was instrumental in crafting much of the legislation that passed through Congress. A gifted negotiator, Clay helped resolve the problems in the Missouri Compromise of 1820 and designed the Compromise of 1833 and Compromise of 1850. He led the Whig Party until his death in 1852.

Clayton Antitrust Act   The 1914 Clayton Antitrust Act, spearheaded by Woodrow Wilson, improved upon the vague Sherman Antitrust Act by enumerating a series of illegal business practices.

Bill Clinton   Bill Clinton, a Democrat, served as president from 1993 to 2001, during a period of intense partisanship in the U.S. government. Clinton's few major domestic and international successes were overshadowed by the sex scandal that led to his impeachment and eventual acquittal.

Christopher Columbus   Columbus sailed to the New World under the Spanish flag in 1492. Although not the first European to reach the Americas, he is credited with the journey across the Atlantic that finally opened the New World to exploration. In 1493, he established Santo Domingo on the island of Hispaniola as a base for further exploration.

Committee to Defend America First   Isolationists who were opposed to FDR's reelection in 1940 sponsored the Committee to Defend America First. Committee members urged neutrality, claiming that the U.S. could stand alone regardless of Hitler's advances on Europe.

Committees of Correspondence   Committees of Correspondence, organized by New England patriot leader Samuel Adams, comprised a system of communication between patriot leaders in the towns of New England and eventually throughout the colonies. Committees of Correspondence provided the political organization necessary to unite the colonies in opposition to Parliament. These committees were responsible for sending delegates to the First Continental Congress.

Common Sense   Thomas Paine published the pamphlet *Common Sense* in 1776, in which he argued that the colonists should free themselves from British rule and establish an independent government based on Enlightenment ideals—one that would protect man's natural rights. *Common Sense* became so popular and influential in the colonies that many historians credit it with dissolving the final barriers to the fight for independence.

Glossary

Compromise of 1833   In response to the escalating Nullification Crisis, Andrew Jackson signed two laws aimed at easing the crisis. Together, these laws were known as the Compromise of 1833. The first measure provided for a gradual lowering of import duties over the next decade, and the second measure, known as the Force Bill, authorized the president to use arms to collect customs duties in South Carolina. South Carolina considered the new tariff a valid concession and rescinded its previous nullifications.

Compromise of 1850   Designed by Henry Clay and pushed through Congress by Stephen A. Douglas, the Compromise of 1850 aimed to resolve sectional conflict over the distribution of slave-holding versus free states. The compromise included the admission of California as a free state; the division of the remainder of the Mexican cession into two separate territories, New Mexico and Utah, without federal restrictions on slavery; the continuance of slavery but abolition of the slave trade in the District of Columbia; and a more effective Fugitive Slave Law. The compromise, however, proved unable to stem controversy over slavery's expansion.

Congregationalism   Congregationalism was a church system set up by the Puritans of the Massachusetts Bay Colony, in which each local church served as the center of its own community. This structure stood in contrast to the Church of England, in which the single state church held sway over all local churches. Congregationalism assured many colonists a role in directing the individual congregations, which became the center of religious, and often political, life in New England communities.

Congress of Industrial Organizations (CIO)   The CIO emerged from within the American Federation of Labor in 1938. The CIO became an influential labor group, operating during an era of government and business cooperation. In 1955, it merged with the AFL to become the AFL-CIO.

Congressional caucus   The congressional caucus met during the early years of the United States to choose presidential candidates. The caucus is significant in that it denied the population any real say in the nomination process, instead leaving the choice up to a centralized group of politicians based in Washington, DC. By the election of 1824, the congressional caucus had become a symbol of undemocratic elitist rule. Resented by much of the American public, the caucus lost its political influence in the early 1820s.

Connecticut Compromise   Ending weeks of stalemate, the Connecticut Compromise reconciled the Virginia Plan and the New Jersey Plan for determining legislative representation in Congress. The Connecticut Compromise established equal representation for all states in the Senate and proportional representation by population in the House of Representatives.

Conquistador   Conquistador is a general term for any one of a group of Spanish explorers in the New World who sought to conquer the native people, establish dominance over their lands, and prosper from natural resources, including its gold. The Conquistadors established a large Hispanic empire stretching from Mexico to Chile and wreaked havoc among native populations.

Constitution   The Constitution is the document that outlines the operation and central principles of American government. As opposed to the Articles of Confederation, which it replaced, the Constitution created a strong central government with broad judicial, legislative, and executive powers, though it purposely restricted the extent of these powers through a system of checks and balances. Written at the Constitutional Convention, the Constitution was ratified by the states in 1789.

Constitutional Convention   In response to the Annapolis Convention's suggestion, Congress called for the states to send delegates to Philadelphia to amend the Articles of Confederation. Delegates came to the convention from every state except Rhode Island in May 1787, and decided to draft an entirely new framework of government that would give greater powers to the central government. This document became the Constitution.

Calvin Coolidge   Calvin Coolidge, president from 1923 to 1929, was nicknamed "Silent Cal." The reticent Coolidge believed that government should interfere with the economy as little as possible and spent his time in office fighting congressional efforts to regulate business.

Corrupt bargain   Although Andrew Jackson won the most popular and electoral votes in the 1824 election, he failed to win the requisite majority and the election was thrown to the House of Representatives. Speaker of the House Henry Clay backed John Quincy Adams for president, ensuring Adams's victory, and Adams rewarded Clay by making him secretary of state. Jackson and his supporters, enraged that the presidency had been "stolen" from them, denounced Adams and Clay's deal as a "corrupt bargain."

James Fennimore Cooper   James Fennimore Cooper was an influential American writer in the early nineteenth century. His novels, *The Pioneers* (1823), *The Last of the Mohicans* (1826), and others, employed distinctly American themes.

Glossary

Glossary

Cotton gin   Invented in 1793 by Eli Whitney, the cotton gin separated the fibers of short-staple cotton from the seeds. The mechanization of this task made cotton plantations much more efficient and profitable, giving rise to a cotton-dominated economy in the South.

Court Packing scheme   Early in 1937, FDR tried to pass a court reform bill designed to allow the president to appoint an additional Supreme Court justice for each current justice over the age of seventy, up to a maximum of six appointments. Though he claimed the measure was offered in concern for the workload of the older justices, the proposal was an obvious attempt to dilute the power of the older, conservative justices. The Senate voted against the proposal later that year. Many historians argue that the proposed bill resulted in a loss of credibility for FDR, which helped slow the New Deal to a standstill.

Confederate States of America   The seceded states formed the Confederate States of America during the Civil War.

Containment   The policy of containment called for the preservation of post–World War II conditions, meaning the U.S. would not challenge nations currently in the Soviet sphere of influence, but also would not tolerate any further Soviet expansion. Established during Truman's presidency, containment initially applied primarily to Europe. It soon evolved into a justification for U.S. global involvement against communism.

Jim Crow laws   Jim Crow laws were state laws that institutionalized segregation in the South from the 1880s through the 1960s. Along with segregating schools, buses, and other public accommodations, these laws made it difficult or impossible for southern blacks to vote and often forbade intermarriage.

Cuban Missile Crisis   In 1962, a year after the failed Bay of Pigs Invasion, the U.S. government learned that Soviet missile bases were being constructed in Cuba. President John F. Kennedy demanded that the USSR stop shipping military equipment to Cuba and remove the bases. The Kennedy administration considered numerous options to force Soviet compliance, from bombings to amphibious assaults, but ultimately opted for a naval blockade preventing Soviet ships from reaching Cuba without inspection. After a stressful waiting period during which nuclear war seemed imminent, Soviet Premier Khrushchev backed down and began dismantling the bases in return for a U.S. promise not to invade Cuba.

George Armstrong Custer   Custer, a Civil War hero, was dispatched to the hills of South Dakota in 1874 to fight off Native American threats. When gold was discovered in the region, the federal government announced that Custer's forces would hunt down all Sioux not in reservations after January 31, 1876. Many Sioux refused to comply, and Custer began to mobilize his troops. At the Battle of Little Bighorn, the Sioux wiped out an overconfident Custer and his men.

Clarence Darrow   Clarence Darrow, a Chicago trial lawyer, earned fame in the 1925 Scopes Monkey Trial. Although Darrow's client, John Scopes, lost the case, Darrow argued masterfully in court, and in so doing weakened the influence and popularity of fundamentalism nationwide.

Dartmouth College v. Woodward   In the case of *Dartmouth College v. Woodward*, the Supreme Court under Chief Justice John Marshall ruled that the state of New Hampshire could not convert the college to a state university because doing so would violate the college's contract, granted by King George III in 1769, and the Constitution forbids states from interfering with contracts. Republicans interpreted the decision and phrasing of the opinion as a shocking defeat for states' rights. The exposed political conflicts concealed under the facade of cooperation during the Era of Good Feelings.

Jefferson Davis   A former secretary of war, Davis was elected president of the Confederacy shortly after its formation. Davis was never able to garner adequate public support and faced great difficulties in uniting the Confederate states under one central authority.

Dawes Plan   The Dawes Plan, devised by banker Charles G. Dawes in 1924, scaled back U.S. demands for debt payments and reparations from World War I and established a cycle of U.S. loans to Germany. These loans provided Germany with funds for its payment to the Allies, thus funding Allied debt payments to the U.S.

Dawes Severalty Act   Passed in 1887, the Dawes Severalty Act called for the breakup of the reservations and the treatment of Native Americans as individuals rather than as tribes. Any Native American who accepted the act's terms received 160 acres of farmland or 320 acres of grazing land and was guaranteed U.S. citizenship in twenty-five years. Intended to help Native Americans integrate into white society, in practice the Dawes Act caused widespread poverty and homelessness.

Espionage Act   Passed in 1917, the Espionage Act enumerated a list of antiwar activities warranting fines or imprisonment.

Glossary

Eugene Debs   Debs was a prominent socialist leader and five-time presidential candidate. He formed the American Railway Union in 1893 and led the Pullman Strike a year later. He helped found the Industrial Workers of the World, or Wobblies, in 1905. A pacifist, he opposed the government's involvement in World War I. In 1918, he was imprisoned for denouncing the government's aggressive tactics under the Espionage Act and Sedition Amendment; he was released in 1921.

Declaration of Independence   The most celebrated event in American history, the Declaration of Independence was approved by Congress on July 4, 1776. Drafted by Thomas Jefferson, the declaration enumerated the reasons for the split with Britain and laid out the Enlightenment values (best expressed by John Locke) of natural rights to "life, liberty, and the pursuit of happiness" upon which the American Revolution was based.

Declaration of the United Nations   On January 1, 1942, prompted by American entry into World War II, representatives of twenty-six nations signed the Declaration of the United Nations. They pledged support for the Atlantic Charter and vowed not to make separate peace agreements with the enemy.

Declaratory Act   Passed in 1776 just after the repeal of the Stamp Act, the Declaratory Act stated that Parliament could legislate for the colonies in all cases. Most colonists interpreted the act as a face-saving mechanism and nothing more. Parliament, however, continually interpreted the act in its broadest sense in order to legislate in and control the colonies.

Deep Throat   "Deep Throat" was the name used to mask the identity of an informant who helped *Washington Post* reporters Bob Woodward and Carl Bernstein as they delved into the Watergate scandal. Deep Throat's true identity remains a mystery to this day.

Deists   Influenced by the spirit of rationalism, Deists believed that God, like a celestial clockmaker, had created a perfect universe and then stepped back to let it operate according to natural laws.

Democratic Party   The Democratic Party was the party of Andrew Jackson, organized at the time of the election of 1828. Throughout the mid- and late 1800s, the Democrats championed states' rights and fought against political domination by the economic elite. They opposed tariffs, federal funding for internal improvements, and other extensions of the power of the federal government. The party found its core support in the South. The party underwent a major transformation in the 1930s during Franklin Delano Roosevelt's presidency, when Democrats began to embrace a more aggressive and involved role for the federal government. FDR's New Deal policies cost Democrats the support of the white South—their traditional stronghold—and won them the support of many farmers, urban workers, blacks, and women. This Democratic support base remains in place today.

Détente   Détente refers to a relaxation of tensions between the U.S. and USSR in the 1960s and 1970s. During this period, the two powers signed treaties limiting nuclear arms productions and opened up economic relations. One of the most famous advocates of this policy was President Richard Nixon's secretary of state, Henry Kissinger.

Dollar diplomacy   William Howard Taft's foreign policy was called "dollar diplomacy." Taft sought to address international problems by extending American investment overseas, believing that such activity would both benefit the U.S. economy and promote stability abroad.

Dorothea Dix   Dorothea Dix, a Massachusetts schoolteacher, studied the condition of the insane in poorhouses and prisons. Her efforts helped bring about the creation of insane asylums, where the insane could be more humanely treated.

Domino theory   The domino theory expressed the idea that if any nation fell to communism, the surrounding nations would likely fall to communism as well. The domino theory, expounded by Dwight D. Eisenhower, served to justify U.S. intervention in Vietnam. According to the theory, if Vietnam became communist, much of Southeast Asia would as well, thus justifying U.S. military opposition to the Vietcong.

Stephen A. Douglas   Stephen A. Douglas first rose to national prominence as Speaker of the House, when he pushed the Compromise of 1850 through Congress. Douglas became the leading Northern Democrat and supporter of popular sovereignty and authored the Kansas-Nebraska Act. He battled Abraham Lincoln for a seat in the Senate (successfully) in 1858, and for president (unsuccessfully) in 1860.

Frederick Douglass   Frederick Douglass is perhaps the most famous of all abolitionists. An escaped slave, Douglass worked closely with William Lloyd Garrison to promote abolitionism in the 1830s.

Dred Scott v. Sandford   In the 1857 *Dred Scott* case, the Supreme Court ruled that no black, whether slave or free, could become a citizen of the United States or sue in federal court. The decision further argued that the Missouri Compromise was unconstitutional because it violated the Fifth Amendment's protection of property, including slaves, from being taken away without due process.

Glossary

W.E.B. Du Bois   Du Bois was the African-American leader most opposed to the gradual approach of achieving equal rights presented by Booker T. Washington. Du Bois advocated immediate equal treatment and equal educational opportunities for blacks. He helped initiate the founding of the National Association for the Advancement of Colored People (NAACP) in 1909.

Dust bowl   The name given to the southern Great Plains region (Arkansas, Texas, Missouri, and Oklahoma) during the 1930s, when a severe drought and fierce winds led to violent dust storms that destroyed farmland, machinery, and houses, and led to countless injuries. Roughly 800,000 residents migrated west from the dust bowl toward California during the 1930s and 1940s.

Dynamic conservatism   President Eisenhower called his philosophy of government "dynamic conservatism" to distinguish it from the Republican administrations of the past, which he deemed backward-looking and complacent. He was determined to work with the Democratic Party rather than against it and at times opposed proposals made by more conservative members of his own party.

Economic Opportunity Act   An element in Lyndon B. Johnson's Great Society, the Economic Opportunity Act established an Office of Economic Opportunity to provide young Americans with job training and created a volunteer network devoted to social work and education in impoverished areas.

Eighteenth Amendment   The Eighteenth Amendment, ratified on January 16, 1919, prohibited the manufacture, transport, or sale of alcoholic beverages. It was sporadically enforced, violated by many, and repealed in 1933.

Dwight D. Eisenhower   Eisenhower, a Republican, served as president from 1953 to 1961. Along with Secretary of State John Foster Dulles, Eisenhower sought to lessen Cold War tensions. One notable success in this realm was the ending of the Korean War. Before serving as president, Eisenhower was the supreme commander of the Allied Expeditionary Force in World War II, coordinating Operation Overlord and the American drive from Paris to Berlin.

Eisenhower Doctrine   Announced in 1957, the Eisenhower Doctrine committed the U.S. to preventing Communist aggression in the Middle East, with troops if necessary.

Elastic clause   Article I, Section VIII of the Constitution states that Congress shall have the power "to make all laws which shall be necessary and proper for carrying into execution . . . powers vested by this Constitution in the government of the United States." This clause, known as the elastic clause, was a point of much contention between those who favored a loose reading of the Constitution and those who favored a strict reading.

Emancipation Proclamation   Abraham Lincoln issued the Emancipation Proclamation on January 1, 1863 to free all slaves under rebel (Confederate) control. The proclamation did not affect the slave states within the Union or the parts of the Confederacy in Union hands, and therefore in practice freed very few slaves. Nevertheless, the proclamation gave the war a new objective—emancipation—and crystallized the tension between the Union and the Confederacy.

Embargo Act   In response to the *Chesapeake-Leopard* affair, Thomas Jefferson endorsed the Embargo Act. Passed in December 1807, the act ended all of America's importation and exportation. Jefferson hoped the embargo would put enough economic pressure on the French and British that the two nations would be forced to recognize U.S. neutrality rights in exchange for U.S. goods. The embargo, however, hurt the American economy more than it did Britain's or France's, leading to the act's repeal in March 1809.

Emergency Banking Relief Act   The opening act of the New Deal, the Emergency Banking Relief Act provided a framework for the many banks that had closed early in 1933 to reopen with federal support.

Emergency Committee for Unemployment   The Emergency Committee for Unemployment was Herbert Hoover's principal effort to lower the unemployment rate. Established in October 1930, the committee sought to organize unemployment relief by voluntary agencies, but Hoover granted the committee only limited resources with which to work.

Ralph Waldo Emerson   Ralph Waldo Emerson was a leader of the transcendentalist movement and an advocate of American literary nationalism. He published a number of influential essays during the 1830s and 1840s, including "Nature" and "Self Reliance."

Enforcement Acts of 1870 and 1871   Passed largely in response to the activities of the Ku Klux Klan, the Enforcement Acts of 1870 and 1871 protected black suffrage.

Glossary

Enlightenment   Also known as the Age of Reason, the Enlightenment was an intellectual movement that spread through Europe and America in the eighteenth century. Followers of the Enlightenment championed the principles of rationalism and logic in all areas of thought—religious, political, social, and economic. Their skepticism toward beliefs that could not be proved by science or clear logic naturally led to Deism.

Era of Good Feelings   The Era of Good Feelings is the name used to describe the period between the end of the War of 1812 and the rise of Andrew Jackson in 1828, during which the United States was governed under a one-party system that promoted nationalism and cooperation. The era centers on the period of James Monroe's presidency, as Monroe strove to avoid political conflict and strengthen American nationalism and pride.

Leif Ericson   Leif Ericson is the alleged leader of a group of Icelandic people who sailed to the eastern coast of Canada and unsuccessfully attempted to colonize the area around the year 1000, nearly 500 years before Columbus arrived in the Americas.

Erie Canal   Begun in 1817 and finished in 1825, the Erie Canal was America's first major canal project. The canal stretched from Albany to Buffalo, New York, measuring a total of 363 miles.

Eugenics   The field of eugenics, popularized during the Progressive Era, was founded on the premise that the "perfect" human society could be achieved through genetic tinkering. Writers on eugenics often used this theory to justify a supremacist white Protestant ideology, which advocated the elimination of what they considered undesirable racial elements from American society.

Fair Deal   The Fair Deal was Harry S. Truman's attempt to extend the policies of the New Deal. Beginning in 1949, the Fair Deal included measures to increase the minimum wage, expand Social Security, and construct low-income housing.

Fair Labor Standards Act   The 1938 Fair Labor Standards Act provided for a minimum wage and restricted shipment of goods produced with child labor, symbolizing the FDR administration's commitment to working together with labor forces.

Farmers' Alliance   During the 1880s, the Farmers' Alliance took the place of the Grange as a support group for the nation's farmers. The alliances were politically active in the Midwest and South, and were central to the founding of the Populist Party.

Federal Deposit Insurance Corporation (FDIC)   The FDIC was created as a part of the first New Deal to increase faith in the banking system by insuring individual deposits with federal funds.

Federal Emergency Relief Act   The Federal Emergency Relief Act (FERA), one of the New Deal's most comprehensive measures, appropriated $500 million to support state and local treasuries that had run dry. The FERA was passed in May 1933.

Federal Home Loan Bank Act   A late attempt by Hoover to address the problems of the destitute, the 1932 Federal Home Loan Bank Act established a series of banks to make loans to other banks, building and loan associations, and insurance agencies, in an attempt to prevent foreclosures on private homes.

Federalists   Led by Alexander Hamilton, the Federalists believed in a strong central government at the expense of state powers. The Federalists were the staunch supporters of the Constitution during the ratification process, and remained a political force throughout the first thirty or so years of the United States. The Federalists entered into decline after the election of the Republican Thomas Jefferson to the presidency and basically disappeared as a political party after the debacle of the Hartford Convention, at the close of the War of 1812.

The Federalist Papers   A series of newspaper articles written by John Jay, James Madison, and Alexander Hamilton, the *Federalist Papers* enumerated the arguments in favor of the Constitution and refuted the arguments of the Anti-federalists.

Federal Reserve Act   Woodrow Wilson's most notable legislative success, the 1913 Federal Reserve Act reorganized the American banking system by creating a network of twelve Federal Reserve banks authorized to distribute currency.

Federal Reserve Board   The Federal Reserve Board (a.k.a. "the Fed") is responsible for making monetary policy in the United States—that is, the policy affecting the money supply. The Fed operates mainly through the mechanisms of buying and selling government bonds and adjusting the interest rates. During the Great Depression, the Fed was given greater power and freedom to directly regulate the economy.

Federal Securities Act   The May 1933 Federal Securities Act made corporate executives liable for any misrepresentation of securities issued by their companies. It paved the way for future acts to regulate the stock market.

Federal Trade Commission Act   The 1914 Federal Trade Commission Act created the Federal Trade Commission to monitor and investigate firms involved in interstate commerce and to issue "cease and desist" orders when business practices violated free competition. The act was a central part of Wilson's plan to aggressively regulate business.

The Feminine Mystique   Betty Friedan's *The Feminine Mystique*, published in 1963, was a rallying cry for the women's liberation movement. It denounced the belief that women should be tied to the home and encouraged women to get involved in activities outside their home and family.

Fifteenth Amendment   Ratified in March 1870, the Fifteenth Amendment prohibited the denial of voting rights to any citizen based on "race, color, or previous condition of servitude."

Millard Fillmore   When Zachary Taylor died on July 9, 1850, Vice President Millard Fillmore took over as president and served out the remainder of Taylor's term, until 1853. He helped to push the Compromise of 1850 through Congress.

Fireside chats   "Fireside chats" refers to FDR's radio broadcasts to the citizens of the United States during his presidency. Through these broadcasts he encouraged confidence and national unity and cultivated a feeling of governmental compassion.

First Continental Congress   The First Continental Congress convened on September 5, 1774, with all colonies but Georgia sending delegates chosen by the Committees of Correspondence. The congress endorsed the Suffolk Resolves, voted for an organized boycott of British imports, and sent a petition to King George III that conceded to Parliament the power of regulation of commerce, but stringently objected to Parliament's arbitrary taxation and unfair judicial system.

First Great Awakening   The First Great Awakening was a time of religious fervor during the 1730s and 1740s. The movement arose in reaction to the rise of skepticism and the waning of religious faith brought about by the Enlightenment. Protestant ministers held revivals throughout the English colonies in America, stressing the need for individuals to repent and urging a personal understanding of truth instead of an institutionalized one. The Great Awakening precipitated a split within American Protestantism.

First hundred days   The first hundred days of FDR's presidency, from March 4 to June 16, 1933, encompassed a period of dramatic legislative productivity. During this period, FDR laid out the programs that constituted the New Deal.

F. Scott Fitzgerald   A prominent author during the Roaring Twenties, F. Scott Fitzgerald wrote stories and novels that both glorified and criticized the wild lives of the carefree and prosperous. His most famous works include *This Side of Paradise*, published in 1920, and *The Great Gatsby*, published in 1925.

Flapper   A central stereotype of the Jazz Age, the flapper was a flamboyant, liberated, pleasure-seeking young woman seen more in media portrayals than in reality. The archetypal flapper look was tomboyish and fashionable: short bobbed hair; knee-length, fringed skirts; long, draping necklaces; and rolled stockings.

Force Bill   Part of the Compromise of 1833, the Force Bill authorized President Jackson to use arms to collect customs duties in South Carolina.

Gerald Ford   Gerald Ford, a Republican, took over the presidency from Richard Nixon after Nixon resigned on August 9, 1974 because of the Watergate scandal. Ford pardoned Nixon and pushed a conservative domestic policy but was little more than a caretaker of the White House until his defeat in the election of 1976.

Fourteen Points   On January 8, 1918, Woodrow Wilson outlined a liberal and idealistic peace program with his Fourteen Points. His plan called for unrestricted sea travel, free trade, arms reduction, an end to secret treaties, the territorial reorganization of Europe in favor of self-rule, and, most importantly, the creation of "a general association of nations" to protect peace and resolve conflicts.

Fourteenth Amendment   Ratified in July 1868 (ratification was a prerequisite for ex-Confederate states' readmission into the Union), the Fourteenth Amendment guaranteed the rights of citizenship to all people born or naturalized in the United States, black and white, and provided for the loss of congressional representation for any state that denied suffrage to any of its male citizens.

Francisco Franco   Francisco Franco controlled the rightist forces during the Spanish Civil War. His fascist government ruled Spain form 1939 until 1975.

Benjamin Franklin   Benjamin Franklin was an inventor, patriot, and statesman. During the Revolutionary War, he served as an ambassador to France, playing a key role in getting France to recognize the United States' independence. Franklin was the oldest delegate to the Constitutional Convention. The other delegates admired his wisdom, and his advice proved crucial in the drafting of the Constitution. Franklin has often been held up as the paradigm of Enlightenment thought in Colonial America because of his fascination with and contributions to the fields of science and philosophy.

Freedmen's Bureau   Established in 1865 and staffed by Union army officers, the Freedmen's Bureau worked to protect black rights in the South and to provide employment, medical care, and education to Southern blacks.

Freedom ride   The freedom ride was a 1961 program led by the Congress of Racial Equality and the Student Nonviolent Coordinating Committee, in which black and white members of the two organizations rode through the South on public buses to protest illegal segregation in interstate transportation.

Freeport Doctrine   The Freeport Doctrine was Democrat Stephen A. Douglas's attempt to reconcile his belief in popular sovereignty with the *Dred Scott* decision. In the famed Lincoln-Douglas debates of 1858, Douglas argued that territories could effectively forbid slavery by failing to enact slave codes, even though the *Dred Scott* decision deprived government of the right to restrict slavery in the territories.

Free-Soil Party   A political party supporting abolition, the Free-Soil Party formed in 1848 from the merger of a northern faction of the Democratic Party, the abolitionist Liberty Party, and antislavery Whigs. The Free Soilers nominated Martin Van Buren as their candidate for president. The party did not come close to winning the election but did pull ten percent of the national popular vote, an impressive showing for a third party. The relative success of the Free-Soil Party demonstrated that slavery had become a central issue in national politics.

French and Indian War   The French and Indian War in North America (1754–1763) mirrored the Seven Years War in Europe (1756–1763). English colonists and soldiers fought the French and their Native American allies for dominance in North America. England's eventual victory brought England control of much disputed territory and eliminated the French as a threat to English dominance in the Americas.

Fugitive Slave Act   The Fugitive Slave Act, originally passed in 1793 and strengthened as part of the Compromise of 1850, allowed Southerners to send posses onto Northern soil to retrieve runaway slaves. During the early 1850s, Northerners mounted resistance to the act by aiding escaping slaves and passing personal liberty laws.

Fundamentalism   Fundamentalism emerged in the early 1900s as a reaction against the many scientific and social challenges facing conservative American Protestantism. Protestant fundamentalists insisted upon the divine inspiration and truth of every word in the Bible and sought to discredit or censure those who questioned the tenets of Protestant faith. Fundamentalism peaked in the 1920s with the anti-evolution movement, culminating in the Scopes Monkey Trial.

Gag rule   During the 1830s, abolitionists sent endless petitions to Congress demanding the outlawing of slavery in Washington, D.C. In 1836, Southerners pushed the gag rule through Congress, which tabled all abolitionist petitions in Congress and thereby prevented antislavery discussions. The gag rule was repealed in 1845, under increased pressure from Northern abolitionists and from those concerned with the rule's restriction of the right to petition.

William Lloyd Garrison   William Lloyd Garrison, the founder of the abolitionist newspaper *The Liberator*, was the most famous white abolitionist of the 1830s. Known as a radical, he pushed for equal legal rights for blacks and went so far as to encourage good Christians to abstain from all aspects of politics, including voting, in protest against the nation's corrupt and prejudicial political system.

Marcus Garvey   Marcus Garvey, a powerful African American leader during the 1920s, founded the Universal Negro Improvement Association (UNIA) and advocated a mass migration of African Americans back to Africa. His radical movement won a substantial following. Garvey was convicted of fraud in 1923 and was deported to Jamaica in 1927. The UNIA collapsed without his leadership.

Gettysburg Address   In a speech that began "Four score and seven years ago," Abraham Lincoln recast the war as a historic test of the ability of a democracy to survive. He delivered the speech on November 19, 1863, at the dedication of a cemetery for casualties of the Union victory at the Battle of Gettysburg.

Gibbons v. Ogden   This 1824 Supreme Court case involved state versus federal licensing rights for passenger ships between New York and New Jersey. A devoted Federalist, Chief Justice Marshall ruled that the states could not interfere with Congress's right to regulate interstate commerce. He interpreted "commerce" broadly to include all business, not just the exchange of goods.

Samuel Gompers   Gompers was the founding leader of the American Federation of Labor. Under Gompers, the AFL rarely went on strike, but rather took a more pragmatic approach based on negotiating for gradual concessions.

"Good Neighbor" policy   In 1933, FDR announced the "Good Neighbor" policy toward Latin American. He pledged that no nation, not even the U.S., had the right to interfere in the affairs of any other nation.

Mikhail Gorbachev   Mikhail Gorbachev was the last Soviet political leader, becoming general secretary of the Communist Party in 1985 and then president of the USSR in 1988. Gorbachev helped ease tension between the U.S. and the USSR, work that earned him the Nobel Peace Prize in 1990. He oversaw the fall of the Soviet Union and resigned as president on December 25, 1991.

Gospel of Success   The Gospel of Success was one justification for the enormous and growing gap between rich and poor in the U.S. during the so-called Industrial Revolution. The Gospel of Success centered on the claim that anyone could become wealthy with enough hard work and determination. This ideology was supported by writers like Horatio Alger.

Grange   The Patrons of Husbandry, known as "the Grange," was formed in 1867 as a support system for struggling western farmers. The Grange offered farmers education and fellowship, providing a forum for homesteaders to share advice and emotional support at biweekly social functions. The Grange also represented farmers' needs in dealings with big business and the federal government.

Ulysses S. Grant   Grant was the commanding general of the Union forces in the West for much of the war and of all Union forces during the last year of the war. Grant later became the nation's eighteenth president, serving from 1869 to 1877 and presiding over the decline of Reconstruction. His administration was marred by corruption.

Great Debate   The so-called Great Debate was an eight-month discussion in Congress over Henry Clay's proposed compromise to admit California as a free state, allow the remainder of the Mexican cession (Utah and New Mexico territories) to be decided by popular sovereignty, and strengthen the Fugitive Slave Act. Clay's solution was passed as separate bills, which together came to be known as the Compromise of 1850.

Great Society   Lyndon B. Johnson's program for domestic policy, the Great Society, aimed to achieve racial equality, an end to poverty, and improvements in health-care. Johnson pushed a number of Great Society laws through Congress early in his presidency, but the Great Society failed to materialize fully, as the administration turned its attention toward foreign affairs.

Gulf of Tonkin Resolution   Passed by the Senate in 1964 following questionable reports of a naval confrontation between North Vietnamese and U.S. forces, the Gulf of Tonkin Resolution granted President Johnson broad wartime powers without explicitly declaring war.

Gulf War   The Gulf War, named for its location near the Persian Gulf, began when Iraqis under the leadership of Saddam Hussein invaded Kuwait in August 1990. In January 1991, the U.S. attacked Iraqi troops, supply lines, and bases. In late February, U.S. ground troops launched an attack on Kuwait City, successfully driving out the Iraqis. A total of 148 Americans died in the war, while over 100,000 Iraqis died, both military personnel and civilians.

Alexander Hamilton   Hamilton emerged as a major political figure during the debate over the Constitution, as the outspoken leader of the Federalists and one of the authors of *The Federalist Papers*. Later, as secretary of treasury under Washington, Alexander Hamilton spearheaded the government's Federalist initiatives, most notably through the creation of the Bank of the United States.

Warren G. Harding   President from 1921 until his death in 1923, Harding ushered in a decade of Republican dominance in the U.S. He accommodated the needs of big business and scaled back government involvement in social programs. After Harding's death, his administration was found to be rife with corruption.

Harlem Renaissance   The Harlem Renaissance refers to the flowering of black culture in New York's Harlem neighborhood during the 1920s. Black writers and artists produced plays, poetry, and novels that often reflected the unique African-American experience in America and in Northern cities in particular.

Harpers Ferry   In 1859, John Brown led twenty-one men in seizing a federal arsenal in Harpers Ferry, Virginia, in a failed attempt to incite a slave rebellion.

Hartford Convention   The Hartford Convention was a meeting of Federalists near the end of the War of 1812, in which the New England–based party enumerated its complaints against the ruling Republican Party. The Federalists, already losing power steadily, hoped that antiwar sentiment would lead the nation to support their cause and return them to power. Perceived victory in the war, however, turned many against the Federalists, whose actions in Hartford were labeled traitorous and antagonistic to the unity and cooperation of the Union.

Nathaniel Hawthorne   Nathaniel Hawthorn was an early American fiction writer. His most famous work, *The Scarlet Letter* (1850), explored the moral dilemmas of adultery in a Puritan community.

Hayes-Tilden Compromise   This compromise resolved the conflict arising from the election of 1876, in which Democrat Samuel J. Tilden won the popular vote but Republican leaders contested some states' election returns, thereby ensuring the Republican candidate Rutherford B. Hayes's victory. To minimize protest from the Democratic Party, Republicans agreed to end Reconstruction by removing federal troops from the last two occupied states in the South.

Haymarket riot   In 1886, workers held a rally in Chicago to protest police brutality against strikers. The riot erupted in violence after someone threw a bomb, killing seven policemen and prompting a police backlash. After the riot, leaders of the Knights of Labor were arrested and imprisoned, and public support for the union cause plunged.

Glossary

William Randolph Hearst   Hearst bought the *New York Journal* in the late 1890s. His paper, along with Joseph Pulitzer's *New York World*, engaged in yellow journalism, printing sensational reports of Spanish activities in Cuba designed to win a circulation war between the two newspapers.

Helsinki Accords   In 1975, Gerald Ford and Soviet Premier Leonid Brezhnev, along with the leaders of thirty-one other states, signed the Helsinki Accords to solidify European boundaries and promise to respect human rights and the freedom to travel.

Ernest Hemingway   Ernest Hemingway was one of the best-known writers of the 1920s' "lost generation." An expatriate, Hemingway produced a number of famous works during the 1920s, including *The Sun Also Rises* in 1926 and *A Farewell to Arms* in 1929. A member of the Popular Front, Hemingway fought in the Spanish Civil War, and his 1940 novel *For Whom the Bell Tolls* depicts an American involved in that bloody war. Hemingway's work, like that of many of his contemporaries, reflects the disillusionment and despair of the time and the desire to return to a simpler time of traditional morality.

Hiroshima   A Japanese city, Hiroshima is the site of the first-ever atomic bomb attack. On August 6, 1945, the U.S. used an atomic bomb to destroy the Japanese city, killing 70,000 of its citizens instantaneously and injuring another 70,000, many of whom later died of radiation poisoning.

Alger Hiss   In 1948, *Time* editor Whitaker Chambers accused longtime government worker Alger Hiss of spying for the USSR. After a series of highly publicized hearings and trials, Hiss was convicted of perjury in 1950 and sentenced to five years imprisonment, emboldening conservatives to redouble their efforts to root out subversives within the government.

Adolph Hitler   Hitler became Chancellor of Germany in January of 1933. As chancellor, he led the nation to economic recovery by mobilizing industry for the purposes of war. His fascist Nazi Party undertook measures of mass genocide and, through efforts to gain global hegemony, ushered Europe into World War II.

Holocaust   The Holocaust is the name for the Nazis' systematic persecution and extermination of European Jews from 1933 until 1945. More than 6 million Jews died in concentration camps throughout Germany and Nazi-occupied lands.

Homestead Act   The Homestead Act, passed in 1862, encouraged settlement of the West by offering 160 acres of land to anyone who would pay $10, live on the land for five years, and cultivate and improve it.

Glossary

Homestead strike   In 1892 near Pittsburgh, steel workers staged the Homestead strike against the Carnegie Steel Company to protest a pay cut and the 70-hour workweek. Ten workers were killed in a riot that began when 300 "scabs" from New York (Pinkerton detectives) arrived to break the strike. Federal troops were called in to suppress the violence.

Herbert Hoover   Hoover served as president from 1929 to 1933, during the stock market collapse and the height of the Great Depression. A conservative, Hoover made only limited efforts to control the economic and social problems of the nation, efforts that were generally considered to be too little, too late. Hoover did, however, set the stage for many future New Deal measures during the last year of his presidency.

J. Edgar Hoover   J. Edgar Hoover served as head of the FBI from 1924 until his death in 1972. He aggressively investigated suspected subversives during the Cold War.

Hooverville   Hoovervilles were communities of destitute Americans living in shanties and makeshift shacks. The homeless constructed Hoovervilles around most major U.S. cities in the early 1930s, providing a stark reminder of Hoover's failure to alleviate the poverty of the Great Depression.

House of Burgesses   The House of Burgesses, established in Jamestown, Virginia, in 1619, is considered to be the first representative government in the New World. It consisted of 22 representatives from 11 districts of colonists.

House Un-American Activities Committee   During the period of McCarthyism, the House Un-American Activities Committee (HUAC) provided the congressional forum in which many hearings about suspected communists in the government took place.

Henry Hudson   An English explorer sponsored by the Dutch East India Company, Hudson sailed up the river than now bears his name, in 1609, nearly reaching present-day Albany. His explorations gave the Dutch territorial claims to the Hudson Bay region.

Hull House   Hull House was an early settlement house founded in Chicago in 1889 by Jane Addams. Hull House provided education, health care, and employment aid to poor families.

Saddam Hussein   Saddam Hussein is the leader of Iraq. In August 1990, he led an Iraqi invasion of Kuwait, sparking the Gulf War.

Glossary

Anne Hutchinson   Anne Hutchinson was a dissenter in the Massachusetts Bay Colony who caused a schism in the Puritan community. Eventually, Hutchinson's faction lost out in a power struggle for the governorship. She was expelled from the colony in 1637 and traveled southward with a number of her followers, establishing the settlement of Portsmouth, Rhode Island.

Impressment   In the early 1800s, the British practiced a policy known as "impressment" whereby the British boarded American ships in search of British naval deserters, whom they would force (or impress) back into service. Often, naturalized or native-born Americans were also seized, provoking outrage in America. Impressment was one of a string of British violations against U.S. neutrality rights in the early 1800s that helped spark the War of 1812.

Indentured servitude   Indentured servants were usually adult white males who bound themselves to labor on plantations for a fixed number of years (three to seven years, generally) in order to secure their freedom. Some immigrants came to the colonies willingly, while others were manipulated into coming or even kidnapped and forced to come in order to remedy the severe labor shortage in the colonies. The first Africans brought to the colonies were also brought as indentured servants, though that practice was not long-lived. During the seventeenth century, slavery replaced indentured servitude as the preferred means of securing labor in the South, as tobacco plantations spread throughout the South and required massive amounts of labor.

Independent Treasury Bill   Hailed by Martin Van Buren and his supporters as a second Declaration of Independence, the Independent Treasury Bill was signed into law in 1840. The bill established an independent treasury to hold public funds in reserve and prevent excessive lending by state banks, thus guarding against inflation. The Independent Treasury Bill was a response to the panic of 1837, which many blamed on the risky and excessive lending practices of state banks.

Indian Removal Act   Passed in 1830, the Indian Removal Act granted Jackson the funds and authority to move Native Americans to assigned lands in the West. The Indian Removal Act primarily targeted the Cherokee tribe in Georgia, as part of the federal government's broad plan to claim Native American lands inside the boundaries of the states.

Industrial Workers of the World (Wobblies)   The IWW, or Wobblies, as they were nicknamed, was a radical labor organization. Founded in 1905, the IWW advocated revolution and massive societal reorganization. The organization faded away around 1920.

Inflation   Inflation is the increase of available paper money and bank credit, leading to higher prices and less-valuable currency.

Interstate Commerce Act   In 1887, Congress passed the Interstate Commerce Act, which forbade price discrimination and other monopolistic practices of the railroads.

Intolerable Acts   The Intolerable Acts, passed in 1774, were the combination of the four Coercive Acts, meant to punish the colonists after the 1773 Boston Tea Party, and the unrelated Quebec Act. The Intolerable Acts were seen in the American colonies as the blueprints for a British plan to deny the Americans representative government and were the impetus for the convening of the First Continental Congress.

Iran-Contra affair   A series of investigations in 1987 exposed evidence that the U.S. had been selling arms to the anti-American government in Iran and had been using profits from these sales to secretly and illegally finance the Contras in Nicaragua. The Contras were a rebel group fighting against the Sandinista regime in Nicaragua, which had communist ties. Oliver North, a member of the National Security Council, had organized this illegal operation from within the White House. There was no proof that Ronald Reagan was aware of North's actions.

Iron curtain   The "iron curtain," a term coined by Winston Churchill, referred to the area of Eastern Europe controlled indirectly by the USSR, usually through puppet governments. This area was cut off from noncommunist Europe.

Andrew Jackson   President from 1829 to 1837, Andrew Jackson presided over a time of great political change. A strong-willed and determined leader, Jackson opposed federal support for internal improvements and the Second Bank of the United States and fought for states' rights and Native American removal. His opponents nicknamed him "King Andrew I" because of his extensive and unprecedented use of the veto power, which they deemed to be tyrannical and against the spirit of democracy. Before becoming president, Jackson gained popularity as a general who launched aggressive military campaigns against Native Americans and led the U.S. to a stunning victory over British forces at the Battle of New Orleans in January 1815.

John Jay   John Jay played an important role in the establishment of the new government under the Constitution. One of the authors of *The Federalist Papers*, he was involved in the drafting of the Constitution.

Glossary

Jay's Treaty   Jay's Treaty, signed in 1795, provided for the removal of British troops from American land and opened up limited trade with the British West Indies, but said nothing about British seizure of American ships or the "impressment" of American sailors. While much of the American public criticized the treaty for being too favorable to Britain, the treaty may have been the greatest diplomatic feat of the Washington administration, since it preserved peace with Britain.

Jazz Age   The 1920s are often called the Jazz Age because of the development and flourishing of jazz music in that decade, as well as the highly publicized (if exaggerated) accounts of wild parties, drinking, and dancing.

Thomas Jefferson   A prominent statesman from Virginia, Jefferson became George Washington's first secretary of state, but later resigned from that post in opposition to Alexander Hamilton's continued efforts to centralize power in the national government and strip states of their rights. Along with James Madison, Jefferson took up the cause of the strict constructionists and the Republican Party, advocating the limitation of federal government. As the nation's third president from 1801 to 1809, Jefferson organized the national government by Republican ideals, doubled the size of the nation through the Louisiana Purchase, and struggled to maintain American neutrality in foreign affairs.

Andrew Johnson   Johnson became president upon Lincoln's death in 1865 and remained in office until 1869. Johnson's plan for presidential Reconstruction was too lenient in the eyes of a Congress heavily influenced by Radical Republicans. Congress fought his initiatives and undertook a more stringent and retributive Reconstruction plan. Johnson's relationship with Congress declined steadily during his presidency, culminating in impeachment proceedings in 1868.

Lyndon B. Johnson   Lyndon B. Johnson was Kennedy's vice president, and became president in 1963 after Kennedy's assassination. He remained president until 1968, when he declined to run again. Johnson's presidency is most known for his attempts to enact his Great Society program at home and his decision to commit troops to fighting in the Vietnam War.

Joint Chiefs of Staff   FDR created the Joint Chiefs of Staff in February 1942 to oversee the rapidly growing military. The Joint Chiefs included representatives from the army, navy, and air force.

Joint-stock companies   By 1600, the English crown and parliament were hesitant to spend money on colonization, having exhausted much time and money in the battle against the Spanish for position in North America. In the absence of government funding, joint-stock companies formed to accrue funding for colonization through the sale of public stock. These companies dominated English colonization throughout the seventeenth century.

Judicial review   Established by Chief Justice John Marshall in *Marbury v. Madison* (1803), the principle of judicial review held that the Supreme Court could declare an act of Congress unconstitutional.

Judiciary Act of 1789   The Judiciary Act of 1789 created the court system. The act established a federal district court in each state and affirmed that the Supreme Court exercised final jurisdiction in all legal matters.

Kansas-Nebraska Act   The Kansas-Nebraska Act, passed in 1854, divided the Nebraska territory into two parts, Kansas and Nebraska, and left the issue of slavery in the territories to be decided by popular sovereignty. The Kansas-Nebraska Act nullified the prohibition of slavery above 36°30'–latitude provided for in the Missouri Compromise of 1820.

John F. Kennedy   John F. Kennedy, a Democrat, served as president from 1961 until his assassination in November 1963. A young and charismatic leader, he cultivated a glorified image in the eyes of the American public. Kennedy's primary achievements came in the realm of international relations, most notably the peaceful resolution of the Cuban Missile Crisis.

King George III   King George III, the King of England from 1760–1820, exercised a greater hand in the government of the country than had many of his predecessors. Colonists were torn between loyalty to the king and resistance to acts carried out in his name. After George III rejected the Olive Branch Petition, the colonists came to see him as a tyrant.

Martin Luther King Jr.   King first rose to national prominence as a Civil Rights leader during the 1956 Montgomery bus boycott. Throughout the late 1950s and early 1960s, King tirelessly led the struggle for integration and full equality through nonviolent means. He was assassinated in 1968.

Henry Kissinger   Henry Kissinger served as national security adviser and secretary of state under Nixon. A major proponent of détente, Kissinger often met secretly with communist leaders in efforts to improve East-West cooperation.

Kitchen Cabinet   Opponents of Jackson dubbed his cabinet the "Kitchen Cabinet" because the members he appointed were all his close political allies and many had questionable political skill. Instead of serving as a policy forum to help shape the president's agenda, as previous cabinets had done, Jackson's cabinet assumed a mostly passive and supportive role.

Knights of Labor   Founded in 1869, the Knights were one of the first major labor organizations in the U.S. The Knights fell into decline after one of several leaders was executed for killing a policeman in the Haymarket riot of 1886.

Know-Nothing Party   The American, or "Know-Nothing," Party largely took the place of the Whig Party between 1854 and 1856, after the latter's demise. The Know-Nothings focused on issues of antislavery, anti-Catholicism, nativism, and temperance. The party collapsed during the latter half of the 1850s, in part because of the rise of the Republicans.

Korean War   On June 24, 1950, troops from the Soviet-supported People's Democratic Republic of Korea, known as North Korea, invaded the Republic of Korea, known as South Korea. Without asking for a declaration of war, Truman committed U.S. troops as part of a United Nations "police action." The Korean War was conducted by predominantly American forces under the command of General Douglas MacArthur. Limited fighting continued until June 1953, when an armistice basically restored the prewar border between North and South Korea.

Korematsu v. U.S.   In the 1944 case of *Korematsu v. U.S.*, the Supreme Court upheld FDR's 1942 executive order for the evacuation of all Japanese-Americans on the West Coast into internment camps. The camps operated until March 1946.

Ku Klux Klan (KKK)   The most prominent of the many southern vigilante groups, the Klan was founded in 1866 in Tennessee, and was soon controlled by Democratic politicians. By 1868, the Klan operated in all Southern states. The Klan often conducted raids to intimidate black voters and Republican officials. The Klan faded away in the late nineteenth century and then made a resurgence beginning in 1915. Capitalizing on middle-class Protestant dismay at changing social and economic conditions in America, the Klan took root throughout the South, and in Western and Midwestern cities and was dominated by white native-born Protestants. Membership and influence again declined in 1925, when corruption among Klan leaders was exposed.

Laissez-faire   By the doctrine of laissez-faire (which literally means in French, "let do"), the government took a "hands-off" approach to the economy and let the market regulate itself.

League of Nations   The brainchild of Woodrow Wilson, the League of Nations was a collective security body meant to provide a forum for the resolution of conflict and to prevent future world wars. The League's covenant was written into the Treaty of Versailles. The U.S. Senate, however, voted against joining the League, leaving it a weak international force.

Robert E. Lee   The commanding general of the Confederate Army of Northern Virginia, Lee was a brilliant strategist, an excellent commander, and a brave fighter. Many historians believe that the Confederacy held out as long as it did only because of Lee's skill and the loyalty he earned from his troops.

Lend-Lease Act   A key move in support of the Allied cause before the U.S. formally entered the war, the Lend-Lease Act of March 1941 allowed the president to lend or lease supplies to any nation deemed "vital to the defense of the United States," such as Britain. Lend-lease was extended to Russia in November 1941 after Germany invaded Russia.

Letters from a Pennsylvania Farmer   This series of twelve letters published by John Dickinson denounced the Townshend Duties by demonstrating that many of the arguments employed against the Stamp Act were valid against the Townshend Duties as well. The letters inspired anti-British sentiment throughout the colonies.

Lewis and Clark   Meriwether Lewis and William Clark, known collectively as Lewis and Clark, were commissioned by Thomas Jefferson to explore the new territory of the Louisiana Purchase. They traveled 3,000 miles between 1804 and 1806, collecting scientific data and specimens and charting the territory to the west of the Mississippi. Their journey spurred national interest in exploration and settlement of the West.

Liberal Republicans   Formed as a party in 1872, the Liberal Republicans split from the ranks of the Republican Party in opposition to President Ulysses S. Grant. Many Liberals argued that the task of Reconstruction was complete and should be put aside. The defection of the Liberals served a major blow to the Republican Party and shattered what congressional enthusiasm remained for Reconstruction.

The Liberator   Radical abolitionist William Lloyd Garrison published *The Liberator* from 1831 until 1865. An influential newspaper within the growing abolition movement, *The Liberator* expressed new and controversial opinions such as the belief that blacks deserved legal rights equal to those of whites.

Limited Test-Ban Treaty   In July 1963, JFK and Soviet Premier Nikita Khrushchev agreed to the Limited Test-Ban Treaty, which prohibited undersea and atmospheric testing of nuclear weaponry. This agreement was characteristic of a period of lessening tensions between the world's two superpowers, known as détente.

Abraham Lincoln   Abraham Lincoln emerged during the late 1850s as the nation's top Republican. His eloquent and forceful performance in the Lincoln-Douglas Debates of 1858 earned him the Republican nomination for president in 1860. His victory in the election precipitated the secession of the first southern states, paving the way for the Civil War. A moderate Republican, Lincoln's primary goal during and after the Civil War was to restore the Union. He began planning for a lenient Reconstruction in 1863, but was assassinated before it was clear how Reconstruction would have developed had he lived.

Lincoln-Douglas Debates   A series of seven debates held between August 21 and October 15, 1858 between senatorial candidates, the Lincoln-Douglas debates pitted Abraham Lincoln, a free-soil Republican, against Stephen A. Douglas, a Democrat in favor of popular sovereignty. The debates were hard-fought, highly attended, and in the end, inconclusive, but they crystallized the two dominant positions of the North in regard to slavery and propelled Lincoln onto the national scene.

Henry Cabot Lodge   Henry Cabot Lodge led the group of senators known as "reservationists" during the 1919 debate over the League of Nations. Lodge and his followers would support U.S. membership in the League of Nations only if major revisions were made to the covenant (part of the Treaty of Versailles). Wilson, however, refused to compromise, and the treaty was rejected. The U.S. never joined the League of Nations.

Huey Long   Huey Long, a Senator from Louisiana, was one of the most vocal critics of the New Deal. His liberal "Share Our Wealth" program proposed a 100 percent tax on all income over $1 million, and large redistribution measures. His passionate orations won him many devoted followers and many bitter enemies. He was assassinated in September of 1935 at the capitol building in Baton Rouge.

Loose constructionists   Loose constructionists favored a loose reading of the Constitution, especially of the elastic clause, in order to expand the powers of the central government to include implied constitutional powers, not just enumerated ones. Led by Alexander Hamilton, loose constructionists formed the core of the Federalist Party.

Lost generation   The term "lost generation" describes a small but prominent circle of writers, poets, and intellectuals during the 1920s. These artists, including Ernest Hemingway, F. Scott Fitzgerald, and Ezra Pound, grew disillusioned with America's postwar culture, finding it overly materialisticl and spiritually void. Many of these artists moved to Europe to write, and their writings often expressed their disgust with America's materialism and superficiality.

Louisiana Purchase   Negotiated in April 1803, during Thomas Jefferson's presidency, the Louisiana Purchase nearly doubled the size of the nation and opened the West to exploration and settlement. With the Louisiana Purchase came not only expansion but also strife: border disputes with foreign powers as well as congressional debates over the admission of new states from the region (whether the states would be slave-holding or free).

Lusitania   The *Lusitania* was a British vessel sunk by a German U-boat in May 1915, killing more than 120 American citizens. This event prompted Woodrow Wilson to plan for a military buildup and encouraged American alliance with Britain and France in opposition to Germany.

Douglas MacArthur   Douglas MacArthur was an American general who commanded the United States army in the Pacific during World War II. After the war, he oversaw the American occupation of Japan and later led American troops in the Korean War. Though MacArthur pushed for total victory in the Korean War, seeking to conquer all of Korea and perhaps move into China, Harry S. Truman held him back from this aggressive goal. After a month of publicly denouncing the administration's policy, MacArthur was relieved from duty in April 1951.

Machine politics   Machine politics refers to the means by which political parties during the Industrial Revolution controlled candidates and voters through networks of loyalty and corruption. In machine politics, party bosses exploited their ability to give away jobs and benefits (patronage) in exchange for votes.

Macon's Bill No. 2   Macon's Bill No. 2 was James Madison's 1810 ploy to induce either Britain or France to lift trade restrictions. Under Macon's Bill No. 2, U.S. trade sanctions were lifted with the promise that if one country agreed to free trade with the U.S., sanctions would be reimposed against the other nation.

Glossary

James Madison   Madison began his political career as a Federalist, joining forces with Alexander Hamilton during the debate over the Constitution. He was one of the authors of *The Federalist Papers* and a staunch advocate of strong central government. He later became critical of excessive power in central government and left the Federalist Party to join Thomas Jefferson in leading the Republican Party. As a Republican he served as the nation's fourth president, from 1809 to 1817.

Maine   The *Maine* was a U.S. battleship sunk by an explosion in Havana harbor in February 1898. Though later investigations suggested that an onboard fire had caused the blast, at the time the American people believed a Spanish mine was responsible. The sinking of the *Maine* combined with the effect of yellow journalism led the American public to push strongly for war against Spain.

Manhattan Project   The Manhattan Project was a secret American scientific initiative to develop an atomic bomb. Working for almost three years at Los Alamos, New Mexico, the project succeeded in detonating the first atomic blast over the desert on July 16, 1945. The bombs produced by the Manhattan project were subsequently dropped on the Japanese cities of Hiroshima and Nagasaki.

Manifest destiny   "Manifest destiny" refers to the belief of many Americans in the mid-nineteenth century that it was the nation's destiny and duty to expand and conquer the West in the name of God, nature, civilization, and progress. Journalist John L. O'Sullivan first coined the phrase "manifest destiny" in 1845, as he wrote of "our manifest destiny to overspread and to possess the whole of our continent which Providence has given us for the development of the great experiment of liberty."

Horace Mann   Horace Mann was the most prominent proponent of public school reform. Appointed secretary of the Massachusetts Board of Education in 1837, he reformed the school system by increasing state spending on schools, lengthening the school year, dividing the students into grades, and introducing standardized textbooks, among other changes. Mann set the standard for public school reform throughout the nation.

Mao Zedong   A Chinese political leader, Mao Zedong (1893-1976) founded the Chinese Communist Party (CCP) in 1921. In 1949, Mao's communist forces defeated Chinese nationalist forces uder Chiang Kai-shek and established the People's Republic of China (PRC).

Marbury v. Madison   In this 1803 case, Chief Justice John Marshall ruled that the Judiciary Act of 1789 was unconstitutional because Congress had overstepped its bounds in granting the Supreme Court the power to issue a writ of mandamus (an ultimatum from the court) to any officer of the United States. This ruling established the principle of judicial review.

March Against Death   The March Against Death was a high point for the student antiwar movement and a poignant symbol of antiwar sentiment in the U.S. In November 1969, 300,000 people marched in a long, circling path through Washington, D.C., for 40 hours straight, each holding a candle and the name of a soldier killed or a village destroyed in Vietnam.

John Marshall   John Marshall served as Chief Justice of the Supreme Court from 1801 until his death in 1835. Under his leadership, the Court became as powerful a federal force as the executive and legislative branches. During Thomas Jefferson's presidency, Marshall's most notable decision came in *Marbury v. Madison*, in which he asserted the principle of judicial review. During James Monroe's term in office, Marshall delivered two rulings in 1819 that curtailed states' rights and exposed the latent conflicts in the Era of Good Feelings.

Thurgood Marshall   Thurgood Marshall, a black attorney, successfully argued the case of *Brown v. Board of Education of Topeka* in front of the Supreme Court in 1954. In 1967, Marshall became the first African-American appointed to the Supreme Court.

Marshall Plan   Begun in 1948, the Marshall Plan was a four-year plan of American aid for the economic reconstruction of Europe. The U.S. government hoped that this plan would prevent further communist expansion by eliminating economic insecurity and political instability in Europe—the very instability that had made it possible for communists to set up several puppet governments in eastern Europe. By 1952, Congress had appropriated some $17 billion for Marshall Plan aid, and the Western European economy had largely recovered.

Mayflower   The *Mayflower* was the ship that carried the Pilgrims across the Atlantic from the Netherlands to Plymouth Plantation in 1620 (remember that the Pilgrims had fled England to the Netherlands before heading to the New World).

Mayflower Compact   The Mayflower Compact is often cited as the first example of self-government in the Americas. The Pilgrims, having arrived at a harbor far north of the land that was rightfully theirs, signed the Mayflower Compact to establish a "civil body politic" under the sovereignty of James I.

Glossary

McCarthyism   McCarthyism refers to the extreme anticommunism in American politics and society during the early 1950s. The term derives from the actions of Senator Joseph McCarthy, who led an intense campaign against alleged subversives during this period.

McCulloch v. Maryland   In the case of *McCulloch v. Maryland* (1819), the Supreme Court under Chief Justice John Marshall ruled that states could not tax federal institutions such as the Second Bank of the United States. The ruling asserted that the federal government wielded supreme power in its sphere and that no states could interfere with the exercise of federal powers. A denunciation of states' rights, this ruling angered many Republicans.

William McKinley   Republican William McKinley defeated Democratic and Populist candidate William Jennings Bryan in the 1896 election, becoming the nation's twenty-fifth president. A supporter of big business, McKinley pushed for high protective tariffs. Under his leadership, the U.S. became an imperial world power. He was assassinated by an anarchist in 1901.

McKinley Tariff   As a congressman, William McKinley wrote and engineered passage of the tariff that bears his name, the McKinley Tariff, in 1890. The act raised protective tariffs by nearly fifty percent. These tariffs are the highest the U.S. has ever placed on imports.

Meat Inspection Act   The 1906 Meat Inspection Act set federal regulations for meatpacking plants and established a system of federal inspection. This act and other measures aimed at improving the quality of food products were undertaken in response to the muckrakers' exposés of the unsanitary and often hazardous conditions of food processing plants.

Medical Care Act   An element of President Johnson's Great Society program, in 1965, the Medical Care Act created Medicare to provide senior citizens with Medical insurance and Medicaid to provide welfare recipients with free health care.

Herman Melville   Herman Melville was a prominent American fiction writer in the 1840s and 1850s. His best-known novel is *Moby Dick* (1851).

H.L. Mencken   Mencken's magazine *American Mercury* served as the journalistic counterpart to the "lost generation" of writers, such as F. Scott Fitzgerald, who grew disillusioned and even disgusted with American postwar life. Mencken used satire to critique political leaders and American society during the 1920s.

Mercantilism   Mercantilism was a theory of trade stressing that a nation's economic strength depended on exporting more than it imported. British mercantilism manifested itself in the triangular trade and in a series of laws passed between the mid-1600s and the mid-1700s aimed at fostering British economic dominance. These laws included the Navigation Acts (1651–1673).

Mexican War   Tension mounted between the U.S. and Mexico after Texas accepted the U.S. Congress's offer of admission to the Union despite the Mexican government's opposition. After Mexican troops crossed the Rio Grande, the U.S. declared war against Mexico in 1846. The U.S. won the war easily. The Treaty of Guadalupe Hidalgo, which ended the war, granted the U.S. possession of Texas, New Mexico, and California in exchange for $15 million.

Minutemen   "Minutemen" was the nickname given to local militiamen who fought against the British during the Revolutionary War. They were called minutemen because of their supposed ability to be ready for battle at a minute's notice.

Missouri Compromise   The Missouri Compromise resolved one of the United States' earliest sectional conflicts, involving the status of Missouri as a slave or free state once admitted to the Union. The Missouri Compromise of 1820 admitted Missouri as a slave state, admitted Maine as a free state, and prohibited slavery in all land north of 36°30' in the remainder of the Louisiana Territory.

James Monroe   Monroe served as president from 1817 until 1825. His presidency formed the core of the Era of Good Feelings, characterized by the consolidation of the one-party system, an upsurge of American nationalism encouraging political harmony, and Monroe's efforts to avoid political controversy and conflict.

Monroe Doctrine   President Monroe issued the Monroe Doctrine in December 1823. The doctrine asserted U.S. ascendancy in the Western Hemisphere.

J.P. Morgan   Morgan was a Wall Street financier and business leader involved in many of the most profitable business ventures during the era of industrialization. In 1901, he bought Carnegie Steel and established the world's first billion-dollar corporation, U. S. Steel Corporation.

Glossary

Mormonism   Joseph Smith founded the Church of Latter-Day Saints, also known as Mormonism, in 1831. The core of the church's tenets derives from the Book of Mormon, a book of revelation similar in style and form to the Bible. Led by Smith, the Mormons moved steadily westward during the early 1830s, seeking to escape persecution and to convert the Native Americans en route. During the late 1840s, a new leader, Brigham Young, led the Mormons to present-day Utah, where they settled and still live.

Lucretia Mott   Lucretia Mott was an outspoken proponent of women's rights, and with Elizabeth Cady Stanton organized the Seneca Falls Convention in 1848.

Muckrakers   Muckrakers were investigative journalists who worked during the early 1900s to uncover the corruption and misdeeds in American industry and politics. Their writings and publications encouraged widespread political and social reform. Important muckrakers include Upton Sinclair, Ida Tarbell, and Lincoln Steffens.

Munich Pact   When Hitler declared his intention to take the Czech Sudetenland by force, British and French leaders acceded to his demands by signing the Munich Pact on September 30, 1938. Intended to appease Hitler and avoid war, the pact only emboldened Hitler further. Bent on conquest, Hitler soon sent troops into many European nations.

Benito Mussolini   Mussolini rose to power as a fascist Italian dictator in 1922. He allied with Hitler in the Rome-Berlin Axis in 1936, uniting the two fascist forces and paving the way for World War II.

Mutual Assured Destruction (MAD)   The U.S. Cold War policy of Mutual Assured Destruction, or MAD, acknowledged that both the U.S. and the Soviet Union had large enough nuclear arsenals to destroy each other many times over. The policy, developed in the early 1960s, was America's form of defense against Soviet attack: MAD promised that whoever launched a nuclear attack would, in turn, be attacked with nuclear weapons, resulting in absolute nuclear devastation on both sides—hence the title, "Mutual Assured Destruction."

Nagasaki   The site of the second U.S. atomic bomb attack on Japan, Nagasaki was devastated by a nuclear blast on August 9, 1945. The explosion led to 40,000 immediate deaths and 60,000 injuries.

National Association for the Advancement of Colored People   In 1909, a group of blacks led by W.E.B. Du Bois joined with a group of white reformers to form the National Association for the Advancement of Colored People (NAACP). The NAACP called for an end to racial discrimination, attacked Jim Crow laws, and fought to overturn the 1896 Supreme Court decision in *Plessy v. Ferguson*. Led by middle-class blacks, the NAACP continued to advocate integration and equal treatment for American blacks throughout the 1900s and continues to do so today. In the 1920s, it served as a counterpoint to the more radical black rights group, the UNIA, led by Marcus Garvey.

National Conservation Commission   Created in 1909 by Theodore Roosevelt, the National Conservation Commission aimed to achieve more efficient and responsible management of the nation's resources.

National Defense Act   The National Defense Act, passed in June 1916, called for the buildup of military forces in anticipation of war. The National Defense Act was largely a response to German threats to American neutrality.

National Labor Relations Act   Popularly known as the Wagner Act, the National Labor Relations Act of 1935 provided a framework for collective bargaining. It granted workers the right to join unions and engage in bargaining, and forbade employers from interfering with, or discriminating against, union rights. The act demonstrated the support of FDR's administration for labor needs and unionization.

National Origins Act   The epitome of anti-immigrant sentiments in the 1920s, the National Origins Act restricted immigration from any one nation to two percent of the number of people already in the U.S. of that national origin in 1890. This law severely restricted immigration from southern and eastern Europe, and excluded Asians entirely.

National Organization for Women (NOW)   The National Organization for Women, formed in 1966, lobbied Congress, initiated lawsuits, and raised public awareness of women's issues. NOW was a central part of the 1960s' women's liberation movement.

National Recovery Administration (NRA)   The NRA, perhaps the most important element of the first New Deal, established a forum in which business and government officials met to set regulations for fair competition. These regulations bound industry from 1933 until 1935, when the Supreme Court declared the NRA unconstitutional.

Glossary

Glossary

National Republican Party   Led by Henry Clay and John Quincy Adams, the National Republicans were one of the two new political parties that emerged in the late 1820s to challenge the dominant Republican Party (the other being the party of Andrew Jackson, the Democrats). The party found its core support in the industrializing Northeast. During Jackson's second term in office, the National Republican Party reconfigured itself as the Whig Party.

National War Labor Board   The National War Labor Board monitored and regulated the efforts of organized labor during World War II. Although the board restricted wage increases, it encouraged the extension of many fringe benefits to American workers.

Navigation Acts   Passed under the mercantilist system, the Navigation Acts (1651–1673) regulated trade in the colonies in order to benefit the British economy exclusively. The acts restricted trade between England and English colonial ports to English or colonial ships, required certain colonial goods to pass through England or Scotland before being exported to foreign nations, provided subsidies for the production of certain raw goods in the colonies, and banned the colonists from competing with the English in large-scale manufacturing.

Neutrality Acts   To keep the U.S. out of another world war, Congress passed a series of Neutrality Acts between 1935 and 1937. The acts made arms sales to warring countries illegal and forbade American citizens to travel aboard the ships of belligerent nations.

New Deal   Coined by FDR in 1932, the phrase "New Deal" came to stand for FDR's strategy for relief and recovery in the United States during the Great Depression. Most New Deal measures emerged during the first hundred days of FDR's presidency.

New England Confederation   New England colonists formed the New England Confederation in 1643 as a defense against local Native American tribes and the encroaching Dutch. The colonists formed the alliance without the English crown's authorization.

New freedom   "New freedom" characterized Woodrow Wilson's approach to foreign relations. Unlike Roosevelt's big stick policies and Taft's dollar diplomacy, Wilson's foreign policy sought to bring morality to foreign relations. Wilson denounced imperialism and economic meddling, and focused instead on spreading democracy throughout the world.

New Frontier   John F. Kennedy's domestic policy, the "New Frontier" focused on reform at home and victory in the Cold War abroad.

New Jersey Plan   The New Jersey Plan was presented at the Constitutional Convention as an alternative to the Virginia Plan. The New Jersey Plan favored small states in that it proposed a unicameral Congress with equal representation for each state.

New Look   Reflecting Eisenhower's preference for nuclear deterrence rather than ground force involvement against the Soviet Union, the New Look emphasized the massive retaliatiory potential of a large nuclear stockpile. Eisenhower worked to increase nuclear spending and decrease spending on ground troops.

Nineteenth Amendment   The Nineteenth Amendment, ratified in August 1920, granted women the right to vote.

Richard Nixon   Richard Nixon, a Republican, served as president from 1969 until his resignation on August 9, 1974. Nixon oversaw a moderately conservative domestic program, gradually pulled troops out of Vietnam, and improved relations with the nation's communist enemies. He was forced to resign after being implicated in the Watergate scandal.

Nixon Doctrine   Announced in July 1969 as a corollary to Nixon's efforts to pull American troops out of Vietnam, the Nixon Doctrine pledged a change in the U.S. role in the Third World from military protector to helpful partner.

Non-Intercourse Act   After the repeal of the Embargo Act, this 1809 law restricted trade with Britain and France only, opening up trade with all other foreign ports.

Oliver North   Lieutenant Colonel Oliver North, a member of the National Security Council, was involved in the Iran-Contra scandal. In 1987, investigations revealed that North had headed the initiative to funnel funding secretly and illegally to the contras in Nicaragua, who fought against an anti-U.S. regime.

North American Free Trade Agreement (NAFTA)   Passed narrowly by Congress in November 1993, the North American Free Trade Agreement (NAFTA) removed trade barriers between Canada, the U.S., and Mexico. Bill Clinton championed this and other efforts to integrate the U.S. more fully into the international economy.

North Atlantic Treaty Organization (NATO)   Formed in 1949 to counter the Soviet threat in Eastern Europe, the North Atlantic Treaty Organization prepared Western European powers and the U.S. to fight as a unified coalition. Throughout the Cold War, NATO was the primary Western alliance in opposition to communist forces.

Glossary

Northwest Ordinance   The 1787 Northwest Ordinance defined the process by which new states could be admitted into the Union from the Northwest Territory. The ordinance forbade slavery in the territory but allowed citizens to vote on the legality of slavery once statehood had been established. The Northwest Ordinance was the most lasting measure of the national government under the Articles of Confederation.

Nullification Crisis   Like the tariff bills of 1816 and 1824, the Tariff of 1828 hurt the Southern economy while benefiting Northern and Western industries. For this reason, Southerners called it the "Tariff of Abominations." Vice President John C. Calhoun denounced the tariff as unconstitutional on the grounds that federal laws must benefit all states equally, and urged that states nullify, or override, the tariff within their own borders. South Carolina did so in November 1832, punctuating a debate over tariffs and states' rights that raged within the administration and the entire federal government between 1828 and 1833.

Nuremberg Trials   The Nuremberg Trials of Nazi war criminals began in November 1945. More than 200 defendants were indicted in the thirteen trials. All but thirty-eight of the defendants were convicted of conspiring to wage aggressive war and of mistreating prisoners of war and inhabitants of occupied territories.

Oil embargo   In the OPEC (the Organization of Petroleum Exporting Countries) oil embargo of 1973, OPEC nations refused to export oil to Western nations. The embargo, in effect from October 1973 to March 1974, sparked rapid inflation in the West and had a crippling effect on the U.S. economy. The ensuing economic crisis plagued Gerald Ford's time in office.

Office of Censorship   The Office of Censorship, created in December 1941, reflected U.S. government worries about information leaks to the enemy during World War II. The office examined all letters sent overseas and worked with media firms to control information broadcast to the people.

Office of Strategic Services (OSS)   The Office of Strategic Services, or OSS, was established by the Joint Chiefs of Staff in 1942 to conduct espionage, collect information crucial to strategic planning, and assess the strengths and weaknesses of the enemy.

Office of War Information   The Office of War Information employed artists, writers, and advertisers to shape public opinion concerning World War II. The Office publicized reasons for U.S. entry into the war, often portraying the enemy Axis powers as barbaric and cruel.

Open Door policy   Developed by Secretary of State John Hay, the Open Door policy aimed to combat the European spheres of influence that threatened to squeeze American business interests out of Chinese markets. The Open Door policy consisted of pressuring European powers to open key ports within their spheres of influence to U.S. businessmen.

Operation Overlord   Operation Overlord refers to the Allied air, land, and sea assault on occupied France. The operation centered on the "D-Day" invasion (June 6, 1944), in which American, British, and Canadian troops stormed the beaches at Normandy. These Allied forces sustained heavy casualties but eventually took the beach and moved gradually inland.

J. Robert Oppenheimer   Oppenheimer headed the Manhattan Project, the secret American operation to develop the atomic bomb.

Thomas Paine   Thomas Paine published his pamphlet *Common Sense* in January 1776, exhorting Americans to rise in opposition to the British government and establish a new type of government based on Enlightenment ideals. Historians have cited the publication of this pamphlet as the event that finally sparked the Revolutionary War. Paine also published rational criticisms of religion, most famously in *The Age of Reason* (1794–1807), a work mainly inspired by Enlightenment ideals.

Palmer Raids   In 1910, in an operation coordinated by Attorney General A. Mitchell Palmer, police and federal marshals raided the homes of suspected radicals and the headquarters of radical organizations in thirty-two cities. The Palmer Raids resulted in more than 4,000 arrests, 550 deportations, and uncountable violations of civil rights.

Panama Canal   Built by the U.S. between 1904 and 1914, the Panama Canal is an articifial waterway stretching across the isthmus of Panama that connects the Atlantic and Pacific Oceans. By a treaty signed in 1977, Panama gained full control of the canal in 1999.

Panic of 1819   The panic of 1819 was the start of a two-year depression caused by extensive speculation, the loose lending practices of state banks, a decline in European demand for American staple goods, and mismanagement within the Second Bank of the United States. The panic of 1819 exacerbated social divisions within the United States and is often called the beginning of the end of the Era of Good Feelings.

Glossary

Panic of 1837   The panic of 1837 punctured the economic boom sparked by state banks' loose lending practices and overspeculation. Contraction of the nation's credit in 1836 led to widespread debt and unemployment. Martin Van Buren spent most of his time in office attempting to stabilize the economy and ameliorate the depression.

Panic of 1873   In 1873, because of overexpansion and overspeculation, the largest bank in the nation collapsed, followed by the collapse of many smaller banks, business firms, and even the stock market. The panic of 1873 precipitated a five-year national depression.

Panic of 1893   The panic of 1893 began when the railroad industry faltered during the early 1890s, followed by the collapse of many related industries. Confidence in the U.S. dollar plunged. The depression lasted roughly four years.

Paris Accords   Signed on January 27, 1973, the Paris Accords settled the terms of U.S. withdrawal from Indochina, ending the war between the U.S. and North Vietnam. The treaty left the conflict between North and South Vietnam unresolved.

Rosa Parks   Rosa Parks was a quiet black seamstress who sparked the Montgomery bus boycott by refusing to give up her bus seat for a white man in December 1955.

Peace Corps   The Peace Corps, created by JFK in 1961, sends volunteer teachers, health workers, and engineers on two-year aid programs in Third World countries.

Pearl Harbor   On December 7, 1941, Japan bombed Pearl Harbor, the site of an American naval base in Hawaii. The surprise attack resulted in the loss of more than 2,400 American lives, as well as many aircraft and sea vessels. The following day, on December 8, the U.S. declared war against Japan, officially entering World War II.

Pendleton Act   Passed in 1883, the Pendleton Act established a civil service exam for many public posts and created hiring systems based on merit rather than on political favors, or patronage. The act aimed to eliminate the corrupt hiring practices that had so long plagued the U.S. government.

William Penn   Penn, an English Quaker, founded Pennsylvania in 1682, after receiving a charter from King Charles II the year before. He launched the colony as a "holy experiment" based on religious tolerance.

Ross Perot   Ross Perot, a third-party candidate in the presidential election of 1992, won nineteen percent of the public vote. His strong showing demonstrated voter disaffection with the two major parties.

Personal liberty laws   During the 1850s, nine northern states passed personal liberty laws to counteract the Fugitive Slave Act. These state laws guaranteed all alleged fugitives the right to trial by jury and to a lawyer and prohibited state jails from holding alleged fugitives.

Franklin Pierce   Franklin Pierce, a Democrat, served as president of the United States from 1853 to 1857. He was the last president until 1932 to win the popular and electoral vote in both the North and South. Pierce's performance in office can best be described as perfunctory. He was little more than a caretaker in the years leading up to the Civil War.

Pilgrims   The Pilgrims were a group of English Separatists who had originally sought refuge in the Netherlands. In 1620, they sailed to Plymouth on the Mayflower and established the colony of Plymouth Plantation.

Platt Amendment   The Platt Amendment authorized American withdrawal from Cuba only on the following conditions: Cuba must vow to make no treaty with a foreign power limiting its independence; the U.S. reserved the right to intervene in Cuba when it saw fit; and the U.S. could maintain a naval base at Guantánamo Bay.

Plessy v. Ferguson   The 1896 Supreme Court Decision in *Plessy v. Ferguson* ruled that segregation was not illegal as long as facilities for each race were equal. This "separate but equal" doctrine served to justify Southern laws separating blacks and whites on trains, in restaurants, in schools, and in other public facilities throughout the early and mid-1900s. In 1954, the Supreme Court overturned the "separate but equal" doctrine in the landmark *Brown v. Board of Education* case.

Edgar Allen Poe   Edgar Allen Poe was a fiction writer who gained popularity in the 1840s as a writer of horrific tales. He published many famous stories, including "The Raven" (1844) and "The Cask of Amontillado" (1846).

James K. Polk   Polk served as U.S. president from 1845 to 1849. A firm believer in expansion, Polk led the U.S. into the Mexican War in 1846, in which the U.S. acquired Texas, New Mexico, and California. Many Northerners saw Polk as an agent of Southern will aiming to expand the nation in order to extend slavery into the West.

Popular Front   The Popular Front was a political group active in aiding the leftist forces in the Spanish Civil War. Prominent American intellectuals and writers, including Ernest Hemingway and John Dos Passos, joined the group.

Glossary

Popular sovereignty   First espoused by Democratic presidential candidate Lewis Cass in 1848 and eventually championed by Stephen A. Douglas, popular sovereignty was the principle stating that Congress should not interfere with the issue of slavery's expansion, but rather leave the question up to each territory. By this principle, each territory, when seeking admission into the Union, would draw up a constitution declaring slavery legal or illegal as it saw fit. Popular sovereignty became the core of the Democratic position on slavery's expansion during the 1850s.

Populist Party   The farmers' Alliances in the Midwest and South joined with poor laborers to form the core of the People's Party of the United States, begun in 1892. The Populist Party agitated for various reforms that supported farmers and the poor, including "free silver" (the unlimited coinage of silver), which would ease debt payments. In 1896, the Democrats appropriated parts of the Populist platform and nominated William Jennings Bryan for president. Bryan lost the election despite the joint backing of the Democrats and Populists.

Potsdam Conference   Although relations between Truman, Churchill, and Stalin grew increasingly strained as World War II wound to its close, during the Potsdam Conference (July 17–August 2, 1945) they coordinated the division of Germany into occupation zones and planned for the Nuremberg Trials. Potsdam was the final meeting between the Big Three powers under the pretense of a wartime alliance.

Elvis Presley   Elvis Presley was the most famous rock star of the 1950s. His sexually charged dance moves and unique musical sound played a major role in defining the growing genre of rock and roll, which became prominent during the 1950s.

Proclamation of American Neutrality   In the early 1790s, Britain and France went to war with each other. The American public was torn over which nation to support: the South pulled for a pro-French foreign policy while the North advocated a pro-British policy (mostly for reasons of trade). Issued in April 1793, the Proclamation of American Neutrality was George Washington's response to the division of the nation, stating that the U.S. would stay out of the war.

Public Works Administration   (PWA) Created by the National Industrial Recovery Act as part of the New Deal, the PWA spent over $4 million on projects designed to employ the jobless and reinvigorate the economy.

Joseph Pulitzer   Joseph Pulitzer owned the *New York World*, the main competitor of William Randolph Hearst's *New York Journal* at the time of the Spanish-American War. Though the *World* was the slightly more reputable of the two papers, both engaged in yellow journalism, exaggerating facts and sensationalizing stories about Spanish atrocities in Cuba.

Pullman strike   In 1894 in Chicago, Eugene Debs led thousands of workers in a strike against the Pullman Palace Car Company after wages were slashed and union representatives were fired. The boycott completely crippled railroad traffic in Chicago. The courts ruled that the strikers had violated the Sherman Antitrust Act and issued an injunction against them. When the strikers refused to obey the injunction, Debs was arrested and federal troops marched in to crush the strike. In the ensuing frenzy, thirteen died and fifty-three were injured.

Puppet governments   During the Cold War, both the U.S. and the Soviet Union set up puppet governments in developing countries in order to maintain influence over the nation in question. The superpowers each supported and funded leaders of their choice.

Pure Food and Drug Act   After muckrakers exposed the questionable packaging and labeling practices of food and drug industries, Congress passed the Pure Food and Drug Act of 1906, which prohibited the sale of adulterated or inaccurately labeled foods and medicines.

Puritans   The Puritans were a Protestant group aiming to purify the Anglican Church from within. In the early 1600s, the Puritans suffered such dire religious persecution in England that many chose to emigrate to the Americas rather than endure further troubles. The first group of Puritans to immigrate established the Massachusetts Bay Colony, centered in Boston. From Boston, Puritan influence in North America spread throughout the region of New England and with it came a focus on family life and a pious restraint of passion.

Quasi-war   Quasi-war was the term widely used to describe French and American naval conflicts occurring between 1798 and 1800. Although neither nation declared war on the other, they carried out hostile naval operations against each other.

Glossary

Radical Republicans The Radical Republicans were a minority group that emerged in Congress during the Civil War. Led by Congressman Thaddeus Stevens and Senator Charles Sumner, the Radicals demanded a stringent Reconstruction policy in order to punish the Southern states for seceding. They also called for extended civil rights in the South. The Radicals, often aligned with moderate Republicans during the early years of Reconstruction, were a dedicated and powerful force in Congress until the mid-1870s.

Railroad strike The railroad strike of 1877 was the first major nationwide strike in the U.S., spreading from New York to Pittsburgh to St. Louis, Chicago, and San Francisco. Railroad workers for nearly every rail line struck to protest wage cuts and firings. The riots provoked widespread violence and resulted in more than 100 deaths. President Hayes sent in federal troops to subdue the angry mobs and restore order.

Rationalism Heavily influenced by the Enlightenment, rationalists criticized most traditional religion as irrational and thus unfounded. Proponents of rationalism held that religious beliefs should not simply be accepted but should instead be acquired through investigation and reflection.

Ronald Reagan Ronald Reagan, a Republican, occupied the White House from 1981 to 1989. His presidency revolved around two goals: economic prosperity and victory in the Cold War. In pursuit of these goals, he initiated major tax cuts and a massive military buildup.

Reaganomics Reaganomics refers to Ronald Reagan's economic philosophy that a capitalist system free from taxation and government involvement would be most productive. Reagan believed that the prosperity of a rich upper class would "trickle down" to the poor.

Reconstruction Act of 1867 The central law passed during congressional Reconstruction, the Reconstruction Act of 1867 invalidated state governments established under Lincoln's and Johnson's plans, provided for military occupation of the former Confederacy, and bound state governments to vote for black suffrage.

Reconstruction Finance Corporation (RFC) Hoover created the RFC in 1932 to make loans to large economic institutions such as railroads and banks. The RFC loaned over $2 billion in 1932, but that amount is generally considered to have been too little, too late in Hoover's fight against the Great Depression. The RFC continued operation under FDR.

Redemption   Redemption was the term used to describe the return of Democratic rule in the South. It meant not only the transition of power in state governments from Republican to Democratic hands, but also the undoing of Republican legislature and the oppression of freedmen.

Republican Party   Rising up as the opposition party to the dominant Federalists during the Washington administration, Republicans (sometimes known as Democratic-Republicans) aimed to limit the power of central government in favor of states' rights and individual liberty. A long period of Republican dominance began with Thomas Jefferson's election in 1800 and ended with Democrat Andrew Jackson's election in 1828. A new Republican Party was formed in the mid-1850s after the collapse of the Whig Party. A sectional party concentrated in the North, the Republican Party focused primarily on promoting the issue of free soil. In 1860, the party successfully elected Abraham Lincoln president, and dominated politics during the Civil War and early Reconstruction. Because of its origin as an antislavery party, the Republican Party held the black vote for over sixty years, until FDR's New Deal policies caused black voters to shift to FDR's party, the Democrats.

Revenue Act of 1942   The Revenue Act of 1942 raised taxes to help finance the war effort. The act hiked rates for the wealthiest Americans and included new middle- and lower-income tax brackets, vastly increasing the number of Americans responsible for paying taxes.

Revolutionary War   The Revolutionary War lasted from the Declaration of Independence in 1776 until the Treaty of Paris in 1783. The American colonists defeated the British and won independence. (If you don't know this, you should be *really* glad you're studying for this test.)

Robber barons   "Robber barons" was the name given to wealthy entrepreneurs and businessmen during the Industrial Age. Among the more famous robber barons were Andrew Carnegie and John D. Rockefeller.

John D. Rockefeller   Rockefeller served as chairman of the Standard Oil Trust, which grew to control nearly all of the United States' oil production and distribution.

Roe v. Wade   The 1973 Supreme Court case *Roe v. Wade* legalized most first- and second-trimester abortions in the U.S. This landmark decision represented a major achievement for the women's liberation movement.

John Rolfe   John Rolfe was an English settler in Jamestown. He married the daughter of the chief of the Native American Powhatan tribe, Pocahontas, and introduced the Jamestown colonists to West Indian tobacco in 1616. Tobacco soon became the lifeblood of Jamestown colony, bringing in much revenue and many immigrants eager for a share in the colony's expanding wealth.

Roosevelt Corollary to the Monroe Doctrine   Expounded in Roosevelt's State of the Union address in 1904, the Roosevelt Corollary declared that the United States, not Europe, should dominate the affairs of Latin America and that although the U.S. had no expansionist intentions, any "chronic wrongdoing" by a Latin American nation would justify U.S. intervention as a global police power.

Franklin Delano Roosevelt   FDR served as president from 1933 until his death in 1945, breaking the unofficial tradition initiated by George Washington of presidents serving no more than two terms in office. FDR was the architect of the New Deal, and the visible force behind the United States' efforts at recovery from the Great Depression. In forging the New Deal, FDR exercised greater authority than perhaps any president before him, giving rise to a new understanding of the role and responsibility of the president. Under FDR's leadership, the modern Democratic Party was formed, garnering support from labor unions, blacks, urban workers, and farmers. In the later years of his presidency, FDR heavily supervised both the civilian and military effort in World War II. He has been called the most popular president in American history.

Tecumseh   A Shawnee chief, Tecumseh and his brother, the Shawnee Prophet, tried to unite Native American tribes in Ohio and Indiana to keep the region under native control and ward off white rule. His forces, however, were defeated in the 1811 Battle of Tippecanoe. Tecumseh later allied with the British during the War of 1812.

Theodore Roosevelt   Theodore Roosevelt rose to fame as the leader of the Rough Riders, a volunteer unit during the Spanish-American War. He went on to become the governor of New York and was Vice President to William McKinley during the first months of McKinley's second term in office. After McKinley's assassination in 1901, Roosevelt assumed the presidency, and served until 1909 (he won the 1904 election). A Progressive reformer, he worked to regulate the activities of corporations and protect consumers and workers. Roosevelt also pursued an aggressive style of foreign relations known as "big stick" diplomacy.

The Rosenbergs   In 1950, the Rosenbergs were accused of spying for the Soviets. They countered the accusation by saying they were being persecuted because of their Jewish background and leftist beliefs. In a trial closely followed by the American public, the Rosenbergs were convicted and sentenced to death. They were executed on June 19, 1953.

Rosie the Riveter   A well-muscled woman holding a pneumatic rivet gun, Rosie the Riveter was a popular advertising character during World War II. Rosie symbolized the important role American women played in the war effort at home, and portrayed a vastly different picture of American womanhood than had been seen before.

Russo-Japanese War   The Russo-Japanese War of 1904–1905 pitted Russia against Japan in a battle over Manchuria, in China. Roosevelt aided in the negotiation of a peace treaty, signed in September 1905, in the interest of maintaining the balance of power in the Far East, an area recently opened to American business through the Open Door policy.

Sacajawea   Sacajawea proved an indispensable guide to the Lewis and Clark expedition, from 1804 to 1806. She showed the men how to forage for food and helped them maintain good relations with the Native American tribes in the Northwest.

Sacco-Vanzetti case   Sacco and Vanzetti, anarchists and Italian immigrants, were charged with an April 1920 murder in Massachusetts and sentenced to death. The case against Sacco and Vanzetti was circumstantial and poorly argued, although evidence now suggests that they were in fact guilty. The case was significant for its demonstration of nativist and conservative forces in America, as well as of the liberal forces beginning to align against them.

Salutary neglect   Salutary neglect describes the English government's stance toward the trade laws of the mercantilist system throughout the late seventeenth and early eighteenth centuries. By this policy, the English government generally did not enforce those trade laws that most harmed the colonial economy. The purpose of salutary neglect was largely to ensure the loyalty of the colonists in the face of the French territorial and commercial threat in North America (the French and British were competing for dominance of North America). Following British victory in the French and Indian War, the English ceased practicing salutary neglect because they no longer needed so urgently to maintain colonial allegiance and because they needed to make up the debts they had incurred in the war (the trade laws, when enforced, were profitable for Britain).

Glossary

Glossary

Salvation Army   Formed in England, the Salvation Army was imported to the U.S. in 1880. The organization provides food, shelter, and employment to the urban poor while preaching temperance and morality.

Scalawags   "Scalawags" is a derisive term that Democrats used to designate Southern moderates who cooperated with Republicans during Reconstruction.

Scopes Monkey Trial   The Scopes Monkey Trial of 1925 concerned a Tennessee statute prohibiting the teaching of evolution in public schools. Anti-evolution forces rallied behind William Jennings Bryan, while pro-evolution forces rallied behind lawyer Clarence Darrow. Darrow and Bryan faced off during the highly publicized trial, and although Darrow lost his case, he made a fool out of Bryan, substantially weakening the anti-evolution cause throughout the U.S.

Second Bank of the United States   Under James Madison, Congress chartered the Second Bank of the United States in 1816. The Bank served as a depository for federal funds and a creditor for state banks. It became unpopular after being blamed for the panic of 1819, and suspicion of corruption and mismanagement haunted it until its charter expired in 1836. Its president, Nicholas Biddle, had sought recharter early, in 1832, but President Jackson vetoed the recharter. Jackson fought against the bank's power throughout his presidency, proclaiming the bank to be an unconstitutional extension of the federal government and a tool that rich capitalists used to corrupt American society.

Second Continental Congress   After fighting had broken out in Massachusetts, the Second Continental Congress convened in May 1775. Most delegates still opposed the drastic move toward complete independence from Britain despite the outbreak of violence. In an effort to reach a reconciliation, the Congress sent the Olive Branch Petition to King George III, offering peace under the conditions that there be a cease-fire in Boston, that the Coercive Acts (part of the Intolerable Acts) be repealed, and that negotiations between the colonists and Britain begin immediately. After King George III rejected the petition, the Second Continental Congress created the Continental Army and elected George Washington its commander in chief.

Second Great Awakening   The Second Great Awakening emerged in the early 1800s partly as a backlash against America's growing secularism and rationalism. A wave of religious revivals spread throughout the nation, giving rise to a number of new (largely Protestant) denominations during the second quarter of the nineteenth century. Revivalist ministers often stressed self-determination and individual empowerment.

Second New Deal   After the first New Deal began to crumble in the face of opposition and antagonistic Supreme Court rulings, FDR laid out plans for the Second New Deal in 1935. The Second New Deal was characterized by greater government spending and increased numbers of work relief programs. The most lasting measure of the Second New Deal was the creation of the Social Security system.

Sedition Amendment   Passed in 1918, the Sedition Amendment to the Espionage Act provided for punishment anyone using "disloyal, profane, scurrilous, or abusive language" in regard to the U.S. government, flag, or military.

Selective Service Act   The Selective Service Act instituted a draft to build up U.S. military forces. Passed in May 1917, the act required all men aged 21 to 30 to register for military duty.

Selective Service and Training Act   Passed September 16, 1940, the Selective Service and Training Act anticipated the war by calling the nation's first peacetime draft.

Seneca Falls Convention   Organized by Lucretia Mott and Elizabeth Cady Stanton in 1848, the Seneca Falls Convention issued a Declaration of Sentiments, modeled on the Declaration of Independence, that declared that all men and women were created equal.

Separatists   The Separatists were English Protestants who would not accept allegiance in any form to the Church of England. One Separatist group, the Pilgrims, founded Plymouth Plantation and went on to found other settlements in Rhode Island and elsewhere in New England. Other notable Separatist groups included the Quakers and Baptists.

Seventeenth Amendment   The Seventeenth Amendment, ratified in 1913, provided for the direct election of U.S. senators rather than their selection by state legislatures.

Sexual revolution   The sexual revolution refers to the easing of sexual taboos in some segments of society during the 1920s. Female sexuality was accentuated, fashion became more liberal, divorce laws were liberalized in many states, and casual dating became more common.

Sharecropping system   After the Civil War, sharecropping replaced the plantation system as the primary method of agricultural production in the South. The sharecropping system consisted of plantations, subdivided into small farms, that were rented to freedmen for leases paid in the form of a share (usually half) of the crop produced. The system gave freedmen a measure of independence while at the same time ensuring that whites maintained control of their land.

Shays's Rebellion   When economic depression struck Massachusetts in the mid-1780s, farmers in particular suffered. In August 1786, western Massachusetts farmers violently tried to shut down three county courthouses in order to prevent foreclosure proceedings. The rebellion was easily put down, but it alerted many government officials to the weaknesses of the nation under the Articles of Confederation.

Sherman Antitrust Act   This 1890 law made illegal "every contract, combination in the form of trust or otherwise, or conspiracy in the restraint of trade." Although intended to break up business monopolies, the Sherman Antitrust Act was used to break up union strikes in the 1890s. Not until the early 1900s did the government invoke the act to launch an aggressive antitrust campaign.

Sherman's March to the Sea   Union general William T. Sherman led his forces on a march from Atlanta to Savannah and then to Richmond. General Sherman brought the South "to its knees" by ordering large-scale destruction.

Shoot-on-sight order   A response to German submarine attacks on American ships in the Atlantic, the 1941 shoot-on-sight order authorized naval patrols to fire on any Axis ships found between the U.S. and Iceland.

Silent majority   Richard Nixon portrayed himself as the voice of the "silent majority" during the campaign of 1968. According to Nixon, the silent majority was tired of chaos, student protests, and civil rights agitation and was eager for a conservative federal government.

Silent Spring   Rachel Carson's *Silent Spring*, published in 1962, exposed the environmental hazards of the pesticide DDT. Her influential book helped spur an increase in environmental awareness and concern among the American people.

Upton Sinclair   Upton Sinclair, a famous muckraker, published *The Jungle* in 1906, which exposed the unsanitary conditions in several meatpacking plants. This novel and other exposés led to the passage of laws designed to ensure the safety of foods and medicines.

Sixteenth Amendment   Ratified in 1913, the Sixteenth Amendment allowed the federal government to collect a direct income tax. Shortly thereafter, Congress instituted a graduated income tax with an upper tax rate of seven percent.

Smith Act   The Smith Act of 1940 made it illegal to speak of or advocate overthrowing the U.S. government. During the presidential campaign of 1948, Truman sought to demonstrate his aggressive stance against communism by prosecuting eleven leaders of the Communist Party under the Smith Act.

Glossary

John Smith   John Smith effectively saved Jamestown when the colony was on the verge of collapse in 1608, its first year of existence. Smith's initiatives to improve sanitation and hygiene and to organize work gangs to gather food and build shelters dramatically lowered mortality rates among Jamestown colonists.

Smith-Connolly War Labor Disputes Act   The generally amiable relationship between the government and organized labor during World War II eroded with the passage of the Smith-Connolly War Labor Disputes Act in June 1943. The act limited the right to strike in key industries and authorized the president to intervene in any strike.

Smoot-Hawley Tariff   The Smoot-Hawley Tariff of 1930 was one of Herbert Hoover's early efforts to protect the nation's farmers following the onset of the Great Depression, although the act wound up hurting farmers more than it helped them. The tariff raised rates to an all-time high. Ninety-four percent of the imports taxed were agricultural imports.

Social Darwinism   Social Darwinism applies Darwin's theories of evolution and survival of the fittest to human societies. Andrew Carnegie and others cited Social Darwinist theories to justify the widening disparities in wealth between the rich and the poor during the era of industrialization.

Social Security   Established by the Social Security Act of August 1935, Social Security provides benefits to the elderly and disabled. These benefits are subsidized by income tax withholdings.

Sons of Liberty   The Sons of Liberty led colonial opposition to the Stamp Act. The organization brought a new level of sophistication to mass demonstrations, forbidding followers to carry weapons and using strict discipline and military formations to direct protesters.

Southern Christian Leadership Conference (SCLC)   In 1957, Martin Luther King Jr. and other prominent clergymen founded the SCLC to fight against segregation using nonviolent means.

Spanish-American War   The Spanish-American War broke out in 1898 over U.S. concerns for the Cuban independence movement. The U.S. decisively won the war, gaining the territories of Puerto Rico, Guam, and the Philippines, and securing independence for Cuba. The victory also marked the entrance of the United States as a power onto the world stage.

Speakeasies   Speakeasies were hidden bars during the Prohibition Era that offered live jazz music and hard liquor to customers. They were often run by organized crime rings.

Glossary

Specie Circular   In 1836, Jackson issued the Specie Circular, an executive order, in an attempt to stabilize the economy, which had been dramatically expanding since the early 1830s as a result of state banks' excessive lending practices and over-speculation. The Specie Circular required that all land payments be made in gold and silver rather than in paper money or credit. The resulting contraction in credit precipitated an economic depression known as the panic of 1837.

Spheres of influence   The term "sphere of influence" refers to a group of nations or territories in the unofficial economic, political, and social orbit of a greater power. NATO countries were in the U.S. sphere of influence, while the Communist bloc countries of the Warsaw Pact were in the USSR's sphere of influence. The term "sphere of influence" is also used to describe European and Russian influence in China at the end of the nineteenth century, when certain countries had exclusive trade and development rights in key Chinese ports and regions.

Spoils system   The name "the spoils system" arose from the adage, "To the victor go the spoils." Also known as rotation in office, the spoils system provided for the removal and replacement of all high-ranking officials within the executive office who were members of a new president's opposition. These offices would then be filled by loyal members of the winning party. Andrew Jackson was not the first president to use the spoils system, but was the first to use it as extensively as he did and the first to justify it by claiming it was necessary to liberty.

Sputnik   Launched by the USSR on October 4, 1957, *Sputnik* was the first artificial satellite to orbit the earth. Its launching prompted the space race between the U.S. and USSR, because Americans were both jealous of Soviet technological skill and afraid that the same rockets that launched *Sputnik* would be used to deliver nuclear warheads anywhere on the globe.

Square Deal   "Square Deal" was the name Theodore Roosevelt gave to his social policies, especially his intended relationships with capital and labor. Roosevelt wanted to treat everyone fairly, and, in particular, eliminate government favors to big business.

Joseph Stalin   Stalin was dictator of the Soviet Union from 1928 until 1953. He coordinated Soviet involvement in World War II, at first displaying eagerness to cooperate with U.S. forces but eventually becoming antagonistic. After the war, he oversaw the escalation of Cold War tensions between his country and the U.S.

Stamp Act   The 1765 Stamp Act required colonial Americans to buy special watermarked paper for newspapers and all legal documents. Violators faced juryless trials in vice-admiralty courts, as under the 1764 Sugar Act. The Stamp Act provoked the first organized response to British impositions.

Stamp Act Congress   Angered over the Stamp Act, representatives of nine colonial assemblies met in New York City at the Stamp Act Congress in October 1765. The colonies agreed widely on the principles that Parliament could not tax anyone outside of Great Britain and could not deny anyone a fair trial, both of which had been dictates of the Stamp Act. The meeting marked a new level of colonial political organization.

Elizabeth Cady Stanton   A prominent advocate of women's rights, Stanton organized the 1848 Seneca Falls Convention with Lucretia Mott.

John Steinbeck   John Steinbeck was a major American author of the 1930s. His novels glorify a simpler, rural way of life, as demonstrated in his most famous work, *The Grapes of Wrath*, published in 1939.

Thaddeus Stevens   The leader of the Radical Republicans in Congress, Thaddeus Stevens was a gifted orator and an outspoken legislator devoted to stringent and punitive Reconstruction. Stevens worked toward social and political equality for Southern blacks.

Strategic Arms Limitation Treaty (SALT)   In May 1972, Nixon signed SALT I, which limited each of the superpowers to 200 antiballistic missiles and set quotas for intercontinental and submarine missiles. Though largely symbolic, the agreement spawned hope for cooperation on both sides.

Strict constructionists   Strict constructionists favored a strict reading of the Constitution, especially of the elastic clause, in order to limit the powers of the central government. Led by Thomas Jefferson, strict constructionists comprised the ideological core of the Republican Party.

Students for a Democratic Society (SDS)   Students for a Democratic Society, created in 1962, united college students throughout the country in a network committed to achieving racial equality, alleviating poverty, and most importantly, ending the Vietnam War.

Suez Canal   In 1956, the Egyptian president Gamal Abdel Nasser tried to nationalize the Suez Canal, which had been owned by British and French interests. In response, Britain, France, and Israel invaded Egypt. The U.S., United Nations, and USSR condemned the intervention and pressured the forces to withdraw in November 1956.

Suffolk Resolves   The First Continental Congress endorsed Massachusetts's Suffolk Resolves, which declared that the colonies need not obey the 1773 Coercive Acts, since they infringed upon basic liberties.

Glossary

Sugar Act   The Sugar Act (1764) lowered the duty on foreign-produced molasses as an attempt to discourage colonial smuggling. The act further stipulated that Americans could export many commodities, including lumber, iron, skins, and whalebone, to foreign countries only if the goods passed through British ports first. The terms of the act and its methods of enforcement outraged many colonists.

Charles Sumner   Sumner was the leading Radical Republican senator throughout the Civil War and Reconstruction. Perhaps the most distinguished member of the radical faction, he ensured the faction's position in the federal government and argued ardently for civil rights for blacks. Sumner went on to lead the defection of the Liberal Republicans.

***Sussex* Pledge**   In 1916, Woodrow Wilson threatened to break off diplomatic relations with Germany following a German U-boat attack against the French ship *Sussex*, which carried U.S. civilians. Germany responded with the *Sussex* Pledge, promising not to attack merchant ships without warning and temporarily easing the diplomatic tension between the U.S. and Germany.

William Howard Taft   William Howard Taft was president from 1909 to 1913. Though handpicked by Roosevelt, he was not as enthusiastic as Roosevelt about progressive reform, and soon allied himself with the conservative wing of the Republican Party by raising tariffs. In doing so, he offended many Progressive Republicans, including Roosevelt himself, and precipitated a split in the Republican Party.

Taft-Hartley Act   The centerpiece of a congressional effort to restrict union activity, the Taft-Hartley Act of 1947 banned certain union practices and allowed the president to call for an eighty-day cooling off period to delay strikes thought to pose risks to national safety. Truman vetoed the measure, and though his veto was overridden, his actions roused the support of organized labor, a group crucial to his election victory in 1948.

Tallmadge Amendment   In 1819, Representative Tallmadge proposed an amendment to the bill for Missouri's admission, which the House then passed but the Senate blocked. The amendment would have prohibited the further introduction of slaves into Missouri and would have mandated the emancipation of slaves' offspring born after the state was admitted to the Union. The proposal sparked intense congressional debate over the balance of slave and free states. In 1821, Congress reached a compromise for Missouri's admission known as the Missouri Compromise.

Roger B. Taney   Taney served as chief justice of the Supreme Court from 1836 to 1864. In support of slavery laws, he delivered the majority opinion on *Dred Scott v. Sanford*.

Tariff of Abominations   Southern politicians called the 1828 tariff the "Tariff of Abominations" because it seriously hurt the South's economy while benefiting Northern and Western industrial interests. Resistance to the tariff in South Carolina led to the Nullification Crisis.

Zachary Taylor   Zachary Taylor, a Whig, served as president from 1849 until his death in 1850. Taylor advocated popular sovereignty and in 1849 encouraged California to apply for statehood as a free state, thereby igniting the controversy that led to the Compromise of 1850.

Tea Act   The 1773 Tea Act eliminated import tariffs on tea entering England, and allowed the British East India Company to sell directly to consumers rather than through merchants. This act lowered the price of British tea to below that of smuggled tea, which the British hoped would end the boycott. The British government hoped to use revenue from the Tea Act to pay the salaries of royal governors in the colonies, a plan that outraged many colonists and prompted the Boston Tea Party.

Teapot Dome scandal   Exposed after Warren G. Harding's death in office in 1923, the Teapot Dome scandal involved Harding's secretary of the interior, Albert B. Fall, who had secretly leased government oil reserves to two businessmen in exchange for a $400,000 payment. Teapot Dome came to symbolize government corruption.

Tehran Conference   The Tehran Conference, November 28 to December 1, 1943, was the first major meeting between the Big Three leaders. At the conference, Churchill, FDR, and Stalin planned the 1944 assault on France and agreed to divide Germany into zones of occupation after the war.

Ten percent plan   Known as the "ten percent plan," Lincoln's plan for Reconstruction was more lenient than many members of Congress, especially the Radical Republicans, hoped to impose. Under Lincoln's 1863 Proclamation of Amnesty and Reconstruction, Southern states would be readmitted to the Union once ten percent of the state's voting population took an oath of loyalty to the Union and the states established new non-Confederate governments. Congress proposed its own more punitive Reconstruction plan with the 1864 Wade-Davis Bill.

Glossary

Tenements   The exponentially increasing population of urban poor during the era of industrialization led to the construction of tenements—narrow, four- or five-story buildings with few windows and limited electricity and plumbing. The poor, mostly ethnic minorities and immigrants, were packed into crowded, dirty apartments. ·

Tennessee Valley Authority (TVA)   Part of FDR's New Deal, the TVA worked to develop energy production sites and conserve resources in the Tennessee Valley. Although the TVA pumped money into the economy and completed a number of major projects, environmentalists, advocates of energy conservation, and opponents of nuclear power all eventually found reason to oppose the TVA.

Tet Offensive   On January 31, 1968, the first day of Tet, the Vietnamese New Year, the Vietcong and North Vietnamese Army launched a general offensive throughout South Vietnam. Although the forces did not succeed in capturing the cities, they did wreak widespread devastation, killing many thousands of American troops. The month-long attack led the American public to believe that victory in Vietnam was unattainable.

Thirteenth Amendment   Ratified December 6, 1865, the Thirteenth Amendment prohibited slavery in the United States.

Three-fifths clause   During the framing of the Constitution, Southern delegates argued that slaves should count toward representative seats, while the delegates of Northern states argued that to count slaves as members of the population would grant an unfair advantage to the Southern states in Congress. The result of this debate was the adoption of the three-fifths clause, which allowed three-fifths of all slaves to be counted as people.

Henry David Thoreau   A disciple of Ralph Waldo Emerson, Henry David Thoreau was a prominent transcendentalist writer. Two of his most famous writings are *Civil Disobedience* (1849) and *Walden* (1854). Thoreau advocated living life according to one's conscience, removed from materialism and repressive social codes.

Tiananmen Square   On June 3 and 4, 1989, China's communist army brutally crushed a pro-democracy protest in Beijing's Tiananmen Square. Diplomatic relations between the U.S. and China significantly soured as a result of the attack.

To Secure These Rights   A sign of progress for the civil rights movement during Truman's presidency, the Presidential Committee on Civil Rights formed in 1956. In 1957, the Committee produced a report, *To Secure These Rights*, that called for the elimination of segregation.

Tories   The Tories were colonists who disagreed with the move for independence and did not support the Revolution.

Townshend Duties   Popularly referred to as the Townshend Duties, the Revenue Act of 1767 taxed glass, lead, paint, paper, and tea entering the colonies. The colonists objected to the fact that the act was clearly designed to raise revenue exclusively for England rather than to regulate trade in a manner favorable to the entire British Empire.

Trail of Tears   Despite the Supreme Court decision in *Worcester v. Georgia*, federal troops forced bands of Cherokee Indians to move west of the Mississippi between 1835 and 1838. Their journey, in which between 2,000 and 4,000 of the 16,000 Cherokee died, became known as the Trail of Tears.

Transcendentalism   Transcendentalism was a spiritual movement that arose in the 1830s as a challenge to rationalism. Transcendentalists aimed to achieve an inner, emotional understanding of God rather than a rational, institutionalized one. They believed concepts such as absolute truth and freedom were inborn, and were accessible through intuition and sudden insight. Among the more prominent transcendentalists were the writers Ralph Waldo Emerson and Henry David Thoreau.

Transcontinental railroad   On May 10, 1869, the first transcontinental railroad was completed when the Union Pacific and Central Pacific railroads joined their tracks at Promontory Point, Utah. The railroad dramatically facilitated western settlement, shortening to a single week a coast-to-coast journey that had once taken six to eight months by wagon.

Transcontinental Treaty   Also known as the Adams-Onís Treaty, the Transcontinental Treaty was signed in 1819 between the U.S. and Spain. By the terms of the treaty, Spain ceded eastern Florida to the U.S., renounced all claims to western Florida, and agreed to a southern border of the U.S. west of the Mississippi extending all the way to the Pacific Ocean.

Treaty of Ghent   Signed on Christmas Eve in 1815, the Treaty of Ghent ended the War of 1812 and returned relations between the U.S. and Britain to the status quo ante bellum (in other words, the way things were before the war).

Treaty of Greenville   After their defeat at the Battle of Fallen Timbers in 1794, 12 Native American tribes signed the Treaty of Greenville, which cleared the Ohio territory of tribes and opened it up to U.S. settlement.

Treaty of Guadalupe Hidalgo   The Treaty of Guadalupe Hidalgo ended the Mexican War. It granted the U.S. control of Texas, New Mexico, and California. In return, the U.S. assumed all monetary claims of U.S. citizens against the Mexican government and paid Mexico $15 million.

Treaty of Paris (1763)   The 1763 Treaty of Paris ended the Seven Years War in Europe and the parallel French and Indian War in North America. Under the treaty, Britain won all of Canada and almost all of the modern United States east of the Mississippi.

Treaty of Paris (1783)   There have been many Treaties of Paris throughout history. For the SAT II, the most important is the treaty signed in September 1783 and ratified by Congress in January 1784, which ended the Revolutionary War and granted the United States its independence. It further granted the U.S. all land east of the Mississippi River, and contained clauses that bound Congress to urge state legislatures to compensate loyalists for property damage incurred during the war and to allow British creditors to collect debts accrued before the war. While generally accepted, the Treaty of Paris opened the door to future legislative and economic disputes.

Treaty of San Lorenzo   Signed with Spain in 1795, the Treaty of San Lorenzo granted the U.S. unrestricted access to the Mississippi River and removed Spanish troops from American land.

Treaty of Tordesillas   Queen Isabella of Castile and King John II of Portugal signed the Treaty of Tordesillas in 1494, dividing all future discoveries in the New World between their respective nations. This treaty soon proved unworkable because of the flood of expeditions to the New World and the proliferation of different countries' claims to territory.

Treaty of Versailles   The Treaty of Versailles was signed in June 1919 at the end of World War I. Woodrow Wilson had hoped for a generous peace settlement to promote democracy, peace, and liberalism throughout war-torn Europe instead of simply punishing the Central Powers. The treaty, however, proved more vindictive against Germany than Wilson would have liked, for he could not check the spirit of revenge that motivated the other Allies. The treaty punished the Germans severely, forcing Germany to assume blame for the war and to pay massive reparations. Other elements of the treaty included demilitarization of the west bank of the Rhine, the creation of new nations to grant autonomy to oppressed geographic and ethnic groups, and the formation of the League of Nations.

Triangular trade Triangular trade routes under the mercantilist system linked England, its colonies in North America, the West Indies, and Africa. At each port, ships were unloaded of goods from another port along the trade route, and then re-loaded with goods particular to that site. New England rum was shipped to Africa and traded for slaves, who were brought to the West Indies and traded for sugar and molasses, which went back to New England. Under this system, all ports prospered, with the exception of Africa, which provided only cargoes of slaves.

Tripartite Pact Signed in September 1940, the Tripartite Pact allied Germany, Italy, and Japan, all of which were engaged in aggressive expansion. These nations comprised the Axis powers.

Harry S. Truman Truman succeeded FDR as president after FDR died in office in April 1945, and served until 1953. Truman is known for his decision to drop the atomic bomb on Japan and for his subsequent role in the Cold War conflict, when he proved instrumental in committing the U.S. to action against the threat of Soviet aggression in Europe. At home, Truman attempted to extend the New Deal policies of his predecessor in what he called the Fair Deal.

Truman Doctrine In March 1947, Truman proclaimed before Congress that the U.S. would support people anywhere in the world facing "attempted subjugation by armed minorities or by outside pressures." The Truman Doctrine committed the U.S. to a role as a global policeman.

Trust A trust is a conglomerate of businesses that tends to reduce market competition. During the Industrial Age, many entrepreneurs consolidated their businesses into trusts in order to gain control of the market and amass great profit, often at the expense of poor workers and consumers.

Harriet Tubman A former slave, Harriet Tubman helped establish the Underground Railroad, a network of safehouses and escorts throughout the North to help escaped slaves to freedom.

Mark Twain The author of *The Gilded Age* (1873), *The Adventures of Tom Sawyer* (1876), and *The Adventures of Huckleberry Finn* (1884), among other books, Mark Twain was a leading literary figure during the era of industrialization.

John Tyler Tyler became president of the United States in 1841, when William Henry Harrison died after one month in office.

Glossary

U-boat German submarines in World War I were known as U-boats. Germany called for indiscriminate use of submarines during World War I, leading to the sinking of many French and British passenger ships carrying American citizens. German U-boat attacks provoked outrage among the American public, strengthening calls for the U.S. to join the war against the Central Powers.

Uncle Tom's Cabin *Uncle Tom's Cabin*, written by Harriet Beecher Stow, portrayed the evils of the institution of slavery. Published in 1852, the novel sold 1.2 million copies in two years and reached millions more through dramatic adaptations. *Uncle Tom's Cabin* aroused sympathy for runaway slaves among all classes of Northerners and hardened many Northerners against the South's insistence upon continuing slavery.

Underground Railroad The Underground Railroad was a network of safe houses and escorts established by Northern abolitionists to foil enforcement of the Fugitive Slave Act. The network helped escaped slaves reach freedom in the North and in Canada.

Underwood Tariff Pushed through Congress by Woodrow Wilson in 1913, the Underwood Tariff reduced average tariff duties by almost fifteen percent, and established a graduated income tax to cover the lost tariff revenue.

Union A general term for the combined states of the United States during the Civil War, "Union" referred to the government and troops of the North.

United Nations Fifty-one countries founded the United Nations on October 24, 1945. Its central mission was to preserve peace and global stability through international cooperation and collective security. Still in operation today, the UN now claims 189 countries as members.

United Negro Improvement Association (UNIA) In 1916, Marcus Garvey brought the United Negro Improvement Association from Jamaica to the U.S. The UNIA urged economic cooperation among African Americans.

Unrestricted submarine warfare Unrestricted submarine warfare referred to the German U-boat policy in which submarines attacked any ship—military, merchant, or civilian—without warning. After a period during which Germany practiced limited submarine warfare as promised by the *Sussex* Pledge, the resumption of unrestricted submarine warfare in January 1917 pushed the U.S. even closer to war.

Utopian communities Utopian communities sprang up in the U.S. beginning in the late 1820s. In these small experimental communities, American reformers attempted to build perfect societies and present models for other communities to emulate. Most of these communities collapsed by the late 1840s.

Martin Van Buren Martin Van Buren served as secretary of state during Jackson's first term in office and as vice president during his second. As Jackson's handpicked successor, Van Buren won the presidency in 1836. Beset by the panic of 1837 and unable to win over Jackson's opposition, the Whigs, Van Buren lost his bid for reelection in 1840.

Vietcong The Vietcong was a pro-communist guerrilla force working secretly within South Vietnam. Extremely difficult to find and target, the Vietcong was unlike any other enemy U.S. troops had ever faced.

Virginia and Kentucky Resolutions Written by James Madison and Thomas Jefferson, respectively, the Virginia and Kentucky Resolutions (1798) condemned the Federalists' broad interpretation of the Constitution and instead put forth a compact theory of the Union, which stated that states' rights superseded federal powers. Virginia and Kentucky endorsed these resolutions in opposition to the Alien and Sedition Acts. The arguments outlined in these resolutions—concerning states' rights and nullification—would resurface in the mid-nineteenth century in the political crises involving tariff issues and slavery, issues that divided the North and South and led to the Civil War.

Virginia Plan The Virginia Plan was the first major proposal presented to the Constitutional Convention concerning congressional representation. It proposed the creation of a bicameral legislature with representation in both houses proportional to population. The Virginia Plan favored the large states, which would have a much greater voice than the small states under this plan. In opposition, the small states proposed the New Jersey Plan. In the end, the two sides found common ground through the Connecticut Compromise.

Virginia Resolves In response to the 1765 Stamp Act, Patrick Henry persuaded the Virginia House of Burgesses to adopt several strongly worded resolutions that denied Parliament's right to tax the colonies. Known as the Virginia Resolves, these resolutions persuaded many other colonial legislatures to adopt similar positions.

Glossary

Virtual representation   Prime Minister George Grenville invoked the concept of virtual representation to explain why Parliament could legally tax the colonists even though the colonists could not elect any members of Parliament. The theory of virtual representation held that the members of Parliament did not only represent their specific geographic constituencies but also took into consideration the well-being of all British subjects when deliberating on legislation.

Voting Rights Act   The Voting Rights Act of 1965 guaranteed the right to vote to all Americans. It allowed the federal government to intervene in elections in order to ensure that minorities could vote.

Wade-Davis Bill   In July 1864, Congress passed the Wade-Davis Bill, setting forth stringent requirements for Confederate states' readmission to the Union. President Lincoln, who supported a more liberal Reconstruction policy, vetoed the Wade-Davis Bill by leaving it unsigned more than ten days after the adjournment of Congress.

Wagner Act   See the National Labor Relations Act.

George Washington   The commander in chief of the Continental Army, Washington is perhaps the best-known figure of the Revolution. A born leader, sharpened by his mishaps and successes as a youth in the French and Indian War, Washington led the Continentals to victory. He was rewarded in 1789, when he became the nation's first president. Washington took on the task of defining the presidency, which he did by setting precedents. He intervened little in legislative affairs and concentrated mostly on diplomacy and finance. A Federalist, he granted Alexander Hamilton a great deal of support in his Federalist economic campaign. Washington officially resigned from office in 1796 after serving two terms in office, establishing a convention that presidents serve no more than two terms in office.

War Hawks   A group of westerners and southerners led by John Calhoun and Henry Clay, the War Hawks pushed for war against Britain. They objected to Britain's hostile policies against U.S. ships, including impressment and the seizure of shipping goods, and advocated fighting instead of submitting to this disgraceful treatment. They also hoped that, through war, the U.S. would win some western, southwestern, and Canadian territories.

War of 1812   The War of 1812, between the U.S. and Great Britain, lasted until 1814. Although it ended in stalemate with the Treaty of Ghent, the American public believed the U.S. had won the war after news spread of General Andrew Jackson's decisive victory at the Battle of New Orleans, which occurred two weeks after the signing of the treaty. For years following this apparent victory, an ebullient spirit of nationalism and optimism pervaded America.

War Production Board   Created in 1942, the War Production Board oversaw the production of the thousands of planes, tanks, artillery pieces, and munitions that FDR requested once the U.S. entered the war. The board allocated scarce resources and shifted domestic production from civilian to military goods.

Earl Warren   Earl Warren served as chief justice of the Supreme Court from 1953 to 1969. During this time, the liberal Warren Court made a number of important decisions, primarily in the realm of civil rights. The most important contribution of the Warren Court during the 1950s was the 1954 decision in *Brown v. Board of Education of Topeka*.

Warsaw Pact   The Warsaw Pact, a Communist bloc treaty from 1955, officially linked the USSR and its Eastern European satellites—Albania, Bulgaria, Czechoslovakia, East Germany, Hungary, Poland, and Romania—in a single Soviet-controlled military command, and allowed the stationing of Soviet troops in Warsaw Pact countries. The Warsaw Pact was seen as the Soviet response to the formation of NATO.

Booker T. Washington   Washington was an African American leader and the first principal of the Tuskegee Institute (1881). Washington adopted a moderate approach in addressing racism and segregation, urging his fellow blacks to learn vocational skills and strive for gradual improvements in their social, political, and economic status.

Watergate   On June 17, 1972, burglars broke into Democratic National Committee headquarters in the Watergate office complex in Washington, DC, to plant bugs. It was later discovered that these burglars had been employed by Nixon's Committee to Re-elect the President (CREEP). In the ensuing investigation, it became clear that Nixon had known of such illegal activity and had participated in a cover-up attempt. Faced with near-certain impeachment, Nixon resigned the presidency on August 9, 1974.

Daniel Webster   One of country's leading statesmen in the first half of the nineteenth century, Webster was a Federalist lawyer from New Hampshire who won, most notably, the *Dartmouth College* (1819) and *McCulloch v. Maryland* (1819) cases in the Supreme Court. First elected to Congress in 1822, Webster became a

Glossary

powerful defender of northern interests, supporting the 1828 tariff and objecting to nullification. Webster, who opposed many of Jackson's policies, became a leader of the Whig Party. He was instrumental in pushing through the Compromise of 1850.

Whigs   The term "Whigs" refers to two distinct entities in U.S. history. During the Revolutionary War, the Whigs were colonists who supported the move for independence. In the mid-1830s, the Whigs arose in opposition to Jackson. The Whig Party consisted of the core of the National Republican Party as well as some Northern Democrats who had defected from their party in protest against Jackson's strong-armed leadership style and policies. The Whigs promoted protective tariffs, federal funding for internal improvements, and other measures that strengthened the central government. Reaching its height of popularity in the 1830s, the Whig Party disappeared from the national political scene by the 1850s, when its Northern and Southern factions irrevocably split over the slavery issue.

Whiskey Rebellion   In 1791, Alexander Hamilton pushed a high excise tax on whiskey as part of his Federalist economic policy. In July 1794, violence broke out in western Pennsylvania, the area most hurt by the tax. In a show of national strength, George Washington himself led a force of militiamen to crush the rebellion.

Walt Whitman   Walt Whitman was an avid reader and disciple of Ralph Waldo Emerson. His major work, *Leaves of Grass*, published in 1855, celebrated the diversity and democracy of America.

Roger Williams   A dissenter, Roger Williams clashed with Massachusetts Puritans over the issue of separation of church and state. After being banished from Massachusetts in 1636, he traveled south, where he founded a colony in Rhode Island that granted full religious freedom to its inhabitants.

Wilmot Proviso   Proposed in 1846 before the end of the Mexican War, the Wilmot Proviso stipulated that slavery be prohibited in any territory the U.S. gained from Mexico in the upcoming negotiations. With strong support from the North, the proviso passed in the House of Representatives but stalled in the Senate.

Woodrow Wilson   Woodrow Wilson, a Democrat, served as president from 1913 to 1921. An enthusiastic reformer, he supported measures to limit corporate power, protect laborers, and aid poor farmers. In foreign relations, he advocated the principles of "new freedom," supporting democracy and capitalism worldwide. During the early years of World War I, Wilson struggled to preserve

American neutrality. Once the U.S. entered the war, he charged ahead aggressively. Wilson's key contributions to the war, beyond furnishing American forces, were the elucidation of his Fourteen Points and his advocacy of the League of Nations.

John Winthrop As governor of Massachusetts Bay Colony, Winthrop (1588-1649) was instrumental in forming the colony's government and shaping its legislative policy. He envisioned the colony, centered in present-day Boston, as a "city upon a hill" from which Puritans would spread religious righteousness throughout the world.

Woman's Christian Temperance Union Founded in 1874, the Woman's Christian Temperance Union (WTCU) worked alongside the Anti-Saloon League to push for temperance. Notable women activists included Susan B. Anthony and Frances Elizabeth Willard.

Women's Strike for Equality In August 1970, tens of thousands of women around the country held demonstrations to demand the right to equal employment and legal abortions. This coordinated effort was known as the Women's Strike for Equality.

Worcester v. Georgia In the case of *Worcester v. Georgia* (1832), Chief Justice John Marshall ruled that the Cherokee tribe comprised a "domestic dependent nation" within Georgia and thus deserved protection from harassment—in this case, from forced migration out of Georgia. Known as a vehement Indian hater and eager to secure Native American land for U.S. settlement, Andrew Jackson refused to abide by the decision, reportedly sneering, "John Marshall has made his decision; now let him enforce it." The Cherokee removal continued on unabated and as aggressively as ever.

Works Progress Administration (WPA) Much of the $5 billion allocated to FDR by the Emergency Relief Allocation Act of 1935 went to the creation of the WPA. Over eight years, the WPA provided work for the unemployed of all backgrounds, from industrial engineers to authors and artists. Partially owing to WPA efforts, unemployment fell by over five percent between 1935 and 1937.

Writs of assistance Legalized by Parliament during the French and Indian War, writs of assistance were general search warrants that allowed British customs officers to search any colonial building or ship that they believed might contain smuggled goods, even without probable cause for suspicion. The colonists considered the writs to be a grave infringement upon their personal liberties.

Malcolm X   A major advocate of Black Power, Malcolm X helped lead the Nation of Islam to national prominence. In 1965, he was assassinated after a well-publicized break with the Nation of Islam over his newfound dedication to cross-cultural unity.

XYZ affair   In response to continued French aggression at sea, John Adams sent a diplomatic envoy to France to negotiate for peace in 1797. Charles de Tallyrand, the French foreign minister, refused to meet with the U.S. delegation and instead sent three anonymous agents, X, Y, and Z, to try to extort money from the Americans (over $12 million) in exchange for negotiation rights. This widely publicized attempt at extortion aroused public outrage among the American people, some of whom called for war.

Yalta Conference   The Big Three, represented by FDR, Churchill, and Stalin, met at the Yalta Conference from February 4 to February 11, 1945. Although FDR and Churchill's bargaining power with Stalin was severely hindered by the presence of Soviet troops in Poland and Eastern Europe, Stalin did agree to declare war on Japan soon after Germany surrendered and did approve plans for a United Nations conference in April 1945.

Yellow journalism   Yellow journalism refers to the exaggerated and sensationalized stories about Spanish military atrocities against Cuban rebels that the *New York World* and *New York Journal*, among other newspapers, published in the period leading up to the Spanish-American War (1898). Yellow journalism swayed American public opinion in favor of war against Spain.

Boris Yeltsin   Boris Yeltsin was president of the Russian Republic in 1991, when hard-line Communists attempted to overthrow Mikhail Gorbachev. After helping to repel these hard-liners, Yeltsin and the leaders of the other Soviet republics declared an end to the USSR, forcing Gorbachev to resign. Yeltsin played an increasingly important role in global politics from that time onward.

Young Men's Christian Association (YMCA)   The YMCA, and later the YWCA (Young Women's Christian Association), came to America from England in 1851. It attempted to alleviate some of the strains of destitution in American cities by providing young people with affordable shelter and recreational facilities.

Zimmerman Telegram   In 1917, British intelligence intercepted the Zimmerman Telegram, sent from the German foreign minister to the German ambassador in Mexico. The telegram urged Mexico to enter the war against the U.S. in exchange for a German pledge to help restore Mexico's former territories of Arizona, New Mexico, and Texas. The unmasking of Germany's aggressive war plans, coupled with Germany's resumption of unrestricted submarine warfare, pushed the U.S. into World War I.

PRACTICE
TESTS

Practice Tests Are Your Best Friends

I~N THIS CRAZY WORLD OF OURS,~ there is one thing that you can always take for granted: the SAT II U.S. History will stay the same. From year to year and test to test, the SAT II U.S. History will cover the same eras to the same degree. Obviously, there are different versions of the SAT II U.S. History. Individual questions will never repeat from test to test. But the topics that those questions test and the way in which the questions test those subjects *will* remain constant.

This constancy can be of great benefit to you as you study for the test. To show how you can use the similarity between different versions of the SAT II U.S. History to your advantage, we provide a case study.

Using the Similarity of the SAT II U.S. History for Personal Gain

One day, an eleventh grader named Molly Bloom sits down at the desk in her room and takes a practice test for the SAT II U.S. History. Because it makes this example much simpler, she takes the entire test and gets only one question wrong. Molly checks her answers and then jumps from her chair and does a little dance that would be embarrassing if anyone else were around to see her.

After her euphoria passes, she begins to wonder which question she got wrong and returns to her chair. She discovers that the question dealt with the Populist movement.

Looking over the question, Molly at first thinks the test made a mistake and that she was actually right, but then she realizes that she answered the question wrong because she had mistakenly believed that the Populist Party wanted to raise protective tariffs, when in fact they wanted them lowered. Molly thinks about why she got the question wrong: she knew that the Populist Party arose among farmers in the 1890s, primarily because of falling prices for agricultural produce, and had assumed these falling prices were the result of foreign competition. Her logic made perfect sense, but it was wrong. In thinking about the question, Molly realizes she didn't have a good grasp of what was going on in the 1890s and looks in her books to figure out the truth. She studies up on the Populist Party, learns what policies they stood behind, and studies *why* they stood behind those policies. All this takes her about 10 minutes, after which she vows never to make a mistake about the Populists again.

Analyzing Molly Bloom

Molly's actions here seem like a minor thing. All she did was study a question she got wrong until she understood why she got it wrong and what she should have done to get it right. But think about the implications. Molly answered the question incorrectly because she didn't understand the topic it was testing. The practice test had pointed out her mistaken understanding in the most noticeable way possible: she got the question wrong. After doing her admittedly goofy little dance, Molly wasn't content simply to see what the correct answer was and get on with her day; she wanted to see *how* and *why* she got the question wrong and what she should have done, or needed to know, in order to get it right. So, with a look of determination, telling herself, "I will figure out why I got this question wrong, yes I will, yes," she spent a little while studying the question, discovered her mistaken understanding of the Populist movement and the issues facing 1890s America in general, and learned the truth of the historical situation. If Molly were to take that same test again, she definitely would not get that question wrong.

"But she never will take that test again, so she's never going to see that particular question again," some poor sap who hasn't read this guide might sputter. "She wasted her time. What a dork!"

Why That Poor Sap Really Is a Poor Sap

In some sense, that poor sap is correct: Molly never will take that exact practice test again. But the poor sap is wrong to call Molly derogatory names, because, as we know, the SAT II U.S. History is remarkably similar from year to year, both in the topics it covers and in the way it poses questions about those topics. Therefore, when Molly taught herself about the Populist movement and 1890s America, she actually learned how to answer the similar questions dealing with the Populist movement and 1890s

America that will *undoubtedly* appear on every future practice test, and on the real SAT II U.S. History.

In studying the results of her practice test, in figuring out exactly why she got her one question wrong and what she should have known and done to get it right, Molly has targeted a weakness and overcome it.

Molly and You

Molly has it easy. She took a practice test and got only one question wrong. Less than one percent of all people who take the SAT II U.S. History will be so lucky. Of course, the only reason Molly got so few questions wrong was because we wanted to use her as an easy example.

So, what if you take a practice test and get 15 questions wrong, and your errors span a number of different eras? Well, you should do exactly what Molly did. Take your test and *study it*. Identify every question you got wrong, figure out why you got it wrong, and then teach yourself what you should have done to get the question right. If you can't figure out your error, find someone who can.

A wrong answer on the SAT II U.S. History identifies a weakness in your test taking, whether that weakness is an unfamiliarity with a particular topic or a tendency to be careless. If you got 15 questions wrong on a practice test, then each of those 15 questions identifies a weakness in your ability to take the SAT II U.S. History or your knowledge about the topics the SAT II U.S. History tests. As you study each question you got wrong, you are actually learning how to answer the very questions that will appear in similar form on the real SAT II U.S. History. You are discovering your exact U.S. History weaknesses and addressing them, and you are learning to understand not just the knowledge behind the question, but also the way the test writers ask their questions.

True, if you got 15 questions wrong, studying your first practice test will take some time. But if you invest that time and study your practice test properly, you will be eliminating future mistakes. Each successive practice test you take should have fewer errors, meaning less time spent studying those errors. Also, and more importantly, you'll be pinpointing what you need to study for the real SAT II U.S. History, identifying and overcoming your weaknesses, and learning to answer an increasing variety of questions on the specific topics covered by the test. Taking practice tests and studying them will allow you to teach yourself how to recognize and handle whatever the SAT II U.S. History throws at you.

Practice Tests

Taking a Practice Test

Through the example of Miss Molly Bloom, we've shown you why studying practice tests is an extremely powerful stratgey. Now we're going to explain how you should take practice tests in order to best put that tool to use.

Controlling Your Environment

Although no one but you needs to see your practice test scores, you should do everything in your power to make the practice test feel like the real SAT II U.S. History. The closer your practice resembles the real thing, the more helpful it will be. When taking a practice test, follow these rules:

Take the tests timed. Don't give yourself any extra time. Be stricter with yourself than the meanest proctor you can think of. Also, don't give yourself time off for bathroom breaks. If you have to go to the bathroom, let the clock keep running; that's what'll happen on the real SAT II.

Take the test in a single sitting. Training yourself to endure an hour of test taking is part of your preparation.

Find a place to take the test that offers no distractions. Don't take the practice test in a room with lots of people walking through it. Go to a library, your bedroom, a well-lit closet, anywhere quiet.

Now, having stated the rules of practice test taking, we can relax a little bit: don't be so strict with yourself that studying and taking practice tests becomes unbearable. The most important thing is that you actually study. Do whatever you have to do in order to make your studying interesting and painless enough for you to actually do it.

Ultimately, if you can follow all of the above rules to the letter, you will be better off. But, if following those rules makes studying excruciating, find little ways to bend them that won't interfere too much with your concentration.

Practice Test Strategy

You should take each practice test as if it were the real SAT II U.S. History. Don't be more daring than you would be on the actual test, guessing blindly even when you can't eliminate an answer. Don't carelessly speed through the test. Don't flip through this book while taking the practice exam just to sneak a peek. Follow the rules for guessing and for skipping questions that we outlined in the chapter on strategy. The more closely your attitude and strategies during the practice test reflect those you'll employ during the actual test, the more predictive the practice test will be of your strengths and weaknesses and the more fruitful your studying of the test will be.

Scoring Your Practice Test

After you take your practice test, you'll no doubt want to score it and see how you did. When you score your test, don't just write down how many questions you answered correctly and tally your score. Instead, keep a list of every question you got wrong and every question you skipped. This list will be your guide when you study your test.

Studying Your...No, Wait, Go Take a Break

You know how to have fun. Go do that for a while. Come back when you're refreshed.

Studying Your Practice Test

After grading your test, you should have a list of the questions you answered incorrectly or skipped. Studying your test involves going through this list and examining each question you answered incorrectly. When you look at each question, you shouldn't just look to see what the correct answer is, but rather why you got the question wrong and how you could have gotten the question right. Train yourself in the process of getting the question right.

Why Did You Get the Question Wrong?

There are three reasons why you might have gotten an individual question wrong.

- **Reason 1**: You thought you knew the answer, but actually you didn't.

- **Reason 2**: You managed to eliminate some answer choices and then guessed among the remaining answers; sadly, you guessed wrong.

- **Reason 3**: You knew the answer but made a careless mistake.

You should know which of these reasons applies to every question you got wrong.

What You Could Have Done to Get the Question Right?

The reasons you got a question wrong affect how you should think about it while studying your test.

If You Got a Question Wrong for Reason 1—Lack of Knowledge

A question answered incorrectly for Reason 1 identifies a weakness in your knowledge of the material tested on the SAT II U.S. History. Discovering this wrong answer gives you an opportunity to target your weakness. When addressing that weakness, make sure that you don't just look at the facts.

For example, if the question you got wrong refers to the election of 1912, which Woodrow Wilson won, don't just memorize the facts of the election; learn *why* Wilson won, study up on the split in the Republican party between Taft and Roosevelt, get some understanding of the ideological split between those two men and how the social and political realities of the U.S. at the time influenced this split. Remember, you will *not* see a question exactly the same as the question you got wrong. But you probably *will* see a question that covers the same topic as the practice question. For that reason, when you get a question wrong, don't just figure out the right answer to the question. Learn the broader topic of which the question tests only a piece.

If You Got a Question Wrong for Reason 2—Guessing Wrong

If you guessed wrong, review your guessing strategy. Did you guess intelligently? Could you have eliminated more answers? If yes, why didn't you? By thinking in this critical way about the decisions you made while taking the practice test, you can train yourself to make quicker, more decisive, and better decisions.

If you took a guess and chose the incorrect answer, don't let that sour you on guessing. Even as you go over the question and figure out if there was any way for you to have answered the question without having to guess, remind yourself that if you eliminated at least one answer and guessed, even if you got the question wrong you followed the right strategy.

If You Got a Question Wrong for Reason 3—Carelessness

If you discover you got a question wrong because you were careless, it might be tempting to say to yourself, "Oh, I made a careless error," and assure yourself you won't do that again. That is not enough. You made that careless mistake for a reason, and you should try to figure out why. Whereas getting a question wrong because you didn't know the answer constitutes a weakness in your knowledge of the test subject, making a careless mistake represents a weakness in your *method of taking the test.*

To overcome this weakness, you need to approach it in the same critical way you would approach a lack of knowledge. Study your mistake. Reenact your thought process on the problem and see where and how your carelessness came about: were you rushing? Did you jump at the first answer that seemed right instead of reading all the answers? Know your error and look it in the eye. If you learn precisely what your mistake was, you are much less likely to make that mistake again.

If You Left the Question Blank

It is also a good idea to study the questions you left blank on the test, since those questions constitute a reservoir of lost points. If you left the question blank, a different thinking applies. A blank answer is a result either of:

1. Total inability to answer a question

2. Lack of time

In the case of the former, you should see if there was some way you might have been able to eliminate an answer choice or two and put yourself in a better position to guess. In the second case, look over the question and see whether you think you could have answered it. If you could have, then you know that you are throwing away points by working too slowly. If you couldn't, then carry out the steps above: study the relevant material (time period, movement, political leader, etc.) and review your guessing strategy.

The Secret Weapon: Talking to Yourself

Yeah, it's embarrassing. Yeah, you may look silly. But talking to yourself is perhaps the best way to pound something into your brain. As you go through the steps of studying a question, you should talk them out. When you verbalize something to yourself, it makes it much harder to delude yourself into thinking that you're working if you're really not.

SAT II U.S. History

Practice Test I

UNITED STATES HISTORY TEST I

Directions: Each of the questions or incomplete statements below is followed by five suggested answers or completions. Select the one that is best in each case and then fill in the corresponding oval on the answer sheet.

1. British joint-stock companies primarily served what function in the colonies?

    (A) they funded British colonization efforts through the sale of public stock
    (B) they brought slaves from Africa to the New England colonies
    (C) they developed trade agreements between English and French colonies
    (D) they funded Spanish colonization efforts by establishing mining operations
    (E) they funded French efforts during the French and Indian War by selling furs from North America in Europe

2. Which of the following best characterizes immigration to Britain's North American colonies after 1680?

    (A) England was the primary source of new immigrants
    (B) immigration decreased dramatically
    (C) immigration to the New England colonies increased while immigration to the Southern colonies decreased
    (D) immigrants attempted to assimilate into well-established settlements
    (E) continental Europe was the primary source of new immigrants

3. All of the following accurately describe the emergence of political parties in the United States EXCEPT

    (A) the origin of the two parties is traced to the debate between strict constructionists and loose constructionists
    (B) George Washington favored the creation of political parties because he vowed to uphold the political ideals of the framers of the U.S. Constitution
    (C) the opposition political party during Washington's presidency effectively used the media to draw supporters
    (D) Federalists and Republicans differed mostly in their views about whether power should rest in state governments or in a strong central power
    (E) whil, geographically, Federalists were centered in the Northeast, Republicans were centered in the agrarian South

4. All of the following pushed the United States toward entering World War I EXCEPT

    (A) President Wilson's political sympathy with Western European liberal democracies
    (B) a blockade of allied ports by German U-boats
    (C) growing U.S. investment in and aid to Allied Europe
    (D) the Democratic Party's war-mongering
    (E) the sinking of the ocean liner *Lusitania*

5. Which of the following best explains the motivation behind the Missouri Compromise of 1820?

    (A) the desire to prevent the entry of more slave states into the Union
    (B) the desire to prevent the entry of more free states into the Union
    (C) the desire to preserve the balance between free states and slave states in the Union
    (D) the desire to prevent Missouri from seceding from the Union
    (E) the desire to prohibit slavery in the Louisiana Territory

6. President Jackson opposed the recharter of the Second Bank of the United States because

    (A) he felt the Bank was unconstitutional
    (B) he realized the Whigs were using the Bank as a political tool against him
    (C) he personally disliked the Bank's president, Nicholas Biddle
    (D) he felt that the Bank hurt Western interests and was monopolistic
    (E) he felt that the Bank would collapse the national economy

7. A muckraker would most likely be interested in

    (A) the free coinage of silver
    (B) a labor shortage caused by strikes
    (C) farmers' economic interests
    (D) a meat-packing plant putting rats in its sausage
    (E) the foundation of settlements like Hull House

GO ON TO THE NEXT PAGE ▶

8. Which of the following is most INCONSISTENT with American isolationism before World War II?

(A) the Lend-Lease Act
(B) immigration restrictions
(C) the Committee to Defend America First
(D) the Ludlow Amendment
(E) the Neutrality Acts

9. "It looks for the liberation of the spirit of woman and through woman of the child. To-day [sic] motherhood is wasted, penalized, tortured. Children brought into the world by unwilling mothers suffer an initial handicap that cannot be measured by cold statistics. Their lives are blighted from the start"

Margaret Sanger, the author of this passage, used this argument, among others, in her quest to

(A) secure women's suffrage
(B) increase women's wages in the workplace
(C) outlaw sexual harassment
(D) legalize and popularize contraceptives
(E) open labor unions to female industrial workers

10. Colonists used the cry "no taxation without representation" to protest against each of the following acts EXCEPT

(A) The Stamp Act
(B) The Townshend Duties
(C) The Declaratory Act
(D) The Sugar Act
(E) The Intolerable Acts

11. All of the following motivated the War Hawks in Congress to push for the War of 1812 EXCEPT

(A) the desire to eliminate the French presence in New Orleans
(B) resentment over the continued impressment of American soldiers
(C) resentment over the recession in southern and western states that had been caused by Macon's Bill No. 2
(D) the desire to eliminate the British presence in North America by annexing Canada
(E) the desire to open up new western lands for settlement

12. All of the following were reform movements during the mid-nineteenth century EXCEPT

(A) the eugenics movement
(B) the temperance movement
(C) the prison reform movement
(D) the public school reform movement
(E) the abolitionist movement

13. Issued during the Civil War, the Emancipation Proclamation freed all black slaves

(A) living in the North and South
(B) living in Union-controlled Southern states
(C) living in areas of the Confederacy still under rebellion
(D) living in the North
(E) captured by Union soldiers

14. The election of 1824 was called the "first modern election" because

(A) it was the first election in which only two candidates ran against each other
(B) it was the first election in which the president was elected by the Electoral College
(C) it was the first election in which party leaders no longer had exclusive control over the presidential candidate nomination process
(D) it was the first election in which women could vote
(E) it was the first election in which the candidate who received the second largest number of votes did not become vice president

15. Which of the following is characteristic of black American political involvement during the 1930s?

(A) black Americans began holding important government positions in the South for the first time since Reconstruction
(B) the number of black American voters dropped by half since the 1920s
(C) most black Americans left the Democratic Party in protest over FDR's New Deal policies
(D) most black Americans backed third party candidates
(E) most Black Americans shifted political allegiances from the Republican Party to the Democratic Party

GO ON TO THE NEXT PAGE

16. "I believe that it must be the policy of the United States to support free peoples who are resisting subjugation by armed minorities or by outside pressures."

This foreign policy statement was issued during the

(A) 1790s
B) 1820s
(C) 1920s
(D) 1940s
(E) 1990s

17. The primary difference between the Constitution and the Articles of Confederation was that the Constitution

(A) created a much stronger national government
(B) reserved explicit powers for the states
(C) created a loose confederation of states
(D) protected civil liberties
(E) provided for a federal legislative body

18. Because Andrew Jackson made extensive use of his executive veto power to overrule Congress, the president's critics often referred to him as

(A) King Andrew I
(B) Old Hickory
(C) Andrew the Tyrant
(D) Unjust Jackson
(E) Andrew the Autocrat

19. In the years leading up to the Civil War, northern and Southern state interests were generally in conflict on all of the following issues EXCEPT

(A) slavery
(B) the denial of suffrage to women
(C) nullification
(D) tariffs and other restrictions on trade
(E) the doctrine of states' rights

20. The Platt Amendment of 1901

(A) secured land for the construction of the Panama Canal
(B) restricted Cuban sovereignty by giving the U.S. the right to intervene in Cuban affairs
(C) opened up trade relations with China
(D) established diplomatic relations with Japan
(E) provided American support for Nicaraguan rebels

21. The term "iron curtain" was coined by Winston Churchill to describe

(A) the U.S. nuclear deterrent
(B) the Soviet-imposed division of Eastern Europe from the West
(C) Stalin's negotiating position at Yalta
(D) Britain's air defense against Germany
(E) the repression of democratic freedoms in the USSR

22. In the late 1800s, all of the following celebrated capitalism and served to justify the growing gap between the rich and poor EXCEPT

(A) Horatio Alger's popular tales
(B) Jacob Riis's *How the Other Half Lives*
(C) Andrew Carnegie's "Gospel of Wealth"
(D) the hero status of men like John D. Rockefeller
(E) Social Darwinist theory

23. Which of the following organizations was founded to support reform efforts in the early nineteenth century?

(A) the National Association of Colored People (NAACP)
(B) the Populist Party
(C) the American Temperance Society
(D) the Bull Moose Party
(E) the Congress of Industrial Organizations (CIO)

24. Which of the following factors helped motivate public school reform efforts in the mid-nineteenth century?

(A) the increasing need to prepare students for work in technologically sophisticated industries
(B) pressure from Protestant groups to give children a good moral education
(C) rationalism's critique of religion in public schools
(D) the desire to decrease poverty and crime
(E) the desire, stemming from the expansion of suffrage, to produce an educated and literate citizenry

GO ON TO THE NEXT PAGE

25. For President Wilson, the most important element of the Treaty of Versailles was

    (A) the plan for a League of Nations
    (B) the redistribution of German territory
    (C) the German commitment to repay the U.S. for the damage wrought by German U-boat attacks
    (D) The creation of Czechoslovakia
    (E) German disarmament

26. Which of the following was a major result of the New Deal?

    (A) many tenant farmers and sharecroppers in the South and Midwest received much-needed economic assistance
    (B) the American financial system was changed in the hopes of preventing future stock crashes and bank failures
    (C) labor unions recognized the importance and value of female workers
    (D) the structure of the Supreme Court was altered
    (E) women achieved the right to vote in national elections

27. Which of the following figures was NOT associated with the Harlem Renaissance?

    (A) Langston Hughes
    (B) James Weldon Johnson
    (C) Zora Neale Hurston
    (D) Claude McKay
    (E) Richard Wright

28. The 1920's Ku Klux Klan differed from the earlier, Reconstruction-era Klan in that the 1920's Klan

    (A) lynched people
    (B) was hostile to immigrant Catholics and Jews from southern and eastern Europe, as well as to African-Americans
    (C) was a secret society dedicated to white supremacy
    (D) had members dress in white robes and hoods
    (E) concentrated its activities exclusively in the South

29. In accordance with the policy of containment after World War II, the U.S.

    (A) worked diplomatically to force the Red Army out of Eastern Europe
    (B) did not attempt to change the post-war make-up of Europe, but rather to prevent further Soviet advances
    (C) worked to overthrow communist countries
    (D) planned a massive offensive to free Eastern Europe from communist rule
    (E) accepted that communism would eventually spread across all of Europe

30. The labor force used to staff northern industries in the 1840s and 1850s consisted primarily of

    (A) slaves from Africa
    (B) indentured servants from Europe
    (C) young girls from areas surrounding the factories
    (D) immigrants from Europe
    (E) young boys from distant towns

GO ON TO THE NEXT PAGE

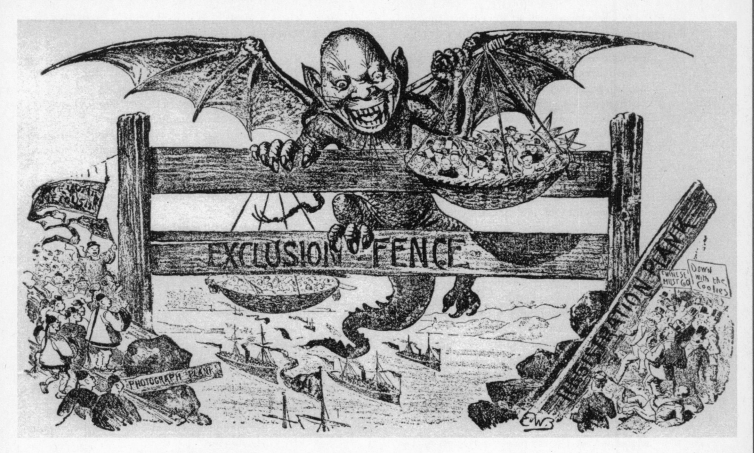

31. The above cartoon most likely refers to

 (A) the internment of Japanese-Americans during World War II
 (B) the Chinese Exclusion Act of 1882
 (C) the influx of immigrants to the U.S. who had been exiled from their own countries
 (D) America's exclusion of immigrants from the West Coast
 (E) America's aggressive campaign to deport Chinese communists after World War II

GO ON TO THE NEXT PAGE

32. All of the following were true of slave life in the South during the early to mid-nineteenth century EXCEPT

   (A) marriage between slaves was discouraged by slave owners
   (B) slaves attempted to form kinship networks with other slaves who were not blood relatives
   (C) female slaves primarily did housework and raised slave children while male slaves worked primarily in the fields
   (D) house servants had better living conditions than field workers
   (E) slave children were often separated from their families and sold to different owners

33. In *Walden* (1854), Henry David Thoreau advocated

   (A) reforming federal environmental protection laws
   (B) establishing national parks
   (C) assessing religious beliefs through logic and rational reflection
   (D) living a simple, contemplative life rather than one steeped in luxury and materialism
   (E) establishing communities in nature to promote social harmony and utopian ideals

34. As chief justice of the Supreme Court, John Marshall

   (A) weakened the Court's power in respect to the executive and legislative branches of government
   (B) led the Court to expand states' rights and limit the power of the central government
   (C) led the Court to side with abolitionists in cases involving slavery
   (D) exerted a strong Federalist influence and enhanced the Supreme Court's power in federal government
   (E) enraged and alienated his Federalist supporters

35. The concept of Manifest Destiny would most likely have been used to justify

   (A) government subsidies of industry in the Ohio river valley
   (B) regulating railroad companies in interstate trade disputes
   (C) forced removal of Native American populations to western lands
   (D) redesigning the nation's capital to better represent America's new influence in the world
   (E) extending popular sovereignty on the slavery question to newly admitted western states

36. The Marshall Plan helped the U.S. in its Cold War efforts by

   (A) providing massive funds for scientific research
   (B) aggressively promoting democracy in Latin America
   (C) giving military aid to countries fighting against communist insurgents
   (D) promoting political stability through economic assistance designed to rebuild European countries after World War II
   (E) controlling the proliferation of nuclear technology

37. "I am not a friend to energetic government."

   The author of the statement above would most likely have considered himself a(n)

   (A) Know-Nothing
   (B) Whig
   (C) Progressive
   (D) Federalist
   (E) Anti-federalist

38. Dissenter Roger Williams was banished from the Massachusetts Bay Colony for advocating

   (A) the complete separation of church and state
   (B) theocracy
   (C) an inner, emotional understanding of religious truth
   (D) legal separation of church and state, but with substantial cooperation between the two
   (E) the utter depravity of human nature

39. Britain's policy of salutary neglect toward the colonies was primarily motivated by

   (A) Britain's desire to establish a favorable balance of trade
   (B) Britain's need to pay off the war debt accumulated during the French and Indian War
   (C) Britain's need to raise funds to support colonial expansion past the Appalachian mountains
   (D) Britain's desire to thwart colonial independence
   (E) Britain's desire to maintain colonist loyalty in the face of possible war against France

GO ON TO THE NEXT PAGE

40. John Brown's activity in the years preceding the Civil War can best be characterized as

(A) providing hope to slaveholders that pro-slavery forces would impel the capture and return of escaped slaves

(B) evidence that the debate over slavery could turn explosive and violent

(C) emblematic of the poor treatment of Native Americans by U.S. government officials

(D) a model of the type of civil disobedience encouraged by abolitionist thinker Henry David Thoreau

(E) representative of the antislavery opinions quietly harbored by many Northerners at the time

41. Following the system of triangular trade

(A) New England rum was shipped to Africa and traded for slaves

(B) African slaves were traded in the West Indies for rum

(C) New England sugar and molasses were shipped to Africa and traded for slaves

(D) New England rum was shipped to England and traded for sugar and molasses

(E) West Indies sugar and molasses were shipped to Africa and traded for slaves

42. Which of the following statements best describes American foreign policy during the mid-1930s?

(A) supportive of German expansionism

(B) aiming to avoid involvement in European affairs

(C) fully tolerant of Japanese aggression toward China

(D) aiming to impede Russian expansion

(E) supportive of Britain's anti-German campaign

43. Which of the following statements is most INCONSISTENT with transcendentalist beliefs?

(A) God created a perfect universe and then allowed it to operate independently according to natural laws

(B) knowledge is gained through the senses

(C) the concepts of God, freedom, and absolute truth are inborn

(D) truth is accessible through sudden insight

(E) spontaneous and vivid expression are favored over purely intellectual analysis

44. American society in the 1950s is best characterized by

(A) intense conflict between social classes

(B) its broad and unprecedented affluence

(C) a declining population

(D) a rejection of consumerism

(E) a spirit of nonconformity

45. Which of the following served as the foundation for the creation of affirmative action programs that favored minorities and women?

(A) Brown v. Board of Education

(B) the Taft-Hartley Act

(C) the Civil Rights Act of 1964

(D) *Roe v. Wade*

(E) the Voting Rights Act

46. Which of the following best characterizes the Populist Party's political efforts in the early 1890s?

(A) the Populists secured control over a number of state legislatures and elected a number of governors, senators, and congressmen to office

(B) as a third party, the Populists could not break the Republican and Democratic stranglehold on state and federal offices

(C) much of the Populist platform was co-opted by the Democratic Party, and the two parties soon merged

(D) Populist candidates fared well at first, but in-fighting within the party lessened the party's power and led to poor showings in state and federal elections

(E) the Populists swept control of northern states, but fared poorly in the South and the West

47. Which of the following was NOT an important issue in the United Sates during the 1920s?

(A) immigration restriction

(B) prohibition of alcohol

(C) the possibility of electing a Catholic president

(D) the halting of German rearmament

(E) corruption in the Harding administration

GO ON TO THE NEXT PAGE

48. All of the following were motivations of the Spanish conquistadors EXCEPT

   (A) to challenge English dominance in the New World
   (B) to establish lucrative trade routes
   (C) to win fame
   (D) to exploit natural resources including gold
   (E) to conquer the native people

49. From the 1870s through the 1930s, which of the following political groups would be LEAST likely to claim Midwestern farmers as a major constituency?

   (A) The Republican Party
   (B) The Grange
   (C) The Greenback Party
   (D) The Populist Party
   (E) The New Deal Coalition

50. The outcome of Colonel George Armstrong Custer's attacks against the Sioux in 1876 were representative of which of the following?

   (A) the ability of some Native American tribes to resist the removal policy fiercely and with a sustained effort
   (B) the total superiority of American arms and the American army over the fighting methods of the Native Americans
   (C) the end of Native American resistance to the policy of removal
   (D) the beginning of the violent expulsion of Native Americans from their lands west of the Mississippi
   (E) the Sioux tribe's cooperation with other major tribes in a unified resistance against the American government

51. Many of President Franklin Roosevelt's New Deal policies were based on economist John Maynard Keynes's theories, which stated that

   (A) government saving could revive a failing economy
   (B) government spending could revive a failing economy
   (C) a failing economy will revive itself if the government does not interfere
   (D) the government should encourage consumers to save money in order to revive a failing economy
   (E) the government should encourage consumers to spend money in order to revive a failing economy

52. Which of the following arguments is LEAST characteristic of the 1960's campaigns against the Vietnam War?

   (A) the horror and devastation shown on television proved that the government's assurances of an easy, winnable war were false
   (B) the U.S. should have become militarily committed to freeing Eastern Europe from Soviet control rather than wasting energy in a minor part of the globe
   (C) the war unfairly asked poor Americans to risk their lives in combat while rich Americans stayed home and prospered
   (D) there was no way to really win such a war without a massive loss of life and expenditure of resources
   (E) the war was essentially a Vietnamese civil war and therefore none of America's business

53. One result of the Hartford Convention of 1814 was

   (A) the founding of the Republican Party
   (B) the decline of the Federalist Party's prominence
   (C) the surge in antiwar sentiments, as Americans nationwide protested against the deadlocked war with Britain
   (D) in-fighting among the Federalists, leading to the party's eventual split into two factions
   (E) the founding of the Populist Party

54. In the 1832 Nullification Crisis, Vice President John C. Calhoun did all of the following EXCEPT

   (A) resign from his position as Vice President
   (B) argue that because the states had ratified the Constitution, they had the final say over whether laws affecting their regions were constitutional
   (C) draft the Ordinance of Nullification, which passed in the South Carolina legislature in 1832
   (D) encourage Southern states to secede from the Union
   (E) argue that federal laws needed to benefit everyone in order to be constitutional

GO ON TO THE NEXT PAGE

55. The presence of "scalawags" and "carpetbaggers" in the Southern state governments during Reconstruction illustrated that

(A) Reconstruction was working
(B) many Southern Reconstruction governments were inefficient and corrupt
(C) many Southern Reconstruction governments were extremely efficient and effective
(D) Southerners worked hard to reunite with the Union
(E) Northerners did not desire reunification with the South

56. All of the following improved the lives of city dwellers and urban workers in the late 1800s and early 1900s EXCEPT

(A) electric streetcars
(B) sanitary tenement housing
(C) the spread of parks and other green spaces
(D) the efforts of the CIO to raise factory wages
(E) the efforts of the Salvation Army to provide shelter and food to the poor

57. How did the U.S. government respond to an alleged attack on U.S. Navy ships by North Vietnamese in the Gulf of Tonkin?

(A) the U.S. immediately launched an intensive bombing campaign, known as Rolling Thunder, against North Vietnam
(B) Congress passed a resolution granting President Johnson the authority to escalate U.S. military involvement in Vietnam
(C) Congress urged President Johnson to withdraw all forces from Southeast Asia
(D) U.S. Marines were sent to attack North Vietnam
(E) Congress issued a formal declaration of war against North Vietnam

58. All of the following encouraged the huge wave of immigration to the U.S. between 1870 and 1920 EXCEPT

(A) the spread of pogroms against the Jews in Eastern Europe
(B) intense population pressures in Europe
(C) the efforts of American political officials, who encouraged immigration with their "streets are paved with gold" campaign
(D) the hopes of peasants, who were eager to begin a better life on American shores
(E) the urgings of established immigrant families in the U.S., who would send word for the rest of the family to join them

GO ON TO THE NEXT PAGE

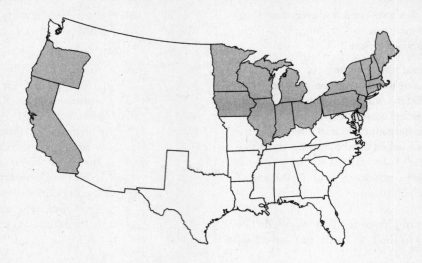

59.   The shaded states represent

(A)   all the states that Abraham Lincoln won in the election of 1860

(B)   the Federalist stronghold in the early 1800s

(C)   the areas unaffected by the Emancipation Proclamation

(D)   the support base for Andrew Jackson

(E)   the states most opposed to the doctrine of popular sovereignty

60. Federalists generally believed that the new national government under the Constitution

   (A) should have no executive office, but a legislative and a judicial branch
   (B) should be strong and centralized
   (C) should have less power than the state governments
   (D) should be headed by a president elected for life and have no legislative body
   (E) should invest absolute power in the federal government and disband state governments

61. Which of the following is considered an affect of the First Great Awakening?

   (A) the separation of American Protestants from the Anglican Church
   (B) the so-called democratization of religion
   (C) the exclusion of women from religious revivals
   (D) systematic and intense training of clergy
   (E) heightened intolerance of dissenters

62. All of the following are included in the Constitution and its amendments EXCEPT

   (A) the three-fifths Clause
   (B) freedom of speech
   (C) judicial review
   (D) representation in the House of Representatives proportionate to state population
   (E) the Electoral College

63. Which of the following foreign actions most directly challenged Washington's policy of neutrality?

   (A) the outbreak of the French Revolution
   (B) the Spanish enlistment of Native American tribes in Florida
   (C) the Spanish attempts to plunder American trade vessels
   (D) the French attempts to control the forts and posts along the Mississippi River
   (E) the British seizure of American ships, the impressment of American sailors, and the building of British forts on American territory

64. Southern states reacted to the Supreme Court's decision in *Brown v. Board of Education* by

   (A) immediately but begrudgingly desegregating schools across the South
   (B) calling in federal troops to assist in desegregation
   (C) having *Brown v. Board* overturned on appeal
   (D) boycotting public buses
   (E) resisting integration and denying funding to school districts working to desegregate

65. The Declaration of Independence embodies the general ideas found in

   (A) Enlightenment philosophy
   (B) Social Darwinism
   (C) Egalitarianism
   (D) Aristotlian philosophy
   (E) Calvinism

66. Which of the following characterized colonial Pennsylvania in the 1700s?

   (A) its highly developed banking and commercial networks
   (B) the lowest death rate in the colonies
   (C) its large population of German settlers who became skilled farmers and tradesmen
   (D) its exceptionally friendly relations with local Native American tribes
   (E) the New World's first successful cultivation of West Indian tobacco

GO ON TO THE NEXT PAGE

Average Life Expectancy at Age 20 During the Seventeenth Century

Married Women in Middlesex County, Virginia	39
Married Men in Middlesex County, Virginia	48
Women in Andover, Massachusetts	62
Men in Andover, Massachusetts	64
Women in Plymouth, Massachusetts	62
Men in Plymouth, Massachusetts	69

Source: www.gilder-lehrman.org

67. The chart above lends support to which of the following statements?

(A) Virginia's many slave uprisings made the colony a veritable death trap

(B) marriage tended to shorten colonial life spans—especially for women, because childbirth was dangerous and often fatal

(D) a scarlet fever epidemic ravaged the Southern colonies but spared much of New England

(D) New Englanders generally had much longer life spans than colonists living in the Southern colonies, in part because of better diets

(E) New England's climate prevented the spread of diseases like tuberculosis

GO ON TO THE NEXT PAGE

68. Booker T. Washington believed that

  (A) African-Americans must aggressively pursue equal rights in order to obtain them
  (B) the best way for African-Americans to improve their status in the United States is to work hard, learn vocational skills, and acquire property
  (C) African-Americans should withdraw from mainstream U.S. society and form their own cities and separate laws
  (D) the smartest African-Americans, or the "talented tenth" as they were often known, should provide a good example and help elevate the status of all African-Americans
  (E) legal action is more effective than education at securing equal rights for African-Americans

69. In the 1840s, all the following states or territories were the subject of heated congressional debate over the issue of extending slavery EXCEPT

  (A) Kentucky
  (B) Oregon
  (C) Texas
  (D) Utah
  (E) California

70. What provided the biggest obstacle to union success in the latter half of the nineteenth century?

  (A) federal laws, mostly passed during the Cleveland administration, forced labor unions to meet all sorts of criteria in order to organize
  (B) as industry spread throughout the country, workers were dispersed, so the labor movement consisted of only tiny, isolated uprising.
  (C) Andrew Carnegie won over the hearts of middle-class America with his "Gospel of Wealth," so that workers won little or no win sympathy from the general public
  (D) the Civil War left the country struggling with civil rights issues, so the plight of industrial workers was not a national priority
  (E) most laborers, both skilled and unskilled, were not members of unions, rendering the labor movement largely ineffective

71. After President Truman endorsed a report from the Presidential Committee on Civil Rights entitled *To Secure These Rights*, he

  (A) sent federal troops to the Deep South to begin desegregation
  (B) did little to enact the report's recommendations
  (C) moved to protect black voting rights, but refused to desegregate the military
  (D) lost the political support of many southern whites
  (E) won the support of white southern Democrats in Congress

72. All of these people would likely be members of the Populist Party EXCEPT

  (A) a debt-ridden worker
  (B) a man living in suburban Philadelphia
  (C) a farmer in Nebraska
  (D) a silver mine owner
  (E) a member of the Knights of Labor

73. The final draft of the Constitution was the product of

  (A) a series of compromises
  (B) power politics
  (C) the dominance of the Anti-federalists
  (D) only a few delegates rather than all the delegates at the convention
  (E) elite politics in early America

74. Aside from territorial expansion, the debate over the acquisition of the Oregon territory during President Polk's administration was politically important because

  (A) it threatened to prolong the Mexican War
  (B) future statehood for Oregon would affect the ratio of free states to slave states
  (C) it caused lasting hostilities between America and Great Britain
  (D) the discovery of gold in the territory portended a massive population shift
  (E) it improved American relations with imperial Russia, which had carved out a sphere of influence over western Canada

GO ON TO THE NEXT PAGE

75. Which of the following presidents is correctly paired with an event that took place during his administration?

    (A)   Richard Nixon . . . the launching of the "Great Society" social welfare program

    (B)   Jimmy Carter . . . the Watergate scandal

    (C)   Ronald Reagan . . . the U.S. invasion of Grenada

    (D)   George H. Bush . . . the taking of U.S. hostages by the Iranians

    (E)   Bill Clinton . . . the end of the Gulf War

76. In which decade did the suburban population of the U.S. nearly double?

    (A)   the 1940s

    (B)   the 1950s

    (C)   the 1970s

    (D)   the 1930s

    (E)   the 1980s

77. Parliament passed the Proclamation Line in 1763 in order to

    (A)   prohibit colonists from settling west of the Allegheny Mountains

    (B)   allow for French occupation of parts of the Northeastern territory

    (C)   extend the colonists' claim to westward lands

    (D)   set up a boundary at which traders would have to proclaim goods subject to taxation

    (E)   void Native American claims to land in the colonies

78. Abraham Lincoln's success in the Lincoln-Douglas debates in 1858 signaled

    (A)   the end of Senator Stephen A. Douglas's political career

    (B)   the inevitability of Lincoln's election to the presidency that same year

    (C)   the increasing popularity of Lincoln's opinions favoring popular sovereignty

    (D)   the rise to national prominence of the Republican Party

    (E)   a large-scale loss of popular support for the Democratic Party

79. How did industrialization proceed in the South after the Civil War?

    (A)   the South became America's industrial leader, owing to its rapid development of the mill economy and the introduction of the iron, steel, and oil industries

    (B)   the South developed advanced manufacturing plants, using raw goods shipped from the North

    (C)   industrialization bypassed the South entirely, leaving the region much the same as it had been before the Civil War

    (D)   despite the introduction of heavy industry and the development of the mill economy, the South industrialized only gradually, and lagged far behind the North

    (E)   free blacks in the South embraced industrialization, but free whites feared its potentially adversary effects on agriculture

GO ON TO THE NEXT PAGE

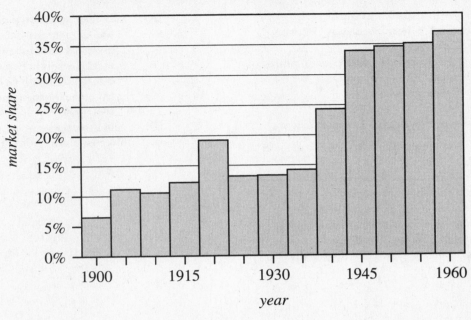

U.S Private Sector Trade Union Membership, 1900-1960

Source: U.S. Department of Labor

80. Which of the following statements best explains the data in the above graph?

   (A) automation and mass production in the late 1950s severely weakened the labor movement

   (B) union membership swelled from 1935 to 1940 because of government policies favoring unionization

   (C) the huge influx of immigrants in the late 1930s led to the sharp increase in union membership

   (D) the advent of the "open shop" policy in industry stimulated union growth from 1940 to 1960

   (E) decreasing wages in the 1920s helped fuel the labor cause and expand union membership

GO ON TO THE NEXT PAGE

81. The administration of President Theodore Roosevelt invoked the Sherman Antitrust Act to

    (A) regulate the meatpacking industry
    (B) break up the Northern Securities Company railroad monopoly
    (C) establish the Interstate Commerce Commission
    (D) strengthen the Pure Food and Drug Act
    (E) put down labor strikes

82. The primary goal of Progressive Era feminists was

    (A) the repeal of laws prohibiting the use of birth control
    (B) the passage of laws prohibiting discrimination against women in the workplace
    (C) the regulation of child care facilities
    (D) the passage of a constitutional amendment providing for women's suffrage
    (E) the passage of state laws liberalizing divorce

83. Alexander Hamilton primarily designed his financial policy in order to

    (A) establish good national credit with domestic and foreign creditors and stimulate the growth of new manufacturing
    (B) protect the southern cotton industry from competition with Great Britain
    (C) prevent northern manufacturers from exporting their goods
    (D) generate higher revenue from income taxes
    (E) increase the amount of currency in circulation

GO ON TO THE NEXT PAGE

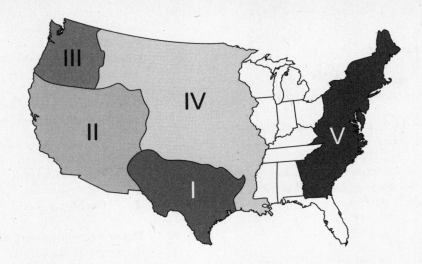

84. Which territory did Thomas Jefferson purchase from France?

(A) I
(B) II
(C) III
(D) IV
(E) V

GO ON TO THE NEXT PAGE

85. The regulation of the economy during World War I affected American labor by

    (A) lowering workers' wages
    (B) outlawing unions for the duration of the war
    (C) ensuring that unions had a legal right to strike
    (D) forcing unions to root out all communist members
    (E) allowing more than a million blacks and women to enter the labor force

86. Since the 1970s, all of the following groups have had an easier time entering the workforce and earning competitive salaries EXCEPT

    (A) women
    (B) African-Americans
    (C) young people with advanced degrees in law and medicine
    (D) high school graduates without college degrees
    (E) Asian-Americans

87. The 1924 National Origins Act was intended to

    (A) restrict immigration from Southern and Eastern Europe and Asia
    (B) encourage immigration from Asia
    (C) ensure that the genealogy of Americans was studied and recorded
    (D) acknowledge the claims of Native Americans to lands in the West
    (E) block further immigration of Protestants into the U.S.

88. "We will walk on our own feet; we will work with our own hands; we will speak our own minds... A nation of men will for the first time exist, because each believes himself inspired by the Divine Soul which also inspires all men."

    This statement was probably made by a member of which of the following schools of American writers?

    (A) The Dark Romantics
    (B) The Expatriates
    (C) The Romantics
    (D) The Transcendentalists
    (E) The Muckrakers

89. The primary purpose of the United Nations, when it was created, was to

    (A) prosecute war crimes
    (B) collect reparations from the Axis powers
    (C) halt Soviet expansion
    (D) rebuild Europe after World War II
    (E) maintain global peace through collective security

90. Which of the following was NOT true of the Untied States during World War II?

    (A) the economy slumped and unemployment rose
    (B) Americans grew "victory gardens"
    (C) industries shifted from the production of civilian goods to the production of military goods
    (D) wage increases were limited to prevent inflation
    (E) some consumer goods were rationed

S T O P

IF YOU FINISH BEFORE TIME IS CALLED, YOU MAY CHECK YOUR WORK ON THIS TEST ONLY.
DO NOT TURN TO ANY OTHER TEST IN THIS BOOK.

SAT II U.S. History

Practice Test I

Explanations

Answers to SAT II U.S. History Practice Test I

Question Number	Correct Answer	Right	Wrong	Question Number	Correct Answer	Right	Wrong
1.	A	___	___	51.	B	___	___
2.	E	___	___	52.	B	___	___
3.	B	___	___	53.	B	___	___
4.	D	___	___	54.	D	___	___
5.	C	___	___	55.	B	___	___
6.	D	___	___	56.	D	___	___
7.	D	___	___	57.	B	___	___
8.	A	___	___	58.	C	___	___
9.	D	___	___	59.	A	___	___
10.	E	___	___	60.	B	___	___
11.	A	___	___	61.	B	___	___
12.	A	___	___	62.	C	___	___
13.	C	___	___	63.	E	___	___
14.	C	___	___	64.	E	___	___
15.	E	___	___	65.	A	___	___
16.	D	___	___	66.	C	___	___
17.	A	___	___	67.	D	___	___
18.	A	___	___	68.	B	___	___
19.	B	___	___	69.	A	___	___
20.	B	___	___	70.	E	___	___
21.	B	___	___	71.	D	___	___
22.	B	___	___	72.	B	___	___
23.	C	___	___	73.	A	___	___
24.	E	___	___	74.	B	___	___
25.	A	___	___	75..	C	___	___
26.	B	___	___	76.	B	___	___
27.	E	___	___	77.	A	___	___
28.	B	___	___	78.	D	___	___
29.	B	___	___	79.	D	___	___
30.	D	___	___	80.	B	___	___
31.	B	___	___	81.	B	___	___
32.	C	___	___	82.	D	___	___
33.	D	___	___	83.	A	___	___
34.	D	___	___	84.	D	___	___
35.	C	___	___	85.	E	___	___
36.	D	___	___	86.	D	___	___
37.	E	___	___	87.	A	___	___
38.	A	___	___	88.	D	___	___
39.	E	___	___	89.	E	___	___
40.	B	___	___	90.	A	___	___
41.	A	___	___				
42.	B	___	___				
43.	A	___	___				
44.	B	___	___				
45.	C	___	___				
46.	A	___	___				
47.	D	___	___				
48.	A	___	___				
49.	A	___	___				
50.	A	___	___				

Calculating Your Score on
SAT II U.S. History
Practice Test 1

Your raw score for the SAT II History test is calculated from the number of questions you answer correctly and incorrectly. Once you have determined your composite score, use the conversion table on page 19 of this book to calculate your scaled score.

To Calculate Your Raw Score

Count the number of questions you answered correctly: _____
A

Count the number of questions you answered incorrectly, and multiply that number by $\frac{1}{4}$:

_____ X $\frac{1}{4}$ = _____
B   C

Subtract the value in field C from value in field A: _____
D

Round the number in field D to the nearest whole number. This is your raw score: _____
E

1. **(A)** The Colonial Period

Fact Question

England exhausted a lot of time and money fighting Spain for position in North America. As a result, by 1600, the English government was hesitant to spend money on colonization. Joint-stock companies formed to raise funds for colonization efforts through the sale of public stocks. Joint-stock companies dominated English colonization efforts throughout the seventeenth century.

2. **(E)** The Colonial Period

Trend Question

After 1680, continental Europe replaced England as the primary source of new immigrants to the colonies. Immigrants from continental Europe left to escape war and poverty at home and to seek new economic and religious opportunities in colonial America.

3. **(B)** A New Nation

Except Question

Washington actually opposed the development of political parties because he feared that they would weaken and even destroy the government. The framers of the U.S. Constitution likewise considered political parties unnecessarily divisive, and so intentionally left them out of their plan for the new nation. Note that (C) is true because Republicans gained support for their party primarily through the use of the publication *The National Gazette*.

4. **(D)** World War I

Except Question

Although war increasingly loomed on the horizon from 1914 on, America's traditional isolationist position was the dominant one across the nation. All of the factors mentioned made U.S. neutrality difficult except the Democratic Party's position on war—which was to avoid war. In fact, in 1916, Democratic President Woodrow Wilson ran his winning reelection campaign on his record of keeping America out of war. Wilson's sympathies toward Britain and France (A) did indeed challenge his pledge to maintain neutrality. The U-boat blockade (B) cost America lives and money and pushed America toward joining the Allies. During the early years of the war, U.S. investment in Allied Europe surged (C), while it declined dramatically in Germany. The sinking of the *Lusitania* (E) provoked the U.S. to commence a military buildup.

5. **(C)** A New Nation

Fact Question

The Missouri Compromise was designed to keep the number of free and slave states in the Union equal by allowing Missouri to enter as a slave state while Maine entered as a free state. (A), (B), and (E) only represent the view of one side of the compromise. (D) is incorrect because the Missouri Compromise was about Missouri's entrance into, not secession from, the Union.

6. **(D)** The Age of Jackson

Fact Question

President Jackson opposed Biddle's efforts to obtain a second charter for the Second Bank of the United States because he felt that the Bank was monopolistic, elitist, and harmful for Westerners. In his attempt to dismantle the Bank, Jackson moved much of the money in the national bank to state banks and also encouraged the creation of new state banks. With the 1836 Deposit Act, he further tried to decentralize the national banking system.

7. **(D)** Industrial Revolution   *Trend Question*

Theodore Roosevelt first coined the phrase "muckraker" in a speech in 1906 to describe the journalists who rooted out (or "muckraked") filth when writing their alarming exposés on various political and corporate evils. Muckrakers helped spur many of the reforms of the Progressive Era, including consumer protection laws, conservation laws, and child labor laws. Upton Sinclair, who wrote *The Jungle* to expose the unsanitary and hazardous working conditions at a meat processing plant, was the most famous muckraker of his time.

8. **(A)** World War II   *Except Question*

The 1941 Lend-Lease Act allowed the president to lend or lease supplies to any nation deemed important to the defense of the United States. FDR used the Lend-Lease Act to help the Allied nations in World War II, thus involving the U.S. in the war. The remaining answers are examples of isolationist policies and initiatives meant to keep the U.S. out of war.

9. **(D)** The Progressive Era   *Quotation Question*

Margaret Sanger used this passage to argue for the legalization of contraceptives. She believed that women were oppressed because society condemned the notion of female sexual desires. She also believed that the constant fear of becoming pregnant was an unnecessary burden that most women carried.

10. **(E)** Revolution & Constitution   *Except Question*

Colonial Americans created the slogan "no taxation without representation" in the mid 1760s and continued to use the phrase until the beginning of the Revolutionary War. The colonists believed that Parliament should not tax the colonists unless the colonists received rights to represent themselves as official members of Parliament. The colonists would have used the cry "no taxation without representation" to respond to every act except for the Intolerable Acts because those acts did not concern taxation, but were instead intended to punish Bostonians for the Boston Tea Party (by closing Boston Harbor and enforcing the Quartering Act, among other measures). The Stamp Act was a tax on printed material, the Townshend Duties taxed multiple goods, and the Sugar Act was a tax on molasses. Although the Declaratory Act did not tax any specific goods, it did give Parliament the authority to tax the colonies on any item at any time.

11. **(A)** A New Nation   *Except Question*

The United States tried to maintain neutrality as Britain and France battled against each other in the Napoleonic Wars, but both powers drew the United States into the conflict by blocking U.S. trade and seizing neutral American ships. Macon's Bill No. 2 led to an embargo against Britain, hurting the U.S. economy especially in southern and western states. The U.S. eventually went to war against Britain and fought British, not French, troops in New Orleans.

12. **(A)** Cultural Trends: 1781–Mid-1800s   *Except Question*

The eugenics movement, which aimed to reform society through genetic manipulation, was a dark side of the Progressive movement in the early twentieth century. (E) should be eliminated because abolitionism was important in the years leading up to the Civil War.

13. **(C)** Civil War & Reconstruction
Fact Question

The Emancipation Proclamation freed only black slaves living in the Confederacy under rebel control. It did not free slaves in the North (four Union states were slave states), nor did it emancipate slaves in Southern lands conquered by the Union prior to the Proclamation. In reality, the Emancipation Proclamation freed very few slaves, but it did bolster the Union Army and morale. After the Proclamation, more than 200,000 free blacks in the North joined the Union Army, giving the North an even greater military advantage.

14. **(C)** The Age of Jackson
Fact Question

The election of 1824 is called the "first modern election" because it was the first in which the party leaders did not have exclusive control over the nominating process. Although the congressional caucus did nominate a presidential candidate, William Crawford, for the 1824 election, its choice was not a very popular one. Instead, five candidates emerged to compete for the president, representing the nation's growing regional differences and the fracturing of the Republican Party.

If you did not immediately recognize the answer to this question, you can use your knowledge of political trends in American history to eliminate some answer choices. For example, you can quickly eliminate (D) because women were not granted the right to vote until nearly a hundred years later. Also, you can cross out (B) because presidents have always been elected by the Electoral College under the rules of the Constitution. (E) is incorrect because the runner-up had not become vice president since the Twelfth Amendment modified the election process in 1804. (A) is incorrect because there were several prior elections in which only two candidates ran against each other.

15. **(E)** The Great Depression & New Deal
Trend Question

During the 1930s, black American political participation was marked by a drastic shift in party allegiance from the Republican Party to the Democratic Party. Until the Depression Era, blacks generally supported the Republican Party because of the party's emancipation and enfranchisement policies during the aftermath of the Civil War. During the Great Depression, Democratic President Franklin Delano Roosevelt's New Deal policies helped blacks tremendously (although black Americans still suffered tremendously during the Depression). In allegiance to FDR, many blacks switched parties to become Democrats. Their support in the 1936 election helped secure FDR his reelection victory.

16. **(D)** The 1950s
Quotation Question

President Harry S. Truman made the above statement in the 1940s after World War II. This question is difficult because it requires you to identify what type of foreign policy it describes—in this case, it stems from the Truman Doctrine—and then asks you to identify the time period during which the United States conducted international relations according to this policy. When doing similar quotation-format questions, remember that many Americans during the Cold War used the term "outside pressure" to refer to the Soviet Union.

17. **(A)** Revolution & Constitution
Trend Question

The Constitution was different from the Articles of Confederation primarily because it established a strong national government with authority over the state governments. Under the Articles of Confederation, the states retained their sovereignty; the central government consisted of only a legislative body (no judicial or executive branch) with *very* limited authority over the states: Congress lacked the power to levy taxes, raise an army, regulate commerce, and sign and enforce national treaties.

18. **(A)** The Age of Jackson   *Fact Question*

Because Jackson made extensive use of the executive powers to override Congress's actions, Jackson's critics gave him the name "King Andrew I," in reference to colonial days under a somewhat tyrannical British monarchy. Another of Jackson's nicknames was Old Hickory (B), but he did not earn this nickname from exercising his veto powers.

19. **(B)** Westward Expansion & Sectional Strife   *Except Question*

In the antebellum years, Southern and Northern states did not oppose each other on the question of women's suffrage. All states uniformly opposed the idea at this time.

20. **(B)** The Age of Imperialism   *Fact Question*

The Platt Amendment of 1901 restricted Cuban sovereignty by giving the U.S. the right to intervene in Cuban affairs and to maintain a naval base at Cuba's Guantanamo Bay. Many Cubans were outraged, but the Cuban Constitutional Convention ultimately accepted the amendment.

21. **(B)** The 1950s   *Fact Question*

The term "iron curtain" refers to the Soviet-imposed division of Europe.

22. **(B)** Industrial Revolution   *Trend Question*

In *How the Other Half Lives*, Jacob Riis exposed the horrendous conditions of European immigrants living in NYC tenements. Horatio Alger, who wrote popular tales about hardworking men going from "rags to riches," was the most prominent proponent of the "Gospel of Success," the theory that anyone in American society could improve his societal position if only he tried hard enough. Andrew Carnegie's essay, "Gospel of Wealth," applied Darwin's theory of evolution to human society, arguing that economic competition benefited America: specifically, that the rich were the harworking and "fittest" of the species, and therefore should be allowed to flourish without government regulation or intervention. Carnegie's essay was one example of Social Darwinist theory.

23. **(C)** Cultural Trends: 1781–Mid-1800s   *Trend Question*

The American Temperance Society was founded in 1826 to advocate complete abstinence from alcohol. It is possible to answer this question by eliminating answers, since none of the other movements listed originated in the early nineteenth century. The Populist Party (B) was founded in 1892 in response to the plight of farmers. In 1909, W.E.B. Du Bois and a group of white reformers founded the NAACP (A) to push for an end to racial discrimination. In 1912, Theodore Roosevelt, in protest against President Taft's pro-business policies, founded the Bull Moose Party (D) to challenge President Taft for the presidency. The CIO (E) formed in 1938 and fast became one of the country's most successful and prominent labor unions.

24. **(E)** Cultural Trends: 1781–Mid-1800s   *Trend Question*

The nineteenth century saw the expansion of suffrage to all free males. Politicians feared the possibly corrupting effects that an uneducated, illiterate citizenry would have on the political process. One of the primary motivations for school reform was therefore the desire to mold students into responsible citizens.

25. (A) World War I   *Fact Question*

The creation of a League of Nations was Wilson's one major victory at the Versailles Peace Conference. Otherwise, the conference was mostly a debacle for Wilson. Angry, war-torn Allies bent on punishing Germany succeeded in taking away German territory and forcing German disarmament and heavy reparation payments. True, Wilson did favor the creation of independent states (such as Czechoslovakia) out of the remains of the Austro-Hungarian Empire, but the League of Nations was his primary achievement. In many ways, the League embodied his vision for the post-war world order.

26. (B) The Great Depression & New Deal   *Trend Question*

Many New Deal policies and programs, including the Federal Securities Act, the FDIC, and the SEC, altered the American financial system in an attempt to prevent future bank failures and stock market crashes.

27. (E) The Roaring Twenties   *Except Question*

Richard Wright, an African-American writer of great acclaim, was not associated with the Harlem Renaissance. The Renaissance faded with the onset of the Great Depression, in the early 1930s, and Wright wrote during the late 1930s and 1940s. His most famous novel, *Black Boy*, was published in 1945. The others authors listed—Hughes, Johnson, Hurston, and Mckay—were among the most famous associated with the movement.

28. (B) The Roaring Twenties   *Trend Question*

In the 1920s, the KKK no longer targeted blacks alone, but extended its hostility to immigrants and non-Protestants as well, especially in the West and Midwest. The Klan continued to be a secret white supremacist society (C) whose members staged lynchings and engaged in other terrorizing activities (A). The Klan's costume of white robes and hoods also did not change (D).

29. (B) The 1950s   *Fact Question*

After World War II, the U.S. opposed Soviet dominance of Eastern Europe by seeking to contain Soviet territorial advances. Rather than liberate areas that had already fallen under the Soviet sphere of influence, the U.S. worked to prevent any further advancement by the Soviets, while at the same time preparing militarily for the possibility of war.

30. (D) Cultural Trends: 1781–Mid-1800s   *Trend Question*

After the 1830s, the labor force staffing industries in the North was largely comprised of immigrants from Europe. Prior to the 1830s, factories were staffed using the Lowell System: hiring young girls from nearby towns and housing them in on-site dormitories. Unlike the South, the North never had a large slave population.

31. (B) Industrial Revolution   *Cartoon Question*

This cartoon refers the 1882 Chinese Exclusion Act, which placed a ten-year ban on Chinese immigration. Congress passed the act amid an atmosphere of rising nativism, as Americans grew to resent the influx of immigrants to the U.S., especially the influx of "new" immigrants from eastern and southern Europe and Asia. American workers resented the immigrants for flooding the job market and driving down wages, while the Protestant general public feared the disruptive social and religious effects these "new" (that is, ethnically unfamiliar) immigrants might have.

32. **(C)** Cultural Trends: 1781–Mid-1800s   *Except Question*

Both male and females slaves both worked primarily in the fields—although a small percentage worked as house servants—and enjoyed better living conditions as a result. Slave owners discouraged marriage between slaves and often sold slave children to other owners, fragmenting families. As a result, many slaves worked to establish surrogate families through kinship networks with other slaves who were not blood relatives.

33. **(D)** Cultural Trends: 1781–Mid-1800s   *Fact Question*

In *Walden*, Thoreau recounted his two years spent living alone in the woods away from civilization. He advocated living a simple, solitary life in nature, far removed from materialism and luxury, which he thought corrupted one's contemplation of and quest for truth.

34. **(D)** A New Nation   *Trend Question*

Under the leadership of Chief Justice John Marshall, the Supreme Court became a powerful federal force equal to the executive and legislative branches. Marshall was a staunch Federalist whose rulings enhanced federal power at the expense of states' rights, enraging many Republicans.

35. **(C)** Westward Expansion & Sectional Strife   *Trend Question*

Forced removal of the Native Americans to western lands was a policy closely aligned with the concept of Manifest Destiny. By this concept, white Americans viewed westward expansion as their God-given right. Removing the Native Americans to more distant lands facilitated U.S. expansion.

36. **(D)** The 1950s   *Fact Question*

Formulated in 1948, the Marshall Plan promised U.S. financial assistance to Europe in order to stimulate an economic recovery and to insure political stability. The plan was intended to strengthen European governments against possible communist threats.

37. **(E)** A New Nation   *Quotation Question*

The author of the above statement is Thomas Jefferson, the primary leader of the Anti-federalist movement during the late eighteenth and early nineteenth century. You can recognize the statement as Anti-federalist because the Anti-federalists opposed powerful centralized government and instead favored individual liberties and states' rights.

38. **(A)** The Colonial Period   *Fact Question*

In Massachusetts, Puritans followed a system of legal separation but substantial cooperation between church and state. Roger Williams argued for a complete separation between church and state because without this separation the state could corrupt the church. Banished from Massachusetts, Williams established the colony of Rhode Island in 1647.

39. **(E)** The Colonial Period   *Trend Question*

The British policy of salutary neglect was motivated by a desire to maintain colonist loyalty in case war broke out with the French. Because salutary neglect meant the lax enforcement of trade laws against the colonies, the policy did not generate a favorable balance of trade (A), and it actually helped foster colonial independence (the reverse of (D)). The need to pay off the war debt accrued during the French and Indian War (A) prompted England to abandon the policy of salutary neglect and enforce strict taxation and regulatory measures against the colonies.

40. **(B)** Westward Expansion & Sectional Strife   *Except Question*

John Brown crusaded violently in the cause of abolition, first in Kansas, in 1856, and then at Harper's Ferry, Virginia, in 1859. His activities signaled to many people that the debate over slavery was explosive and quickly turning violent.

41. **(A)** The Colonial Period   *Fact Question*

Under the system of triangular trade, New England rum was shipped to Africa and traded for slaves, who were brought to the West Indies and traded for sugar and molasses, which were in turn shipped back to New England. Raw materials were also shipped from the colonies to England, where they were traded for manufactured goods.

42. **(B)** World War II   *Trend Question*

Isolationism most characterized American foreign policy during the mid-1930s, which meant that the United States avoided entanglement in European affairs. You might have been tempted by (C), but despite its generally isolationist tendencies, the United States *was* concerned about Japan's expansionism. The U.S. tried to counter Japan's aggressive policy through trade embargoes.

43. **(A)** Cultural Trends: 1781–Mid-1800s   *Except Question*

The belief that God created a perfect universe and then allowed it to operate according to natural laws is a tenet of Deism, which is a rationalist religion. All of the other statements are true of transcendentalist belief.

44. **(B)** The 1950s   *Trend Question*

In American society, the 1950s was a time of unprecedented affluence and consumerism, and the population boomed. It was marked more by conformity and peace than by counterculture and rebellion.

45. **(C)** The 1960s   *Trend Question*

The Civil Rights Act of 1964 provided the legal basis for affirmative action programs that favored women and minorities.

46. **(A)** Industrial Revolution   *Fact Question*

By 1894, the Populists had elected four U.S. senators and four U.S. representatives to office, as well as almost 500 state senators and representatives, primarily in the South and West (the reverse of (E)). The Populists did align with the Democratic Party—but only briefly—in support of Democratic presidential candidate William Jennings Bryan in the 1896 election.

47. **(D)** The Roaring Twenties   *Except Question*

German rearmament was not considered an issue in America in the 1920s, when isolationism dominated U.S. political policy and public sentiment. Immigration restriction (A) and prohibition (B) were major concerns. When Al Smith ran for President in 1928, his Catholic faith was highly controversial (C). Finally, the Harding administration was plagued by corruption scandals (E).

48. **(A)** The Colonial Period   *Except Question*

Conquistador is the general term for any one of a group of Spanish explorers who went to the New World to find and exploit natural resources including gold, conquer native populations, develop trade routes, and earn fame. England became interested in the New World later than Spain and many other European powers. When England first tried to establish a settlement in 1584 off the coast of North Carolina, Spain was already a dominant force in the New World.

49. **(A)** Industrial Revolution
Except Question

Midwestern farmers would be least likely to support the Republican Party. The Republican Party found its core support in the cities of the Northeast because it favored measures to benefit industrial society, sometimes at the expense of agriculture.

Midwestern farmers found a political voice in the Grange (1867), then the Greenback Party (1976), then the Populist Party (1892). Farmers generally supported FDR's New Deal because its relief and regulatory measures (most notably the AAA) were aimed at helping the nation's agricultural sector.

50. **(A)** Westward Expansion & Sectional Strife
Trend Question

At the Battle of Little Bighorn in 1876, the Sioux tribe wiped out General Armstrong and his troops. The battle marked the tribe's sustained, fierce effort against American removal, which American forces did not successfully quell until the Battle at Wounded Knee in 1890.

51. **(B)** The Great Depression & New Deal
Trend Question

Most of Franklin Delano Roosevelt's New Deal policies stemmed from the theoretical writings of British economist John Maynard Keynes. Keynes argued that government spending could revive a failing economy. This question is difficult, but you can answer it even if you don't remember Keynes's theories. Many of FDR's programs—such as the Tennessee Valley Authority, the Public Works Administration, the Works Progress Administration, Civil Works Administration, and the Agricultural Adjustment Administration—involved the government spending money in order to hire workers and/or subsidize farmers. These programs thus relied on the theory that, by spending money, the government would pull the country out of the Great Depression.

52. **(B)** The 1960s
Except Question

Hardly anyone thought that the U.S. should commit militarily to freeing Eastern Europe from Soviet control, since most Americans supported the containment strategy of the Cold War. The other arguments listed were used to question America's military involvement in Southeast Asia.

53. **(B)** A New Nation
Fact Question

At the Hartford Convention, Federalist leaders met to draft a resolution listing their grievances against the ruling Republican Party. Among other complaints, the Convention members opposed the War of 1812 and its accompanying trade restrictions, which most hurt New England, a Federalist stronghold. The Federalists hoped their opposition to the war would tap into the nation's growing antiwar sentiment. But by the time the Federalists arrived in Washington, D.C., to deliver their petition to President Madison, news had spread of the American victory at the Battle of New Orleans and the signing of the Treaty of Ghent. In this celebratory atmosphere, as Americans rejoiced their perceived victory over Britain, the antiwar Federalists were branded as disloyal and traitorous. The political careers of these Federalists never recovered from the debacle. The Hartford Convention thus led to the death of the Federalist Party. Note that the Populist Party (E) was not founded until 1892.

54. **(D)** The Age of Jackson
Except Question

Vice President Calhoun did all of the above except encourage southern states to secede from the Union. Calhoun and South Carolina *threatened* to secede from the Union, but never actually encouraged others to do so. In fact, South Carolina itself quickly acquiesced in its fight to secede when President Jackson threatened to send armed forces into the state to collect taxes.

55. **(B)** Civil War & Reconstruction *Trend Question*

To answer this question correctly, you must first remember what "scalawags" and "carpetbaggers" were. Scalawags were Southern moderates who helped the Northern Radical Republicans during Reconstruction. Carpetbaggers were Northern opportunists who came to the South after the Civil War in order to grab political power and make a profit through bribes. After remembering the definitions of these terms, you can easily answer the question or at least eliminate several answers. To begin, (D) and (E) can be eliminated because they are not relevant: Southerners' and Northerners' desires have nothing to do with the Southern state governments. (C) can also be eliminated because the presence of scalawags and carpetbaggers did not help the government; their presence only illustrated the extent of corruption in the Reconstructed South.

56. **(D)** Industrial Revolution *Trend Question*

All of the answer choices except (D) transformed and improved the lives of city-dwellers and urban workers in the late 1800s and early 1900s. The CIO did not officially form until 1938, when it became one of the nation's two premier unions (the other was the AFL), striking and negotiating for better working conditions, wages, and benefits for industrial workers.

57. **(B)** The 1960s *Fact Question*

In August 1964, two American destroyers allegedly clashed with North Vietnamese patrol boats in the Gulf of Tonkin, off of North Vietnam. President Johnson announced that Americans had been attacked without cause, and ordered air strikes. Congress passed the Gulf of Tonkin Resolution in August 1964, which was nearly equivalent to a declaration of war: it authorized Johnson to escalate American troops' involvement in Vietnam as he saw fit. Rolling Thunder (A) was a bombing campaign begun in 1965.

58. **(C)** Industrial Revolution *Except Question*

American political officials did not campaign to encourage foreigners to move to the United States. If anything, many Americans viewed the influx of immigrants with unease and suspicion, even hostility. Nativist sentiment swelled among many native workers, who feared job competition from immigrants, and among many Protestants, who feared that foreign religious beliefs would weaken and corrupt America's dominant religious values.

59. **(A)** Civil War & Reconstruction *Map Question*

In the election of 1860, Lincoln carried all eighteen free states, defeating Democratic nominee Stephen Douglas. Lincoln's election victory alienated the South, for he had not even appeared on the ballots of a number of slave states and in ten slave states had not received a single popular vote. Almost immediately after the election results were known, South Carolina voted to secede from the Union. Six other Southern states soon followed.

Note that the Federalist stronghold (B) was in the Northeast only and did not include California and Oregon. In fact, the Federalist Party faded from the national political scene around 1815, long before California and Oregon were admitted as states (in 1850 and 1859, respectively). As for (D), Jackson's support base was in the rural and agrarian West and South, not the Northeast.

60. **(B)**   Revolution & Constitution   *Trend Question*

The Federalists generally believed that the new national government should be strong, powerful, and centralized, and that it should have authority over the state governments. Although some Federalists were very radical (some believed that the Constitution should eliminate state governments entirely), the general consensus was to retain the state governments as subordinate governments under the president, Congress, and Supreme Court. Opposing the Federalists, the Anti-federalists pushed for a relatively weak federal government so that states could have more sovereignty.

61. **(B)**   The Colonial Period   *Trend Question*

The First Great Awakening is credited with democratizing religion because revival ministers stressed that all men and women who repented could be saved, even if they were not prominent members of the established church. Revival ministers pushed an emotional, personal understanding of religious truth rather than an institutionalized one. Women, blacks, and Native Americans participated heavily in the revivals.

62. **(C)**   Revolution & Constitution   *Except Question*

The concept of judicial review is not included in the Constitution. Judicial review—the power of the Supreme Court to interpret the Constitution and declare acts of Congress unconstitutional—was established by the Court in the case of *Marbury v. Madison* (1803).

63. **(E)**   A New Nation   *Trend Question*

From 1793 until the end of his presidency, Washington strove hard to keep the U.S. out of the conflict raging between France and joint British and Spanish forces. In 1793, he issued the Proclamation of American Neutrality. In spite this policy, some American settlers in the Southwest aided French military efforts against the British navy. In retaliation, the British seized over 250 American vessels in 1794 and forced the ships' crews into service in the British navy—a policy known as "impressment." Tension further flared when British troops began building forts on U.S. territory. These aggressive and antagonistic British policies most directly challenged Washington's Proclamation of American Neutrality.

64. **(E)**   The 1950s   *Fact Question*

The southern states resisted integration and denied funding to school districts trying to desegregate. In fact, Eisenhower had to dispatch the National Guard to some states, including Arkansas, to escort the first black students to desegregated schools.

65. **(A)**   Revolution & Constitution   *Trend Question*

The Declaration of Independence embodies the general philosophies of the Enlightenment, also known as the Age of Reason. Prominent writers of the Enlightenment period include Locke, Rousseau, and Montesquieu. Locke's philosophy on sovereignty of the people and consent of the governed, in particular, is reflected in the Declaration of Independence. You can eliminate choices (B), (D), and (E) easily because Social Darwinism was a late-nineteenth-century American concept and becuase it is highly unlikely that Jefferson would have based the Declaration of Independence on ancient Greek philosophy or religious Puritanism. Using this process of elimination increases your chances of choosing the correct answer.

66. **(C)**   The Colonial Period   *Fact Question*

In the eighteenth century, colonial Pennsylvania and the entire southern Appalachian region was characterized by its high population of German and Scots-Irish settlers. Many of these German immigrants became highly skilled farmers and craftsmen—weavers, shoe makers, and cabinet makers. Note that (E) is true of Jamestown in the early 1600s.

67. **(D)** The Colonial Period   *Chart Question*

New Englanders generally lived fifteen to twenty-five years longer than colonists from other regions, in part because of better diets. Comparative death rates were as follows: 40–50 per thousand in Jamestown after 1630 and 24–26 per thousand in New England (source: www.gilder-lehrman.org). (C) and (E) are incorrect because scarlet fever and tuberculosis in fact ravaged New England, with scarlet fever claiming the lives of roughly 30 per thousand New Englanders in the mid-eighteenth century, and tuberculosis killing roughly twenty percent of New England colonists in the 1700s (source: www.gilder-lehrman.org). As for (A), while various slave uprisings did erupt in Virginia (most notably, Nat Turner's Rebellion in 1831), they were not widespread until the early to mid-nineteenth century and would not explain Virginia's high death rates/short life spans in the seventeenth century.

68. **(B)** Industrial Revolution   *Fact Question*

Booker T. Washington founded the Tuskegee Institute in Alabama to promote his philosophy that African-Americans can prove their worth through hard work: specifically, through learning vocational skills and acquiring property. Black activist W.E.B. Du Bois most famously countered Washington's views, arguing that agitation (not education) was the best way for African-Americans to elevate their status.

69. **(A)** Westward Expansion & Sectional Strife   *Except Question*

In the 1840s, Kentucky (a state since 1792) was a confirmed slave state and therefore not the subject of heated debate when Congress discussed the extension of slavery into the newly acquired territories and newly admitted states.

70. **(E)** Industrial Revolution   *Trend Question*

Although some unions boasted a large membership base—the Knights of Labor (1869), for example, boasted some half million members—the labor movement, on the whole, was very limited. Nationwide, less than three percent of American workers were unionized. Unable to harness the power of the working class, unions were largely ineffective.

71. **(D)** The 1950s   *Fact Question*

After Truman endorsed the 1947 report *To Secure These Rights*, he lost considerable political support from southern whites, but gained support from black voters. His support base continued to shift in this direction as he worked to desegregate the federal government and the army.

72. **(B)** Industrial Revolution   *Except Question*

Middle-class Americans, such as a man living in suburban Philadelphia, never really supported the Populist Party in any substantial way. Farmers and laborers ((C) and (E), respectively) comprised the majority of the Populist Party base. A debt-ridden worker (A) would have supported the Populist push for an expanding, or inflationary, money supply, which would have made debt payments easier. A silver mine owner (D) would have supported the Populist push for the silver standard.

73. **(A)** Revolution & Constitution   *Trend Question*

The final draft of the Constitution represented a series of political compromises. Many groups brought their concerns to the Philadelphia Convention. Small states fought with large states, for example, over congressional representation, while Anti-federalists and Federalists fought over how much power to invest in the central government. The Constitution incorporated aspects of each of these opposing arguments in order to make a government generally suited to all.

74. **(B)** Westward Expansion & Sectional Strife *Trend Question*

The Oregon debate tapped into the larger debate over the ratio of free states to slave states. Oregon became a free state when admitted into the Union in 1859.

75. **(C)** 1970s–2000 *Fact Question*

Ronald Reagan ordered the invasion of Grenada in 1983, which resulted in the toppling of the country's newly installed pro-Soviet government.

76. **(B)** The 1950s *Trend Question*

The American suburban population nearly doubled in the 1950s. The boom in the automobile industry greatly increased Americans' mobility, allowing them to live in areas once thought to be too far from their work places in urban centers. Middle-class and wealthy Americans began to flee the poverty and congestion of the cities for outlying areas, or suburbs, that offered clean, homogenous, child-friendly, and safe environments.

77. **(A)** Revolution & Constitution *Fact Question*

The British established the Proclamation Line in 1763 to prohibit colonists from settling west of the Allegheny Mountains in Pennsylvania and to demand that colonists already living west of the Proclamation Line remove themselves and return to the East. This proclamation deeply angered most colonists who had been expanding their colonial territories westward. Despite their outrage, the colonists took no direct political action at the time.

78. **(D)** Westward Expansion & Sectional Strife *Trend Question*

Lincoln's success in the debates for the 1858 Illinois Senate seat—an election that he in fact lost to his opponent, Democrat Stephen A. Douglas—signaled the rise to national prominence of the Republican Party, which had been founded only four years before. After 1858, the Republican and the Democratic Parties dominated national politics as the two major parties.

79. **(D)** Industrial Revolution *Trend Question*

The mill economy, the harvesting of southern timber, and the founding of iron, steel, and oil production facilities did much to push the South toward industrialization. The South, however, lagged far behind the North in industrial capacity and production, as it still does today.

80. **(B)** The Great Depression & New Deal *Chart Question*

As the graph indicates, union membership did, in fact, swell in the late 1930s, mostly because FDR's New Deal policies so favored unionization. The National Industry Recovery Act of 1933 and the National Labor Relations Act of 1935 (also known as the Wagner Act) protected the right of laborers to join unions and collectively bargain.

(C) incorrectly identifies one of the causes of union growth during the 1930s. In truth, there was no influx of immigration during the 1930s; instead, immigration markedly declined during the decade because of the enforcement of immigration quota laws as well as the onset of economic depression. Furthermore, many unions were not particularly immigrant-friendly, so even if the decade had seen an influx of immigrants, this change would in no way guarantee a rise in union membership. (A) is incorrect because even though the labor movement did in fact lose some influence and power during the late 1950s (owing, in part, to the rise of automation and the accompanying decrease in blue-collar jobs), the graph does *not* show a sharp decline in union membership. (D) is incorrect because the "open shop" policy, widespread in the 1920s, actually barred unions from many workplaces, so would not have promoted union grpwth. (E) is an incorrect reading of the graph: unions lost, not gained, members in the 1920s.

81. **(B)** The Progressive Era
Fact Question

Theodore Roosevelt's administration first successfully used the Sherman Antitrust Act to break up the Northern Securities Company railroad monopoly in 1904. His administration went on to file many other suits under the Sherman Antitrust Act, earning Roosevelt the nickname of "trust-buster."

82. **(D)** The Progressive Era
Fact Question

The primary goal of feminists during the Progressive Era was the promotion of women's suffrage. The Nineteenth Amendment granted women the right to vote in 1920.

83. **(A)** A New Nation
Fact Question

Hamilton's overall goal was to use both the explicit and implied powers of the federal government to establish a strong financial and economic base for the new nation. Knowing full well that a strong economy required a foundation of good credit, Hamilton sought to pay back in full all debts and loans accrued during the American Revolution. This policy would encourage creditors to loan to the United States again, stimulating the nation's economic growth.

Hamilton did not want to increase the amount of money in circulation (E) because doing so would only increase inflation and destabilize the economy. As for (B), Hamilton was not as concerned about protecting the southern cotton industry as he was with helping the northern industrial economies compete worldwide with Great Britain, which he did by imposing tariffs on manufactured goods imported from other nations. He did not, however, aim to prevent northern manufacturers from exporting their goods, so you can eliminate (C). During Hamilton's time, the new nation was still quite unhappy with the idea of taxation; in fact, the only form of taxation that Congress imposed was the tariff. (D) is therefore incorrect, leaving you with (A), the correct answer.

84. **(D)** A New Nation
Map Question

In 1803, Jefferson authorized the Louisiana Purchase from France. The purchase nearly doubled the size of the United States.

85. **(E)** World War I
Trend Question

Because of severe labor shortages during World War I, many jobs previously closed to blacks and women were opened to them. As a result, more than a million blacks and women joined the workforce. Wages actually rose during the war (the reverse of (A)). As for (B) and (C), unions were supported by the National War Labor Board but not permitted to strike. The wave of anticommunist activity did not occur until after the war (D).

86. **(D)** 1970s–2000
Except Question

A major trend since the 1970s has been the increasing value of college degrees in the general job market. Individuals without higher education have faced more trouble than ever before getting well-paying jobs.

87. **(A)** The Roaring Twenties
Fact Question

The National Origins Act of 1924 heavily curtailed the immigration of Eastern and Southern Europeans to the U.S., and excluded Asians entirely. This nativist legislation set immigration quotas based on the national origin of U.S citizens in 1890, a time when there were very few Americans of Asian, Italian, Eastern European, or Jewish descent.

88. **(D)** Cultural Trends: 1781–Mid-1800s *Quotation Question*

This statement was made by Ralph Waldo Emerson, who belonged to the Transcendentalist school of writing in the 1840s and 1850s. Although you probably do not recognize the passage, you can infer the Transcendentalist influence because the author talks about the inspiration that transcends from the greater Divine Soul.

89. **(E)** World War II *Fact Question*

The United Nations, founded in 1945, aimed to maintain global peace and collective security. The UN charter established a General Assembly to make policy and a Security Council to settle disputes.

90. **(A)** World War II *Except Question*

During World War II, war production and war spending actually stimulated the economy, generating many new jobs and raising the GNP. As a result, the unemployment rate declined during these years.

SAT II U.S. History

Practice Test II

UNITED STATES HISTORY TEST II

Directions: Each of the questions or incomplete statements below is followed by five suggested answers or completions. Select the one that is best in each case and then fill in the corresponding oval on the answer sheet.

1. Which colonial power established the first successful European settlement in North America?

    (A) Portugal
    (B) Spain
    (C) England
    (D) the Netherlands
    (E) France

2. Which of the following contributed most to the success of the Progressive movement?

    (A) support from union critics
    (B) the publicity generated by the muckrackers
    (C) the economic boom generated by high protective tariffs
    (D) support from prominent business leaders and entrepreneurs
    (E) support from nativists

3. All of the following helped England establish a colonial presence in North America EXCEPT

    (A) the English defeat of the Spanish Armada
    (B) funding from joint-stock companies
    (C) settlements founded by religious groups
    (D) the successful cultivation of tobacco
    (E) the mapping of paths through the Appalachian Mountains

4. Indentured servants in the British colonies of North America

    (A) bound themselves to work on plantations for a fixed number of years
    (B) were mostly Africans
    (C) were mostly orphaned adolescents and criminals
    (D) moved to the New England colonies after serving their labor term
    (E) often became plantation owners once they earned their freedom

5. All of the following are true of the Puritans EXCEPT

    (A) they wanted to found a "city upon a hill" to help spread religious righteousness
    (B) they established a government closely aligned with the church
    (C) they believed in the innate goodness of man
    (D) they persecuted religious dissenters
    (E) they enforced strict education and training of the clergy

6. During the First Great Awakening, revivalist ministers preached about the need to

    (A) purify the Anglican Church
    (B) repent immediately for one's sins
    (C) spread religious tolerance
    (D) have a clergy that is extensively trained and well-studied
    (E) reach a rational understanding of God

7. The 1770 Boston Massacre marked the peak of colonial resistance to

    (A) the Stamp Act
    (B) the Sugar Act
    (C) the Townshend Duties
    (D) the Intolerable Acts
    (E) the Declaratory Act

GO ON TO THE NEXT PAGE

8. In response to colonists' cry of "no taxation without representation," Prime Minister George Grenville justified the Stamp, Sugar, Tea, and Declaratory Acts by saying

   (A) that the colonies must disband their own forms of colonial government before they could be represented in Parliament
   (B) that the colonies could never be represented in Parliament because American colonists were not loyal enough to the Crown to merit representation
   (C) that the colonies could never be represented in Parliament because only people living in Great Britain were represented
   (D) that colonists were "virtually represented" because Parliament remembered the interests of all those under British rule
   (E) that royal governors in each colony relayed the interests of the colonists directly to King George III and therefore the colonies did not require Parliamentary representation

9. The Articles of Confederation established a government for the United States that can best be described as

   (A) strong and powerful
   (B) centralized and federalized
   (C) weak and decentralized
   (D) financially strong but politically and militarily weak
   (E) authoritarian

10. "If one of them be a minute late, he will be docked an hour's pay, and if he be many minutes late, he will be apt to find his brass check turn to the wall, which will send him out to join the hungry mob that waits every morning at the gates of the packing houses, from six o'clock until nearly half-past eight. There is no exception to this rule, not even little Ona—who has asked for a holiday the day after her wedding day, a holiday without pay, and been refused. While there are so many who are anxious to work as you wish, there is no occasion for incommoding yourself with those who must work otherwise."

   This passage is an example of

   (A) yellow journalism
   (B) dark romantic literature
   (C) nationalist propaganda
   (D) muckraker literature
   (E) existentialist philosophy

11. ". . . recall that the proposed capitalization of $15,000,000, caused by the merging of the Boston and Worcester and the Western railroads, was widely denounced as 'monstrous' and as a corrupting force that would destroy our Republican institution."

   Those Americans who deemed such a merger as "monstrous" would most likely have supported which of the following Congressional acts?

   (A) The Sherman Antitrust Act
   (B) The Federal Reserve Act
   (C) The Homestead Act
   (D) The Intolerable Acts
   (E) The National Recovery Act

12. Despite the Thirteenth, Fourteenth, and Fifteenth Amendments, many Southern governments hindered the rights of freed slaves by passing laws known as

   (A) Anti-Suffrage Laws
   (B) Former Slave Laws
   (C) Jim Crow Laws
   (D) John Doe Laws
   (E) Carpetbagger Laws

GO ON TO THE NEXT PAGE

13. Hamilton's proposal for a national bank was supported mostly by

   (A) strict constructionists, Anti-federalists, and southerners
   (B) Washington, Madison, and Jefferson
   (C) northerners, westerners, and strict constructionists
   (D) Federalists, loose constructionists, and northerners
   (E) bankers, lawyers, and plantation owners

14. During the Civil War, the North had all of the following advantages over the South EXCEPT

   (A) better transportation
   (B) a larger military
   (C) better military leadership
   (D) a stronger economy
   (E) more food sources

15. All of the following are true of the Second Great Awakening EXCEPT

   (A) it fueled social activism among its followers
   (B) it urged followers to reach a personal, emotional understanding of God
   (C) its meetings were more animated on the western frontier than in New England
   (D) it emphasized gradual and systematic spiritual growth
   (E) it increased the popularity of Methodism

16. All of the following are true of the Missouri Compromise EXCEPT

   (A) Maine was admitted to the Union as a free state
   (B) Missouri was admitted to the Union as a slave state
   (C) the doctrine of popular sovereignty was established in southern Louisiana Territory
   (D) slavery was prohibited in the Louisiana Territory north of 36° 30', except in Missouri
   (E) Missouri was not allowed to block free blacks from entering its borders

17. All of the following were evidence of the rising democratic spirit in American politics during the 1820s EXCEPT

   (A) the demise of the congressional caucus
   (B) the use of written ballots instead of verbal votes
   (C) the elimination of property requirements for suffrage
   (D) the election of many formerly appointed officials
   (E) the extension of suffrage to women

18. Which president is most closely associated with the spoils system?

   (A) James A. Garfield
   (B) Woodrow Wilson
   (C) Theodore Roosevelt
   (D) Andrew Jackson
   (E) Richard Nixon

19. Jackson's response to the Supreme Court's 1832 ruling that the president did not have authority to forcefully remove the Cherokee people from their lands demonstrated that

   (A) the Supreme Court is dependent on the president to enforce its decisions
   (B) the Supreme Court did not have the authority to declare the Cherokee an "independent nation"
   (C) even the president of the United States must follow the Supreme Court's rulings
   (D) Jackson did not believe the Supreme Court had the authority to interpret the Constitution
   (E) Jackson believed the Supreme Court was the ultimate authority on United States law

20. Which of the following forms of entertainment is most closely associated with the 1950s?

   (A) radio
   (B) internet
   (C) television
   (D) movies
   (E) theater

21. A Congressional commission in 1907 found that virtually every major industry was dominated by laborers who were

   (A) Southern Civil War veterans
   (B) raised on farms in the Midwest
   (C) European immigrants
   (D) trained as tailors or bakers
   (E) content with their quality of life

GO ON TO THE NEXT PAGE

22. The Wilmot Proviso of 1846 and the Compromise of 1850 addressed which of the following issues?

    (A) the acquisition of western territories from Great Britain and Russia
    (B) the proposed statehood of Kansas
    (C) the abolition of slavery in all American states
    (D) the establishment of popular sovereignty in newly acquired territories
    (E) the extension of slavery into the territories acquired from Mexico

23. Betty Freidan's *Feminine Mystique*, published in 1963, called for women to

    (A) break out of their domestic roles and pursue other opportunities and interests in life
    (B) work hard to stay sexually appealing to their spouses
    (C) use their position in society to work for social justice between the races
    (D) follow a series of rules designed to snare a desirable mate
    (E) remain strongly devoted to maternity and domesticity because it was the foundation of society

24. Which of the following was a goal of reformers during the mid-nineteenth century?

    (A) the federal regulation of food and medicines
    (B) women's suffrage
    (C) the dismantling of monopolies
    (D) legalizing abortion
    (E) the establishment of national parks

25. "In those days also there were 'scabs', often called 'rats' or 'dung'. Places under ban were systematically picketed, and warnings like the following were sent out: 'We would caution all strangers and others who profess the art of horseshoeing, that if they go to work for any employer under the above prices, they must abide by the consequences.' Usually consequences were a fine imposed by the union, but sometimes they were more severe."

    Those who sent out the warnings to "scabs" would most likely have supported

    (A) the government's labor policies that were part of the New Deal
    (B) the "open shop" policy in business
    (C) the merger of the AFL and CIO
    (D) the repeal of the Sherman Antitrust Act
    (E) the Palmer Raids

26. All of the following explain why the economy in the north came to rely on industry after the American Revolution EXCEPT

    (A) poor soil made large-scale farming unprofitable
    (B) extensive waterways provided power for mills
    (C) the Lowell System of crop rotation failed in the North
    (D) northern trade networks grew immensely
    (E) a steady flow of immigrants provided an ample labor supply

27. Which of the following was NOT a concession that the North made to the South between 1787 and 1797?

    (A) the nation's capital was built in Washington, D.C., a region carved out in a southern territory between Maryland and Virginia
    (B) slaves counted as three-fifths of a person for purposes of calculating representation in Congress
    (C) Hamilton's tariff, proposed in 1791, did not pass in Congres
    (D) the slave trade was not to be outlawed before 1808
    (E) the passage of the Bill of Rights

28. Nat Turner's Rebellion in Virginia in 1831 led to

    (A) heightened tension between wealthy plantation owners and poor, small-scale farmers in the South
    (B) increased fear among Southern slave-holders of a violent and massive slave revolt
    (C) tension between American colonists and British officials
    (D) increased fear among New England colonists of Native American attacks
    (E) tension between factory owners and labor unions in the North

GO ON TO THE NEXT PAGE →

29. Which of the following is true of late-nineteenth-century leisure activities, such as vaudeville, dance halls, and amusement parks?

   (A)   incomes were not high enough for workers to enjoy any of these modern pleasures
   (B)   workers did not have enough free time to squander hours on frivolity
   (C)   progressive leaders like Lillian Wald and Jane Addams discouraged these immoral activities and placed a greater emphasis on religious education
   (D)   these amusements became widespread and highly popular, as did spectator sports
   (E)   modes of transportation were not adequate at this time to bring most workers to places of leisure

30. President Eisenhower's "domino theory" asserted that

   (A)   if one country fell to communism, in turn the whole region would fall
   (B)   if one nation's economy crashed, then the economies of its neighbors would be in great risk
   (C)   economic aid given to one nation helps each nation with which the first nation trades
   (D)   if attacked in one country, communist governments would collapse one after another
   (E)   if England or France became involved in war, then so too would the U.S.

31. All of the following represent the end of isolationism in the United States before its entry into World War II EXCEPT

   (A)   the adoption of the "cash and carry" policy
   (B)   the passage of the Ludlow Amendment
   (C)   the approval of a peacetime draft
   (D)   the extension of aid to Russia after the German invasion there
   (E)   the passage of the Lend-Lease Act

GO ON TO THE NEXT PAGE

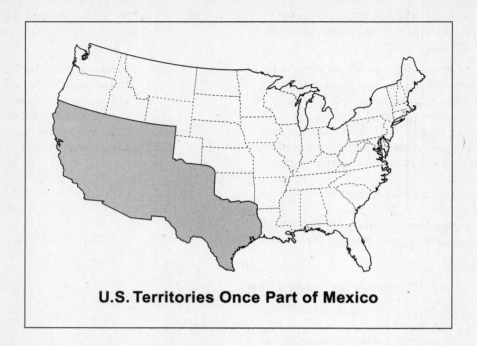

U.S. Territories Once Part of Mexico

32.   The U.S. acquired the shaded region after

(A)   the Mexican War
(B)   lengthy negotiations with the Spanish
(C)   a series of wars against the Sioux and the French
(D)   the War Hawks in U.S. Congress threatened war against the British unless the British agree to cede their land holdings in the Southwest
(E)   the Transcontinental Treaty

33. In the debate over the Constitution, the Anti-federalists fought for all of the following EXCEPT

   (A) the inclusion of a Bill of Rights in the Constitution
   (B) the granting of more power to the states
   (C) a system of checks and balances in order to prevent the national government from becoming tyrannical
   (D) a strong executive office to head the new government under the Constitution
   (E) the writing of a new draft of the Constitution to explicitly limit federal power

34. During the Progressive Era (1900–1917), what was the Socialist movement able to accomplish?

   (A) it secured the temporary nationalization of steel processing plants
   (B) it helped nationalize major railroad and telegraph industries
   (C) it blocked the passage of laws restricting immigration of suspected socialists
   (D) it prevented the establishment of independent labor unions
   (E) it won control of several city governments and elected some members of state legislatures and U.S. Congress

35. Literature written during the Great Depression generally incorporates themes of

   (A) anger and hatred
   (B) faith and prayer
   (C) excitement and optimism
   (D) disillusionment and cynicism
   (E) fear and anxiety

36. In 1844, the U.S. Congress repealed the gag rule of 1836, which had forbidden congressional debates on

   (A) the acquisition of the Oregon territory
   (B) the importation of new slaves from Africa
   (C) the Native American removal policies of state governments
   (D) slavery and its accompanying political questions
   (E) the annexation of and possible statehood for Texas

GO ON TO THE NEXT PAGE

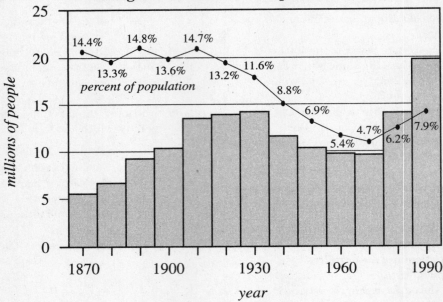

Immigrant Totals in U.S. Population, 1870-1990

Source: U.S. Census

37. Which of the following statements is most consistent with the data in the above graph?

(A) proportionate to the population, there were more immigrants in the U.S. in 1970 than in 1940

(B) immigration peaked during the Great Depression

(C) immigration quotas, combined with economic depression, led to declining immigration rates in the 1930s

(D) the Immigration Act of 1924, also known as the National Origins Act, failed to curtail or otherwise affect immigration rates

(E) despite tight regulatory measures, immigration rates have risen dramatically since 1940

GO ON TO THE NEXT PAGE

38. Of the following, who would have been LEAST likely to support the Know-Nothing Party in the mid-1850s?

 (A) a Presbyterian minister who favored temperance, or the outlawing of liquor sale
 (B) a northern businessman who favored the abolition of slavery
 (C) an Irish Catholic recent immigrant
 (D) a Bostonian who favored restrictions on immigration
 (E) a former member of the Whig Party

39. All of the following were discussed at the 1848 Seneca Falls Convention EXCEPT

 (A) the idea of universal suffrage
 (B) the relationship of the women's rights movement to the antislavery movement
 (C) the liberalization of divorce laws
 (D) the need to reform laws affecting property held by married couples
 (E) the sanctioning of a woman's right to an abortion

40. Which of the following pairs of foreign nations quietly helped the Confederate States of America during the first half of the Civil War?

 (A) Spain and Mexico
 (B) Prussia and Italy
 (C) Russia and Holland
 (D) Great Britain and France
 (E) Great Britain and Spain

41. The primary cause of the 1919 race riots was

 (A) black civil rights groups' anger over the continuing segregation of American society
 (B) tension in northern cities between white factory workers returning from the war and black workers who had migrated north to fill these jobs during the war
 (C) President Wilson's decision to integrate the armed forces
 (D) a wave of lynchings across the South led by the Ku Klux Klan
 (E) the arrest and incarceration of Marcus Garvey

42. Radical Republicans in Congress after the Civil War pushed for all of the following EXCEPT

 (A) Union military occupation in former Confederate states
 (B) Suffrage for blacks
 (C) the readmission of former Confederate states according to Lincoln's ten percent plan
 (D) Union control of former Confederate estates and plantations
 (E) the passage of laws barring former high-ranking Confederates from holding offices in the U.S. Government

43. Students for a Democratic Society began as

 (A) a communist front during the Great Depression
 (B) an organization of Czech dissidents during the Cold War
 (C) a group dedicated to supporting the Democratic Party and its leader, President Lyndon Johnson
 (D) a group of students who supported Richard Nixon and the so-called "silent majority"
 (E) an organization articulating a "new left" politics in America, opposed to the war in Vietnam and in favor of racial equality

44. During his presidency, Washington's major accomplishments included

 (A) keeping the young nation out of foreign entanglements and appointing the first official cabinet members
 (B) firmly establishing the president's veto power over Congress and protecting the young nation from French invasion
 (C) pursuing diplomatic ties with the nations of Europe and devising the new nation's financial policy
 (D) encouraging the nation to support the strict constructionist view of James Madison
 (E) encouraging the formation of political parties to best represent the various and opposing interests of U.S. citizens

GO ON TO THE NEXT PAGE

45. All of the following is true of the Knights of Labor union, founded in 1869, EXCEPT

    (A) it aimed to create an alliance among everyone involved in industry
    (B) it was open to women, blacks, and immigrants
    (C) it lost influence and power after the disastrous Haymarket Riot of 1886
    (D) it merged with the AFL, since it shared the AFL's labor goals and membership base
    (E) it successfully backed a number of politicians for election

46. Which of the following is most INCONSISTENT with a Progressive politician's aims?

    (A) to implement direct primaries
    (B) to regulate railroad rates
    (C) to ensure tax equity
    (D) to promote big business
    (E) to conserve the nation's resources

47. The Interstate Commerce Act of 1887 helped reform the railroad industry in all of the following ways EXCEPT

    (A) it prohibited agreements between companies compeing for control of the market
    (B) it provided for public ownership of the railroads
    (C) it stopped the practice of railroads giving rebates to large shippers
    (D) it discontinued the incongruent practice of charging high prices on short routes and low prices on long ones
    (E) it provided for the creation of the Interstate Commerce Commission

48. Senator Joseph McCarthy rose to national prominence in 1950 when he

    (A) claimed to have a list of 205 members of the Communist Party working in the State Department
    (B) helped convict Alger Hiss of perjury
    (C) launched a blacklisting campaign against suspected communists in Hollywood
    (D) aggressively pushed for U.S. military involvement in Korea to contain the spread of communism
    (E) denounced the House of Un-American Activities Committee (HUAC) as undemocratic and tryannical

49. Of the following, who would most likely have been a member of the National Association for the Advancement of Colored People (NAACP) when it was founded in 1909?

    (A) a robber baron
    (B) a graduate of the Tuskegee Institute in Alabama and follower of Booker T. Washington
    (C) an educated black man from Harlem
    (D) a destitute black sharecropper
    (E) a 37-year-old French man

50. All of the following are reasons the Populist Party decided to push for the silver standard EXCEPT

    (A) the issue was easier to explain to voters than some of the party's more complicated ideas
    (B) silver mine owners were more willing to finance the Populist campaigns if the issue had prominence
    (C) farmers widely supported the idea, hoping to generate inflation
    (D) the issue appealed to prominent industrialists and bankers, securing for the party a broad base of support
    (E) like all politicians, Populist candidates wanted to win and they thought the silver standard issue would guarantee them victory

51. William Lloyd Garrison's *The Liberator*

    (A) wished to establish Liberia as a slave colony
    (B) advocated total and immediate emancipation of slaves
    (C) preached "moral suasion"
    (D) advocated gradual emancipation of slaves and vocational training for freed blacks
    (E) aimed to petition Congress to end the importation of slaves

52. In the early twentieth century, muckrakers like Ida Wells led highly publicized campaigns against southern mobs for

    (A) the forced slavery of children in textile factories
    (B) the lynching of African-Americans
    (C) the killing of immigrants
    (D) the rape of female suffragists
    (E) the beating of men involved in the temperance movement

GO ON TO THE NEXT PAGE

53. "The American continents... are henceforth not to be considered as subjects for future colonization by any European powers. We should consider any attempt on their part to extend their [political] system to any portion of this hemisphere as dangerous to our peace and safety."

This statement was made by

(A) James Monroe
(B) James Polk
(C) Franklin Roosevelt
(D) Woodrow Wilson
(E) James Madison

54. In business, an example of horizontal integration is

(A) a meat-processing company that acquires livestock, slaughterhouses, and refrigerator cars
(B) a textile company that teaches a new technique to some workers, who will then teach the technique to others
(C) whiskey distillers and beer producers who combine their operations into one factory
(D) an oil company that gradually takes over other competing oil companies
(E) a steel producer that switches to making copper depending on market needs

55. In 1963, Martin Luther King Jr. made his famous "I have a dream speech" in Washington, D.C., in support of

(A) the Voting Rights Act
(B) the Great Society
(C) the Equal Rights Amendment
(D) the freedom ride
(E) the Civil Rights Act

56. America's Open Door Policy was primarily motivated by

(A) the desire to open Latin America to U.S. entrepreneurs
(B) the desire to open ports in China to American businesses
(C) the desire to overthrow the Spanish government in Cuba
(D) the desire to promote trade with Mexico
(E) the desire to compete with Europe for colonial holdings in Asia

57. President Polk compromised the aims of the expansionists by

(A) signing the Treaty of Guadalupe Hidalgo with Mexico
(B) opposing statehood for Texas
(C) withholding support from the Mexican War
(D) agreeing with the British to divide the Oregon territory along the forty-ninth parallel
(E) setting limitations on the migrations to California during the Gold Rush of 1848

58. Which of the following reforms was NOT part of Truman's domestic policy known as the Fair Deal?

(A) a higher minimum wage
(B) universal health insurance coverage
(C) expanded social security
(D) the construction of more public housing
(E) more extensive rights for labor unions

59. What was most significant about the election of President Jefferson in 1800?

(A) it marked the strengthening of the Federalist Party
(B) it underlined the weaknesses of the Constitution
(C) it was the first time a Virginian was elected president
(D) it unified Americans under a single political faction
(E) it marked the first power shift from the Federalist to the Republican Party

GO ON TO THE NEXT PAGE

Speaker Reed to McKinley—" You've got to bank the fire some way or other: I can't hold in this steam much longer."

Minneapolis "Tribune."

60. The above cartoon suggests that

(A) McKinley was an ineffective leader who had no authority over Congress
(B) Congress was an explosive body under Speaker of the House Reed, filled with in-fighting and controversy
(C) the so-called War Hawks controlled Congress, pushing for war to expand America's colonial holdings
(D) McKinley and Reed were on opposite sides of the war debate, one pushing for war with Spain and the other opposing it
(E) McKinley and Reed could not avoid war with Spain much longer, for they faced extreme pressure from Congress and the American public

GO ON TO THE NEXT PAGE

61. In the mid-nineteenth century, the American Temperance Society's reform efforts resulted in

    (A) the passage of the Eighteenth Amendment
    (B) the repeal of state laws regulating the sale of alcohol
    (C) a hike in the sales tax on alcohol
    (D) a decrease in the consumption of alcohol
    (E) intensive and highly coordinated police efforts targeting drunken behavior

62. Before 1914, President Woodrow Wilson's agenda included all of the following EXCEPT

    (A) corporate regulation
    (B) banking reform
    (C) lower tariffs
    (D) heavy economic investment overseas
    (E) promoting morality in international affairs

63. How did the U.S. raise most of its army for World War I?

    (A) the U.S. already had a large standing army in anticipation of joining the war as part of its program of military preparedness
    (B) thousands of men volunteered to fight overseas
    (C) National Guard units were called up across the country
    (D) black Americans volunteered heavily, serving in the U.S. Army for the first time
    (E) the government instituted a draft

64. In seventeenth-century America, proprietary colonies

    (A) were owned by the king of England
    (B) included Rhode Island and Connecticut
    (C) formed when the British government conferred land grants to individuals
    (D) formed when the king granted a charter to a joint-stock company, which in turn set up its own independent government
    (E) first formed in Virginia

65. In World War I, all of the following were elements of U.S war policy EXCEPT

    (A) the establishment of a pro-war propaganda agency called the Committee on Public Information
    (B) government regulation of food and fuel production and consumption
    (C) the internment of German-Americans
    (D) legislation prohibiting a range of antiwar activities
    (E) Liberty Bond campaigns

66. As part of America's isolationist policy after World War I, the 1928 Kellogg-Briand Pact called for

    (A) the establishment of a world court to adjudicate disputes between nations
    (B) the repayment of Allied World War I debt to the U.S.
    (C) the drastic reduction of immigration to America
    (D) the outlawing of war
    (E) a better working relationship between big business and labor

67. During the 1920s, business experienced all of the following EXCEPT

    (A) a massive consolidation of firms
    (B) the rise of a professional managerial class
    (C) dramatic increases in productivity resulting from assembly line manufacturing
    (D) a rise in protective tariffs against foreign competition
    (E) an increase in union membership

68. The Scopes Monkey Trial of 1925 pitted religious fundamentalism versus

    (A) the socially progressive reforms of William Jennings Bryan
    (B) the goals of the women's liberation movement
    (C) the "loosened" morals of the Jazz Age
    (D) the "robber baron" mentality of favoring economic profit and efficiency over spirituality
    (E) the evolutionary theories of Charles Darwin

69. All of the following were results of the Great Depression EXCEPT

    (A) bank failures
    (B) increased wages for unskilled workers
    (C) soaring unemployment
    (D) widespread poverty
    (E) business failures

GO ON TO THE NEXT PAGE

70. In the sixteenth century, the French search for a Northwest Passage in North America led to

    (A) the discovery of a river route from the Atlantic Ocean to the Pacific Ocean
    (B) the establishment of Spanish territorial claims around the St. Lawrence River
    (C) early French dominance of major North American waterways
    (D) the establishment of the first permanent French settlement in North America
    (E) the discovery of vast silver deposits

71. During the Great Depression, female workers faced much opposition from

    (A) political machines
    (B) the U.S. Government
    (C) black workers
    (D) migrant workers
    (E) organized labor

72. The 1936 New Democratic Coalition, which helped Franklin Delano Roosevelt win his second term in office, was comprised primarily of

    (A) wealthy white northerners
    (B) previously underrepresented minority groups
    (C) impoverished white southerners
    (D) westerners
    (E) big business and industry

73. James Fennimore Cooper is often credited with

    (A) writing the first serial mystery series
    (B) creating the first western hero
    (C) writing the first history of the frontier
    (D) leading the American impressionist movement
    (E) establishing the first American literary magazine

74. "Congress had powers which were only recommendatory, and its recommendations were ignored by the local legislatures. The treaties of the new nation were flouted by every State in the Union. Tariff wars and conflicting land grants embittered the relations of sister States."

    This passage reflects the weaknesses of the

    (A) U.S. Constitution
    (B) Bill of Rights
    (C) Articles of Confederation
    (D) First Continental Congress
    (E) Second Continental Congress

75. The Lend-Lease Act of 1941

    (A) authorized the sale of arms to the Allies in World War II
    (B) authorized the lending and leasing of arms to American merchant ships
    (C) allowed the president to lend or lease supplies to any nation deemed important to the defense of the United States
    (D) allowed the president to lend or lease supplies to any nation under German attack
    (E) required that private manufacturers lend or lease supplies that the U.S. government needed for the war effort

76. The primary goal of the Manhattan Project was to develop

    (A) nuclear submarines
    (B) surface-to-air missiles
    (C) biological weapons
    (D) atomic bombs
    (E) hydrogen bombs

77. Which of the following factors did NOT contribute to the baby boom in the 1950s?

    (A) the rising fertility rate
    (B) the sexual revolution
    (C) the falling infant mortality rate
    (D) conservative views on the role of women in the home
    (E) general prosperity

78. Why did President Monroe's term of office become known as the "Era of Good Feelings"?

    (A) a series of trade agreements between the U.S. and Great Britain greatly stimulated the U.S. economy
    (B) great political cooperation arose out of the one-party political system and patriotic fervor that spread after the War of 1812
    (C) an economic boom followed the French and Indian War
    (D) an unprecedented level of cooperation arose between the Republican and Federalist Parties
    (E) the nation celebrated following victory in the Spanish-American War

GO ON TO THE NEXT PAGE

79. The Oregon Trail was one of the most famous

(A) migratory routes for Canadians during the Gold Rush of 1848
(B) forced passage routes for Native Americans who were relocated to reservations in the Northwest
(C) routes for American settlers who migrated to the Northwestern territories from the East
(D) escape routes for runaway slaves
(E) early railroad routes

80. The 1948 Marshall Plan was primarily intended to

(A) provide aid to communist governments willing to hold monitored free elections
(B) give military support to nations resisting communism
(C) help rebuild the economies of Western Europe and promote political stability there
(D) help the nations of Latin America industrialize
(E) secure the oilfields of Arabia from communist control

81. All of the following innovations helped promote a culture of consumerism in America in the late nineteenth century EXCEPT

(A) home iceboxes, which allowed families to purchase more perishable goods
(B) the sewing machine, which allowed manufacturers to mass-produce clothing
(C) so-called "consumption communities," developed by advertisers so that customers would develop brand loyalty
(D) department stores that bought in bulk and sold a wide array of products
(E) the credit card, which allowed people to shop without cash

82. Industrial growth and technological advances in the 1950s were primarily the result of

(A) increased consumer demands
(B) automation
(C) weaker unions
(D) the spread of laptop computers
(E) massive defense spending

83. All of the following trends characterized the years of Jimmy Carter's presidency EXCEPT

(A) increased concern for human rights issues in American foreign policy
(B) improved relations between Israel and Egypt
(C) a general slowdown of the economy
(D) double-digit inflation
(E) increasing popular confidence in the American ideals of democratic freedom and limitless economic opportunity

84. All of the following were associated with the 1920's sexual revolution EXCEPT

(A) higher hemlines on women's clothing
(B) liberalized divorce laws
(C) college parties full of drinking, smoking, and dancing
(D) more common use of makeup among women
(E) widespread acceptance of premarital sex

85. The military campaign known as the Tet Offensive refers to

(A) General MacArthur's expansion of the Korean War
(B) a massive wave of attacks by communist insurgents against American forces in South Vietnam
(C) the U.S. Army's invasion of Germany, led by George S. Patton, at the end of World War II
(D) Nixon's bombing campaign against Cambodia
(E) Japan's invasion of the Philippines

86. The New Deal was a collection of liberal programs designed to accomplish all of the following EXCEPT

(A) provide short-term economic relief
(B) inject money into the national economy
(C) constrict the national money supply
(D) prevent the nation from sliding deeper into economic depression
(E) regulate the banking industry

GO ON TO THE NEXT PAGE

87. Which of the following civil rights leaders went from advocating non-violent resistance in the service of integration to espousing militant armed separatism?

    (A) Stokely Carmichael
    (B) Huey Newton
    (C) Malcom X
    (D) Jesse Jackson
    (E) Andrew Young

88. Which of the following immigrants was statistically most likely to have passed through Ellis Island in 1904?

    (A) a young man from Russia
    (B) a little girl from Mexico
    (C) an older woman from Scandinavia
    (D) a young woman from Japan
    (E) a young man from France

89. Since the 1970s, the U.S. has seen the most immigration from which part of the world?

    (A) Mexico and other Latin American countries
    (B) sub-Saharan Africa
    (C) the Middle East
    (D) southern Europe
    (E) Canada

90. Which of the following was true of American industry during World War II?

    (A) it was overseen by the Office of Strategic Services
    (B) it continued to produce civilian goods at prewar levels
    (C) it produced more war material than all of the Axis powers combined
    (D) it suffered a number of crippling labor strikes
    (E) it refused to employ women despite labor shortages

S T O P

**IF YOU FINISH BEFORE TIME IS CALLED, YOU MAY CHECK YOUR WORK ON THIS TEST ONLY.
DO NOT TURN TO ANY OTHER TEST IN THIS BOOK.**

SAT II U.S. History

Practice Test II

Explanations

Answers to SAT II U.S. History Practice Test II

Question Number	Correct Answer	Right	Wrong	Question Number	Correct Answer	Right	Wrong
1.	B			51.	B		
2.	B			52.	B		
3.	E			53.	A		
4.	A			54.	D		
5.	C			55.	E		
6.	B			56.	B		
7.	C			57.	D		
8.	D			58.	B		
9.	C			59.	E		
10.	D			60.	E		
11.	A			61.	D		
12.	C			62.	D		
13.	D			63.	E		
14.	C			64.	C		
15.	D			65.	C		
16.	C			66.	D		
17.	E			67.	E		
18.	D			68.	E		
19.	A			69.	B		
20.	C			70.	C		
21.	C			71.	E		
22.	E			72.	B		
23.	A			73.	B		
24.	B			74.	C		
25.	A			75.	C		
26.	C			76.	D		
27.	E			77.	B		
28.	B			78.	B		
29.	D			79.	C		
30.	A			80.	C		
31.	B			81.	E		
32.	A			82.	E		
33.	D			83.	E		
34.	E			84.	E		
35.	D			85.	B		
36.	D			86.	C		
37.	C			87.	A		
38.	C			88.	A		
39.	E			89.	A		
40.	D			90.	C		
41.	B						
42.	C						
43.	E						
44.	A						
45.	D						
46.	D						
47.	B						
48.	A						
49.	C						
50.	D						

Calculating Your Score on
SAT II U.S. History
Practice Test II

Your raw score for the SAT II History test is calculated from the number of questions you answer correctly and incorrectly. Once you have determined your composite score, use the conversion table on page 19 of this book to calculate your scaled score.

To Calculate Your Raw Score

Count the number of questions you answered correctly: _____
A

Count the number of questions you answered incorrectly, and multiply that number by $\frac{1}{4}$:

_____ X $\frac{1}{4}$ = _____
    B   C

Subtract the value in field C from value in field A: _____
          D

Round the number in field D to the nearest whole number. This is your raw score: _____
    E

1. **(B)** The Colonial Period *Fact Question*

After Ponce de Leon claimed Florida for Spain in 1513, the Spanish established the first successful European settlement in North America in 1565, in St. Augustine, Florida.

2. **(B)** The Progressive Era *Trend Question*

The success of the Progressive movement owed in no small part to the efforts of the muckrakers—journalists and authors who raised the public's alarm over social injustice, political corruption, and corporate immorality. None of the other choices fits with the Progressive movement.

3. **(E)** The Colonial Period *Except Question*

Early English settlements were concentrated along the Atlantic Coast because dense forests and hostile Native American tribes prevented English settlers from moving west through the Appalachian Mountains. Mapping paths through the Appalachian Mountains was therefore not an important aspect of English settlement.

4. **(A)** The Colonial Period *Fact Question*

Indentured servants were usually adult white males who bound themselves to work on a plantation for a fixed number of years (usually four to seven). After earning their freedom, they were given a small plot of land to farm.

5. **(C)** The Colonial Period *Except Question*

The Puritans believed in man's total depravity, not innate goodness, and stressed man's complete reliance on God for salvation. Settling in Massachusetts, they established a government closely aligned with, though legally separated from, the church (B). Puritan governor John Winthrop envisioned the colony as a "city upon a hill," a beacon of religious righteousness that would shed light on the rest of the world (A). Puritans stressed the need for a well-educated and well-trained ministry (E). Intolerant of outspoken dissenters, Puritan leaders banished Roger Williams, Anne Hutchinson, and others from Massachusetts (D).

6. **(B)** The Colonial Period *Fact Question*

Many revivalist ministers during the Great Awakening stressed the need for all followers to immediately repent their sins in order to achieve salvation. They actually de-emphasized the importance of the established clergy (the reverse of (D)) and instead urged followers to reach a more personal, emotional, even intuitive understanding of God (as opposed to (E)).

7. **(C)** Revolution & Constitution *Fact Question*

The Boston Massacre occurred in March of 1770, when a group of colonists wielding rocks and perhaps more dangerous weapons, gathered to protest a package of taxes collectively known as the Townshend Duties. The colonists challenged British regulars stationed in Boston. It is unknown which group fired first, but five colonists were killed in the massacre. Parliament finally succumbed to colonial pressure and repealed most of the Townshend Duties.

8. **(D)** Revolution & Constitution *Trend Question*

Prime Minister George Grenville believed that the colonists did not need to have representative seats in Parliament because they were already "virtually represented" by Parliament, meaning that Parliament considered the interests of *all* people under British rule when deliberating on legislation. Grenville argued that the American colonists essentially held the same status as landless males living in England, who did not meet the requirements necessary for direct Parliamentary representation.

9. **(C)** Revolution & Constitution   *Trend Question*

The government under the Articles of Confederation can best be described as decentralized and weak. It consisted of one central government composed of one legislative body (no judicial or executive branch) that had very limited authority: most notably, it lacked powers to levy taxes, raise an army, and sign and enforce national treaties. Under the Articles of Confederation, the states retained their sovereignty. Note that the Founding Fathers of America purposefully designed the original U.S. Government to be weak because they feared that a strong government would become tyrannical, as they had accused the royal crown of becoming.

10. **(D)** The Progressive Era   *Quotation Question*

This passage is an excerpt from Upton Sinclair's novel *The Jungle* (1906), which exposed the horrible living and working conditions that immigrant Americans faced in meat-packing towns and stockyards. The book raised the public's alarm over inhumane and unhygienic working conditions, leading to calls for reform. The book is an example of muckraker literature.

11. **(A)** Industrial Revolution   *Quotation Question*

A person who considered the merger and capitalization of several large companies "monstrous" would have approved most the passage of the 1890 Sherman Antitrust Act. The act was designed to regulate the practices of large, domineering companies that sought to gain a monopoly on a single market by driving out the competition.

12. **(C)** Civil War & Reconstruction   *Trend Question*

Despite the Thirteenth, Fourteenth, and Fifteenth Amendments, many Southern governments passed Jim Crow Laws to keep freed slaves from enjoying their new civil rights. These laws enforced racial segregation and discrimination.

13. **(D)** A New Nation   *Fact Question*

In order to answer this question, think about the factions that opposed Hamilton's proposal for a national bank. These included the strict constructionists, who argued that the U.S. Constitution did not explicitly allow for the creation of a national bank. You can therefore eliminate all choices that include strict constructionists ((A) and (C)). If you remember that Jefferson and Madison both objected to the national bank, you can also eliminate (B). In selecting between (D) and (E), you should select the choice that most clearly includes Hamilton's political affiliation—the Federalists—rather than a grouping of professions, some of whom may not fit neatly into one particular political category: that is, select (D).

14. **(C)** Civil War & Reconstruction   *Except Question*

The North had the upper hand in the beginning of the Civil War. The Union had an excellent railroad and shipping based transportation system, more than two million soldiers(compared to the South's 800,000), a much stronger economy, and abundant sources of grains from Northern foodstuffs producers. The North did *not*, however, have better military leadership. Throughout the first half of the Civil War, until Lincoln made Ulysses Grant the head of the Union armed forces, the North was plagued with poor military leadership. The South, by contrast, had many generals and other high-ranking officers who had served distinguished careers in the United States army before secession.

15. **(D)** Cultural Trends: 1781–Mid-1800s   *Except Question*

Revivalists in the Second Great Awakening believed that goodness could come through sudden emotional conversion and insight. The Unitarians, by contrast, argued that goodness could only be achieved through gradual and systematic character development.

16. **(C)** A New Nation *Except Question*

The doctrine of popular sovereignty was incorporated into the Compromise of 1850 and the Kansas-Nebraska Act of 1854, not the Missouri Compromise of 1820. In the Missouri Compromise, Missouri was admitted as a slave state while Maine was admitted as a free state, thus preserving the balance between the number of free and slave states. Also, slavery was forbidden in the Louisiana territory north of the 36° 30' line, and Missouri was barred from discriminating against free blacks from other states.

17. **(E)** The Age of Jackson *Except Question*

All of the above were indications of the 1820's "spirit of democracy" except (E). Women were not granted the right to vote until the beginning of the twentieth century.

Remember that this decade is called "the age of the common man" for many reasons. First, by 1820 most states had relaxed their voting requirements so that all free white males and even some free black males could vote. Also, during this decade, written ballots replaced verbal ballots to prevent social superiors from influencing their inferiors at polling time, and many appointive offices became elective. With the demise of the congressional caucus system in 1824, party leaders no longer had exclusive control over the nominating process, allowing presidential candidates to more directly reflect the interests and wants of the American people.

18. **(D)** The Age of Jackson *Fact Question*

Andrew Jackson is most associated with the spoils system (or office rotation system), which is the practice of removing government officers from the opposite party in order to fill the positions with partisans of one's own party. The name comes from the adage, "To the victor belong the spoils." Jackson is known as the first president to extensively use—or perhaps misuse—this system.

19. **(A)** The Age of Jackson *Fact Question*

This question is particularly difficult because it requires that you first remember how Jackson responded to the Supreme Court's ruling in *Worcester v. Georgia* and then interpret his actions to determine the correct answer. When the Supreme Court declared that President Jackson had no authority to remove the Cherokee people because they constituted an "independent nation," Jackson effectively responded that he did not care what the Supreme Court believed. Instead of obeying the Court's ruling, he continued to forcefully remove the Cherokee and other tribes on the Trail of Tears. His actions demonstrated that the Supreme Court has no real power over government—that although the Court interprets the laws of the United States, it cannot actually enforce these interpretations.

20. **(C)** The 1950s *Trend Question*

The 1950s are considered the golden age of television, as television came to dominate pop culture. By the end of the decade, nearly every household owned at least one television set.

21. **(C)** Industrial Revolution *Trend Question*

The new wave of immigrants that came to the United States around the turn of the century, mostly from Eastern and Southern Europe, moved to urban centers and assumed industrial jobs. Soon, these immigrants held the majority of low-paying positions in almost every industry.

22. **(E)** Westward Expansion & Sectional Strife *Fact Question*

The Wilmot Proviso, passed by the House but rejected by the Senate, proposed that slavery be prohibited in all of the territories acquired from Mexico. The Compromise of 1850 resolved the debate over the extension of slavery into the lands gained from the Mexican War: it provided for the admission of California as a free state and the enforcement of popular sovereignty in New Mexico and Utah.

23. **(A)** The 1960s
Fact Question

Betty Freidan's *Feminine Mystique* urged women to question their domestic roles and pursue other opportunities and interests in life.

24. **(B)** Cultural Trends: 1781–Mid-1800s
Trend Question

Women's rights activists in the mid-nineteenth century actively pushed for women's suffrage, although women would have to wait until 1920 to win the right to vote. (A), (C), and (E) were all goals of the Progressive movement in the early twentieth century. The legalization of abortion (D) was not a prominent goal of the women's movement until the second half of the twentieth century.

25. **(A)** The Great Depression & New Deal
Quotation Question

Because those who sent out warnings to "scabs" were most likely committed union members, they would have backed the labor policies of the New Deal, which supported, even encouraged, unionization. New Deal legislation like the National Industrial Recovery Act (1933) and the Wagner Act (1935) protected workers' rights to form labor unions and to collectively bargain. As a result, union membership swelled during the 1930s. You might have been tempted by (C). While many union members did support the merger of the AFL-CIO in 1955, others did not, which makes (C) a poorer choice than (A)

As for the other answer choices, union members would have opposed the "open shop" policy because it kept unions out of many workplaces. Union supporters also would have opposed the repeal of the Sherman Antitrust Act (1890) because the act was used to restrict big business; its repeal would only have helped large corporations at the expense of laborers and consumers. The Palmer Raids (1920), which led to the arrest of thousands of suspected communists, did not directly involve the labor cause.

26. **(C)** Cultural Trends: 1781–Mid-1800s
Except Question

The Lowell System was a form of labor rotation, not crop rotation. It was successfully used in the early 1800s to staff New England factories with young women who lived near the factory towns. The women worked in very poor conditions, earned very little, and generally returned to their families after a short time.

27. **(E)** A New Nation
Except Question

For a tricky EXCEPT question like this one, work to eliminate all the correct answers. (B) and (D) are correct because they were both major concessions that the North granted to the South during the framing of the Constitution, in order to win the support of southern states. (A) was a concession made to the southern states in exchange for their acceptance of Hamilton's Assumption Bill (the federal assumption of state debts), which favored northern states because they lagged far behind southern states in repaying their war debts. Having eliminated these three answers, you are left to choose between (C) and (E). (C) was, indeed, a concession made by the North to the South, since the tariff would have favored northern industrial interests over the more rural and agrarian South. So you are left with (E): the only choice that was *not* an explicit compromise between the North and the South. Although the Bill of Rights was a concession made to the Anti-federalists, many of whom were southerners, it was not an expressly North-South agreement.

28. **(B)** Cultural Trends: 1781–Mid 1800s
Fact Question

Nat Turner's Rebellion was a slave uprising in Virginia in 1831. It raised fears among Southern plantation owners of widespread and violent slave revolts.

29. **(D)** The Industrial Revolution
Trend Question

In the late nineteenth century, recreation became hugely popular in the form of shows, games, and sports. Places like Coney Island gave urban laborers a much-needed break from the city and from work, as well as a chance to mingle socially. Rapid, citywide transit facilitated such recreation trips.

30. **(A)** The 1950s *Trend Question*

Eisenhower's "domino theory" maintained that if one country fell to communism, in turn the whole region would fall. Eisenhower invoked this theory to justify America's involvement in Vietnam. To block the unification of Vietnam under communist rule, the CIA propped up a separate government in South Vietnam.

31. **(B)** World War II *Except Question*

The Ludlow Amendment (1938) was a proposed amendment to the Constitution that would have required a national referendum on any declaration of war not provoked by a direct attack. The amendment is therefore an example of American isolationist tendencies. FDR helped block its passage.

32. **(A)** Westward Expansion & Sectional Strife *Map Question*

Before the Mexican War broke out in 1846, the U.S. tried unsuccessfully to buy the New Mexican and Californian territories from Mexico. Only after the war ended did the U.S. acquire these lands. By the terms of the Treaty of Guadeloupe Hidalgo, signed in February 1848, Mexico ceded Texas, New Mexico, and California to the U.S. in exchange for 15 million dollars. This ceded territory encompassed present-day Arizona, Nevada, California, Utah, and parts of New Mexico, Colorado, and Wyoming. American land now stretched continuously from the Atlantic to the Pacific Ocean.

Note that the Transcontinental Treaty (E) resolved a conflict between the U.S. and Spain. By the terms of this treaty, signed in 1819, Spain ceded East Florida to the United States, renounced all claims to West Florida, and agreed to a southern border of the United States west of the Mississippi River extending all the way to the Pacific Ocean.

33. **(D)** Revolution & Constitution *Except Question*

The Anti-federalists did not push for a strong executive office to lead the new nation. Instead, they fought to establish more rights for the states, more individual liberties, and a check on national power. They opposed ratification of the Constitution because they believed it gave too much authority to the national government. You may find this question difficult, but think of it this way: all of the choices except (C) reflect the general Anti-federalist attitude that powerful government is undesirable.

34. **(E)** The Progressive Era *Trend Question*

The Socialist movement gained momentum in the U.S. during the Progressive Era; it eventually gained enough power to win control of several city government and to elect some members of state legislatures and U.S. Congress.

35. **(D)** The Great Depression & New Deal *Trend Question*

Literature written during the Great Depression generally incorporates themes of disillusionment and cynicism. Prominent writers during this period include John Steinbeck, Earnest Hemingway, Langston Hughes, Jack Conroy, John Dos Passos, and William Faulkner.

36. **(D)** Westward Expansion & Sectional Strife *Fact Question*

The gag rule, in effect from 1836 to 1844, forbid debate over the issue of slavery. The importation of new slaves had, in fact, been illegal since 1808 (B).

37. **(C)** The Great Depression & New Deal *Chart Question*

Of the answers listed, only (C) is true. Immigration sharply declined in the 1930s for two main reasons: the strict enforcement of immigration quotas linked to the National Origins Act of 1924 and the onset of the Great Depression, which dissuaded emigrants from coming to the United States (the reverse of (B)). (A) is incorrect because, proportionate to the population, there were actually *more* immigrants in 1940 than in

1970 (8.8 percent versus 6.2 percent). (D) is incorrect because the Immigration Law of 1924 dramatically affected both the ethnic makeup of immigrants (by severely limiting immigration from Southern and Eastern Europe and Asia) as well as the nation's immigration totals (notice the sharp reduction when the act was fully enforced in the 1930s). As for (E), while immigration totals have risen since 1940, immigration *rates* have not risen. Keep in mind that the total U.S. population has markedly grown since 1940, so that even though the immigrant population equaled 11,500,000 in 1940 and 19,700,000 in 1990, immigrants still comprised a larger percentage of the population in 1940 (8.8 percent versus 7.9 percent).

38. **(C)**   Westward Expansion & Sectional Strife   *Fact Question*

The Irish Catholic immigrant would have been least likely to support the Know-Nothings, since the party was mostly anti-Catholic and nativist, or opposed to new immigration.

39. **(E)**   Westward Expansion & Sectional Strife   *Except Question*

The early American feminists at the Seneca Falls Convention, famous among them Elizabeth Cady Stanton and Susan B. Anthony, did not believe in a woman's right to an abortion, as did later feminists. In fact, they strongly opposed the idea.

40. **(D)**   Civil War & Reconstruction   *Fact Question*

Throughout the first half of the Civil War, Great Britain and France quietly supported the Confederacy because these countries relied on Southern cotton imports (whereas the countries actually competed against Northern manufacturing interests). Great Britain even went so far as to build several warships for the Confederate States of America. Both countries supported the Confederacy—and nearly officially recognized the South as an independent country—until the North won the Battle of Antietam and issued the Emancipation Proclamation.

41. **(B)**   World War I   *Trend Question*

Tension over factory jobs in northern cities was the primary cause of the 1919 race riots. Whites returning from World War I found that more than 500,000 blacks had migrated north during the war, many of them working in factories and settling in communities that had once been dominated by white immigrants. Note that President Truman did not integrate the armed forces until after World War II (C). Marcus Garvey was imprisoned in 1922 on federal charges for mail fraud and deported to Jamaica in 1927 (E).

42. **(C)**   Civil War & Reconstruction   *Except Question*

Led by Thaddeus Stevens and Charles Sumner, the Radical Republicans wanted to severely punish the South before readmitting former Confederate states into the Union. They pushed for military occupation in the South, confiscation of Southern property, and laws preventing former important Confederates from holding office in the federal government. They also pushed for black suffrage. They did *not*, however, support Lincoln's rather lenient plan (known as the "ten percent plan") for reconstructing the Union, which would have allowed states to be readmitted to the Union if ten percent of the voting population in those states swore allegiance to the Union.

43. **(E)**   The 1960s   *Fact Question*

Students for a Democratic Society (SDS) was an organization of American college students who joined together in 1962 to formulate a "new left" politics for America. The organization was radically opposed to the war in Vietnam and in favor of racial equality. It did not support Johnson or Nixon, nor was it a communist front.

44. (A)   A New Nation   *Trend Question*

As president, Washington was known for maintaining American neutrality in international affairs and for establishing the first cabinet. (B) is incorrect because Washington did not strongly assert his veto power over Congress (having vetoed only twice in his two terms as president), nor did he face any French threat. (C) is wrong because he generally avoided foreign entanglements. (E) is wrong because Washington showed strong disfavor toward political parties, for he feared that such factions would weaken or even destroy the nation. Although Washington discouraged political partisanship, he nonetheless aligned himself with the loose constructionist beliefs of Alexander Hamilton and the Federalists, who promoted a strong central government (the reverse of (D))).

45. (D)   Industrial Revolution   *Fact Question*

The Knights of Labor boasted an open membership policy, which allowed women, blacks, and immigrants to join. Believing the current industrial system to be destructive, the Knights hoped to offer an alternative to capitalism by allying workers with employers. The union also advocated widespread progressive reform: a graduated income tax, equal pay for women, and an end to child labor. Gaining power in the 1870s, the Knights of Labor was able to successfully back politicians for election and push favorable labor laws through Congress. The bloody Haymarket riot of 1886, however, effectively destroyed the union: many of its leaders were imprisoned and public support for the union plummeted. Craft workers who had been members of the Knights broke off and formed the AFL, which, unlike the Knights, catered exclusively to skilled workers and focused on more limited issues (wage increase and hour reduction) rather than widespread, progressive reform.

46. (D)   Industrial Revolution   *Fact Question*

Progressive politicians often opposed big business interests in favor of laborers and consumers. Progressives aimed to regulate monopolies and restrict ruthless business practices, including the exploitation of workers and the over-use of resources. Progressive reformers also agitated for far-reaching reform in politics, poverty relief, and conservation.

47. (B)   Industrial Revolution   *Fact Question*

The Interstate Commerce Act created the ICC to monitor the business practices of the railroads, which had been corrupted in the 1870s and 1880s by pools and unfair price-setting that favored large shippers and big business. While still privately owned, railroad companies were placed under strict federal supervision.

48. (A)   The 1950s   *Trend Question*

In 1950, Senator Joseph McCarthy claimed to have a list of 205 known members of the Communist Party who worked in the State Department. Although he later shortened the list and modified the allegations to merely "bad risks," he nonetheless continued on with his aggressive anticommunist rhetoric. Four years later, McCarthy took his anticommunist fervor too far by accusing the U.S. Army of being infiltrated by spies. In public hearings to investigate these charges, McCarthy appeared bullying and unjust when attacking the reputations of prominent American military officials and war heroes. Following these hearings, the Senate voted to censure McCarthy.

49. (C)   Industrial Revolution   *Trend Question*

W.E.B. DuBois and his friends set up the NAACP to end racial discrimination through legal means. In the beginning, their elitist views about the "talented tenth" turned off poorer, less-educated African-Americans, including sharecroppers and many of Booker T. Washington's followers.

50. **(D)** Industrial Revolution   *Except Question*

Businessmen and bankers tended to oppose the silver standard for its inflationary and economically destabilizing effects, and instead favored the more restrictive gold standard. The silver standard, by providing for an "easy," or expanding, money supply, would have benefited debtors but hurt creditors by making debts payments easier to make (because they would be worth less).

51. **(B)** Cultural Trends: 1781–Mid 1800s   *Fact Question*

William Lloyd Garrison first published *The Liberator*, a radical abolitionist newspaper, in 1831. He called for the immediate emancipation of slaves and equal civil rights for blacks. Garrison also founded the New England Anti-Slavery Society in 1832 and the American Anti-Slavery society in 1833. The importation of slaves (E) ended in 1808, following constitutional mandate.

52. **(B)** Industrial Revolution   *Trend Question*

Lynching was a terrible reality in the South for many decades. While child laborers, suffragists, temperance supporters, and immigrants invariably suffered hardships and discriminatory violence, no issue was as highly publicized as Southern lynching.

53. **(A)** A New Nation   *Quotation Question*

This statement was made by President James Monroe and is known as the Monroe Doctrine (1823). It warned against European interference in Latin America and proclaimed American preeminence in the Western Hemisphere.

54. **(D)** Industrial Revolution   *Fact Question*

Horizontal and vertical integration were two of the primary techniques business owners used to consolidate power and create monopolies during the Industrial Revolution. Horizontal integration occurs when a company takes over all of its competitors one by one and then has control over the entire market. Vertical integration is the technique companies use to control every aspect of the production of one good, as in (A).

55. **(E)** The 1960s   *Fact Question*

In August 1963, a quarter of a million Americans gathered in Washington, D.C., to support the passage of the Civil Rights Act. It was at this "March on Washington" that Martin Luther King Jr. gave his famous "I have a dream" speech, outlining a utopian view of what America could be. Despite this demonstration and King's eloquence, Republicans in Congress blocked the civil rights bill.

56. **(B)** The Age of Imperialism   *Fact Question*

In the nineteenth century, European powers carved China into "spheres of influence" that prevented U.S. businesses from establishing a presence there. In 1899, Secretary of State John Hay announced the Open Door Policy in China in order to open up all "exclusive" ports. European powers, however, refused to comply with or endorse this policy, so China remained largely closed to American businesses. In the years following his unveiling of the policy, Hay continued to try to open up new markets in Asia.

57. **(D)** Westward Expansion & Sectional Strife   *Fact Question*

President Polk agreed to a compromise with Britain to divide Oregon along the forty-ninth parallel, while the expansionists—with whom he was generally aligned—had hoped that America would gain the entire territory up to the fifty-fourth parallel (hence their war cry, "Fifty-four-forty or fight!"). The Treaty of Guadalupe Hidalgo (A), which concluded the Mexican War, actually secured a vast amount of territory for the U.S. in the southwest, and was therefore a major expansionist success. Polk favored statehood for Texas (B), fully supported the Mexican War (C), and did not set any limitations on migrations to California (E).

58. **(B)** The 1950s   *Except Question*

Truman did not include universal heath coverage as part of his Fair Deal.

59. **(E)** A New Nation   *Trend Question*

The election of 1800 was the first election in the history of the new nation to effect a switch from one ruling party to another. The fact that this transition occurred peacefully and without protest from the Federalist Party was one of the most significant indicators of the success of the U.S. Constitution. Although the Federalist Party never again reclaimed power in the White House, Jefferson's election did not wholly eliminate party opposition. With this knowledge, you can cross off (A), (B), and (D)

Of the remaining choices, you can eliminate (C) because Jefferson was the second Virginian, after Washington, to be elected president.

60. **(E)** The Age of Imperialism   *Cartoon Question*

In 1898, war against Spain seemed almost inevitable. The American public was outraged over Spain's much-publicized brutality against Cuban rebels, and over Spain's apparent sinking of the U.S. naval ship, the *Maine*, off the coast of Havana. As the cartoon suggests, Congress aggressively campaigned for war, and McKinley and Reed could do little to contain the steam. The U.S. declared war in April 1898, and won the war within two months. Note that (C) is incorrect because the War Hawks referred to the group of southern and western congressmen, led by John C. Calhoun and Henry Clay, who pushed for war against Britain (what became known as the War of 1812) in order to protest the impressment of American soldiers and to gain control of British-owned territories in Canada and the American West and Southwest.

61. **(D)** Cultural Trends: 1781–Mid 1800s   *Trend Question*

Alcohol consumption decreased in the late 1830s and 1840s as a result of the reform efforts of the American Temperance Society. Several state laws restricting or banning the sale of alcohol were also passed. The Eighteenth Amendment, which prohibited the manufacture, sale and transportation of alcohol in the Unites States, was not passed until 1917 and was repealed in 1933.

62. **(D)** The Progressive Era   *Except Question*

An aggressive progressive reformer, Wilson pushed for corporate regulation, banking reform, and lower tariffs. Woodrow Wilson's foreign policy agenda, known as "new freedom," aimed at promoting morality in international relations. Signaling his opposition to his predecessor's "dollar diplomacy," Wilson withdrew American partnership from a loan consortium in China in 1913.

63. **(E)** World War I   *Fact Question*

Passed by Congress in 1917, the Selective Service Act instituted a draft that called all men from age twenty-one to thirty to serve in the military. By November of 1918, about 3,000,000 men had been drafted. The U.S. had a much smaller standing army. Although volunteers, including African-Americans, made up a significant portion of the army, draftees accounted for the majority—roughly two-thirds—of America's armed forces.

64. **(C)** The Colonial Period   *Fact Question*

Proprietary colonies were land grants from the British government. Individuals were awarded huge tracts of land that they would then supervise and govern, usually in return for political or financial favors. These colonial governors reported directly to the king. (A) is the definition of a royal colony. (D) is the definition of a self-governing colony. Rhode Island and Connecticut were self-governing colonies. Virginia began as a self-governing colony but eventually became a royal colony.

65. **(C)** World War I   *Trend Question*

During World War I, the United States engaged in a number of activities at home designed to support the war. Unlike what occurred in World War II, however, the U.S. did not intern American citizens because of their ethnicity or race. The government did establish a Committee on Public Information to wage a domestic propaganda campaign (A) and it passed the Espionage Act and the Sedition Amendment, which criminalized numerous antiwar activities (D). The government helped to finance the war through the sale of Liberty Bonds (E), and it regulated food and fuel to ensure the armed forces and the allies were properly supplied (B).

66. **(D)** The Roaring Twenties   *Fact Question*

The 1928 Kellogg-Briand Pact, signed by more than 60 nations, was an international agreement calling for the outlawing of war. In the 1920s, the U.S. refused to join a world court (A) created by the League of Nations. The 1924 Dawes Plan provided for repayment of war debt (B).

67. **(E)** The Roaring Twenties   *Trend Question*

Business in the 1920s experienced all of the above except a rise in union membership. Union membership actually declined in the 1920s, as courts ruled against various union activities, and employers raised wages in efforts to keep work places free of union associations.

68. **(E)** The Roaring Twenties   *Fact Question*

The Scopes Monkey Trial of 1925 involved the right to teach Darwin's theory of evolution in the classroom. Clarence Darrow defended Tennessee teacher John Scopes against the prosecution. Aiding the prosecution was William Jennings Bryan, a former presidential candidate was led the national movement to ban Darwin's teachings. Although Bryan, in his debates against Darrow, appeared foolish and unknowledgeable in court, he and the prosecution won a conviction against Scopes.

69. **(B)** The Great Depression & New Deal   *Except Question*

The Great Depression did not result in an increase of wages for unskilled workers. (In an economic recession as devastating as the Great Depression, wages never rise.) Instead, poverty spread throughout the country, unemployment soared to as high as twenty-five percent, and hundreds of banks and thousands of businesses failed.

70. **(C)** The Colonial Period   *Trend Question*

French explorer Jacques Cartier explored the St. Lawrence River region for France between 1534 and 1542 in search of the Northwest Passage, a water route through which ships could cross the Americas and access Asia. Although he found no such passage, his exploration laid the foundation for France's early dominance of American waterways. The first permanent French settlement in North America was not founded until 1608 at Quebec by Samuel de Champlain.

71. **(E)**   The Great Depression & New Deal   *Trend Question*

During the Great Depression, working women faced much opposition from organized labor unions that protected the rights of working men, many of whom were unemployed and blamed women for taking away available jobs.

72. **(B)**   The Great Depression & New Deal   *Trend Question*

Franklin Delano Roosevelt won reelection in 1936, in part because of the support of previously underrepresented minorities, including blacks, women, farmers, and urban laborers. These groups became loyal Democrats largely as a result of FDR's New Deal programs, which benefited the poor and underrepresented tremendously. Together, these groups comprised the New Democratic Coalition.

73. **(B)**   Cultural Trends: 1781–Mid-1800s   *Fact Question*

James Fennimore Cooper is often credited with creating the first western hero. Cooper incorporated distinctly American themes in his books, which included *The Pioneers* (1823) and *The Last of the Mohicans* (1826).

74. **(C)**   Revolution & Constitution   *Quotation Question*

This passage reflects the weaknesses of the Articles of Confederation. Remember: under the Articles, the national government was very weak, which is why the Articles were scrapped and the Constitution was written. A question concerning this political transition will undoubtedly appear in some form on the actual test.

75. **(C)**   The Progressive Era   *Fact Question*

The Lend-Lease Act of 1941 allowed the president to lend or lease supplies to any nation deemed vital to the defense of the United States. Under the Lend-Lease Act, FDR extended aid to Great Britain and Russia.

76. **(D)**   World War II   *Fact Question*

The Manhattan Project, begun in 1941, was a secret Anglo-American project to develop an atomic bomb. The Project ended roughly four years later, in 1945, with the successful detonation of an atomic blast.

77. **(B)**   The 1950s   *Except Question*

The sexual revolution is associated with the Roaring Twenties and the 1960s, not the more conservative 1950s. In the 1950s, advances in health science led to falling infant mortality rates, rising fertility rates, and longer life spans. Conservative views on women and family popularized and promoted motherhood. Widespread prosperity meant that people could afford to have more children, further contributing to the baby boom.

78. **(B)**   A New Nation   *Trend Question*

President Monroe's term of office (1817-1825) became known as the "Era of Good Feelings" for two reasons. First, one-party politics following the demise of the Federalist Party led to high levels of political cooperation. Second, America's seeming victory in the War of 1812 generated patriotic fervor throughout the nation. The French and Indian War (C) took place prior to the American Revolution. The Spanish-American War (E) took place under President McKinley.

79. **(C)**   Westward Expansion & Sectional Strife   *Trend Question*

The Oregon Trail was a famous passageway for American settlers traveling to the West and Northwest.

80. **(C)** The 1950s — *Fact Question*

Under the 1948 Marshall Plan, the U.S. promised financial assistance to Europe in order to stimulate economic recovery and political stability. The U.S. also offered aid to the USSR, but the Communists rejected the offer because of U.S. controls on the financial aid.

81. **(E)** Industrial Revolution — *Except Question*

Credit cards certainly promoted the culture of consumerism in America, but they did not start doing so until 1950. The other innovations mentioned dramatically changed consumer society in the late nineteenth century.

82. **(E)** The 1950s — *Trend Question*

In the 1950s, huge increases in defense spending on aerospace and new military technology generated much of the country's industrial growth and major technological advances.

83. **(E)** 1970s–2000 — *Except Question*

The Carter years were in fact known for a decreasing confidence in American ideals. Carter himself described the years as ones marked by a general "malaise." Contributing to this pessimism were chronic economic problems and the seeming permanence of the Soviet Union's superpower world status.

84. **(E)** The Roaring Twenties — *Except Question*

Although the Jazz Age signaled a loosening moral code for a small segment of society, most of America remained conservative and traditional. Premarital sex was therefore not widely accepted. In fashion, hemlines did rise (A), and wearing make up became more popular (D). Divorce laws were liberalized (B), and young college students did engage in seemingly inappropriate activities at parties (C).

85. **(B)** The 1960s — *Fact Question*

In January 1968, the North Vietnamese Army and the Vietcong launched against U.S. troops a massive offensive known as the Tet Offensive. Many thousands of Americans were killed, and areas thought to be secure were breached by the enemy. After about a month of fighting, American troops repelled the offensive.

86. **(C)** The Great Depression & New Deal — *Except Question*

The New Deal was President Franklin Roosevelt's package of policies and programs aimed at reviving the faltering economy and regulating the nation's banking system to prevent future economic failure (see answers (A), (D), and (E)). Many of the New Deal programs derived from John Maynard Keynes's belief that the government could save a dying economy by injecting money into the market (B), or in other words, by increasing the money supply. With this in mind, (C) makes no sense because Roosevelt wanted to increase the supply of money in the economy, not decrease it.

87. **(A)** The 1960s — *Trend Question*

Stokely Carmichael began his civil rights leadership at the Student Nonviolent Coordinating Committee, but he became more radical in the later 1960s, eventually advocating armed resistance. Huey Newton (B) was a Black Panther who favored separatism. Malcolm X (C) began as separatist but eventually became more positive about working with whites. Jesse Jackson (D) and Andrew Young (E) are integrationists.

88. **(A)** Industrial Revolution   *Trend Question*

Most of the immigrants coming to America in the earliest years of the twentieth century were young men from Eastern Europe. The earlier wave of immigration had come mostly from Western Europe (France, Ireland, Germany, etc.), but by the turn of the century, incoming immigrants were most often "new" immigrants from Italy, Russia, Armenia, and other Eastern and Southern European countries.

89. **(A)** 1970s–2000   *Trend Question*

Mexico and other Latin American countries have supplied the greatest numbers of new immigrants to the U.S. in recent decades. Immigration numbers have been comparatively low from the other parts of the world listed.

90. **(C)** World War II   *Trend Question*

American industry during World War II shifted from the production of civilian goods to the production of military goods, ultimately producing more war material than all of the Axis powers combined. (A) is incorrect because the War Production Board, not the Office of Strategic Services, oversaw American industry. (D) is incorrect because the 1943 Smith-Connolly War Labor Disputes Act limited the right to strike in key industries and authorized the president to intervene in labor disputes by taking control of any firm beset by strikes. Also during the war, women entered the paid workforce in record numbers, to fill the positions left vacant by men who went overseas to fight (E).

SAT II U.S. History
Practice Test III

UNITED STATES HISTORY TEST III

Directions: Each of the questions or incomplete statements below is followed by five suggested answers or completions. Select the one that is best in each case and then fill in the corresponding oval on the answer sheet.

1. Spanish exploration of the American Southwest led to

   (A) the mining of gold on Native American land
   (B) the French conquest of Native American land
   (C) the development of an irrigation system in the Great Plains
   (D) the introduction of horses to the Great Plains
   (E) the mapping of buffalo migratory patterns

2. After completing their contracted period of labor, most indentured servants in the Southern colonies

   (A) were forced into slavery
   (B) farmed small plots of land
   (C) moved to the New England and Middle colonies in search of economic and social opportunities
   (D) became plantation owners
   (E) moved westward to establish new settlements

3. What was the explicit purpose of the Monroe Doctrine of 1823?

   (A) to reinforce that the United States would not get involved in European conflicts
   (B) to open up the ports of Asia to the U.S.
   (C) to protect Latin America from additional European conquest
   (D) to lay the groundwork for the U.S. invasion of Mexico
   (E) to warn the British away from their holdings in Canada

4. Andrew Jackson confronted all of the following issues during his presidency EXCEPT

   (A) American westward expansion through Native American lands
   (B) The battle over the survival of the Second Bank of the United States
   (C) The national tariff
   (D) The growing power of trusts in America
   (E) The crisis over nullification

5. "As a result of this immigrant surge after World War I, nativist appeals intensified. A reorganized Ku Klux Klan emerged calling for '100-percent Americanism.' By redefining its enemies, the Klan broadened its appeal to parts of the North and Midwest, and for a time, its membership swelled."

   The "enemies" of the newly reorganized KKK of the 1920s included all of the following groups EXCEPT

   (A) African Americans
   (B) Jews
   (C) Protestants
   (D) immigrants
   (E) Catholics

6. Around 1910, Henry Ford increased industry productivity by successfully introducing

   (A) the eight-hour workday
   (B) healthcare for workers
   (C) incentive plans for workers
   (D) a non-union workplace
   (E) the assembly line

7. Which of the following best describes the "cash-and-carry" policy enacted by President Franklin Delano Roosevelt?

   (A) cash grants to small businesses to stimulate the economy
   (B) the lending and leasing of supplies to the Allies during World War II
   (C) the sale of arms to warring parties during World War II, provided the purchasing nation pay in cash and transport the arms on its own ships
   (D) cash grants to American entrepreneurs attempting to establish businesses in Asia
   (E) low-interest loans to the Allies during World War II

GO ON TO THE NEXT PAGE

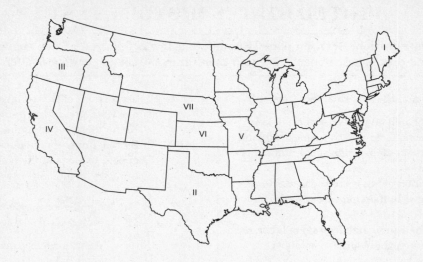

8.   During Polk's presidency, which region did
       expansionists aim to annex from Britain?

       (A)   II
       (B)   III
       (C)   IV
       (D)   VI
       (E)   VII

9. Which of the following countries allied itself with the United States against Britain in 1778, providing the colonists with much-needed military assistance?

   (A) Prussia
   (B) France
   (C) Italy
   (D) Spain
   (E) the Dutch Republic

10. The Marshall Court resolved each of the following constitutional issues EXCEPT

   (A) The Supreme Court has the power to rule an act of Congress unconstitutional
   (B) Congress can constitutionally establish and maintain a national bank
   (C) An individual or a corporation has the right to own private property
   (D) Congress has the rightful authority to regulate interstate commerce
   (E) An individual state has the power to rule an act of Congress unconstitutional

11. The term "Manifest Destiny" was used to justify which of the following wars?

   (A) The Civil War
   (B) The Revolutionary War
   (C) The French and Indian War
   (D) The Mexican War
   (E) The War of 1812

12. All of the following are true of the Republican Party in the years leading up to the Civil War EXCEPT

   (A) its 1860 national platform called for the abolition of slavery
   (B) Abraham Lincoln became its leading spokesman
   (C) it drew its strength primarily from northern sectional interests
   (D) one of its primary positions was favoring free soil
   (E) much of its support came from the former Whig Party

13. "The records of the period show that the outcry against the concentration of capital was furious. Men believed that it threatened society with a form of tyranny more abhorrent than it had ever endured. They believed that the great corporations were preparing for them the yoke of a baser servitude than had ever been imposed on the race, servitude not to men but to soulless machines incapable of any motive but insatiable greed. Looking back, we cannot wonder at their desperation, for certainly humanity was never confronted with a fate more sordid and hideous than would have been the era of corporate tyranny which they anticipated."

   The author of this passage is best considered to be a

   (A) socialist
   (B) capitalist
   (C) Republican
   (D) progressive
   (E) Know-Nothing

14. Throughout the 1890s, the Sherman Antitrust Act was not particularly effective in protecting consumer interests because

   (A) the act asked companies to decide themselves whether or not they were monopolies
   (B) the act's vague language meant that instead of restricting business monopolies it was often used to restrict union activities and strikes
   (C) industry regulators completely refused to enforce the law
   (D) John D. Rockefeller paid off Supreme Court justices to rule in favor of big business
   (E) too many companies hid the fact that they had monopolies over the production and sale of select goods

15. All of the following were elements of the Progressive movement EXCEPT

   (A) limiting immigration
   (B) limiting the power of labor unions
   (C) muckraker exposés
   (D) breaking up monopolies
   (E) regulating medicines and foods

GO ON TO THE NEXT PAGE

16. Franklin D. Roosevelt's New Deal is best described as a package of policies and programs aimed at

    (A) protecting southern industry from northern competition
    (B) curbing the threats of socialism in America
    (C) providing economic relief and reviving the domestic economy
    (D) protecting civil rights
    (E) reviving the economies of depressed Latin American countries

17. At the end of World War II, the Soviet Union moved swiftly to establish a sphere of influence in

    (A) the United Nations
    (B) Asia
    (C) Western Europe
    (D) Eastern Europe
    (E) Latin America

18. Yellow journalism had which of the following effects?

    (A) fueled public support for Cuban nationalist rebels resisting Spanish rule
    (B) drew attention to problems in the meat-packing industry
    (C) generated criticism of American imperialistic tendencies in Latin America
    (D) prompted federal regulation of the food and drug industry
    (E) provoked criticism of U.S. involvement in the Spanish-American War

19. Franklin D. Roosevelt's Good Neighbor Policy pledged that the United States would not intervene in the affairs of

    (A) Europe
    (B) East Asia
    (C) Latin America
    (D) Canada
    (E) Russia

20. The conglomeration of corporations in the 1950s is most attributable to

    (A) the support of President Eisenhower
    (B) the popular teachings at business school
    (C) the boost that automated production gave to big business
    (D) the Korean War effort
    (E) the desegregation of industry

21. Which of the following is true of the pre-Columbian Maya?

    (A) they depended on foraging for survival
    (B) they established a network of towns throughout the Andes
    (C) they developed advanced mathematics, astronomy, and calendar systems
    (D) they developed the bow and arrow
    (E) they built elaborate cliff dwellings

22. Which of the following best explains President Jefferson's support of the Louisiana Purchase?

    (A) the desire to provide territory for the expansion of industries in the North
    (B) the desire to expand the power of the presidency
    (C) the desire to establish a strategic advantage in case of a conflict with British forces in Canada
    (D) the desire to secure western territory in order to achieve his ideal of an agrarian republic
    (E) the desire to promote a strict constructionist view of the U.S. Constitution

23. The concept of containment in U.S. foreign policy is most closely associated with

    (A) the New Deal
    (B) the Monroe Doctrine
    (C) Dollar Diplomacy
    (D) Lend Lease Aid
    (E) the Cold War

24. According to the theory of mercantilism, how must a nation build economic strength?

    (A) by importing manufactured goods
    (B) by exporting raw materials
    (C) by exporting more than it imports
    (D) by establishing a policy of salutary neglect toward its colonies
    (E) by eliminating protectionist tariffs

GO ON TO THE NEXT PAGE

25. What most directly motivated the Puritans' migration to North America?

   (A) their desire to separate from the Anglican Church
   (B) their desire to convert the native population
   (C) their desire to escape religious and political persecution in England
   (D) their desire to promote religious tolerance and pluralism
   (E) their desire to establish a trading port in Boston

26. Relations between the American colonies and Britain in the 1770s were generally marked by

   (A) a mutual indifference
   (B) increasing hostility
   (C) amicability and cooperation
   (D) a reconciliatory tone
   (E) limited and sporadic contact

27. President Andrew Jackson's closest supporters and political advisors were collectively called

   (A) the Tennis Cabinet
   (B) the Kitchen Cabinet
   (C) the Fireside Cabinet
   (D) the Farmers' Cabinet
   (E) the Tennessee Cabinet

28. In the 1870s and 1880s, which theory of economic governance was most prominent?

   (A) direct democracy
   (B) micromanaging
   (C) the Monroe Doctrine
   (D) utilitarianism
   (E) laissez-faire

29. During World War I, black Americans drafted by the U.S. military were

   (A) fully integrated into every branch of the military
   (B) placed mostly on the front lines and forced to assume extremely dangerous combat assignments
   (C) placed in segregated units usually commanded by white officers
   (D) treated better by the army than by civilian authorities
   (E) not ever called up because their labor was needed in factories on the home front

GO ON TO THE NEXT PAGE

BE CAREFUL! IT'S LOADED!
By Victor Gillam in "Judge."

30.   The cartoon above suggests that

(A)   the U.S. should be a global police power in Latin America
(B)   the U.S. must fight in Cuba to protect and advance its economic and political interests there
(C)   the U.S. is a belligerent nation readying for war in Cuba without just cause
(D)   the U.S. has no choice but to go to war against Spain because of Spain's brutal atrocities in Cuba
(E)   the U.S. should be wary of engaging in military conflicts in Cuba that are unnecessarily risky and dangerous

GO ON TO THE NEXT PAGE

31. Which of the following was NOT an element of the Navigation Acts (1651-1673)?

    (A)   only English or English colonial ships could carry cargo between imperial ports
    (B)   certain goods could not be shipped to foreign nations, except through England or Scotland
    (C)   Americans must produce and sell certain goods also produced in England
    (D)   Americans were encourage to produce certain raw goods so that Britain would not have to import these goods from Europe
    (E)   Americans must not directly compete with large-scale British manufacturing

32. Which of the following factors does NOT explain why the American forces were relatively weaker than Great Britain's during the Revolutionary War?

    (A)   the American military was significantly smaller than the British military
    (B)   the American colonists were divided into factions: one that supported revolution and one that still supported Great Britain
    (C)   the Americans did not have financial resources equal to Great Britain's
    (D)   American military forces were undertrained compared to their British counterparts
    (E)   the American population was significantly smaller than Great Britain's

33. In which of the following Supreme Court cases did the Court guarantee a suspect's right to be informed, upon arrest, of his/her right to remain silent and to have an attorney present during questioning?

    (A)   *Miranda v. Arizona*
    (B)   *Gideon v. Wainwright*
    (C)   *Engel v. Vitale*
    (D)   *Roe v. Wade*
    (E)   *Plessy v. Ferguson*

34. Abolitionist Frederick Douglass

    (A)   supported sending freed slaves back to Africa
    (B)   recognized the rights of slave owners but demanded equal treatment of freed slaves
    (C)   rejected the assistance of white abolitionists and insisted on forming an entirely black abolitionist movement
    (D)   supported equal civil rights for blacks and an end to slavery
    (E)   supported the efforts of the National Association for the Advancement of Colored People (NAACP) to provide freed slaves with vocational training

35. The Whig Party was comprised of all of the following interest groups EXCEPT

    (A)   Democrats who disliked Jackson's strong-armed politics
    (B)   merchants who disliked Jackson's antibusiness economic policies
    (C)   southerners who disliked Jackson's high tariffs
    (D)   westerners who disliked Jackson's banking policies
    (E)   northerners who favored a strong national government

36. "With malice towards none; with charity for all; with firmness in the right, as God gives us to see the right, let us strive on to finish the work we are in; to bind up the nation's wounds; to care for him who shall have borne the battle, and for his widow and his orphan . . . to do all which may achieve and cherish a just and lasting peace among ourselves and with all nations"

    Who most likely issued this statement, and to what event was he referring?

    (A)   Harry S. Truman on the end of World War II
    (B)   Woodrow Wilson on the end of World War I
    (C)   Thomas Jefferson on the end of the Revolutionary War
    (D)   Abraham Lincoln on the end of the Civil War
    (E)   Gerald Ford on the end of the Vietnam War

37. All of the following accurately describe the 1787 Northwest Ordinance EXCEPT

    (A)   it forbade slavery in the Northwest Territory
    (B)   it established a process by which the Northwest territories could become states
    (C)   it established a bill of rights for settlers
    (D)   it allowed settlers from the existing states to expand westward
    (E)   it allowed existing states to claim parts of the Northwest territory as their own

GO ON TO THE NEXT PAGE

38. Which of the following was a consequence of the North's rapid industrialization following the American Revolution?

    (A) the increased reliance on slave labor
    (B) the near-total depletion of New England's resources, requiring that raw material be shipped from Britain
    (C) the decline of the mill economy
    (D) the emergence of towns planned around the needs of factory owners and workers
    (E) the decline in foreign trade

39. New Deal legislation established all of the following to help laborers EXCEPT

    (A) a national minimum wage
    (B) restrictions on child labor
    (C) the right to form labor unions
    (D) the right to collectively bargain
    (E) guaranteed benefits for full-time workers

40. Following Japanese surrender in World War II,

    (A) Korea was divided into Soviet Union and U.S. occupation zones
    (B) Japan was occupied by the Soviets
    (C) Vietnam was divided between Soviet Union and U.S. occupation zones
    (D) Japan retained control over Manchuria
    (E) Manchuria became a U.S. colony

41. The 1950's civil rights movement can best be described as

    (A) concentrated on ending the impoverished conditions of African Americans in the North
    (B) using nonviolence to achieve some notable successes in desegregating the American South
    (C) lacking any significant achievements
    (D) led mainly by sympathetic whites
    (E) a period of militant black nationalism

GO ON TO THE NEXT PAGE

Annual Consumer Price Changes, 1980–1998

	Fuel Oil	Medical Care
1980	+38%	+10%
1982	0%	+11%
1984	+1%	+7%
1986	-23%	+9%
1988	0%	+7%
1990	+25%	+9%
1992	-5%	+8%
1994	-3%	+6%
1996	+13%	+5%
1998	-14%	+4%

Source: Historical Abstract of the United States

42.   The chart above lends support to which of the
      following statements?

(A)   medical costs stayed the same, roughly, from 1980–1998,
      while fuel costs rose and fell dramatically
(B)   taxes on fuel were volatile, changing from year to year, while
      healthcare taxes stayed steady
(C)   there is more inflation in medical costs than in fuel costs
(D)   the U.S. suffered two major oil crises, around 1980 and again
      around 1990
(E)   consumers spent more money on medical care than on fuel
      oil

GO ON TO THE NEXT PAGE

43. After he left the Nation of Islam, Malcolm X

    (A) espoused a new philosophy of nonviolence
    (B) embraced orthodox Islam and continued advocating black nationalism and pride
    (C) insisted more aggressively than before that blacks and whites must live separately
    (D) founded the Black Panthers
    (E) concentrated on voter registration drives in the Deep South

44. Which of the following is NOT considered an effect of the First and Second Great Awakenings?

    (A) ministers preached a personal, even intuitive, understanding of God
    (B) organized religion was made more accessible
    (C) Methodists emerged as a dominant revival sect
    (D) the number of Protestant religious sects decreased
    (E) the beliefs helped inspire social activism and widespread reform movements

45. John Jay, James Madison, and Alexander Hamilton wrote *The Federalist Papers* in order to

    (A) convince New Yorkers and other Americans not to ratify the Constitution
    (B) convince New Yorkers and other Americans to ratify the Constitution
    (C) convince New Yorkers and other Americans that the central government under the Articles of Confederation was too weak and required amending
    (D) convince New Yorkers and other Americans that the Articles of Confederation did not require amending because it represented the perfect form of democratic government
    (E) convince New Yorkers and other Americans that they needed to rebel against Great Britain

GO ON TO THE NEXT PAGE

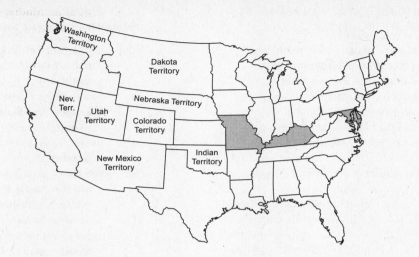

46.   The shaded states represent

(A)   the first states to pass Jim Crow laws
(B)   the only Southern states that Lincoln carried in the 1860
       election
(C)   the only slave states that did not secede from the Union
(D)   the only states in which slaves were freed by the
       Emancipation Proclamation
(E)   the only ex-Confederate states in which Reconstruction had
       a lasting effect

GO ON TO THE NEXT PAGE

47. Why did labor groups like the American Federation of Labor (AFL) push for restriction of immigration?

   (A) because of widespread unemployment, new immigrants would be left homeless and penniless, like most of the underclass
   (B) the disparate immigrant cultures made it difficult to forge working relationships at factories and other large labor bases
   (C) labor groups believed the steady stream of cheap labor would impair unions' organizing and bargaining efforts, and would keep wages low
   (D) because immigrants often brought unique skills to American shores, they generally earned more money and respect than native workers
   (E) labor groups feared immigrants would serve as spies for management because they were so eager to ingratiate themselves to the new country

48. "Our international trade relations, though vastly important, are to point in time and necessity, secondary to the establishment of a sound national economy."

   This statement was probably delivered during

   (A) the War of 1812
   (B) the Civil War
   (C) the Cold War
   (D) the Era of Good Feelings
   (E) the Great Depression

49. In 1890, the Federal Census Office issued the notable declaration that

   (A) more Americans lived in big cities than in rural and suburban areas
   (B) no more Native Americans lived outside reservations
   (C) northern European immigration had for the first time exceeded southern European immigration
   (D) a census would be taken every five years rather than every ten years
   (E) the frontier line no longer existed in the West

50. All of these changes helped extend the life expectancy for people in America after 1900 EXCEPT

   (A) people were eating better than ever before thanks to the wide availability of healthy foods
   (B) the serious consequences of smoking became known, and many smokers took the initiative to quit
   (C) medical advances had severely reduced the number of cases of typhoid and diphtheria
   (D) most people experienced improved living conditions, especially through new forms of waste management
   (E) nutritionists like John H. Kellogg convinced people to eat cereal instead of fatty, traditional breakfast foods

51. The great battle over slavery in Kansas in the 1850s resulted from

   (A) Congress's forbidding slavery in the state
   (B) the Kansas-Nebraska Act's opening of the territory to popular sovereignty
   (C) the Missouri Compromise
   (D) President James Buchanan's refusal to support the Lecompton Constitution
   (E) John Brown's violent pro-slavery raids

52. In 1954, the Warren Court reversed the national policy of "separate but equal" in racial matters with its ruling in

   (A) *Plessy vs. Ferguson*
   (B) *Brown vs. Board of Education*
   (C) the Scopes Monkey Trial
   (D) *Roe vs. Wade*
   (E) *Sacco v. Venzetti*

GO ON TO THE NEXT PAGE

53. Which of the following best explains the concentration of English colonies on the Atlantic coast of North America?

(A) England's defeat of the Spanish Armada led to the English seizure of all Spanish territory on the Atlantic coast

(B) the discovery of vast silver deposits on the Atlantic coast spurred intense colonization efforts there

(C) cooperation with Native Americans made possible the development of trading routes from the Atlantic coast to the Mississippi River

(D) the Atlantic coast had the ideal climate for raising tobacco

(E) other areas in North America had already been claimed by other European powers

54. The Southern colonies differed from the New England colonies in that the Southern colonies

(A) were more religiously and ethnically diverse

(B) had fewer Roman Catholics

(C) had a higher population density

(D) had larger-sized families

(E) had a more powerful and prominent merchant class

55. Which of the following does NOT accurately describe the Alien and Sedition Acts of 1798?

(A) they were designed, in part, as a barrier to freedom of the press

(B) they prevented the Republicans from strengthening their base of power prior to the 1800 election

(C) they were provoked, in part, by the anti-French sentiment propagated by the Federalists

(D) they helped provoke the later articulation of the concept of nullification

(E) among other impositions, they increased the number of years of residency required to become a U.S. citizen

56. Which of the following novels, published in the 1850s, is thought to have had a significant political impact?

(A) *Up From Slavery*

(B) *Walden Pond*

(C) *The Grapes of Wrath*

(D) *Uncles Tom's Cabin*

(E) *The Last of the Mohicans*

57. All of the following characterized labor organizations during the Industrial Revolution EXCEPT

(A) unions achieved moderate success in pushing for higher wages and shorter working days

(B) union power and influence dropped during the 1880s, in part because of an antiunion backlash after a series of bloody labor riots

(C) unions staged a number of strikes against the railroad, steel, and iron industries

(D) unions helped the antitrust movement in successfully invoking the Sherman Antitrust Act to break up several high-powered monopolies

(E) all sorts of workers joined: skilled and unskilled, women, blacks, and immigrants

58. Which artist of the 1950s is most closely associated with the advent of American abstract expressionism?

(A) Gertrude Stein

(B) John S. Copley

(C) Jean Michel Basquiat

(D) Andy Warhol

(E) Jackson Pollack

59. Strong opposition to the Vietnam war first arose among

(A) industrial workers

(B) civil rights groups

(C) students and academics

(D) women

(E) police officers

60. Generally speaking, what effect did Reconstruction have on blacks in Southern society?

(A) no effect because blacks still served as slaves to landowning whites

(B) drastic effect because blacks and whites became social equals

(C) little effect because free blacks in the South still faced widespread oppression and discrimination

(D) little effect because Reconstruction programs immediately fell under Southern white control

(E) no effect because Reconstruction programs helped only former slaves living in the North

GO ON TO THE NEXT PAGE

61. Why were political bosses and so-called party machines so effective at improving urban conditions in the late nineteenth century?

    (A) in exchange for votes, political support, and even bribe money, the parties doled out city contracts to companies to build streets, sanitation systems, parks, and other much-needed city projects

    (B) as immigrants themselves, political bosses were primarily concerned with improving the standard of living for the urban, mostly immigrant poor

    (C) by putting the power in the hands of several people, as opposed to one leader, political machines protected city politics from possible corruption and mismanagement

    (D) the political bosses' close connection to labor unions helped ensure good working conditions for urban workers

    (E) as progressive reformers, political bosses pushed through aggressive legislation to help the less-advantaged

62. In the 1950s, popular culture generally encouraged American women to

    (A) work outside the home
    (B) protest for equality
    (C) pursue higher education
    (D) focus on marriage, motherhood, and domesticity
    (E) use contraception

63. Which of the following is NOT true about U.S. involvement in Vietnam?

    (A) it was the longest conflict in American history
    (B) Congress never issued a formal declaration of war
    (C) the Vietnamese soldiers suffered far greater casualties than U.S. forces
    (D) before entering the conflict, the U.S. military was not prepared or designed for such a long guerilla war
    (E) U.S. forces were briefly able to control most of Vietnam

64. The Voting Rights Act of 1965 helped to increase black enfranchisement in the South by

    (A) requiring that a minimum number of congressional representatives from each southern state be black
    (B) authorizing federal examiners to register qualified voters and to suspend literacy tests in many voting districts.
    (C) double-counting votes cast by blacks
    (D) installing marshals in every electoral district where blacks voted
    (E) barring confirmed white racists from voting

65. Democrats in Congress in the 1980s would most likely have opposed

    (A) an increase in defense spending
    (B) an expansion of social services
    (C) a lift of the economic sanctions against Communist Cuba
    (D) an increase in women's access to abortions
    (E) a reduction in America's nuclear weapons arsenal

66. The increased demand for southern cotton in the early to mid-nineteenth century is most directly linked to

    (A) the increasing use of cotton as insulation for northern homes
    (B) the increasing use of cotton in textile factories in the North and in Great Britain
    (C) the destruction of cotton crops in Europe during the Thirty Years' War
    (D) the destruction of cotton crops in the North during a lengthy and devastating drought
    (E) the increasing use of cotton as a packaging material in transatlantic trade

67. Of the following, who would most likely have supported Social Darwinist theory?

    (A) a poor southern black
    (B) an inhabitant of a New York City tenement
    (C) an urban socialist
    (D) a member of the Ku Klux Klan
    (E) a rich northern businessman

GO ON TO THE NEXT PAGE

68. "I shall strenuously contend for the immediate enfranchisement of our slave population . . . . On this subject I do not wish to think, or speak, or write with moderation . . . . I am in earnest—I will not equivocate—I will not excuse—I will not retreat a single inch and I WILL BE HEARD."

This statement was probably made by which of the following radical abolitionists?

(A) Abraham Lincoln
(B) Thaddeus Stevens
(C) William Lord Garrison
(D) Andrew Johnson
(E) Andrew Jackson

69. The Populist Party primarily supported the needs of farmers and

(A) blacks, with its stance on integration and the abolition of Jim Crow laws
(B) middle-class Americans, with its flat tax proposal
(C) laborers, by demanding shorter hours and attacking the use of strikebreakers
(D) immigrants, with its loose stance on immigration laws
(E) followers of the nationalist philosophy made popular by Edward Bellamy's book *Looking Backward From 2000 to 1887*

70. The main reason Parliament passed the Sugar and Stamp Acts was to

(A) help pay off Britain's war debts accrued during the French and Indian War
(B) promote trade in the colonies
(C) secure the colonists' loyalty against the French threat in North America
(D) hurt the American shipping industry
(E) punish colonists for the Boston Tea Party

71. The Constitution specifically grants all of the following powers to the federal government EXCEPT

(A) the power to raise and maintain armies
(B) the power to levy taxes
(C) the power to conduct international relations
(D) the power to regulate commerce within a state
(E) the power to regulate interstate commerce

72. The Fugitive Slave Act of 1850 stipulated that

(A) escaped slaves had no right to a trial or to testify in their own defense
(B) slaveholders had no right to reclaim their escaped slaves if those slaves had successfully fled to a free state
(C) earlier laws on punishing escaped slaves must be relaxed
(D) opponents of slavery had the right to harbor escaped slaves
(E) southern lawmen could not enter northern states to search for escaped slaves

73. Mid-nineteenth century activists Elizabeth Cady Stanton and Lucretia Mott were principally associated with which of the following reform movements?

(A) the temperance movement
(B) the prison reform movement
(C) the public school improvement movement
(D) the women's rights movement
(E) the abolitionist movement

74. Henry David Thoreau believed in

(A) Deism
(B) Universalism
(C) transcendentalism
(D) Mormonism
(E) evangelicalism

GO ON TO THE NEXT PAGE

75. Strict constructionists and loose constructionists disagreed about the establishment of a national bank primarily because

(A) loose constructionists did not believe that the benefits of a national bank would outweigh the negatives associated with increased debt

(B) strict constructionists were primarily farmers with little currency available to keep in the bank

(C) loose constructionists would have preferred that individual states be responsible for state debts and collecting funds

(D) strict constructionists believed that the U.S. Constitution did not authorize the federal government to establish a national bank

(E) strict constructionists feared that the national bank would interfere with Hamilton's overall financial policy

76. All of the following represent legislative victories for the labor cause between 1865 and 1900 EXCEPT

(A) the abolition of the Contract Labor Law

(B) the passage of a law ensuring job security for workers

(C) the passage of a law restricting Chinese immigration

(D) the establishment of an eight-hour workday for public works projects

(E) a number of state laws that shortened workdays and improved safety conditions

77. Which of the following best describes the U.S position at the Versailles Peace Conference at the close of World War I?

(A) an isolationist stance towards Europe

(B) aggressively seeking to expand its power in global affairs by accumulating more colonies

(C) idealistically seeking to impose its liberal democratic values on a post-war world order

(D) indifferent to the concerns of smaller nations

(E) accommodating to the demands of its European allies

78. Part of America's Cold War policy, the Truman Doctrine is best characterized as

(A) a commitment to help any country defend itself against communist insurgents or outsiders

(B) a declaration that the president has the final authority in international affairs

(C) a proclamation that the U.S. would not rest until the entire world was free from communist rule

(D) the assertion that no European nation had a right to exercise power in the Western Hemisphere

(E) a statement that the U.S. needed to have overwhelming first-strike capability in the event of a nuclear war against the Soviets

79. All of the following are reasons the Anti-Saloon League and the Woman's Christian Temperance Union opposed the consumption of alcohol EXCEPT

(A) the detrimental effects of alcohol on the liver

(B) the danger that drinking posed in the workplace

(C) the presumed links between drinking and poverty

(D) the hazards of drinking and driving

(E) the negative effects of alcohol on work productivity

80. The three-fifths clause in the Constitution dictated that

(A) amending the Constitution requires an affirmative vote from three-fifths of states

(B) three-fifths of the Senate must vote for a piece of legislation in order for it to pass

(C) three-fifths of the House of Representatives must agree in order to impeach a president

(D) slaves counted as three-fifths of a person, when determining a state's population

(E) three-fifths of the population in a territory seeking statehood must be white male property owners

GO ON TO THE NEXT PAGE

81. Woodrow Wilson's "new freedom" foreign policy differed from the foreign policy of his predecessors in that Wilson

    (A) aimed to promote morality in international affairs
    (B) used U.S. investments to generate international stability
    (C) relied on the aggressive use of force
    (D) sought to expand of U.S. colonial holdings
    (E) renewed the American partnership in a loan consortium in China

82. The 1863 Emancipation Proclamation had all of the following effects EXCEPT

    (A) it bolstered support for the Union in Great Britain and France
    (B) it led to almost 200,000 black soldiers enlisting in Union Army
    (C) it demoralized the South
    (D) it freed all the slaves in the Union
    (E) it appeased Radical Republicans in the North

83. In the 1920s, the National Association for the Advancement of Colored People (NAACP) was led by

    (A) Marcus Garvey
    (B) Booker T. Washington
    (C) Martin Luther King Jr.
    (D) Fredrick Douglass
    (E) W.E.B. Du Bois

84. All of the following contributed to the Great Depression EXCEPT

    (A) wild speculation on the stock market
    (B) a decade of economic failure in the agricultural sector
    (C) rising unemployment
    (D) a shortage of gold bullion in the national reserves
    (E) unsound banking practices

85. The federal system of government, as established by the U.S. Constitution, means which of the following?

    (A) Federalists were the party in power when George Washington was elected president
    (B) power is shared equally between a strong national government and individual state governments
    (C) power is balanced between three branches of government at the national level
    (D) power is shared between a federal government and state governments, but the federal government has predominance because it can enact binding national laws
    (E) the United States government consists of a confederation of states that share power equally

86. In the mid-1840s, which idea gained popularity among moderates in Congress as a means to minimize tensions over the slavery issue?

    (A) the doctrine of popular sovereignty, whereby local governments would decide without federal intervention whether their states would be slave-holding or free
    (B) the gradual abolition of slavery in all states and territories
    (C) extending slavery to half of all the new states entering the Union
    (D) a return to the gag rule forbidding congressional debates on slavery
    (E) the doctrine of concurrent majority, whereby individual states could veto federal laws pertaining to slavery

87. In 1867, farmers formed which of the following groups to address their concerns, their financial distress and social isolation?

    (A) the Populist Party, also known as the People's Party
    (B) the Grange movement
    (C) the Carpetbaggers
    (D) the Democratic Party
    (E) the John Birch Society

GO ON TO THE NEXT PAGE

88. When William Jennings Bryan concluded his most famous speech with the words, "You shall not crucify mankind upon a cross of gold," he was defending the Populist stand on

   (A)   the free coinage of silver
   (B)   religious freedom in schools
   (C)   greater government regulation of banking practices
   (D)   the platinum standard
   (E)   antilynching regulation

89. During the 1930s, many facets of American pop culture—including film, radio, comedy, magazines, and photographs—soared in popularity because

   (A)   everyone had money during the economic boom
   (B)   people worked less and had more time to enjoy art and culture
   (C)   such entertainment provided a much-needed diversion from the troubles and anxieties caused by the Great Depression
   (D)   the U.S. experienced an influx of artists from war-torn Europe
   (E)   technological improvements spurred the entertainment industry to new levels of production

90. Which of the following is credited with sparking the modern environmental movement and contributing to passage of the Clean Air Act?

   (A)   Albert Gore's *The Earth in Balance*
   (B)   James Baldwin's *The Fire Next Time*
   (C)   Rachel Carson's *Silent Spring*
   (D)   Abbie Hoffman's *Steal This Book*
   (E)   Jane Jacobs's *Death and Life of Great American Cities*

S T O P

IF YOU FINISH BEFORE TIME IS CALLED, YOU MAY CHECK YOUR WORK ON THIS TEST ONLY.
DO NOT TURN TO ANY OTHER TEST IN THIS BOOK.

SAT II U.S. History

Practice Test III

Explanations

Answers to SAT II U.S. History Practice Test III

Question Number	Correct Answer	Right	Wrong	Question Number	Correct Answer	Right	Wrong
1.	D	___	___	51.	B	___	___
2.	B	___	___	52.	B	___	___
3.	C	___	___	53.	E	___	___
4.	D	___	___	54.	A	___	___
5.	C	___	___	55.	B	___	___
6.	E	___	___	56.	D	___	___
7.	C	___	___	57.	D	___	___
8.	B	___	___	58.	E	___	___
9.	B	___	___	59.	C	___	___
10.	E	___	___	60.	C	___	___
11.	D	___	___	61.	A	___	___
12.	A	___	___	62.	D	___	___
13.	A	___	___	63.	E	___	___
14.	B	___	___	64.	B	___	___
15.	B	___	___	65.	A	___	___
16.	C	___	___	66.	B	___	___
17.	D	___	___	67.	E	___	___
18.	A	___	___	68.	C	___	___
19.	C	___	___	69.	C	___	___
20.	C	___	___	70.	A	___	___
21.	C	___	___	71.	D	___	___
22.	D	___	___	72.	A	___	___
23.	E	___	___	73.	D	___	___
24.	C	___	___	74.	C	___	___
25.	C	___	___	75..	D	___	___
26.	B	___	___	76.	B	___	___
27.	B	___	___	77.	C	___	___
28.	E	___	___	78.	A	___	___
29.	C	___	___	79.	D	___	___
30.	D	___	___	80.	D	___	___
31.	C	___	___	81.	A	___	___
32.	A	___	___	82.	D	___	___
33.	A	___	___	83.	E	___	___
34.	D	___	___	84.	D	___	___
35.	D	___	___	85.	D	___	___
36.	D	___	___	86.	A	___	___
37.	E	___	___	87.	B	___	___
38.	D	___	___	88.	A	___	___
39.	E	___	___	89.	C	___	___
40.	A	___	___	90.	C	___	___
41.	B	___	___				
42.	D	___	___				
43.	B	___	___				
44.	D	___	___				
45.	B	___	___				
46.	C	___	___				
47.	C	___	___				
48.	E	___	___				
49.	E	___	___				
50.	B	___	___				

Calculating Your Score on
SAT II U.S. History
Practice Test III

Your raw score for the SAT II History test is calculated from the number of questions you answer correctly and incorrectly. Once you have determined your composite score, use the conversion table on page 19 of this book to calculate your scaled score.

To Calculate Your Raw Score

Count the number of questions you answered correctly: _____
A

Count the number of questions you answered incorrectly, and multiply that number by $\frac{1}{4}$:

_____ X $\frac{1}{4}$ = _____
B   C

Subtract the value in field C from value in field A: _____
D

Round the number in field D to the nearest whole number. This is your raw score: _____
E

1. **(D)** The Colonial Era *Trend Question*

Spanish explorer Francisco Coronado set out from Mexico in 1540, in search of the mythical Seven Cities of Cibola, which were described as wealthy cities made of gold. Coronado explored the Grand Canyon and Kansas, but failed to find gold or treasure. During his voyage, enough horses escaped from his party to fundamentally transform Native American life on the Great Plains. After a few generations, the Native Americans of the Great Plains became skilled horseback riders, greatly enhancing their hunting and trading capabilities.

2. **(B)** The Colonial Era *Fact Question*

After completing the term of their service (usually three to seven years), indentured servants were given a small plot of land to farm themselves.

3. **(C)** A New Nation *Trend Question*

The Monroe Doctrine (1823) warned European countries against further colonizing or otherwise interfering in Latin America. It stated that the U.S would construe any attempt at European colonization in the New World as an "unfriendly act."

4. **(D)** The Age of Jackson *Except Question*

Andrew Jackson did not have to worry about the rising power of trusts in the United States. Corporate trusts and big business did not gain power in the U.S. until after the Civil War.

5. **(C)** The Roaring Twenties *Quotation Question*

The "enemies" of the newly reorganized KKK of the 1920s included all of the groups listed except Protestants—namely blacks, non-Protestants, and immigrants. KKK members were almost exclusively white Protestants.

6. **(E)** The Roaring Twenties *Fact Question*

Henry Ford is credited with developing the first automated assembly line for his Ford Motor Company's Model T.

7. **(C)** World War II *Fact Question*

In 1939 the Neutrality Acts were revised to allow warring nations to purchase arms from the U.S., as long as they paid in cash and carried the arms away on their own ships—the "cash and carry" policy.

8. **(B)** Western Expansion & Sectional Strife *Map Question*

In 1844, James Polk won the presidency on an expansionist slogan, "Re-annex Mexico and re-occupy Oregon." In the first few years of his presidency, Polk focused mostly on the first half of this slogan. Expansionists, meanwhile, pressured Congress to annex the entire Oregon territory, while Northerners also pushed for its acquisition (since the admission of Oregon as a free state would balance the admission of slave-holding Texas). But Polk, already engaged in tense border disputes with Mexico, did not want to embroil the U.S. in further expansionist conflict. In 1846, he agreed to a compromise with Britain in which the two countries split the Oregon territory at the forty-ninth parallel: south of this line lay the U.S.-owned Oregon territory, and north lay the British-owned Washington territories.

9. **(B)** Revolution & Constitution   *Fact Question*

In 1778, France allied itself with the fledgling United States, against Great Britain. France's alliance with the United States signified the turning point in the Revolutionary War, in which the colonists, up until this point, had been faring badly. Within two years, Spain (D) and the Dutch Republic (E) also declared war on Britain, but their involvement alongside the U.S. was not as pivotal as France's involvement. The German Hessians (A) actually fought alongside the British as hired mercenaries. Italy (C) was not involved in the American Revolution.

10. **(E)** A New Nation   *Except Question*

The Marshall Court never authorized states to declare federal laws unconstitutional. Quite the reverse, the Marshall Court's decisions often enhanced federal powers at the expense of states' rights. The court ruled on Congress's authority to regulate interstate commerce (A) in *Gibbons v. Ogden* (1824) and on the constitutionality of the national bank in *McCulloch v. Maryland* (1819). The court established the power of judicial review (D) in *Marbury v. Madsion* (1803).

11. **(D)** Western Expansion & Sectional Strife   *Fact Question*

First coined in 1845, the term "Manifest Destiny" conveyed the popular belief that Americans had a God-given right to expand the nation's territory throughout the North American continent—to spread American civilization as well as the Protestant faith. This belief was used to justify the Mexican War, declared in 1846, in which America won from Mexico vast territory that encompasses present-day Arizona, Nevada, California, Utah, and parts of New Mexico, Colorado, and Wyoming.

12. **(A)** Western Expansion & Sectional Strife   *Except Question*

The Republican Party did not explicitly call for an abolition of slavery in 1860. Abolitionism was still a minority and politically problematic position at the time, and many Republicans, including President Lincoln, were not yet prepared to call for an end to slavery until well into the Civil War.

13. **(A)** Industrial Revolution   *Quotation Question*

This passage, written by Edward Bellamy in *Looking Backward from 2000 to 1887*, is best described as socialist, since it describes capitalists as greedy tyrants seeking to earn profits at the expense of working-class people.

14. **(B)** Industrial Revolution   *Fact Question*

Because the Sherman Antitrust Act was loosely phrased to prohibit any "conspiracy in constraint of trade," many courts in the 1890s interpreted the act to prohibit strikes and restrain the activities of unions—not business monopolies, as the act intended. It was not until the early 1900s that the act was used as an aggressive antitrust measure to protect consumer interests.

15. **(B)** The Progressive Era   *Except Question*

Progressives generally supported labor unions. Theodore Roosevelt, a Progressive president, defended the rights of labor to organize, collectively bargain, and strike. The remaining choices—limiting immigration, muckracking, breaking up monopolies, and regulating medicines and foods—were all elements of the Progressive movement.

16. **(C)** The Great Depression & New Deal   *Trend Question*

The New Deal was President Franklin Roosevelt's package of policies and programs aimed at reviving the depressed economy and providing short-term relief for the millions of destitute Americans during the Great Depression of the 1930s.

17. (D) The 1950s   *Trend Question*

At World War II's end, Stalin tried to establish a buffer zone of pro-Soviet states in Eastern Europe. The Red Army set up puppet governments in Bulgaria, Romania, Hungary, and Poland.

18. (A) The Age of Imperialism   *Fact Question*

Yellow journalism drew attention to the plight of Cuban nationalists resisting Spanish rule. Sensational news reports about Spanish atrocities fueled public support for the rebels, which led to the Spanish-American War. Muckracking, not yellow journalism, drew attention to problems in the meat packing industry and prompted federal regulation of food and medicines ((B) and (D)).

19. (C) The Great Depression & New Deal   *Fact Question*

The 1932 Good Neighbor Policy pledged that the United States would not intervene in the affairs of Latin American countries.

20. (C) The 1950s   *Trend Question*

The rise of corporations in the 1950s can best be attributed to automation, which favored big business and economies of scale.

21. (C) The Colonial Era   *Fact Question*

The Maya had a flourishing society in Central America. They were known for developing advanced methods of astronomy and mathematic; an elaborate calendar system; and their own form of writing. The tribes of the Great Basin depended on foraging for survival (A). The Incas established a network of towns throughout the Andes (B). The Anasazi of the Southwest were known for their cliff dwellings (E).

22. (D) A New Nation   *Trend Question*

Jefferson wanted to expand the territory in the west in order to fulfill his ideal of the U.S. as an agrarian, decentralized republic. Jefferson was a strict constructionist who did not want to expand the power of the presidency but instead wanted to limit the power of the federal government. He was therefore wary about spearheading the Louisiana Purchase because the Constitution did not explicitly grant him the power to make such a purchase. To allay his concerns, he drafted a constitutional amendment that would give the federal government this power, but was persuaded by fellow Republicans to go ahead and submit the purchase to Congress in case Napoleon retracted his offer of sale before the purchase went through.

23. (E) The 1950s   *Fact Question*

Containment of communist territory and influence was the foundation of U.S. foreign policy during the Cold War.

24. (C) The Colonial Era   *Fact Question*

According to mercantilist theory, a nation must establish a favorable balance of trade in order to build economic strength—that is, it must export more than it imports and then earn its trade deficit in bullion (gold and silver). Through mercantilist trade measures such as the Navigation Acts, England imported raw goods from the colonies and exported manufactured goods to other European markets and back to the colonies (the reverse of (A) and (B)). In keeping with mercantilist theory, England also imposed protectionist tariffs to thwart trade competition (the reverse of (E)). Salutary neglect (D) involved the lax enforcement of trade laws and thus worked against developing a favorable balance of trade.

25. (C) The Colonial Era — *Trend Question*

Increased religious and political persecution in England prompted Puritans to leave for North America. Note that (A) is incorrect because the Puritans wanted to purify, not separate from, the Anglican Church. As for (D)), Puritan colonies urged strict religious conformity, not religious tolerance.

26. (B) Revolution & Constitution — *Trend Question*

Colonial and British feelings for each other in the 1770s can be best be described as increasingly hostile. Colonists grew outraged over Britain's aggressive efforts to tax the colonies exclusively for Britain's profit. The British, for their part, resented colonial protests.

27. (B) The Age of Jackson — *Fact Question*

Andrew Jackson chose his closest supporters and friends to be members of his cabinet, despite the fact that many of them had no knowledge of politics or government. These men were collectively known as the Kitchen Cabinet.

28. (E) Industrial Revolution — *Fact Question*

In the 1870s and early 1880s, the U.S. government mostly pursued a laissez-faire policy, which meant granting companies autonomy and leaving prices up to the free market. This behavior fit in with the major tenet of Social Darwinism, which stated that competition in human society, specifically in the business world, was necessary to produce the "fittest" of species. Because free competition was considered so crucial to the health of the economy, the government did not intervene much in the market.

29. (C) World War I — *Trend Question*

More than 250,000 black soldiers served in American forces in World War I. They were placed in segregated units commanded by white officers and were generally assigned menial labor. Blacks were excluded entirely from the U.S. Marines. Racism in the army was pervasive, and racial tension often flared up at military camps.

30. (D) The Age of Imperialism — *Cartoon Question*

If you look closely at the cartoon, you'll see a ship named the *Maine* sinking in the background. The *Maine* was a U.S. ship that exploded in Havana in February 1898. Although the cause of the explosion was unknown, the Spaniards were blamed. Already, before the sinking of the *Maine*, the American public was agitating for war because of Spain's aggressive actions in Cuba; many alarming, sensationalist reports had spread throughout the U.S. describing the Spanish military's brutality against the Cuban rebels. The sinking of the *Maine* therefore served as the final trigger for a war that already seemed inevitable. Hence the cartoon's message: in the name of patriotism, the U.S. *had* to avenge the loss of the *Maine* and Spain's savagery in Cuba. The U.S. won the Spanish-American War within two months, gaining independence for Cuba.

31. (C) The Colonial Era — *Except Question*

The Navigation Acts were part of British mercantilist policy aimed at establishing a favorable balance of trade: that is, more exports than imports. Specifically, Britain aimed to import raw goods while exporting manufactured goods. To achieve this end, England passed a series of regulatory measures, including the Navigation Acts, that exclusively benefited the British economy by implementing mercantilist theory. (C) would work against this trade policy because America would provide unwanted competition to Britain's manufacturing dominance, lessening Britain's trade profits.

32. **(A)** Revolution & Constitution — *Except Question*

This question is tricky because it requires you to recognize the one false answer out of what seem to be five correct answers. One way to proceed is to eliminate all the answers you know to be true. You can rule out (B) if you remember that the American people were, in fact, divided between the loyalist Tories and the pro-independence Whigs. It is also pretty safe to rule out (C) because Great Britain had a vast global empire while the Americans only controlled a small strip of land on the eastern North American coast; it therefore stands to reason that Britain had more financial resources than the United States. The same reasoning also allows you to eliminate (E) because the British empire's vast size suggests that its population was much larger than the 2.5 million Americans in the colonies. This process of elimination leaves you with two answer choices, (A) and (E). (A) is the correct choice of the two because it is the one false one: the American military forces were *not* smaller than Great Britain's. Numbered at 220,000, American forces roughly equaled the British military.

33. **(A)** The 1960s — *Fact Question*

During the 1960s, the Supreme Court under liberal Chief Justice Earl Warren delivered a number of significant decisions. The 1966 decision in *Miranda v. Arizona* required police to make suspects aware of their rights to remain silent and to have an attorney present during questioning—the so-called Miranda rights.

In the 1963 case *Gideon v. Wainwright*, the Court ruled that defendants who could not afford counsel had the right to court-appointed counsel in criminal trials. In *Engel v. Vitale* (1962), the Court ruled that prayer in public school violated the First Amendment's Establishment Clause. The 1973 *Roe v. Wade* case legalized abortion. The Court's ruling in *Plessy v. Ferguson* (1896) established the "separate but equal" doctrine that upheld the South's discriminatory Jim Crow laws until the doctrine's reversal in *Brown v. Board of Education* (1954).

34. **(D)** Cultural Trends: 1781–Mid-1800s — *Fact Question*

Frederick Douglass worked with both white and black abolitionists during the mid-nineteenth century to bring about an end to slavery and to establish equal civil rights for blacks. The NAACP was not founded until the early twentieth century (1909) and vocational training was not one of its major goals.

35. **(D)** The Age of Jackson — *Fact Question*

Formed in the 1830s, the Whig Party consisted of an eclectic group of individuals and smaller political parties that opposed Andrew Jackson's politics and economics. Northerners generally disliked Jackson because he favored a weaker, decentralized government. Merchants disliked him because he hurt their business interests. Southerners—especially Jackson's vice president, John C. Calhoun—opposed him because of his tariff policies. Even some Democrats in his own party disliked his forceful style of politics. Jackson's primary supporters were westerners who benefited from his banking policies and his self-declared "fight for the common man." (D) was therefore not heavily represented in the formation of the Whig Party.

36. **(D)** Civil War & Reconstruction — *Quotation Question*

The author and speaker of this passage was Abraham Lincoln, and he was referring to the end of the Civil War. Instead of punishing the South for the war, Lincoln argued that former Confederate states should be readmitted to the Union once ten percent of the population in that state had sworn allegiance to the United States. Radical Republicans deemed Lincoln's plan too generous and forgiving; instead, they wanted to impose a more punitive plan. The reference to the "widow" and the "orphan" in the speech imply estrangement, much as the North and the South had been estranged from each other during the war.

37. **(E)** Revolution & Constitution   *Except Question*

The Northwest Ordinance of 1787 forbade slavery in the territories, allowed Americans to expand westward, established a process by which qualifying territories could become states, and created a bill of rights for settlers. It did *not*, however, allow existing states to claim, or annex, part of the Northwest Territory. In fact, Congress passed the Northwest Ordinance (as well as the earlier Land Ordinance of 1785) primarily to prevent states from claiming any territory as their own.

38. **(D)** Cultural Trends: 1781–Mid-1800s   *Trend Question*

The rise of industrialization led to the establishment of so-called "planned towns," which were structured to meet the needs of factory owners and workers. (B) is incorrect because New England's resources seemed nearly inexhaustible in the eighteenth and nineteenth centuries, so there was no need to import raw goods from Britain. (E) is incorrect because the expansion of foreign trade, not its decline, resulted from the North's rapid industrialization. As for (C), precisely the reverse is true: industrialization meant the development of manufacturing and the flourishing, not disintegration, of the mill economy. As for (A), young immigrant men, not slaves, came to dominate the North's workforce.

39. **(E)** The Great Depression & New Deal   *Except Question*

New Deal legislation did not establish guaranteed benefits for full-time employees. The Fair Labor Standards Act (1938) established a national minimum wage and set restrictions on child labor ((A) and (B)). The Wagner Act (1935) encouraged the formation of labor unions and protected union members' right to collectively bargain ((C) and (D)).

40. **(A)** World War II   *Trend Question*

As part of the Japanese surrender in World War II, Korea was divided at the thirty-eighth parallel in an agreement between the Soviet Union and the U.S. The Soviets occupied North Korea and the U.S. occupied South Korea, each supporting governments hostile to each other. This hostility erupted in the Korean War in 1950.

41. **(B)** The 1950s   *Trend Question*

In the 1950s, Martin Luther King Jr. and other black civil rights leaders used nonviolence to achieve some notable successes in desegregating public facilities and accommodations in the American South. Their protest efforts included boycotts and sit-ins.

42. **(D)** World War II   *Chart Question*

As the chart indicates, fuel prices soared around 1980 and around 1990, rising 38 percent and 25 percent, respectively. The cause of these price hikes were two major fuel shortages, the first resulting from actions taken by the Middle East cartel, OPEC, in the late 1970s, and the second connected to the Iraqi invasion of Kuwait in the summer of 1990. You don't have to know this historical background to read the chart, however. You just have to see that the price for fuel oil price spiked remarkably around 1980 and 1990.

43. **(B)** The 1960s   *Fact Question*

After a disagreement with Elijah Muhammad, Malcolm X left the Nation of Islam and started his own mosque. He embraced orthodox Islam and continued on with his political activities. He advocated self-defense and black nationalism, but acknowledged that different races could live together successfully.

44. **(D)** Cultural Trends: 1781–Mid-1800s *Except Question*

The Great Awakenings led to a proliferation of religious sects, the most prominent being Methodism. (B) is true because revival ministers preached that God would save anyone who fully repented—including women, blacks, and Native Americans—and not just the prominent members of established churches. (A) is correct because revivalist ministers preached a personal, emotional understanding of God rather than an institutionalized or rationalized one. (E) is true because many reformers believed that they were doing God's work, and the Second Great Awakening did much to encourage them in their missions.

45. **(B)** Revolution & Constitution *Trend Question*

Federalists John Jay, James Madison, and Alexander Hamilton wrote *The Federalist Papers* as a series of newspaper and pamphlet essays in order to convince New Yorkers and all Americans to ratify the Constitution. The question itself contains a clue to the answer, because the title *The Federalist Papers* implies that the authors were Federalists themselves. Remember that the Constitution was overall a Federalist document because it was written on the Federalist premise that the new national government should be strong and centralized.

46. **(C)** Civil War & Reconstruction *Map Question*

The shaded states represent the border states that did not secede from the Union. (B) is incorrect because Lincoln carried no slave states in the election of 1860, and in fact did not even appear on the ballots of a number of slave states; he won all eighteen free states in the North and West. (D) is incorrect because the Emancipation Proclamation, issued January 1, 1863, only freed slaves in the Confederate states still under rebellion at the time—that is, not yet under Union control.

47. **(C)** Industrial Revolution *Trend Question*

Labor's anti-immigration stance derived mostly from concerns over money and job competition. Coming from miserable existences in Europe, new immigrants were all too eager to take on low-paying jobs with terrible conditions. Because employers had such a steady supply of cheap labor, unions had little leverage with which to demand higher wages and better conditions.

48. **(E)** The Great Depression & New Deal *Quotation Question*

Franklin Delano Roosevelt delivered this speech on March 4, 1933, at his first inauguration, when he pledged to resolve the economic depression devastating the nation. To answer this question, note that the speaker says that international trade relations are secondary to creating a sound economy. Of the time periods listed in the answer choices, you should recognize that the Great Depression was the one with the most economic hardship.

49. **(E)** Western Expansion & Sectional Strife *Fact Question*

The year 1890 marked the closing of the western frontier, as the Census Office declared that the line no longer existed. By 1890, America claimed all land that is now the contiguous U.S. between the Atlantic and Pacific oceans.

50. **(B)** Industrial Revolution *Except Question*

Smoking was not considered a health risk at the turn of the twentieth century. In fact, smoking became more widespread in the early twentieth century with the introduction of mass-produced cigarettes. Nonetheless, between 1900 and 1920, the life expectancy in the United States rose by a full six years and the death rate dropped precipitously, in part because of the other health advances listed.

51. **(B)** Western Expansion & Sectional Strife   *Trend Question*

The Kansas-Nebraska Act's introduction of popular sovereignty to Kansas, in 1854, fueled a heated and violent struggle over the territory's status, whether slave-holding or free. After a fraudulent election in 1855, a pro-slavery government swept into power and created a pro-slavery constitution known as the Lecompton Constitution, which President Buchanan actually supported (the reverse of (D)). The ensuing rash of bloody antislavery raids led by John Brown (E) earned Kansas the nickname "Bloody Kansas." Note that (E) is not the right answer, however, because the battle over slavery did not *result* from John Brown's raids; rather Brown's raids were central parts of this battle. The Missouri Compromise of 1820 (C) had nothing to do with Kansas; instead, it dealt with admission of Maine as a free state, Missouri as a slave state, and the division of the Louisiana Territory into slave-holding and free lands.

52. **(B)** The 1950s   *Trend Question*

With its ruling in *Brown v. Board of Education*, the Warren Court overturned the 1896 *Plessy v. Ferguson* decision and ruled that segregation of schools was unconstitutional on the basis that separate schools are inherently unequal.

53. **(E)** The Colonial Era   *Trend Question*

England began to take an interest in the New World later than many other European powers. By the time England asserted territorial claims, much of the territory in the New World had already been claimed by other countries (mostly Spain and France). England was therefore limited to the Atlantic coast of North America. Early English settlers could not move farther inland because dense forests and hostile Native American tribes prevented them from moving west through the Appalachian Mountains.

You may have been tempted by (D) because tobacco played an important role in the success of the Southern colonies. This choice is not the best answer because tobacco cultivation was only significant in the southern Atlantic coast and does not explain England's colonization of the Atlantic coast as a whole.

54. **(A)** The Colonial Era   *Trend Question*

The Southern colonies were more ethnically and religiously diverse than New England and the Middle colonies because of the vast number of immigrants and slaves needed to work on the South's sprawling, labor-intensive plantations. The South's plantation system prevented the growth of a large merchant class, as well as the growth of large families (because given the plantation system's labor needs, adult males so greatly outnumbered adult females in the region).

55. **(B)** A New Nation   *Except Question*

The Alien and Sedition Acts grew out of the nation's growing anti-French sentiment—the public outrage over the XYZ Affair and the violence of the French Revolution. The laws were pushed into effect by a Federalist majority in Congress, which allows you to eliminate (C) (remember, for EXCEPT questions you choose the *wrong* answer, meaning you can cross out all the *correct* answers). Each act aimed to restrict either the influence of foreigners or of the Republican Party. One of the acts increased the amount of time a foreigner had to wait before becoming eligible for citizenship, so you can eliminate (E). The least popular of the acts, the Sedition Act, prohibited any group or individual from speaking against the president or Congress, in essence serving as a restriction on freedom of the press (A).

Of the remaining two choices, you can eliminate (D) if you know that the Republican Party reacted to the acts by passing the Virginia and Kentucky resolutions and articulating for the first time the concept of nullification of a federal law by a state government. Even if you do not know about the Virginia and Kentucky resolutions, however, you can still select the correct answer by considering the effect of the

Federalists' attempt to restrict individual liberties. Although the acts targeted the Republican Party, they actually increased the Republican Party's popularity because so many citizens objected to the seeming totalitarianism of the Federalist acts. The acts thus encouraged the growth of the Republican Party's power based and paved the way for Jefferson's election in 1800. (B) is therefore the correct choice.

56. **(D)** Western Expansion & Sectional Strife *Fact Question*

Uncle Tom's Cabin was Harriet Beecher Stowe's fictional depiction of the life of slaves on a Southern plantation. The portrayal fueled antislavery sentiments, heightening the tensions between the North and South that eventually erupted in Civil War.

57. **(D)** Industrial Revolution *Except Question*

The antitrust movement did not gain significant force until the Progressive Era, 1900–1917, which was known for its trust-busting. During the Industrial Revolution, monopolies and trusts still flourished, largely unregulated by government and unhindered by unions (apart from business' granting some concessions to unions, in the form of higher wages and/or shorter work days). In fact, during the 1890s, the Sherman Antitrust Act was often used *against* unions, not against monopolies, as courts ruled that labor strikes illegally retrained trade. Not until 1904 was the Sherman Antitrust Act successfully invoked against big business.

58. **(E)** The 1950s *Fact Question*

In the 1950s, painter Jackson Pollack was considered a leader in America's abstract expressionist movement. Rejecting traditional painting techniques, Pollack flung paint and other materials across the canvas.

59. **(C)** The 1960s *Trend Question*

The first serious organized opposition to the war began on college campuses in 1965.

60. **(C)** Civil War & Reconstruction *Trend Question*

Generally speaking, Reconstruction had little effect on protecting rights for blacks because secret societies like the Ku Klux Klan raided black voting booths and conducted mob lynchings and floggings to intimidate free blacks. Discriminatory Jim Crow laws also blocked blacks from fully integrating into Southern society. After Redemption—when Southern Democrats "reclaimed" state governments in the South—Southern blacks lost even more rights.

61. **(A)** Industrial Revolution *Trend Question*

Political bosses often controlled voter loyalty by distributing political and economic benefits such as offices, jobs, and city contracts. These contracts allowed companies to build parks, sanitation systems, and roads, and to provide much-needed public services benefiting the entire urban population.

62. **(D)** The 1950s *Trend Question*

In the 1950s, popular culture encouraged American women to focus on marriage, motherhood, and domesticity. The education system further promoted this portrayal of women. One of the leading advocates of domesticity was Dr. Benjamin Spock, author of the widely successful *Baby and Child Care* (1946). Dr. Spock argued that mothers should devote themselves to the full-time care of their children.

63. **(E)** The 1960s
Except Question

U.S. forces only held control over limited areas in Vietnam. The Vietcong, by contrast, operated all over the country, traveling mostly at night via a network of tunnels. Vietcong tunnels positioned next to U.S. army bases allowed Vietcong forces to breach enemy lines.

64. **(B)** The 1960s
Fact Question

The Voting Rights Act of 1965 authorized federal examiners to register qualified voters and to suspend literacy tests in voting districts where fewer than half of the minority population of voting age was registered. The act effectively eliminated many of the racist practices that had been used to deny generations of southern blacks their voting rights.

65. **(A)** 1970s–2000
Trend Question

In the 1980s, Republican president Ronald Reagan advocated large increases in defense spending as part of his aggressive strategy against the Soviet Union. Congressional Democrats often opposed these increases.

66. **(B)** Cultural Trends: 1781–Mid-1800s
Fact Question

The spread of textile factories in the North and in Great Britain increased the demand for Southern cotton during the early and mid-nineteenth century. Note that the Thirty Years' War (C) ended in 1648.

67. **(E)** Industrial Revolution
Trend Question

According to the tenets of Social Darwinism, Darwin's theories of evolution and survival of the fittest held as true for human society as they did for biological nature. Social Darwinists believed that those who succeeded financially and socially were akin to the "fittest" or "strongest" of the human species, while the struggling poor were "unfit" or "weak." Social Darwinists therefore argued that the gap between rich and poor arose naturally and necessarily from character difference, and, for this reason, they opposed poor relief and other forms of government welfare for disrupting economy's natural selection. Among the choices listed, a rich businessman would most likely have endorsed Social Darwinist thought.

68. **(C)** Cultural Trends: 1781–Mid-1800s
Quotation Question

The question actually tells you the answer: the correct choice is (C), William Lord Garrison, because, of the five choices, only Garrison was a radical abolitionist. Prior to the Civil War, Garrison published *The Liberator* newspaper to demand an end to slavery. The above passage is an 1831 excerpt from his newspaper.

69. **(C)** Industrial Revolution
Trend Question

In addition to supporting issues like national ownership of railroads, a graduated income tax, government-operated banks, and the direct election of senators, the Populist Party also supported popular labor causes—most notably, immigration restriction and an eight-hour working day. As for (A), while many members of the Populist Party did believe that black and white farmers should fight for their rights together, ideas like integration never made it to the platform.

70. **(A)** The Colonial Period
Fact Question

The British Parliament passed the Sugar and Stamp Acts (in 1764 and 1765, respectively) primarily to raise revenue for the British crown. The British government had accumulated a massive debt fighting the French and Indian War and now looked toward the American colonies to help pay it. Revenue acts like the Stamp and Sugar Acts elicited fierce resistance from the colonists, who felt the taxes were unfair (hence their cry of resistance, "No taxation without representation!") What distinguished the Stamp and Sugar Acts from previous tax measures was that these acts were *not* meant simply to regulate trade for the benefit of the entire British Empire; rather, they were taxes specifically aimed at procuring money *from* the colonies *for* Britain.

Note (C) describes Britain's primary motivation for implementing the policy of salutary neglect toward the colonies before the French and Indian War. By this policy, Britain did not enforce taxes that hurt the colonies most. Almost immediately after Britain's victory in the French and Indian War, Parliament revoked this policy and heavily taxed the colonies. Note that (E) is true of the Intolerable Acts of 1773.

71. **(D)** Revolution & Constitution — *Fact Question*

The Constitution does not grant the federal government the power to regulate intrastate commerce, although it does grant the government the power to control interstate commerce. Interstate commerce is trade between states while intrastate commerce is trade within a state itself. Each state has the right to regulate its own intrastate commerce. The national government has all of the other powers listed: the power to raise and maintain armies, levy national taxes, and conduct international relations.

72. **(A)** Western Expansion & Sectional Strife — *Fact Question*

The Fugitive Slave Act strengthened the federal government's position that escaped slaves had no rights under the law. The act denied fugitives the right to a trial and to defend themselves in a court of law. It also required citizens of any state, slave or free, to assist in the capture and return of runaway slaves.

73. **(D)** Cultural Trends: 1781–Mid-1800s — *Fact Question*

Although Stanton and Mott supported abolitionist activities, they were principally associated with the women's rights movement. They organized a women's rights convention, known as the Seneca Falls Convention, in 1848.

74. **(C)** Cultural Trends: 1781–Mid-1800s — *Fact Question*

A transcendentalist, Thoreau believed that knowledge comes through the senses, intuition, and sudden insight rather than solely from the intellect. He advocated living a simple life in contemplation and in harmony with nature.

75. **(D)** A New Nation — *Trend Question*

Strict and loose constructionists disagreed over whether the national bank was constitutional. Strict constructionists argued that since the U.S. Constitution does not explicitly authorize the founding of a national bank, Congress cannot lawfully charter it. Loose constructionists argued that since Congress has the power to tax and to coin and borrow money, it has an *implied* power to charter a national bank.

Even if you don't know why the strict and loose constructionists differed in their views on the national bank, you can still eliminate some choices—for example, those that do not mention a political debate. You can cross out (B) because even if it was true that strict constructionists generally lacked the money to put in the bank, this statement describes a personal or financial argument, not one based on political theory. The remaining answer choices do not correctly match political faction with belief: (A) is wrong because Alexander Hamilton and his followers, the loose constructionists, were in favor of the national bank; (E) is wrong because strict constructionists did not support Hamilton's overall financial policy, and therefore would not oppose anything simply for interfering with it; (C) is wrong because loose constructionists tended to favor a strong central government over decentralized, state-allotted powers.

76. **(B)** Industrial Revolution *Except Question*

There is no law that ensures job security for workers. All the other choices were considered legislative victories for the labor movement. Note that (C) refers to the Chinese Exclusion Act of 1882.

77. **(C)** World War II *Trend Question*

At the Versailles Peace Conference of 1919, President Wilson met much resistance, even antagonism, in attempting to institute his democratic liberal vision embodied in the Fourteen Points. France, Britain, and Italy regarded his plan as naïve and too benevolent toward Germany. Although the Allied demands for retribution did eventually prevail, Wilson still fought hard for the creation of a League of Nations, which he felt might still accomplish his lofty goals of lasting peace and self-determination. (A) is wrong because the U.S. was far from assuming an isolationist stance; in fact, through the League of Nations, Wilson meant to commit the U.S. to active involvement in world affairs. Nor did the U.S. seek more colonial possessions (B) at Versailles.

78. **(A)** The 1950s *Trend Question*

In 1947, President Truman proclaimed that the U.S. would help people anywhere in the world fight against subjugation by armed minorities. The Truman Doctrine thus promised to help countries resist the communist threat.

79. **(D)** Industrial Revolution *Except Question*

Although the WTCU (1879) and the Anti-Saloon League (1893) opposed drinking for a number of reasons, the dangers of drinking and driving was not one of them because cars had not yet been invented. All of the other issues were pressing concerns for temperance reformers of the day.

80. **(D)** Revolution & Constitution *Fact Question*

The three-fifths clause in the Constitution states that slaves only count as three-fifths of a person in the census. During the drafting of the Constitution, free states without slaves feared that slave-holding states would have more representatives in the House of Representatives if they included their slaves in the official populations, thus giving the slave-holding states more power in the House. To compromise, the free and slave-holding states agreed to count each slave as only three-fifths of a person.

81. **(A)** The Progressive Era *Trend Question*

Wilson sought to establish morality in international affairs. He focused on spreading capitalism, democracy, and freedom throughout the world. He rejected the aggressive use of force and vowed not to try to extend U.S. territorial holdings. To signal his departure from the foreign policy of his predecessors, he withdrew American partnership from a loan consortium in China in 1913. The use of investments to generate stability is representative of Taft's "dollar diplomacy."

82. **(D)** Civil War & Reconstruction *Except Question*

The Emancipation Proclamation heralded as a major turning point for the Union in the Civil War. It boosted morale in the North while destroying morale in the South. It encouraged nearly 200,000 former slaves in the South to join the Union Army, which gave the North an even greater military advantage. The proclamation also appeased Radical Republicans in Congress who pushed for emancipation, and pleased Great Britain and France who had only decades earlier outlawed slavery in their own countries. The Proclamation did *not*, however, free black slaves in the four slave states in the Union; in actuality, the Proclamation liberated very few slaves, only those in the Confederate states still in rebellion (not yet under Union control).

83. (E) The Roaring Twenties   *Fact Question*

W.E.B. Du Bois led the National Association for the Advancement of Colored People (NAACP) during the 1920s. It was primarily a northern urban organization. Marcus Garvey's more radical United Negro Improvement Association (UNIA) rivaled the NAACP for the allegiance of northern blacks.

84. (D) The Great Depression & New Deal   *Except Question*

A shortage of gold bullion in the national reserves was *not* a factor contributing to the Great Depression. The Depression was caused by overspeculation in the stock market, unsound banking practices (such as "buying on margin"), the rising unemployment rate, and failures in the agricultural sector of the economy.

85. (D) A New Nation   *Trend Question*

A federal system of government, by definition, is one that combines a system of state governments with a centralized national government. (B) and (D) both describe a federal system of government as shared power between a federal and state governments, but read carefully. (B) indicates equally shared power, whereas (D) places the balance of power in the national government. (D) is correct because the federal government has predominance: it can enact binding national laws.

86. (A) Western Expansion & Sectional Strife   *Trend Question*

Popular sovereignty became a popular position among congressional moderates in the 1840s. The other ideas listed remained marginal positions at that time.

87. (B) Industrial Revolution   *Fact Question*

The Grange became extremely popular among farmers in the 1870s, garnering a member base of over 800,000 people by 1875 and securing passage of a few "Granger" laws that protected farming interests. In the 1880s, the group was gradually replaced by farmers' alliances, which were, in turn, replaced by the Populist Party.

88. (A) Industrial Revolution   *Fact Question*

Bryan and his fellow Populists believed that the free coinage of silver would help struggling farmers and laborers pay off their debts, since the silver standard was inflationary—that is, it would expand the money supply. The gold standard, by contrast, was more restrictive. *The Wizard of Oz* is believed to be an allegory of the silver/gold standard debate.

89. (C) The Great Depression & New Deal   *Trend Question*

Pop culture exploded in the 1930s primarily because Americans needed diversion from their troubles caused by the Great Depression. If you were confused by the answer choices, reread the question: the keyword "1930s" gives you a major clue. The Great Depression was one of the most significant events during the 1930s, so it is a good bet that the correct answer will somehow involve the depression.

90. (C) The 1960s   *Fact Question*

Rachel Carson's publication of *Silent Spring* in 1962, which exposed the environmental hazards of DDT, touched off a broad movement to push environmental measures through Congress. In 1963, this effort spurred the passage of the Clean Air Act to regulate factory and automobile emissions. This act, along with the 1960 Clean Water Act, marked the beginning of a period during which the federal government became increasingly invested in environmental matters.

SparkNotes Literature Study Guides

1984

The Adventures of
  Huckleberry Finn

The Adventures of
  Tom Sawyer

The Aeneid

All Quiet on the
  Western Front

And Then There
  Were None

Angela's Ashes

Animal Farm

Anne of Green Gables

Antony and Cleopatra

As I Lay Dying

As You Like It

The Awakening

The Bean Trees

The Bell Jar

Beloved

Beowulf

Billy Budd

Black Boy

Bless Me, Ultima

The Bluest Eye

Brave New World

The Brothers Karamazov

The Call of the Wild

Candide

The Canterbury Tales

Catch-22

The Catcher in the Rye

The Chosen

Cold Mountain

Cold Sassy Tree

The Color Purple

The Count of Monte Cristo

Crime and Punishment

The Crucible

Cry, the Beloved Country

Cyrano de Bergerac

Death of a Salesman

The Diary of a Young Girl

Doctor Faustus

A Doll's House

Don Quixote

Dr. Jekyll and Mr. Hyde

Dracula

Dune

Emma

Ethan Frome

Fahrenheit 451

Fallen Angels

A Farewell to Arms

Flowers for Algernon

The Fountainhead

Frankenstein

The Glass Menagerie

Gone With the Wind

The Good Earth

The Grapes of Wrath

Great Expectations

The Great Gatsby

Gulliver's Travels

Hamlet

The Handmaid's Tale

Hard Times

Harry Potter and the
  Sorcerer's Stone

Heart of Darkness

Henry IV, Part I

Henry V

Hiroshima

The Hobbit

The House of the
  Seven Gables

I Know Why the
  Caged Bird Sings

The Iliad

Inferno

Invisible Man

Jane Eyre

Johnny Tremain

The Joy Luck Club

Julius Caesar

The Jungle

The Killer Angels

King Lear

The Last of the Mohicans

Les Misérables

A Lesson Before Dying

The Little Prince

Little Women

Lord of the Flies

Macbeth

Madame Bovary

A Man for All Seasons

The Mayor of Casterbridge

The Merchant of Venice

A Midsummer
  Night's Dream

Moby-Dick

Much Ado About Nothing

My Ántonia

Mythology

Native Son

The New Testament

Night

The Odyssey

The Oedipus Plays

Of Mice and Men

The Old Man and the Sea

The Old Testament

Oliver Twist

The Once and Future King

One Flew Over the
  Cuckoo's Nest

One Hundred Years
  of Solitude

Othello

Our Town

The Outsiders

Paradise Lost

The Pearl

The Picture of Dorian Gray

A Portrait of the Artist as a
  Young Man

Pride and Prejudice

The Prince

A Raisin in the Sun

The Red Badge of Courage

The Republic

Richard III

Robinson Crusoe

Romeo and Juliet

The Scarlet Letter

A Separate Peace

Silas Marner

Sir Gawain and the
  Green Knight

Slaughterhouse-Five

Snow Falling on Cedars

The Sound and the Fury

Steppenwolf

The Stranger

A Streetcar Named Desire

The Sun Also Rises

A Tale of Two Cities

The Taming of the Shrew

The Tempest

Tess of the d'Urbervilles

Their Eyes Were
  Watching God

Things Fall Apart

To Kill a Mockingbird

To the Lighthouse

Treasure Island

Twelfth Night

Ulysses

Uncle Tom's Cabin

Walden

Wuthering Heights

A Yellow Raft in
  Blue Water